THE FRAGMENTATION OF U.S. HEALTH CARE

THE FRAGMENTATION OF U.S. HEALTH CARE

CAUSES AND SOLUTIONS

EDITED BY EINER R. ELHAUGE

OXFORD

UNIVERSITY PRESS

OXFORD
UNIVERSITY PRESS

Oxford University Press, Inc., publishes works that further Oxford University's objective
of excellence in research, scholarship, and education.

Oxford   New York
Auckland   Cape Town   Dar es Salaam   Hong Kong   Karachi   Kuala Lumpur   Madrid
Melbourne   Mexico City   Nairobi   New Delhi   Shanghai   Taipei   Toronto

With offices in
Argentina   Austria   Brazil   Chile   Czech Republic   France   Greece   Guatemala   Hungary
Italy   Japan   Poland   Portugal   Singapore   South Korea   Switzerland   Thailand
Turkey   Ukraine   Vietnam

Published by Oxford University Press, Inc.
198 Madison Avenue, New York, New York 10016

Oxford is a registered trademark of Oxford University Press
Oxford University Press is a registered trademark of Oxford University Press, Inc.

Library of Congress Cataloging-in-Publication Data.

Elhauge, Einer
The fragmentation of U.S. health care : causes and solutions/edited by Einer Elhauge.
    p. cm.
  Includes bibliographical references and index.
  ISBN 978-0-19-539013-1 ((hardback) : alk. paper)
1. Health care reform—United States. I. Title.
  RA395.A3E415 2010
  362.1'0425--dc22
                                    2009035088

1 2 3 4 5 6 7 8 9

Printed in the United States of America on acid-free paper

CONTENTS

CONTRIBUTORS

James F. Blumstein is University Professor of Constitutional Law and Health Law & Policy and Director of the Health Policy Center at the Vanderbilt University Law School.

Lawrence P. Casalino is the Livingston Farrand Associate Professor of Public Health at Weill Cornell Medical College.

Randal Cebul is Director of the Center for Health Care Research & Policy at MetroHealth Medical Center, and Professor of Medicine at Case Western Reserve University.

Arthur Daemmrich is Assistant Professor of Business Administration at Harvard Business School.

Einer Elhauge is the Founding Director of the Petrie-Flom Center for Health Law Policy, Biotechnology and Bioethics and the Carroll and Milton Petrie Professor of Law at Harvard Law School.

Alain Enthoven is the Marriner S. Eccles Professor of Public and Private Management, Emeritus and Core Faculty Member of the Centers for Health Policy and Primary Care and Outcomes Research at Stanford University.

Thomas Greaney is the Chester A. Myers Professor of Law and Director of the Center for Health Law Studies at Saint Louis University School of Law.

Jeremy Greene is Assistant Professor in the Department of the History of Science at Harvard University and an Instructor in Medicine in the Division of Pharmacoepidemiology and Pharmacoeconomics of the Department of Medicine at Brigham & Women's Hospital and Harvard Medical School

Daniel Grossman is an Associate in Research in the Department of Economics at Duke University.

Mark A. Hall is the Fred D. & Elizabeth L. Turnage Professor of Law at Wake Forest University School of Law.

Eric Helland is Professor of Economics at Claremont McKenna College and Senior Economist at the RAND Corporation.

David A. Hyman is the Richard W. and Marie L. Corman Professor and Director of the Epstein Program in Health Law and Policy at the University of Illinois College of Law.

David W. Johnson is a Senior Managing Director for Chicago-based Ziegler Capital Markets.

Timothy Stoltzfus Jost is the Robert L. Willett Family Professor of Law at the Washington and Lee University School of Law.

Nancy M. Kane is Professor of Management and Associate Dean for Educational Programs in the Department of Health Policy and Management at Harvard School of Public Health.

Jonathan Klick is a Professor of Law at the University of Pennsylvania Law School.

Kristin Madison is Professor of Law at the University of Pennsylvania Law School and a Senior Fellow at the Leonard Davis Institute of Health Economics.

Theodore R. Marmor is Professor Emeritus of Public Policy and Management & Professor Emeritus of Political Science at the Yale School of Management.

Frank Pasquale is Associate Professor of Law and, Associate Director of the Center for Health and Pharmaceutical Law and Policy at Seton Hall Law School.

James B. Rebitzer is Professor of Economics and Chair of the Business Policy and Law Department at the Boston University School of Management, Research Associate at NBER, the Levy Institute and IZA.

Barak Richman is Professor of Law at Duke Law School.

Kevin A. Schulman is the Director of the Center for Clinical and Genetic Economics, and Professor at the Duke University School of Medicine, and the Fuqua School of Business.

Frank Sloan is the J. Alexander McMahon Professor of Health Policy and Management and Professor of Economics at Duke University.

Lowell J. Taylor is Professor of Economics and Public Policy at the Carnegie Mellon Heinz School.

Mark Votruba is Associate Professor of Economics at the Case Western Reserve University Weatherhead School of Management and the Director of the Health Economics Unit at the Center for Health Care Research & Policy at MetroHealth Medical Center.

1. WHY WE SHOULD CARE ABOUT HEALTH CARE FRAGMENTATION AND HOW TO FIX IT

EINER ELHAUGE

THE MEANING AND DIMENSIONS OF FRAGMENTATION

What does health care fragmentation mean? I take the term to mean having multiple decision makers make a set of health care decisions that would be made better through unified decision making. Just as too many cooks can spoil the broth, too many decision makers can spoil health care. Individual decision makers responsible for only one fragment of a relevant set of health care decisions may fail to understand the full picture, may lack the power to take all the appropriate actions given what they know, or may even have affirmative incentives to shift costs onto others. All these forms of fragmentation can lead to bad health care decisions. It is my privilege to introduce a terrific series of chapters by leading scholars on this topic. In this chapter, I hope to elucidate some common themes in their work, build on them by connecting them to general theories of firm integration and team production, outline some areas of difference, and recommend some reforms.

As the chapters of this book show, fragmentation can occur along many dimensions. Looking at the most narrow dimension, we might be concerned about fragmentation in treating particular *illnesses,* such as the lack of coordination among the various professionals involved in treating a patient during a single hospital stay. This might occur if, for example, a patient tells one nurse she is allergic to some medicine, but the nurse does not communicate this information, so the nurse on the next shift administers that medicine. A somewhat broader conception would focus on fragmentation in treatments for particular *patients* at any give time, such as a lack of coordination between different providers that a patient might see for different illnesses. This might occur if, say, a surgeon used a high-sugar intravenous therapy after an operation on a diabetic patient without consulting with the diabetic specialist treating the patient. Even more broadly, we might worry about fragmentation for patients *over time,* such as when a private health insurer underfunds preventive care because the costs will be borne later by Medicare. Most broadly of all, we might worry about fragmentation for a *patient group.* This would be the case if disintegration resulted in care being misallocated to patients in the group who needed it less than others. The last dimension also invites the question of whether the appropriate group should be broadened to include others in the state, nation, or even world.

Under my definition, the fragmentation concept presupposes some normative content, because determining when fragmentation exists turns on baseline assumptions about when we think integrated decision making would produce better decisions.[1] Likewise, positions regarding the proper dimensions of fragmentation to worry about depend on which health care decisions we think should be made in a unified fashion. Worries about fragmentation at the community level raise controversial issues about the extent to which we should have unified decision making about health care allocations across patients. It is less controversial that the care received by an individual patient should reflect some sort of coherent common plan. It is probably for this reason that the chapters of this book focus on the latter dimensions of fragmentation; because there is more consensus about the desirability of more unified decision making regarding these dimensions, there is more consensus about what counts as fragmentation along these dimensions.

However, even at the patient level there may be controversy or tradeoffs about which set of decisions are best integrated. As Professor Hyman's chapter points out, retail health clinics separate some routine health care from other health care, but if we think retail clinics are desirable because they deliver quality care with lower cost, hassle, or delay (the last of which can have important health effects), we would not want to object to retail clinics as "fragmenting" health care. On the other hand, if we thought retail clinics led to care that is inconsistent with the care provided by primary physicians in a way that harmed patient health, then we would likely regard retail clinics as a form of harmful fragmentation.

We thus cannot simply assume that all reductions in health care integration are bad and worthy of the pejorative label "fragmentation." This should not be surprising. After all, other markets feature mixes of integration and disintegration that raise no necessary hackles. Many services provided by, say, a hotel, are integrated into a common company; after checking into the hotel, one does not have to select the housekeeper, concierge, or phone service for one's stay. On the other hand, other hotel services are disintegrated: one can often select among various hotel restaurants or activities with various prices, or choose non-hotel substitutes for either. Further, it seems unproblematic that hotel services are not integrated with the company that provides the air travel that contributes to the common vacation "episode," or with the wireless carrier that provides mobile

---

1. Some chapters in this book instead use the term "fragmentation" interchangeably with "disintegration," but I find it clearer to use the term "fragmentation" as a normative term, referring to disintegration that is undesirable, and to use the terms "distintegration" or "integration" as descriptive terms, referring to states of less or more unified decision making that may or may not be desirable. My conclusions about what might constitute fragmentation should be compared to what some other chapters would refer to as undesirable fragmentation.

phones to a common individual. Nor does it seem problematic that services provided by one hotel are not integrated over time with the hotel one uses on the next vacation. For many services, aggregation by a series of separate individual consumer decisions seems preferable.

Thus, in order to know which disintegrations to object to as "fragmenting" health care in an undesirable fashion, we need either (1) a theory about the optimal integration of decision making, or (2) evidence of the sort of bad results that must reflect excessive disintegration. The latter unfortunately tells us only which direction in which to travel, rather than what our destination should be: that is, it tells us to fragment less than we do now, but not necessarily what level of integration is best. However, the latter may well be easier to come by than a convincing theory of optimal disintegration. And even a convincing theory may well focus on providing guidance on the process used to set integration levels, rather than establishing a basis for favoring a particular integration result.

EVIDENCE SHOWING FRAGMENTATION

The chapters of this book provide considerable empirical evidence to suggest that U.S. health care suffers from excessive disintegration that worsens outcomes and thus constitutes fragmentation. At the illness level, as several chapters point out, Institute of Medicine studies show that, within any given hospital, many medical errors result because of a lack of effective data sharing and teamwork among the health care professionals working at that hospital. These studies indicate these errors are a systemic problem caused by hospital structure, rather than reflecting some rogue behavior by particular hospitals or individuals, and thus directly support greater integration within hospitals as a way of improving health care.

At the patient level, Professors Hyman points to evidence that the average Medicare beneficiary sees two physicians and five specialists a year, and that those with chronic illnesses see an average of thirteen physicians a year, "each focused on the discrete symptoms and/or body parts within their jurisdiction." Professors Cebul, Rebitzer, Taylor, and Votruba cite similar evidence that the median Medicare patient sees eight physicians in five distinct practices, and if they have a coronary artery disease, the numbers increase to ten physicians in six distinct practices. They both point to evidence that few physicians are in multispecialty practices. Nor do Medicare and other insurers pay physicians to spend time coordinating care. Patients or family members thus end up saddled with most of the responsibility for coordinating all the physicians. But patients and family cannot do so effectively because they lack the medical expertise, authority over physicians, or control of the purse strings. The result of this lack of coordination among physicians, an Institute of Medicine report finds, is that "patients do not always receive timely care best suited to their needs." Providing an empirical link between fragmentation and poor outcomes, Professors Cebul, Rebitzer, Taylor, and Votruba point to studies showing that the greater the number of physicians treating a Medicare patient following a heart attack, the higher the costs and the lower the survival rates.

One problem this fragmentation creates, as Professors Enthoven and Hyman note, is that the results of prior treatments or tests are often unavailable or treated with distrust by other providers, and that different providers lack a common information technology structure. Professors Cebul, Rebitzer, Taylor, and Votruba add that only four percent of physicians have fully functional electronic medical systems, and that government studies indicate that fragmented care leads to multiple incompatible formats for medical records. Professors Hall and Schulman focus on this issue, showing that few providers use electronic records, and when they do, their electronic records rarely interconnect with others, a problem that is getting worse over time rather than better. They also shows a clear link between the underuse of electronic records and the fragmentation of providers, by observing that electronic medical records are generally used only in integrated delivery systems that have fixed global budgets like Kaiser or the Veteran's administration. Outside of such integrated systems, patients or family members often have to keep track of all their prescriptions and test results, but they don't always have easy access to their medical records and the ability to persuade other providers to accept them. At best, the same records and tests keep getting redone and duplicated, achieving the same health benefit with a wasteful cost increase. At worst, pertinent records and tests end up being ignored, increasing health risks.

At the temporal level, Professors Cebul, Rebitzer, Taylor, and Votruba provide compelling evidence that fragmentation reduces long-term health investments. As they note, "only fifty-five percent of adults receive recommended levels of preventive care, while adults with a chronic illness . . . receive only fifty-six percent of the chronic care recommended by clinical guidelines." Further, they empirically link these low levels of long-term health investments to fragmentation over time by showing that the more frequently that insureds switch insurers, the less those insurers make efficient investments in long-term health like providing preventive care. Likewise, the higher the costs of switching insurers, the more insurers make such investments in long-term health. In addition, as they and Professors Helland and Klick stress, private insurers and state Medicaid plans have incentives to underinvest in care that would prevent illnesses that will materialize after individuals turn sixty-five and become Medicare's responsibility. Professors Helland and Klick demonstrate that this is a distinctive problem, citing evidence that state Medicaid programs also fare poorly in delivering preventive care.

The link between insurance and employment exacerbates the short-termism effect, because many changes in insurance are caused by changes in employment or by employer decisions. Professors Helland and Klick also show that this link creates a different sort of temporal problem, citing empirical evidence that it delays retirement and reduces job mobility.

At the patient group level, Professor Enthoven stresses the RAND study showing that integrated prepaid group practice lowers costs by twenty-eight percent without worsening overall outcomes. I put this evidence at the group level because the RAND study does not actually show that outcomes are unchanged for everyone. Instead, it shows that prepaid integrated practices do provide less beneficial care in many cases, reflecting their incentive to under-care, but also provide less harmful care in other cases, reflecting their elimination of the fee-for-service incentive to provide excessive care.[2] The net effect on health outcomes is neutral only because the health benefits of the latter effect cancel out the health detriments from the former effect. This means that we might regard the overall allocation with prepaid integrated practices as better for the group as a whole than it would be with fee-for-service care. But it also means that prepaid integrated practices create their own perverse incentives for under-treatment that can harm many patients and that could possibly be reduced with a regime that differs from these two extremes, a topic to which I shall return below.

Likewise, Professors Cebul, Rebitzer, Taylor, and Votruba stress that there are enormous variations in health care costs between different areas of the United States, most of which cannot be explained by differences in prices, demographics, health status, or health outcomes, but instead seem to mean that some regions spend more on high-cost ineffective care than others. Professors Richman, Grossman and Sloan demonstrate a similar sort of inter-group variation based on race and income, showing that—even with equal insurance coverage—whites and high-income individuals consume more mental health services, and are more likely to get those services from a mental health professional rather than a general practitioner. They also show that this variation in treatment does not produce a variation in outcomes, thus suggesting that the additional mental health services obtained by whites and high-income individuals are ineffective or have offsetting benefits and harms. A less fragmented system might produce a more effective and equitable allocation of health care.

Cutting across all the levels is other evidence showing harm from fragmentation. For example, Professors Cebul, Rebitzer, Taylor, and Votruba point out that administrative costs in our disintegrated U.S. system are $1059 per capita. The fact that this is an astonishing thirty-one percent of total health care expenditures itself suggests that excessive administrative costs are being imposed. This seems confirmed by the fact that these U.S. administrative costs are $752 more than the administrative costs in the less fragmented Canadian system. Nor are

---

2. *See* Joseph P. Newhouse, Free For All? Lessons From the RAND Health Insurance Experiment 283 (1993).

the costs all borne by insurers: the United State's additional administrative costs are $212 for insurers, $212 for hospitals, $217 for practitioners, and $49 for employers.

Finally, the chapter by Professors Daemmrich and Greene demonstrates an entirely different dimension of fragmentation—fragmentation in gathering information for purposes of making regulatory decisions. Specifically, they focus on fragmentation in monitoring the side effects of drugs after they have been introduced in the marketplace. Traditionally, post-marketing monitoring took the form of centralized collection of individual case reports initiated by physicians or patients. More recently, it has often taken the form of episodic statistical analysis of large databases that either already exist or are created in targeted phase-IV clinical trials. The problem is that these sources can provide conflicting results based on variations in how the analysis is done. They argue that a better, more integrated approach would be to first use standardized case reports collected by pharmacies to identify possible risks, next analyze the probabilities of these risks with statistical analysis of existing databases, and then design and run a large new phase IV clinical trial that would provide the definitive guidance on what the FDA should do about the drug.

Theory Indicating Fragmentation

Does theory also suggest excessive health care fragmentation? I think that the answer is yes given general economic theory on firms and team production, which provides a theoretical framework to understand the observations discussed in the other chapters of this book. Professor Coase first pointed out that the fact that business firms were characterized by centralized control (rather than allocating their resources via internal markets) must mean that such coordinated control had some efficiency advantages over decentralized market transactions for some important set of joint production activity.[3] Professor Alchain and Demsetz followed up by showing that the major efficiency advantage to using firms was that trying to use a market system to reward team production often creates incentives to shirk, because it is often hard for the market to measure and reward each team member's contribution to the team production.[4] Firms minimize this problem by creating an owner who (1) has the power to select, direct, monitor, and reward or punish team members based on their contributions to the joint product and (2) has a residual claim to any profits on the sale of the joint product that are left after all the team members are paid. The easier it is to measure the contribution of inputs without observing them, the more likely a firm is to contract out those activities, such as when a firm buys

3. Ronald Coase, *The Nature of the Firm*, 4 ECONOMICA (n.s.) 386 (1937).

4. Armen Alchain & Harold Demsetz, *Production, Information Costs, and Economic Organization*, 62 AM. ECON. REV. 777 (1972).

pencils or gallons of oil rather than making them itself. But when an activity both requires team production and is easier to assess by observation than with market rewards, then the firm will encompass that activity. The residual claim to profits is important because it gives the owner efficient incentives to police shirking and coordinate the team members efficiently to create the joint product.

Applying this theoretical framework suggests that health care raises the mother of all team production problems where input contributions are difficult to measure. Many doctors, nurses, technicians, drugs, devices, tests, and resources must be combined in complex ways to produce the common result of healthy outcomes for individual patients or groups of them. Yet it is fiendishly difficult without close observation to determine the contribution of each. In health care, shirking seems unlikely to take the form of not working because everyone in health care seems to work pretty hard. Rather, in health care shirking is likely to consist of failing to coordinate with others involved in the team effort on strategy, timing, and information-sharing in order to maximize health benefits per costs expended. The situation thus cries out—even more than most industries—for an owner who can select, direct, and closely monitor the various contributors, and reward or punish them accordingly.

Unfortunately, U.S. health care couples the mother of all team production problems with the mother of all refusals to use centralized ownership structures to solve them, as the chapters in this book show. Even a single hospital stay generally means the patient is treated by multiple physicians who are independent contractors, each paid a fee for their services that is separate from the other physicians and from the fees the hospital receives for providing support. This is so even when the hospital receives flat payments from Medicare for a diagnosis-related group, because those fees cover only hospital support services and not physician fees. The hospital usually cannot direct or monitor the substance of physician decisions, which are instead subject only to medical review by the other physicians who comprise the medical staff. Further, because neither the hospital nor the medical staff pays the physicians, they lack the power to give the sort of significant financial rewards or penalties that might induce compliance with any directions. The hospital and medical staff can perhaps select which physicians have privileges at the hospital, but the law often prohibits selections that are based on grounds other than medical competence, and because hospitals depend on physicians to bring them patients, they have little incentive to make selections on other grounds anyway.

Indeed, hospitals and medical staffs generally have little financial incentive to direct and monitor physicians efficiently because neither is a residual claimant that would gain any additional profit by coordinating physicians and other inputs more effectively. Instead, the hospital's incentive is to allow case management to be controlled by the doctor who brings in the patient, like the surgeon who admits a patient for a procedure, even if the doctor has little incentive or interest in managing the case once the procedure is finished. Not surprisingly, such doctors often spend hardly any time on case management, with the unfortunate result that no is really managing the case. Some hospitals have innovatively begun to hire case managers to deal with this problem, but their ability to do so is limited because case managers lack any real power over the admitting physicians; furthermore, the hospital has strong financial incentives to please those admitting physicians and little incentive to improve case management. The incentives would be different if the hospital got paid a fee for all services necessary to achieve some medical result, like a successful surgery, and then selected and paid the physicians and other inputs out of that payment. But that is not the world we live in.

Instead, the current payment system perversely provides disincentives for any provider to invest in coordination or care that might lessen the need of patients for health care, because (as Professors Hyman and Enthoven note) such investments result in fewer payments for medical or hospital services. One nice example of this, stressed elsewhere by Professor Herzlinger, involves the case of Duke University Hospital, which adopted an integrated program to treat congestive heart failure that reduced health problems and cut costs by forty percent, but lost money because this meant Duke had fewer health problems to treat.[5] In any other market, a new system that provided more value for forty percent less cost would reap enormous rewards; in our fragmented health care system, it was affirmatively penalized.

Outside of a single hospital stay, the problems are even worse. A patient with any complex problem has to visit a series of physicians and care providers, each of which is paid separately and acts autonomously, and who usually are not even in the same building. The patient's primary physician can provide some help in referring the patient to the right specialists. But the primary physician is not a residual claimant who pays those specialists, and thus has little incentive to manage them optimally and little power to do so anyway. Each physician and specialist bills only for its separate services, and no one is paid to manage the case or based on the results of the case. Indeed, the payment system affirmatively discourages the physicians from coordinating with each for the same reason noted above: if coordination lowers the need for services that can be billed, then the physicians will earn less money.

Nor can we count on patients orchestrating the various contributors that will achieve the desired health results, the way we can count on, say, hotel guests to choose the restaurants and activities that will make their vacations enjoyable. The problem is that, unlike consumers in other markets, patients lack the knowledge, power, and incentives to make such decisions optimally. They lack the knowledge because what they are buying *is* knowledge about what health care they need. They lack the power because often they cannot order medical services

---

5. Regina Herzlinger, *Why Innovation in Health Care Is So Hard*, HARV. BUS. REV. 58 (May 1, 2006).

or products without provider or insurer consent. And they lack incentives to make sensible tradeoffs because an insurer generally covers the lion's share of the cost.

One might try to count on insurers to manage cases, as managed care promised to do. But insurers never could direct particular medical decisions, and the backlash against managed care has limited the ability of insurers to monitor or select physicians. Even if one could overcome those problems, the root problem would remain that insurers are not a residual claimant, because they do not receive payment for achieving a particular medical result that they use to pay the team members. Instead, insurers earn more profits the less they cover, even if that worsens medical outcomes in particular cases, which is part of what explains the backlash to insurer case management. This insurer incentive to under-care might be attenuated if benefit denials led insureds to switch to other insurers, but if sicker insureds are more likely than healthier insureds to switch insurers in response to benefit denials, then the switching effect can increase insurer profits and exacerbate incentives to under-care. The latter effect seems plausible because sicker insureds are not only more likely to experience (and thus know about) benefit denials, but also more likely to take seriously any benefit denials they hear about.

Insurers do have some incentives to invest in preventive care that might lower the insurer's costs. But here the fragmentation of insurance over time creates inefficient incentives because, as Professors Cebul, Rebitzer, Taylor, and Votruba show, twenty percent of insureds leave their insurer every year. Thus, an insurer has practically no incentive to invest in preventive care that might avoid health problems five years down the line. Indeed, if the preventive care aims to prevent a problem that will materialize after the age of sixty-five, the insurer has no incentive at all because Medicare will bear the costs of the care. I would add, to their convincing analysis, that even an insurer with a lifetime insurance contract would have suboptimal incentives because the only benefit it reaps from preventive care is avoiding the financial costs of treating the later health problem. The health benefits to the patient from avoiding the health problem are not experienced by the insurer, and thus the insurer will have suboptimal incentives to invest in preventive care.

Even if we had an appropriately incentivized entity to manage patient cases across providers and time, such efforts would be hampered by our fragmented medical records. As Professors Hall and Schulman show, there are strong theoretical reasons to blame our fragmented medical records on fragmented providers. The problem is not simply that no one is paying anyone to incur the costs to consolidate and disseminate records in a universal format. The problem is that disintegrated providers have affirmative incentives not to make their medical records available in a format that other providers could easily access because doing so would make it easier for patients to switch to other providers.

Electronic medical records in a common format may make all the medical sense in the world, but they are bad business in a world of disintegrated providers.

In other industries one might think that, if the current organizational structures did such a poor job of managing team production, then some firm would enter this market, adopt the right structure, and sweep the market. But this brings us to our last theoretical reason to think current levels of health disintegration reflect undesirable fragmentation: namely, the current organizational structures are not the result of free market forces, but rather are dictated by a complex set of laws that prevent different organizational forms from being used. I address that issue in the next section on the causes of fragmentation.

Causes of Fragmentation

Fragmentation might have various causes, and it pays to understand which are the actual causes because that bears on the appropriate solutions. Given that we are talking about medicine, it makes sense to begin by asking: are there sound medical or scientific reasons for the current fragmentation of U.S. health care? Certainly none that appeared in any of the chapters of this book. The fact that other nations have far more integrated health care systems and hospitals dominated by salaried doctors, and achieve similar or better health results at lower cost, belies any claim that medicine or science inherently requires U.S. levels of disintegration. This same fact seems inconsistent with the claim that the sociology of the medical profession inherently requires such fragmentation. Further, Institute of Medicine studies of the U.S. system have condemned fragmentation because it leads to more medical errors, meaning that, if anything, sound medicine and science cuts in the opposite direction and is being overwhelmed by other causes.

This much may seem obvious, but it has an important implication. If medical or scientific reasons are not driving current health care fragmentation, it is unlikely that fragmentation is going to be cured by studies that show how it leads to medical errors, by analyses demonstrating medically optimal team methods, or by new information technologies that help hospitals and physicians coordinate better. Those may help at the margins, but to really tackle fragmentation we are going to have to address the underlying structural cause that has been driving U.S. health care to levels of disintegration that are medically harmful.

Can the current fragmentation of U.S. health care be explained by sound economics or business reasons? Again, none of the chapters offers any support for that possibility. To the contrary, the evidence that fragmentation raises costs, worsens outcomes, and deters efficient investments in long-term health suggests that the economics are to the contrary. And the fact that hospital organization deviates from the sort of business organization used to address team production for other businesses suggests the absence of any sound business rationale for fragmentation either.

Again, this may not be particularly surprising, but it has the important implication that we cannot expect economic or business studies on optimal payment schemes or organizational methods to solve the fragmentation problem. For example, while payment for performance is a popular business strategy for dealing with some of the problems caused by fragmentation, it amounts to trying to cure the fact that core incentives are not producing appropriate conduct by making (or withholding) payments to reward (or punish) some types of conduct. This strategy is unlikely to help much for two reasons. First, it presupposes, contrary to fact, that we do not have a team production problem where contributions are difficult to assess without observation. It basically tries to use a market mechanism to deal with the problem—paying for particular conduct—even though the problem is precisely that market mechanisms are less efficient than ownership monitoring and control. Thus, it is not surprising that, as Professor Hyman notes, pay for performance systems have largely focused on easy to define categories of care that clearly should or should not be provided. This provides little help for the more typical problem of performances whose health contributions are hard to assess or vary a lot from case to case or with what other team members are doing. Second, without an owner with a residual profit claim, no one has incentives to adopt payment methods that encourage only optimal performances even if they can be identified. Participants instead have incentives to adopt payment methods that maximize the profits for their fragmented part of the system, which may encourage undesirable performance and fail to encourage a lot of desirable performance.

The dominant cause of fragmentation instead appears to be the law, which dictates many of the fragmented features described above and thus precludes alterative organizational structures. The law is the culprit even though the payment system is also an important cause of health care fragmentation, as is correctly observed in the chapters by Professors Hyman, Enthoven, Greaney, Cebul, Rebitzer, Taylor, Votruba, Casalino and Jost. The reason is that, as many of these authors recognize, the law dictates that payment system.

Medicare law does so most directly by specifying separate payments for hospitalization, physician services, drugs, and outpatient services that must go directly to each provider. Medicare law thus bars any firm from charging Medicare for everything necessary to treat some illness or to achieve some health outcome. Medicare does not even provide any payments for coordination or case management at all. Indeed, as noted above, the payment system affirmatively discourages effective coordination because any coordination that lowers the need for services also lowers the payments to providers. Medicare reinforces physician control by requiring physicians to certify the need for any services, and by forbidding other firms from making payments to physicians that are designed to cause physicians to alter the care they give or referrals they make. And Medicare prohibits federal officials from supervising the practice of medicine or selecting some providers over others. This disables the federal officials from themselves filling the coordination void by managing the providers or by using provider selection as a carrot or stick. None of these features of Medicare are inevitable—the Medicare laws could be written differently.

Other laws effectively dictate the same sort of regime for cases covered by private insurance. State laws generally make it illegal for physicians to split their fees with anyone other than physicians with which a physician is in a partnership. More important, alternative payment systems, such as paying a hospital (or other firm) to produce some health outcome or set of treatments, would make sense only if it has some control over the physicians and other contributors to that outcome and treatments. And other laws preclude such control, as detailed in the chapters by Professors Blumstein, Greaney, Hyman, Madison, Cebul, Rebitzer, Taylor, and Votruba. The corporate practice of medicine doctrine provides that firms—whether hospitals or HMOs—cannot direct how physicians practice medicine because the firms do not have medical licenses, only the physicians do. Although some states allow hospitals to hire physicians as employees, that change in formal status does not help much if the employer cannot tell the employee what to do. Even if the law did not prohibit such interference, tort law generally penalizes firm decisions to interfere with the medical judgments of individual physicians, making it unprofitable to try, as Professor Blumstein observes. Further, hospital bylaws usually require leaving the medical staff in charge of medical decisions, and those bylaws are in turn required by hospital accreditation standards and often by licensing laws. By dictating autonomy for the various providers involved in jointly producing health outcomes, these rules largely dictate separate payments to each autonomous provider.

Private insurer efforts to directly manage care have likewise been curbed by the ban on corporate practices of medicine and the threat of tort liability. In addition, states have adopted laws requiring insurers to pay for any care (within covered categories) that a physician deemed medically necessary, banning insurers from selectively contracting with particular providers, and restricting the financial incentives that insurers can offer providers.[6]

Although these laws may have been partly motivated by the interest group power of physicians, they also initially had a valid pubic purpose. The general idea, as Professor Madison details, was to preserve physician autonomy to serve the medical needs of their patients and to avoid conflicts of interest that might make physicians disloyal to their patients. But this purpose presupposes a world where treatments and outcomes are largely determined by the individual physician. Today, medical quality is less a function of individual professional action than of complex team production to achieve health results. A legal system that

---

6. Einer Elhauge, *Can Health Law Become a Coherent Field of Law?*, 41 WAKE FOREST L. REV. 365, 373 (2006); Einer Elhauge, *The Limited Regulatory Potential of Medical Technology Assessment*, 82 VA. L. REV. 1525, 1546–64 (1996).

mandates separate payments and autonomy for all team members thus, in the current world, means that each member has incentives to maximize its profits from providing its uncoordinated portion of the treatment, rather than to act in the health interests of the patient by coordinating the care of the team. A legal system that historically preserved autonomous decision making in order to improve medical outcomes and avoid a conflict with patient interests thus, today, perversely worsens medical outcomes and a creates a conflict with the patient interest in quality coordinated care.

The above leads me to a different conclusion than Professor Madison. In her insightful chapter, she argues that, given their rationale, the various laws preserving professional autonomy are most necessary when medical quality is hard to ascertain, because when quality is easy to ascertain, it will be easy to spot and deter deviations from good health care that result from employer control or conflicts of interest. This argument has much intuitive appeal, and yet my conclusion is the opposite. When it is easy to assess the quality of care, then theory of the firm considerations that I outlined above indicate it is likely to be efficient to use a market mechanism rather than an organizational one, so that a decentralized system where each provider acts separately and is paid separately causes little problem. It is when it is difficult to assess the value of each provider's care that a firm structure is more necessary and most hampered by laws that prevent firms from organizing the care and getting the residual profits from it.

To me, then, the absence of good quality measures provides no reason to favor preserving physician autonomy because today uncoordinated autonomous providers worsen medical quality. Moreover, paying a firm for a set of treatments and making that firm responsible for it would make it *easier* to measure quality because then one can just measure the outcomes, without getting into complex issues about the extent to which each participant contributed to those outcomes.

Other possible legal causes strike me as more doubtful explanations for the current state of health care fragmentation. Professor Enthoven's chapter, for example, emphasizes a lack of antitrust enforcement against activities that anticompetitively foreclosed alternatives to traditional medicine. As an antitrust scholar, I am pleased to acknowledge its vital importance, and Professor Enthoven certainly makes a compelling case that antitrust nonenforcement played an important historical role in the development of our current fragmented system. But as Professor Greaney's chapter notes, we have now had decades of serious antitrust enforcement in health care. "There is an expiry date on blaming your parents," J.K. Rowling recently said, and I think we may have similarly reached the expiry date on blaming antitrust nonenforcement for the state of our health care system. We have had antitrust enforcement in health care since the 1943 *American Medical Association* decision and certainly since the 1980s explosion of health care antitrust litigation, and the sad fact is that it has not done much to reduce fragmentation.

This suggests to me that antitrust nonenforcement is no longer a serious cause of our current state of fragmentation, which in turn suggests that the underlying problem is that the above-described laws prevent free competition from driving health care markets towards less fragmented solutions by making such solutions illegal or ineffective given legal limits. If the integrated systems that one could offer under the current set of laws were really much more attractive than the alternatives, then one would think consumers and employers would switch to them in droves. But they haven't. HMOs have lost, rather than gained, market share, and insurers have reduced their use of managed care techniques.[7] Nor have efforts to integrate hospitals with physicians lowered costs. To the contrary, as Professor Blumstein points out, hospitals with physician-hospital organizations have higher prices, higher procedure rates, and higher expenditures. Further, they have not achieved a high level of clinical integration that could improve quality. He posits they have been motivated more by market power rather than improving efficiency or medical quality. Not surprisingly, the share of hospitals with such hospital-physician alliances has declined since 1996.

The problem, I think, is in part that the laws described above have prevented HMOs, insurers, or hospital-physician groups from ever exerting the sort of full control that would be most effective. The other problem is that the profit interest of each does not induce them to use their control optimally. HMOs and insurers, because they are paid a flat fee for any care they provide, have incentives to under-care that make their decisions suspect and unpopular and lead to real health problems. And as noted above, benefit denials may encourage greater disenrollment by sick individuals and thus exacerbate this under-care incentive. Physician-hospital organizations have incentives to over-care that lead to the reverse problems. To really solve the fragmentation problem we are going to have to combine an ownership structure that gives a residual claimant real control with a payment system that makes the incentives created by that residual claim efficient and desirable, a topic to which I shall return below.

Although the above laws seem to be the proximate cause of current fragmentation levels, one might wonder what causes those laws. This I take to be the deeper challenge posed by the two chapters that conclude this book. The chapter by Mr. Johnson and Professor Kane argues that the health fragmentation we get reflects core U.S. values such as individualism and faith in markets and competition. Professor Marmor's chapter argues that our health care system is driven by larger political forces, and that fragmentation has played a modest role in those political debates. If true, these positions indicate that any quest to defragment the health care system may be futile or relatively unimportant. My view is to the contrary, but if one wants to fully understand the skeptical view, one could hardly do better than reading their illuminating chapters.

---

7. Elhauge, *Can Health Law Become a Coherent Field of Law?*, *supra* note 6, at 373.

To me, the problem with saying that current health care fragmentation reflects U.S. values or politics is that this position doesn't explain why those same values and politics do not produce similar levels of fragmentation for other markets like education, air travel, hotels. We don't view individualism or market competition as inconsistent with the fact that we usually buy our products and services from integrated corporations that perform team production functions. The faith in market competition is, after all, a faith in competition among integrated corporations. It also seems to me that the above evidence and theory suggests that the role of fragmentation is large, not modest, and indeed that the fundamental legal framework of fragmented, autonomous, separately-paid providers has undermined many other reform efforts. Even if some of our values and political pressures favor fragmentation, our values and political interests also favor better and more efficient care, so that I think defragmentation reforms can overcome resistance based on values or political interests, though such resistance will no doubt be formidable.

But, assuming such defragmentation reforms are politically possible, what should they be?

Defragmenting Reforms

The most promising reforms, it seems to me, involve ending the legal obstacles to integrated care. Thus, I agree with Professors Madison, Cebul, Rebitzer, Taylor, and Votruba that the corporate practice of medicine doctrine should be eliminated, and that hospital bylaws and other standards that prevent hospitals from controlling physician behavior should be lifted. In addition, Medicare and state laws should be changed to allow payments to firms that would orchestrate all the providers necessary to provide some health outcome, and those firms should be enabled to select which providers they use and to monitor and control their decisions without such control being itself grounds for tort liability.

This doesn't necessarily mean that one should simply repeal laws that prohibit payments for referrals or to alter care decisions. When patients *are* relying on autonomous physician choices, then such side payments undermine that reliance and create a conflict of interest for the physicians whom the patients expect to make the choice. Banning such side payments is no different than the sort of legal bans we have for similar bribes of actors across our legal system. What we need is an exception, much as we have everywhere else in our legal system, for when buyers have contracted with firms that the buyers know control the employees involved in providing some product or service for the buyers.

I am less enthusiastic about reforms that would tend to force more integration. Here, I agree with Professor Blumstein that the law should be neutral about the appropriate organizational form, thus requiring more integrated firms to win over patients by providing cheaper or better coordinated care. Such neutrality, it seems to me, is wise given that we know much more about the direction we need to go than about what level of integration is optimal, and that we don't know precisely what *type* of integration will prove most successful. Indeed, the level and types of integration that are most effective are likely to change over time with changes in technology, costs, and consumer preferences, just as they do in other industries, so it is important to maintain a legal framework that allows such shifts over time.

For similar reasons, I would not favor reforms that try to require some specific type of integration. For example, laws that require Medicare or other insurers to pay physicians to coordinate care seem unwise. They presuppose we know what sort of coordination is optimal and impose it as a centralized choice. A better strategy would be to simply make sure that the total payments to a collection of autonomous providers providing some joint treatment are no higher than the same payment to an integrated firm doing so, and then leave competition between autonomous and integrated providers to determine which forms of coordination are optimal. Nor do payments for coordination seem likely to do much to reduce fragmentation anyway. As Professor Hyman points out, payments for coordination do not really reduce our fragmented system; they just add another fee-for-service payment on top of it. I would add that it is also unclear why otherwise autonomous physicians would listen to a coordinator who lacks the power to control or incentivize physician choices.

Likewise, I don't think legal reforms should try to curb the development of specialty hospitals. Although specialty hospitals disintegrate some procedures from other hospital procedures, Professor Hyman correctly observes that this may well be more efficient. Further, there is probably more integration amongst physicians acting within a specialty hospital than for those acting within a regular hospital, so it isn't even clear which way specialty hospitals cut in terms of overall integration. Professor Pasquale's probing chapter analyzes the specialty hospital issue in depth, arguing for pilot programs that would provide the data to justify various reforms. He argues that if this data showed that specialty hospitals cherry pick the healthiest patients and most lucrative diagnosis categories, we should lower their reimbursements. Although such cherry picking is a real problem, it seems to me that specialty hospitals have no more incentive to cherry pick than other hospitals, and that the better solution for this problem would be to lower reimbursements for these healthier patients and lucrative categories regardless of what sort of hospital provides the treatment. Professor Pasquale also argues that if the data showed that specialty hospitals erode cross-subsidization of emergent or indigent care, then we should tax them and directly subsidize that care. However, it seems to me that no matter what that data showed, directly subsidizing emergent or indigent care would be more desirable than relying on cross-subsidizations that make such care less reliable and create possible inefficiencies in the organization and costs of other care. Nor is it clear why taxing specialty hospitals in particular would be the best source of funds for such a subsidy.

My view on whether it would be advisable, as Professors Blumstein, Cebul, Rebitzer, Taylor, and Votruba suggest, to replace vicarious tort liability doctrine with enterprise liability for hospitals turns on whether other legal changes are made. Under the current regime, where hospitals have little control over physicians whether they are employees or not, making hospitals vicariously liable for torts by physicians only if they are employees makes little sense. Thus, if no other legal changes were made, it would be better to make hospital tort liability for physicians the same whether or not they are employees, which could be accomplished either by eliminating vicarious liability (leaving hospitals liable for neither) or adopting enterprise liability (making hospitals liable for both). But in other markets, where firms are able to control their employees, the traditional vicarious liability doctrine does make sense because it makes liability follow control, and without control it is hard to see what benefit would come from liability. Thus, if other legal changes were adopted to enable integrated firms to exert real control over physician employees, and if disintegrated hospitals really exerted no control over physicians operating on hospital premises, then I doubt it would make sense to adopt enterprise liability. Indeed, such a change would seem to tilt the field in favor of excessive integration because it would provide a powerful liability reason to exert control even where otherwise it would not be merited.

However, I would make some exceptions to the general policy of not forcing forms of integration that cannot succeed on the market. First, assuming we maintain a market system where insurer incentives to provide certain forms of care depend on the extent to which individuals switch insurers, then I think optimal health care will require centralized risk adjustments to the payments those insurers receive.[8] Otherwise, insurers would have incentives to provide care in a way that induces low-risk individuals to enroll (say by emphasizing sports medicine) and high-risk individuals to disenroll (say by giving them poor care). However, such risk-adjustments will necessarily require some centralized group-level decisions about how resources should be allocated among various health care needs.

Second, again assuming a regime where individuals can switch insurers, we are necessarily going to have fragmentation over time, which will lead to under-investment in preventive care with long-term health benefits, as Professors Cebul, Rebitzer, Taylor, and Votruba show. One reform they suggest—reducing search friction costs by having a default insurance policy—would actually worsen this problem by making switching easier and might also reduce competition and innovation in offering varying types of insurance. But trying to make switching insurers more difficult in order to make insurers more long-term oriented also

---

8. Elhauge, *Allocating Health Care Morally*, 82 Calif. L. Rev. 1449, 1533–34 (1994); Elhauge, *Can Health Law Become a Coherent Field of Law?*, *supra* note 6, at 387.

makes insurers less accountable, which hardly seems preferable. One could mandate the provision of preventive care, but they are right that this produces enforcement problems given the inevitable incentive to shirk unfunded mandates. A better solution would be providing centralized funding for care with long-term health benefits, with the funding amount reflecting the expected gain in health outcomes produced.

Third, I agree with Professors Cebul, Rebitzer, Taylor and Votruba that we should mandate or subsidize the creation of a common system of electronic medical records. The reason is that, although integrated providers are certainly more likely to use electronic medical records than nonintegrated plans, Professors Hall and Schulman's analysis indicates that an integrated provider still has incentives to make its electronic records incompatible with other integrated producers because doing so makes it harder for patients to switch providers. Left to its own devices, a free market will thus not produce the optimal common system of electronic medical records, and government regulations to require or induce a common system will help make the market more competitive. Although Professors Hall and Schulman are certainly right to advocate legal changes allowing patients to authorize use of their medical records for a fee, and Professors Cebul, Rebitzer, Taylor, and Votruba are right that insurers and patients can try to assemble some of the data, I doubt that either alternative will be sufficient given providers' affirmative incentives to create incompatible records.

Leaving aside such exceptions, I would lift legal obstacles to integration, but not adopt legal changes that would mandate particular forms of integration. But lifting these obstacles only fixes one half of the problem—allowing the creation of residual claimants who can select, monitor, and control the others involved in health care team production. The other half of the problem is to pay the residual claimants in a way that gives them optimal incentives to produce what we want, which is beneficial health outcomes.

In health care, reforms to encourage integration have normally been coupled with fixed payments for all treatments provided either for an episode of care or for an insured individual in a year. The problem with this approach is that to the extent that integrated providers or insurers have discretion over what treatments to provide, then this system gives them incentives to provide suboptimal care, denying it even when the benefits exceed the costs. We could try to take away that discretion, by defining precisely what care must be provided, which tended to be the legal reaction whenever HMOs denied care. But then the real decisions are being made by centralized regulators, and we lose any advantage from having integrated firms tailor care to specific cases and innovate with different methods of team production. Alternatively, we could try to couple more integrated providers with fee-for-service payments. But then the providers would have an incentive to over-care and little incentive to coordinate care effectively, because a lack of coordination just increases the services for which they can bill.

We can do better. One strategy would be to stop paying per treatments or for promises to cover "necessary" treatments, but instead to define the health outcomes we value and pay for those outcomes. The most plausible such strategy, it seems to me, is to pay providers based on the quality-adjusted life-years their treatments save. Assuming that this was the right measure of the health outcomes we value and that we could measure it, this would give integrated firms the ideal incentives to provide and organize care in a way that provides the greatest health benefit per dollar spent. With those assumptions, the system could even solve the problem of encouraging plans to provide preventive care that has long-term benefits, because that care could be paid based on the expected quality-adjusted life-years it would provide.

Unfortunately, both those assumptions are rather doubtful. As I have pointed out in other work, there is considerable, and quite reasonable, disagreement about whether the health outcome to maximize should be quality-adjusted life-years, or instead lives-saved, life-years saved, the well-being of the worst off, or the odds of reaching a normal life span.[9] Further, there is reasonable disagreement about the quality of life under various conditions, and quality-adjusted life-year measures aggregate quite different views on that crucial issue, with the results turning on just what method is used to aggregate those varying views.[10] Nor does it seem that feasible to reliably measure how many quality-adjusted life-years different providers or plans saved because it is hard not only to measure quality, but also to measure what quality and life expectancy would have been in the but-for world without the treatment.

A second strategy would be to pay plans based on the number of enrollees they attract. To avoid incentives to under-care or over-care, I would separate the payments that plans receive for each enrollment from the payments that plans receive for providing care to their enrollees.[11] The former the plans would keep as profits, but the latter would constitute a fixed budget that the plans would have to spend on care for their enrollees. This would eliminate incentives to over-care (because increased care would not expand the budget) or under-care (because profits could not be retained from unspent portions of this budget). I would also risk-adjust the care payments that plans receive so they do not have incentives to selectively enroll low-risk individuals.

Under this second strategy, plans would have incentives to coordinate and allocate care in the manner that was most attractive to enrollees. This would give plans incentives to squeeze the most health benefit they can out of their budgets. Different plans would also be able to offer different health-maximization goals,

---

9. Elhauge, *Allocating Health Care Morally, supra* note 8, at 1493, 1496–1510.

10. *Id.* at 1509, 1524–25.

11. *Id.* at 1453; Elhauge, *Can Health Law Become a Coherent Field of Law?, supra* note 6, at 388–39.

with individuals permitted to choose among plans based on the health-maximization goals they favor.[12] This would respect reasonable disagreements about how best to measure health outcomes by allowing a diversity of choices on that issue.[13] Plans would instead compete both in being efficient with their budgets and in offering the health-maximization goals that were most attractive to consumers.

I agree with Professors Enthoven, Helland, and Klick that it would be better to sever the link between health insurance and employment. But the above two strategies could also be pursued within the context of our existing system, by any employer or private or public insurer, if the law were changed to allow integrated firm providers and payments that were not for all medically necessary care. Better still in my view would be to have the government set an annual health care budget funded by a tax not linked to employment, out of which it would make payments to whichever provider or plan individuals chose, with the payments made pursuant to one of the above two strategies.[14] Unlike Professors Enthoven, Helland, and Klick, I would not require that each plan offer the same benefits, because that would eliminate the virtue of competition between plans in offering the most efficient set of benefits or the most desired way of trading those benefits off.

In short, for defragmenting health care to really work, we are going to have to couple (1) reforms lifting laws that bar integrated firms from monitoring and controlling a team of medical professionals with (2) payments for the output produced by those integrated firms that give their owners incentives to optimize the coordination of medical professionals. Payments per treatment or for promises to treat are not really payments for output, and respectively incentivize overcare or under-care. We could pay per medical improvement provided if it is measurable and we have a sufficient consensus on how to define it. Or we could define the output as attracted enrollees, and pay per enrollee attracted. Either payment approach would require repealing or preempting laws that require insurers to pay for any "medically necessary" care within a category they cover, and allowing insurers to instead pay per health improvement or be paid per enrollee they can attract with their method for allocating care. But if the above legal restraints were lifted, then this sort of approach could be used by employers or insurers under our current system, as well as by the government in a more thorough reform.

---

12. Elhauge, *Allocating Health Care Morally, supra* note 8, at 1453–56; Elhauge, *The Limited Regulatory Potential of Medical Technology Assessment, supra* note 6, at 1620–22; Elhauge, *Can Health Law Become a Coherent Field of Law?, supra* note 6, at 385–390.

13. Elhauge, *Allocating Health Care Morally, supra* note 8, at 1451, 1456, 1507, 1510, 1524–26.

14. *Id.* at 1453.

2. HEALTH CARE FRAGMENTATION
We Get What We Pay For

DAVID A. HYMAN[1]

I suspect that our collective search for villains—for someone to blame—has distracted us and our political leaders from addressing the fundamental causes of our nation's health-care crisis. All of the actors in health care—from doctors to insurers to pharmaceutical companies—work in a heavily regulated, massively subsidized industry full of structural distortions. They all want to serve patients well. But they also all behave rationally in response to the economic incentives those distortions create. Accidentally, but relentlessly, America has built a health-care system with incentives that inexorably generate terrible and perverse results. Incentives that emphasize health *care* over any other aspect of health and well-being. That emphasize treatment over prevention. That disguise true costs. That favor complexity, and discourage transparent competition based on price or quality.[2]

Compared to other industries that deal with comparably complex products, health care delivery is extremely fragmented. When I flew to Boston to attend the conference on fragmentation at which I presented this paper, I booked and paid for the entire trip by dealing with the Web site of a single entity (American Airlines). I did not have to find, negotiate, contract with, and separately pay the airline, pilot, co-pilot, flight attendant, baggage handler, gate agent, and so on. Instead, I purchased a bundled product—"a round-trip flight from Champaign, Illinois to Boston, Massachusetts"—and the airline took care of dividing the resulting revenue (and hopefully profits) among those entities and individuals whose collective efforts were required to make the flight happen.

Health care delivery presents a radically different picture. A visit to the hospital results in bills from multiple actors—each individually itemized, reflecting the particular goods and services that were provided.[3] An outpatient visit to a physician will similarly result in separate bills for evaluation and management,

1. Richard & Marie Corman Professor of Law and Professor of Medicine, University of Illinois. In the interest of full disclosure, I have been retained as an expert witness in a parallel proceeding to the case described in note 26, *infra*.

2. David Goldhill, How American Health Care Killed My Father, The Atlantic, Sep. 2009, available at http://www.theatlantic.com/doc/200909/health-care.

3. *See, e.g.*, Tom McGrath, *My Daughter's $29,000 Appendectomy*, PHILADELPHIA MAGAZINE, *available at* http://www.phillymag.com/articles/top_doctors_my_daughters_29000_appendectomy/.

clinical laboratory services, imaging, imaging interpretation, and so on. Patients with chronic illnesses will add bills from durable medical equipment providers, home health agencies, physical therapists, and the like. This is not to suggest that the system is fully fragmented; hospitals (and, to a lesser extent, physicians) do aggregate many services under one roof. Yet, the degree of fragmentation is still remarkably high.

The payment system plays an important role in encouraging and maintaining this degree of fragmentation. To be sure, a host of other factors, including physician and consumer preferences, history, path dependence, social norms, law, and the like help explain why health care delivery looks the way that it does.[4] Further, the payment system looks the way that it does, at least in part, because of these other factors. Despite these complications, the payment system is one of the few accessible levers with which to begin to defragment the system.

Part I provides a brief overview of fragmentation. Part II describes the role of the payment system in creating and maintaining this state of affairs. Part III offers several potential reform strategies. Part IV explains why it is necessary to have a theory of optimal fragmentation (and some insight into whether consumers care one way or the other) before settling on a reform strategy. Part V concludes.

I. FRAGMENTATION: WHAT AND WHERE

Numerous commentators have remarked on the degree of fragmentation of the U.S. health care system.[5] Fragmentation manifests itself across every practice setting, in every state, for all types of patients—and where it occurs, it contributes to higher costs and lower quality.[6] For a patient with one or more chronic

---

4. For a glimpse into the history of these controversies, see Jeff Goldsmith, *Driving the Nitroglycerin Truck*, HEALTHCARE FORUM J. 36 (Mar/Apr. 1993), *available at* http://www.healthfutures.net/pdf/w-nitro.pdf.

5. Thomas Bodenheimer, Coordinating Care—*A Perilous Journey through the Health Care System*, 358 NEW ENG. J. MED. 1064 (2008); Alain C. Enthoven & Laura A. Tolen, *Competition in Health Care: It Takes Systems to Pursue Quality and Efficiency*, HEALTH AFF WEB. EXCL., Sept. 7, 2005 at W5-420; A. Mark Clarfield, Howard Bergman & Robert Kane, *Fragmentation of Care for Frail Older People—an International Problem*, 49 J. AM. GERIATRICS SOCIETY 1714 (2001); STEPHEN M. SHORTELL ET AL., REMAKING HEALTH CARE IN AMERICA: BUILDING ORGANIZED DELIVERY SYSTEMS (1996).

6. *See, generally* Katherine Baicker & Amitabh Chandra, Medicare Spending, the Physician Workforce, and Beneficiaries' Quality of Care, 23 HEALTH AFF. 2004;23:w4-184; *Delivery Systems Matter! Improving Quality and Efficiency in Health Care*, March 17, 2004, Kaiser Permanente Institute for Health Policy and Health Affairs, Washington, D.C., *available at* http://www.kpihp.org/publications/docs/delivery_systems.pdf; Barbara Starfield, et al., Contribution of primary care to health systems and health. 83 MILBANK Q. 457 (2005).

illnesses, it is likely to be experienced as the absence of a physician responsible for coordinating the care the patient receives. Instead, care is typically provided by a host of specialists, each focused on the discrete symptoms and/or body parts within their jurisdiction.[7] Whether chronically ill or not, the patient or a family member ends up bearing most of the responsibility for keeping track of their prescriptions, tests received, and physicians seen. Details of past hospitalizations and the results of tests and imaging studies are often unavailable, even when the patient is returning to the same physician. When the records are available, each "new" physician may express skepticism about the quality of the work-up that had been done previously—and so imaging studies and laboratory tests are routinely repeated. Patients without a regular source of care go to emergency rooms, where old records are rarely available.

Physicians are organizationally fragmented as well. Multi-specialty group practices are rare, and accountable care organizations don't exist.[8] Hospitals and physicians occupy separate organizational universes, although the latter profoundly affect the fiscal fate of the former—and increasingly compete with it.

When systems exist, they are integrated to varying degrees—and there is little integration/continuity across systems. For example, we have various safety net systems, but they almost invariably focus on a particular problem (e.g., mental illness, substance abuse, adolescent pregnancy), or a particular demographic group (the poor, pregnant mothers, children). This is not a situation that holds much promise for integrated care across an extended time-period.[9]

---

7. Hoangmai H. Pham et al., *Care Patterns in Medicare and Their Implications for Pay for Performance*, 356 NEW ENG. J. MED. 1130 (2007) (noting that the average Medicare beneficiary saw two primary care physicians and five specialists over the course of a given year, with higher figures for patients with chronic illnesses).

8. Bodenheimer, *supra* note 5; Elliott Fisher, et al., *Creating Accountable Care Organizations: the Extended Hospital Medical Staff*, 26 HEALTH AFF. w44-w57 (2007).

9. The Veterans Health Administration ("VA") is one of the few exceptions. The VA exemplifies both the potential for improvement in quality that can result from delivering coordinated care—as well as the horrendous consequences that can result when a government program does a bad job, and program beneficiaries lack both exit and voice. Compare PHILLIP LONGMAN, BEST CARE ANYWHERE: WHY VA HEALTH CARE IS BETTER THAN YOURS (2007) with David A. Hyman & Charles Silver, *The Poor State of Health Care Quality in the U.S.: Is Malpractice Liability Part of the Problem or Part of the Solution?* 90 CORNELL L. REV. 893, 934–937 (2005) (cataloging several decades of Congressional oversight and GAO investigations in response to quality of care scandals at VA facilities) and Steve Vogel, *Negligence Suits Likely Over VA Procedures*, Wash. Post, Aug. 24, 2009, available at http://www.washingtonpost.com/wp-dyn/content/article/2009/08/23/AR2009082302175.html (documenting failure of VA employees at several facilities to properly sterilize endoscopic equipment, resulting in exposure of roughly 11,000 veterans to cross-contamination, and risk of developing HIV and hepatitis).

The VA is also experiencing problems with its vaunted software. *See* Office of the Inspector General, U.S Department of Veterans Affairs, *Review of Defects in VA's*

Fragmentation also results from our IT infrastructure—or lack thereof, to be more precise. The absence of agreed standards for interoperability and confidentiality are compounded by the unwillingness of individual providers to invest in such systems unless they are paid to do so. Without good information on clinical matters, we are left with billing/claims records as the principal source of data on the performance of the health care system.

Fragmentation also results from our diverse array of coverage/financing arrangements. Even if patients have identified a physician that they trust to coordinate their care, that physician might not be covered by their insurance plan when they need care. This problem is compounded by the regular turn-over of employers' insurance offerings—an effect further magnified by the fact that roughly 60 percent of the non-elderly population obtains health insurance through an employer. The same dynamic operates when an individual changes employers.

The categorical nature of public coverage creates its own silos; children age out of Medicaid even if their income does not rise; low-income women are covered by Medicaid while pregnant, but not (much) thereafter; SCHIP covers children as long as they fall below a certain income and age, with the precise amount to qualify changing with the fiscal fortunes and priorities of the state and federal governments.

Thus, there is fragmentation on both the financing and delivery sides of the market. Both varieties of fragmentation have their own history, political implications, and consequences. The balance of this paper focuses on the impact of the payment system on delivery-side fragmentation.

II. THE IMPORTANCE OF THE PAYMENT SYSTEM IN EXPLAINING FRAGMENTATION

Sorting out the comparative significance of the various drivers of fragmentation is a daunting undertaking. I focus on the manner in which we pay for health care because it is an important enough cause to justify such attention—and it is also easier to fix than many of the other root causes. There is also near-universal agreement that the payment system is not doing its part to ensure that only high-quality care is delivered.[10]

Computerized Patient Record System Version 27 and Associated Quality of Care Issues, Report Np. 09-01033-155 (2009), available at http://www.va.gov/oig/publications/report-summary.asp?id=3444 Office of the Inspector General, U.S Department of Veterans Affairs, *Review of the Award and Administration of Task Orders Issued by the Department of Veterans Affairs for the Replacement Scheduling Application Development Program (RSA)*, Report No. 09-01926-207 (2009).

10. *See, e.g.*, INSTITUTE OF MEDICINE, REWARDING PROVIDER PERFORMANCE: ALIGNING INCENTIVES IN MEDICARE, (2007) ("The current Medicare fee-for-service payment system

The root cause of this failure is fairly obvious: in health care, most compensation arrangements pay health care providers for what they do, not for what they accomplish.[11] The failure to tie compensation to variables that correlate closely with patients' needs and desires means that providers rarely have an economic incentive to invest in quality or prevent error. More concretely, when physicians are paid using a fee-for-service system of compensation for every patient encounter they have, there is no necessary nexus between payment and quality of care.[12]

---

is unlikely to promote quality improvement because it tends to reward excessive use of services; high-cost, complex procedures; and lower-quality care. Through bundled and prospective payment arrangements for institutions, Medicare has attempted to create incentives for efficiencies, but significant price and payment distortions persist.Services that contribute greatly to high-quality care that are labor- or time-intensive and rely less on technical resources, such as patient education in self-management of chronic conditions and care coordination, tend to be undervalued and are not adequately reflected in current payment arrangements. Little emphasis is placed on efficiency (achieving high clinical quality with a given amount of resources). The lack of incentives for comprehensive, coordinated care discourages services targeting early intervention and prevention that can ultimately reduce the use of expensive services, such as avoidable hospitalizations. Providers often miss opportunities for collaboration since the payment system rewards neither team management nor the integration of services across care settings."); INSTITUTE OF MEDICINE, CROSSING THE QUALITY CHASM: A NEW HEALTH SYSTEM FOR THE 21ST CENTURY (2001) ("Current payment methods do not adequately encourage or support the provision of quality health care, and in some instances, they may actually impede local innovations and efforts to improve quality. . . Payment methods should encourage the implementation of care processes based on best practices and the achievement of better patient outcomes. Whenever possible, payment methods should provide an opportunity for providers to share in the benefits of quality improvement."); Senate Finance Committee, Transforming the Health Care Delivery System: Proposals to Improve Patient Care and Reduce Health Care Costs (Apr. 29, 2009), available at http://finance.senate.gov/sitepages/leg/LEG%202009/042809%20Health%20Care%20Description%20of%20Policy%20option.pdf ("It has become increasingly evident that the way health care is paid for in our system does not always encourage the right care, at the right time, for each and every patient. Today's payment systems more often reward providers for the quantity of care delivered, rather than the quality of care and discourage providers from working together to offer patients the best possible care."); Medicare Drifting Toward Disaster, Reuters, April 29, 2008, available at http://www.reuters.com/article/topNews/idUSN2936521220080429 ("Leavitt said paying for each medical action separately is wasteful and "it often results in bad referral decisions, sloppy hand-offs, duplications, fraud, and poor quality of care. The result is inappropriate care and unnecessary cost.").

11. DAVID A. KINDIG, PURCHASING POPULATION HEALTH (1998) (quoting former Assistant Secretary of Health and Human Services Dr. Philip Lee) (providers "get paid for what we do, not what we accomplish."). See also David A. Kindig, Purchasing Population Health: Aligning Financial Incentives to Improve Health Outcomes, 33 HEALTH SERVICES RES. 223, 223 (1988) (same).

12. Julie Salamon, A Year Long Medical Exam, WALL ST. J., May 17–18, 2008, at W8 ("All the things that are really good—diabetes care, asthma care, taking good care of

As a former dean of clinical affairs at George Washington Hospital, turned long-time president of the principal accrediting entity in health care (JCAHO) summarized: "when I came out of school I thought that someone would be measuring my performance, and that I would be paid accordingly. That seemed logical to me. . . But it turned out that I could do as well or as poorly as I wanted and get paid anyway."[13]

Consider Medicare, responsible for roughly $400 billion in health care spending in 2006, and the dominant way in which the federal government sets health policy. Medicare has separate payment systems for hospitalization (Part A), outpatient services (Part B), and pharmaceuticals (Part D).[14] Each has its own rules for coverage, copayments, and deductibles. None are cost-based, but all employ an encounter-based piece-work model of compensation—meaning that the price per unit is controlled, but the volume of billed services is not. Each of these three parts operate as payment silos, focusing only on the bills that they receive. None seek to actively manage or influence care delivery patterns, apart from prohibitions on outright fraud. Each routinely pays quite different amounts for the same services, depending on where the service is rendered. None pay for time spent attempting to coordinate the delivery of services.

In purchasing services, Medicare also has a historical bias toward paying more for certain services. In general, specialists have done better than generalists, and procedural specialists have done better than cognitive specialists.[15] Although there has been some improvement in these patterns in response to various payment system reforms, the rise of imaging-related costs has left payment for cognitive services more or less where it has always been.

By paying for each unit of disaggregated medical services separately, Medicare creates no incentive for providers to consider the whole picture. More broadly, providers have no economic incentive to coordinate their efforts across treatment locations or specialties—and there is often a disincentive to do so.

---

cancer patients—you don't get paid for that . . . you get paid for radiating people, doing complicated surgery, giving them chemotherapy.")

13. Bonnie Darves, *Physician Pay For Performance Programs Taking Hold*, NEW ENG. J. MED., *available at* http://www.nejmjobs.org/career-resources/pay-for-performance.aspx.

14. I exclude Medicare Part C, which combines and delegates these payment functions, because its continued viability remains to be seen, given its status as a political football.

15. Vanessa Furhmans, *Medical Specialties Hit by a Growing Pay Gap*, WALL ST. J., May 13, 2008, at A1 ("Many in health-policy circles have focused on how the current health-care payment system is helping create shortages among primary-care doctors, internists and others on the front lines of medicine. But often lost is how the system is endangering some of the country's most highly trained specialties as well. Endocrinologists, rheumatologists and pulmonologists—specialties that also don't involve performing many procedures—face acute shortages."); American College of Physicians, *Reform of the Dysfunctional Healthcare Payment and Delivery System* (2006), *available at* www.acponline.org/advocacy/where_we_stand/policy/dysfunctional_payment.pdf.

Since each service is separately paid, integration/coordination that lowers the need for such services can result in lower payments to providers. Indeed, under some circumstances, providers can actually do better if their patients do worse. Not surprisingly, providers feel no particular urgency to take steps that will worsen their financial position. Stated differently, our current payment system does not create a "business case" for either quality or integration.[16]

The interaction between Medicare and Medicaid creates additional opportunities for mischief. "Dual eligibles," who qualify for both programs, often have complex medical and chronic care needs. Coordination is a particular challenge when the two programs "have differing incentives and approaches to client care and funding sources and payments."[17] Worse still, because the two programs are separate, each has an incentive to shift costs to the other: "care management in Medicare might shift costs to long-term care services covered by Medicaid . . . and vice versa."[18] The National Governor's Association has similarly observed that "Medicare is at risk if poor care is rendered during a long term nursing home stay (paid by Medicaid) that results in a hospitalization for a fall or a decubitus ulcer. Medicaid is at risk if the lack of access to prescription drug coverage . . . causes unnecessary nursing facility stays."[19] Congress finally acknowledged this problem in 2003, but its preferred solution is decidedly underpowered.[20]

The current state of affairs in Medicare is nicely summarized by the Institute of Medicine (IOM):

The health care Medicare beneficiaries receive is often fragmented as patients move among different physicians and across different care settings (e.g., hospital to home care). As a result, patients do not always receive timely care best suited to their needs. Fragmentation is reinforced by the failure of the current payment system to recognize and pay for care coordination.[21]

---

16. Sheila Leatherman et al., *The Business Case for Quality, Case Studies and An Analysis*, 22 HEALTH AFF. 17 (2003).

17. Medicare and Medicaid Integration, http://www.hhs.state.tx.us/medicaid/Research Papers/MedicareandMedicaidIntegration.pdf.

18. *Id.*

19. Dual Eligibles: Making the Case for Federalization, 8, *available at* www.nga.org/Files/pdf/0505Dual.pdf.

20. Improving Access to Integrated Care For Beneficiaries Who Are Dually Eligible for Medicare and Medicaid, http://www.cms.hhs.gov/apps/media/press/release.asp?Counter=1912.

21. Institute of Medicine, Rewarding Provider Performance: Aligning Incentives in Medicare, Sep. 2007, *available at* http://www.iom.edu/CMS/3809/25241/37232/37236. aspx. *See also* Karen Davis, *Paying for Care Episodes and Care Coordination*, 356 NEW ENG. J. MED. 1166 (2007) ("The fee-for-service system of provider payment is increasingly viewed as an obstacle to achieving effective, coordinated, and efficient care. It rewards the overuse of services, duplication of services, use of costly specialized services, and involvement of multiple physicians in the treatment of individual patients. It does not reward the

Not surprisingly, the IOM recommends payment reform as a strategy for addressing these problems.

Private payers do not have distinct programs for purchasing inpatient versus outpatient services and pharmaceuticals to the same degree as does Medicare, but there are still broad similarities. This is not all that surprising when one considers that Medicare was modeled on the coverage arrangements that prevailed in the private sector in 1965. For example, most insurers appear to outsource responsibility for handling prescription drug coverage to pharmacy benefit managers, and carve-out various parts of the benefit package, such as mental health care. As with dual eligibles within Medicare/Medicaid, such contractual arrangements can result in difficulties at the interface of the covered services—even if the contracted-out services are run efficiently. The demise of capitation has also meant that most payers employ discounted fee-for-service, coupled with soft forms of utilization review. As with Medicare, private payers generally pay for inputs, not outputs.

Of course, payment incentives are not destiny; providers could fully integrate the delivery system on their own—and share the resulting payments within a newly-created firm. The existence of some integrated delivery systems shows that such arrangements are possible, although such arrangements have had difficulty spreading outside their native habitat on the West Coast. Why has an institutional form with such obvious promise not been adopted more widely? In other sectors of the economy, there is a ceaseless process of reinvention, including unbundling and rebundling of products and services, in an attempt to meet (and even create) consumer demand. The opportunity to capture a share of the more than two trillion spent per year on health care creates an obvious spur to such attempts.

Here, the thicket of other regulatory constraints—many of them implicitly built around "traditional" (i.e. fragmented) ways of paying for and delivering health care services—plays an important role. When an innovative arrangement can be labeled "fraudulent and abusive," it tends to chill innovation. Thus, attempts by physicians and hospitals to use gainsharing programs to align their economic incentives were stopped in their tracks by a 1999 OIG Special Advisory Bulletin.[22] Subsequent guidance modestly eased the constraints, and the Medicare Payment Advisory Commission has come out in favor of such

---

prevention of hospitalization or rehospitalization, effective control of chronic conditions, or care coordination.")

22. See Gainsharing Arrangements and CMPs for Hospital Payment to Physicians to Reduce or Limit Services to Beneficiaries (July 1999), reprinted in 64 Fed. Reg. 37,985 (July 14, 1999). See also Gail Wilensky, Nicholas Wolter & Michelle M. Fischer, *Gain Sharing: A Good Concept Getting a Bad Name?* Health Affairs, 26, no. 1 (2007): w58–w67, available at http://content.healthaffairs.org/cgi/content/full/26/1/w58; Betsy McCubrey, *OIG Bulletin Highlights Schizophrenic Attitude in Cost-Saving Measures: Gainsharing Arrangements—Their History, Use, and Future,* 79 N.C. L. Rev. 157 (2000).

arrangements as well—but there is sufficient residual uncertainty that many lawyers advise their clients to obtain individualized advisory opinions from the Office of the Inspector General at HHS. The risks of proceeding without an advisory opinion are substantial; in 2004, a federal judge in New Jersey permanently enjoined a gainsharing demonstration project approved by HHS on the grounds HHS "should have required the proposed participants in the Demonstration Project to secure an Advisory Opinion from the OIG. . . ."[23]

The basic difficulty is that these rules are designed to protect the "integrity" of the program, but "integrity" is defined by reference to traditional (i.e., fragmented) forms of health care delivery, irrespective of whether the result is efficient or not.[24] It is precisely these traditional understandings of how the health care delivery system should be owned and controlled that have brought us to the current state of affairs, with a system that has hard-wired "incentives that inexorably generate terrible and perverse results."[25]

Finally, even if regulators choose not to enforce the letter of these laws, it does not follow that private parties will be so understanding. Between the false claims act, federal and state antitrust and "unfair competition" laws, and tortious interference claims, providers who find themselves losing referrals and revenues as a result of integration have a ready way to push back against their competitors.[26] Part III turns to various strategies for addressing the problem of fragmentation.

III. PAYMENT REFORM STRATEGIES

It is one thing to agree that the current payment system does not create optimal incentives for the efficient delivery of high-quality care, and quite another to come up with a reform proposal that improves on the status quo. Top-down prescriptive strategies have the advantage of concretely specifying the boundaries of acceptable fragmentation; the conditions of participation in Medicare could easily be leveraged into substantive regulation of the degree of fragmentation.

---

23. Robert Wood Johnson University Hospital, Inc. v. Tommy G. Thompson, 2004 WL 3210732 (D. N.J. 2004).

24. David A. Hyman, *Health Care Fraud and Abuse: Market Change, Social Norms, and 'the Trust Reposed in the Workmen,'* 30 J. LEGAL STUD. 531 (2001) ("Providers who wish to partner with one another to deliver higher quality services and share the economic proceeds from that arrangement are forced by the anti-kickback law to structure their relationship to fall within an existing safe harbor, obtain an advisory opinion, or take their chances they will not be prosecuted . . . The anti-kickback laws encourage complete vertical integration but frown on intermediate steps along the way.").

25. *See supra* note 2.

26. Tricia Bishop, *Baltimore Jury Finds Cardiology Practice Guilty of Fraud,* BALT. SUN, Dec. 22, 2005, *available at* http://www.redorbit.com/news/health/337514/baltimore_jury_finds_cardiology_practice_guilty_of_fraud/.

At present, there is neither the political will nor broad agreement on the "right" rules that would be necessary to undertake this step. Even if both preconditions were satisfied, top-down prescriptive regulatory strategies of this sort eliminate flexibility and innovation.

I discuss three possible payment reforms that have the potential to encourage integration, but still allow for flexibility and innovation: paying for coordination of care, paying for performance, and paying for episodes of care. Obviously, direct delivery-side reform, such as the development of "medical homes," or the determination that identifiable physicians will be held responsible for the cost-efficiency of the care received by individual patients may also trigger greater integration of care.[27] However, payment reform is likely to be an important factor in such reforms, regardless.

A. Payment Reform Strategies

1. Payment for coordination of care

As noted previously, our encounter-based fee-for-service system does not pay for coordination of care. The most obvious strategy is to begin paying individuals (typically primary care physicians) or group practices that provide such services. Medicare currently has a demonstration project that does exactly that, involving physician groups. Other models are also available.[28]

To be sure, payment for coordination does not necessarily result in defragmentation of the system—or of the care that is provided. It may just mean that someone is now being paid to attempt to coordinate the delivery of services across a still-fragmented system. Additional fee-for-service payments for coordination will be a benefit to those receiving the new money—but the system will be prone to some of the same abuses (and some new ones) than those currently prevailing.[29] Plus, it is hard to see where we will find "new" money to pay for coordination when the sustainable growth rate formula already creates an annual fight over threatened cuts in physician payments.

---

27. The Tax Relief and Health Care Act of 2006 requires CMS to conduct a demonstration project of the medical home concept of patient care. A medical home is defined as a large or small medical practice where a physician provides comprehensive and coordinated patient centered medical care and acts as the "personal physician" to the patient.

28. Francois de Brantes, Meredith B. Rosenthal & Michael Painter, *Building a Bridge from Fragmentation to Accountability—The Prometheus Payment Model*, 361 New Eng. J. Med. 1033 (2009); Allan H. Goroll et al., *Fundamental Reform of Payment for Adult Primary care: Comprehensive Payment for Comprehensive Care*, 22 J. GEN. INTERNAL MED. 410 (2007).

29. Interview of Glenn Hackbarth, *Care Coordination for Medicare Beneficiaries*, HEALTHCARE FINANCIAL MANAGEMENT (Jan. 2008), *available at* http://findarticles.com/p/articles/mi_m3257/is_1_62/ai_n24381850 ("If Medicare makes a lump-sum payment for 'care coordination,' what exactly is it buying—and how does it verify that care coordination is actually being delivered?")

2. Payment for performance (P4P)

P4P represents an incremental effort to use economic incentives to encourage health care providers to consistently deliver high-quality care.[30] By forcing providers to internalize the costs of low-quality care and enabling them to capture the benefits of high-quality care, P4P attempts to harness the self-interest of providers to improve quality of care. P4P arrangements have become extremely common in recent years. Medicare recently announced it will no longer pay for certain events that should never occur ("never events").[31] Medicare also recently completed a demonstration project that paid modest financial incentives for hospitals that did well (and modest financial disincentives for hospitals that did poorly) on specified measures of quality for five conditions.[32] Medicare has a number of similar bonus programs for managed care plans and physicians.[33]

Employers and private plans have enthusiastically adopted P4P.[34] The Pacific Business Group on Health has been using incentive-based performance targets for many years in its contracts with HMOs.[35] The Leapfrog Group, a coalition of 145 private and public organizations, is using its purchasing power to

---

30. *See, e.g.*, Arnold M. Epstein, *Pay for Performance at the Tipping Point*, 356 NEW ENG. J. MED. 515 (2007); Peter K. Lindenauer et al., *Public Reporting and Pay for Performance In Hospital Quality Improvement*, 356 NEW ENG. J. MED. 486 (2007); Meredith B. Rosenthal et al., *Pay for Performance in Commercial HMOs*, 355 NEW ENG. J. MED. 1895 (2006).

In two prior articles, I called for increased used of result-based compensation arrangements (RBCA's) that would tie providers' compensation to measurable improvements in patients' health or other objective targets. David A. Hyman & Charles Silver, *You Get What You Pay For: Result-Based Compensation for Health Care*, 58 WASHINGTON & LEE L. REV. 1427 (2001) (hereinafter *You Get What You Pay For*); David A. Hyman & Charles Silver, *Just What the Patient Ordered: The Case For Result-Based Compensation in Health Care*, 29 J. L. MED. & ETHICS 170 (2001). Although we appear to have won the war over the propriety and desirability of these arrangements, we lost the battle over acronyms. P4P has swept RBCA from the field.

31. Centers for Medicare and Medicaid Services, *Eliminating Serious, Preventible, and Costly Medical Errors—Never Events*, May 18, 2006), *available at* http://www.cms.hhs.gov/apps/media/press/release.asp?Counter=1863.

32. *See* Centers for Medicare & Medicaid Services, *Premier Hospital Quality Incentive Demonstration*, *available at* http://www.cms.hhs.gov/hospitalqualityinits/35_hospitalpremier.asp; Reed Abelson, *Bonus Pay By Medicare Lifts Quality*, N.Y. TIMES, Jan. 25, 2007, *available at* http://www.nytimes.com/2007/01/25/business/25care.html?_r=1&oref=slogin.

33. Centers for Medicare & Medicaid Services, *Medicare "Pay For Performance (P4P)" Initiatives*, Jan. 31, 2005, *available at* http://www.cms.hhs.gov/apps/media/press/release.asp?counter=1343.

34. *See, e.g.*, The National Pay For Performance Summit, http://www.pfpsummit.com/.

35. Helen Halpin Schauffler et al., *Raising the Bar: The Use of Performance Guarantees by the Pacific Business Group on Health*, 18 HEALTH AFF. 134 (1999) (outlining use of performance contracts by Pacific Business Group on Health).

encourage hospitals to adopt computerized physician order entry ("CPOE"), referrals to high-volume hospitals for certain procedures, and staffing intensive care units ("ICUs") with intensivists.[36] Finally, multiple insurers have decided they will no longer pay for medical treatments that should not have been provided, nor will they pay the medical bills associated with the consequences of such errors.[37]

In theory, P4P can address fragmentation by creating incentives for providers to reorganize their efforts along functional grounds.[38] To date, this promise has not been fulfilled; existing programs have focused on discrete clinical conditions, and not care coordination or increased efficiency over time.[39] More broadly, current P4P programs take the existing (dysfunctional) system of compensation as given, and create incremental incentives to deliver high performance. The core incentives of our current payment system are not altered merely because a modest P4P incentive has been plopped on top of them.[40] Until P4P displaces the core incentives created by our current system of compensation, one should not expect P4P to do much to solve the problem of fragmentation, except at the margins.[41]

3. Payment for episodes of care

Instead of paying for discrete units of service, one can bundle payment temporally, to compensate for all treatment necessary for an episode of care. Pure annual capitation is the logical endpoint of this continuum, but it created significant push-back from providers and patients. An alternative is to pay a global fee for all services required as part of a "care episode"—including all hospital, physician, and ancillary services required. Payment for care episodes creates substantial incentives for providers to organize themselves and integrate

---

36. Kelly J. Devers & Gigi Liu, *Leapfrog Patient-Safety Standards Are a Stretch for Most Hospitals*, Center for Studying Health System Change, Feb. 2004, at 4.

37. Kevin O'Reilly, *No-pay for Never Event Errors Becoming Standard*, AM. MED. NEWS, Jan. 7, 2008, *available at* http://www.ama-assn.org/amednews/2008/01/07/prsco107. htm; Chen May Yee, *Health Partners to Withhold Payment for Errors*, STAR TRIBUNE, Oct. 6, 2004, at 1A.

38. Hyman & Silver, *supra* note 30, at 1477, n. 172 ("we anticipate that the availability of RBCAs is likely to trigger a significant restructuring of the health care delivery system along functional lines. . . ."); William M. Sage, *Pay For Performance: Will it Work in Theory?* 3 IND. HEALTH L. J. 303 (2006) (describing the "productivity theory" of P4P, and its potential to induce organizational change and defragmentation of health care delivery).

39. Davis, *supra* note 21.

40. Robert A. Berenson, Testimony before the Subcommittee on Health, House Ways and Means Committee, Sep. 29, 2005, *available at* http://waysandmeans.house.gov/ hearings.asp?formmode=printfriendly&id=3818.

41. For one such proposal, see John E. Wennberg et al., *Extending the P4P Agenda, Part 2: How Medicare Can Reduce Waste and Improve the Care of the Chronically Ill*, 26 HEALTH AFF. 1574 (2007).

their offerings, since if they can't provide the requisite services, and control their utilization, they either won't get paid at all, or they will suffer losses when they can't control the volume and/or cost of the services they must purchase from others. Obvious challenges arise, including identifying discrete episodes of care, setting payment levels, and policing the boundaries of the system.[42]

Medicare is in the midst of rolling out bundled payment for dialysis care and it has initiated demonstration projects of bundled payment for hospitals and physicians. However, the largest and most successful bundled payment program currently in existence is the "diagnosis-related groups" (DRG) system. For each hospitalization of a Medicare beneficiary, hospitals receive a standard prospective payment tied to the discharge diagnosis (with some adjustment for outliers, geographic variation in the cost of production, and the like). DRGs have had a profound impact on care patterns within hospitals (and an accompanying impact on hospital finances). In some respects, these changes have led to increased coordination/defragmentation: since hospitals may not get paid for some readmissions, and their fee is capped, they became more aggressive at discharge planning and controlling use of services within their four walls.[43] On the other hand, the DRG system simultaneously created incentives for hospitals to disaggregate/unbundle their service offerings, as more-rapid discharge to rehabilitation units and step-down facilities created opportunities for higher profits per admission.

IV. ON THE IMPORTANCE OF THEORY

It is one thing to complain about fragmentation, another to have a theory of optimal fragmentation, and a third to get consumers to accept the results of the theory. Health policy has long been marked by disagreement on normative premises, and the debate over fragmentation is likely to raise many of the same issues. Without a well-worked out theory of optimal fragmentation that accords

---

42. Davis, *supra* note 21.

43. To be sure, there is still a long way to go in preventing avoidable readmissions. In 2003–2004, roughly 20% of Medicare beneficiaries who had been hospitalized were readmitted within thirty days of discharge—and billing records indicated fully half of them had not seen a doctor between discharge and readmission. Stephen F. Jencks et al, *Rehospitalizations among Patients in the Medicare Fee-for-Service Program*, 360 NEW ENGL. J. MED. 1418 (2009). *See also* Arnold M. Epstein, *Revisiting Readmissions*, 360 NEW ENGL. J. MED. 1457 (2009). For one proposal on how to address the issue, see Senate Finance Committee, *supra* note 10, at 14–15.

with actual consumer preferences, reform efforts will be ineffective at best, and turn into egregious rent-seeking at worst.[44]

A few concrete examples help make the point. The rise of retail clinics has spurred opposition from some parts of organized medicine, on the grounds that it fragments health care delivery, and makes it harder for patients to have a "medical home."[45] Medical homes may be the best thing since sliced bread—or they may be this decade's version of virtual integration, primary care gate-keeping, or whatever other fad you prefer.[46] Retail clinics appear exceedingly popular with consumers, judging by the precipitous growth of the sector.[47] If we adhere to a blanket principle of "defragmentation," we would not allow this development— but in doing so we effectively grant incumbent providers a monopoly on deter- mining the optimal level of fragmentation. History indicates that providers are likely to accord great weight to their convenience and self-interest in implement- ing this invitation. The precipitous growth of retail clinics is a powerful demon- stration that consumers do not feel their needs are being met by the existing system that providers have mobilized to defend. Even the least cynical among us should regard the complaints of providers about this particular example of frag- mentation with a jaundiced eye.[48]

---

44. *See* Sage, *supra* note 38; William M. Sage, *Legislating Delivery System Reform: A 30,000 View of the 800-Pound Gorilla*, 26 HEALTH AFF. 1553 (2007).

45. *See* Bruce Japsen, *Doctors, Retailers Square Off: AMA to Seek Probe of In-Store Clinics*, CHI. TRIB., June 26, 2007, sec. 3, at 1; Jay E. Berkelhamer, *Retail Health Clinics Are a Return to an Earlier Form of Medical Care*, WALL ST. J., May 19–20, 2007, at A7 (noting the American Academy of Pediatrics' opposition to retail clinics because they undermine con- tinuity of care); Richard Bohmer, *The Rise of In-Store Clinics—Threat or Opportunity?*, 356 NEW ENG. J. MED. 765, 765, 767 (2007) ("Physicians, however, express concern about the quality of care and the potential impact on their businesses. . . . The effect of this spe- cialized care delivery model on traditional primary care practices may be to remove some patients and services from the doctor's office, leaving a sicker population behind. Some practitioners will see this as "cream skimming" and a threat to their revenue, particularly if they rely on income from short appointments for simple cases to subsidize the cost of more time-consuming appointments for more complex cases").

46. Peter D. Jacobson, *Consumer-Directed Health Care (CDHC)—Not the Next Best Thing Since Sliced Bread (Or, Why Is This Fad Different from All Other Health Policy Fads?)*, available at http://www.pennumbra.com/debates/debate.php?did=10 ("If there's a field of domestic policy that is more subject to the fad-of-the-month than health care, it eludes me.")

47. William M. Sage, *The Wal-Martization of Health Care*, 28 J. LEGAL MED. 503 (2007).

48. Consider the mind-set that motivated the response of one physician to an article in USA Today on retail clinics: "the American public cannot have it both ways. They must decide what is more important—money and time—or comprehensive, appropriate care." D Schell, MEDICINE IS NOT FAST FOOD, USA TODAY, Aug 30, 2006, Cited in Sage, *supra* note 44.

Medical tourism raises the same set of issues as retail clinics. In 2007, an estimated 150,000 Americans traveled abroad for medical care—usually provided at a much lower cost than had they stayed home. A host of intermediaries exist to make the necessary arrangements—and JCAHO has even gotten into the act, accrediting medical facilities in foreign countries.[49] Such practices obviously fragment care—as well as create difficult problems of follow-up if all does not go according to plan. How should health policy address such fragmentation?

A closer question is provided by specialty hospitals and ambulatory surgery centers ("ASCs")—but not for the reasons advanced by those who complain about the impact of such unbundling on general/community hospitals. The issue is typically framed in terms of the economic impact on general/community hospitals from the new competitor—with the entitlement of the incumbent to continued revenues either assumed, or supported with vague claims of community benefit/cross-subsidization. Such strategies assume what has yet to be established. The real issue is whether there are clinical or financial efficiencies from integration (or, conversely, from unbundling); how large (or small) those efficiencies actually are; and whether they actually matter to consumers. Such matters cannot be established on a priori grounds, let alone through quasi-normative claims of the sort that are invariably deployed by incumbent providers and their apologists.

To be sure, it does not follow that we should encourage unbundling by overpaying for cardiac and orthopedic services.[50] There are also compelling arguments for mandatory disclosure of standardized quality and cost information to consumers regardless of where they opt to receive care. That said, the debate over specialty hospitals and ASCs is about money and who gets it—not fragmentation.

Such controversies are not unique to these three settings; similar considerations apply across a host of disputes, including hospitalists, the growing use of para-professionals, consumer interest in complementary and alternative medicine, and telemedicine. The same goes for those perennials of health policy, relaxed antitrust scrutiny for physicians, and certificate of need proceedings for capital investment. The fact that incumbents have long lusted after these reforms, and they now, miraculously enough, turn out to be the solution to fragmentation should raise skepticism. But, the more fundamental problem is that without a theory of optimal fragmentation, we are at sea without a compass in deciding how to frame regulatory and reimbursement policy for health care.

To summarize, defragmenting the health delivery system is not as easy as defragmenting a computer drive. In health care, not all fragmentation is inefficient—and even if some defragmentation is inefficient from a clinical perspective,

---

49. Joint Commission International, http://www.jointcommissioninternational.org/.
50. Paul B. Ginsburg & Joy M. Grossman, *When The Price Isn't Right: How Inadvertent Payment Incentives Drive Medical Care*, HEALTH AFF. W5–376 (2005).

consumers might still prefer it. Before undertaking reform, we need a theory of optimal fragmentation—and we will have to decide whose preferences count in distinguishing between "good" and "bad" fragmentation.

V. CONCLUSION

In health care, we get what we pay for—and what we pay for is the provision of specific services—virtually irrespective of whether they are provided efficiently, or even needed. Because payment is conditioned on the laying of hands (or eyes) upon a patient, time spent coordinating care doesn't create a billing opportunity. When we don't pay for something, it generally doesn't get done. Similarly, providing integrated care doesn't pay better than fragmented care—and in some instances, it pays worse. The results are entirely predictable—and until the incentives created by the payment system are modified, we will continue to get what we've already got: a fragmented non-system for delivering care of highly variable quality at high cost. In our health care delivery non-system, coordination/integration is the dog that doesn't bark—because under our current payment system, no one has any interest in actually buying the dog.[51]

---

51. Arthur Conan Doyle, *Silver Blaze in* The Memoirs of Sherlock Homes ("Is there any point to which you would wish to draw my attention?"
"To the curious incident of the dog in the night-time."
"The dog did nothing in the night-time."
"That was the curious incident," remarked Sherlock Holmes.")

3. ORGANIZATIONAL FRAGMENTATION AND CARE QUALITY IN THE U.S. HEALTH CARE SYSTEM

RANDAL CEBUL, JAMES B. REBITZER, LOWELL J. TAYLOR, AND MARK VOTRUBA

The financing and provision of health care in the United States is distributed across a variety of distinct and often competing entities, each with its own objectives, obligations and capabilities. These fragmented organizational structures lead to disrupted relationships, poor information flows, and misaligned incentives that combine to degrade the quality of health care in important ways. Many goods and services can be readily financed and provided through a series of unconnected transactions, but in health care close coordination improves both health outcomes and the efficiency with which good outcomes are achieved.

In discussing the effect of organizational fragmentation on the quality of health care, it is helpful to separate the financing of health care from the provision of care. Medical expenditures over a lifetime are often large, lumpy, and uncertain, so health insurance plays a central role in financing care. Insurance for individuals under age 65 is provided largely through employers. The employer-based system leads to high rates of turnover in the relationship between insurers and their policy holders. People change their health insurance company either when they move between jobs or when their employer changes insurance companies. For individuals aged 65 and older, insurance is available from a single, government-run insurance program, Medicare, so there is a near-universal exit from commercial insurance policies around age 65. The first section of this paper, "Fragmentation in Health Insurance," investigates the consequences of our fragmented health insurance system. Given the high rates of turnover, we ask whether insurers have appropriate incentives to invest in the future health of their policy holders. We also consider the effect of insurance fragmentation on administrative costs.

The second part of the paper, "Fragmentation in Hospital Governance and Care," concerns the provision of health care in hospitals. Hospitals have a fragmented structure because of the special role played by physicians. Physicians are central to resource allocation and care processes in the hospital, yet they are typically independent of hospital management. The organizational independence and the clinical interdependence of physicians and hospitals inhibit key clinical process improvements. Integrating physicians more tightly into process improvement efforts is made difficult by the sociology of the medical profession and also by legal doctrines that have historically supported arms-length physician-hospital relationships.

Any discussion of organizational fragmentation and care delivery must consider the role of modern information technologies that promise to enhance coordination over time and within care episodes. Unfortunately, the current information infrastructure in health care does not allow for the seamless flow of information between hospitals, providers and insurers. As we discuss in section three, "Organizational Fragmentation and Information Technology," the absence of fully interoperable electronic medical records and personal health records is both a cause and consequence of organizational fragmentation. The absence of fully portable electronic medical records also creates opportunities for insurers to take on the role of information aggregators for their policy holders. The ability of insurers to serve this function is limited by the frequent disruption of their relationships with policy holders as well as the inherent limitations of the billing data they possess.

The paper concludes by considering responses to organizational fragmentation.

FRAGMENTATION IN HEALTH INSURANCE

Disrupted Relationships

Individuals under age 65 largely rely on private insurance plans to finance healthcare. About 63 percent of the population under age 65 obtain health insurance through an employer.[1] More than 1.5 million employer groups purchase health insurance on behalf of their employees from over 1200 registered insurance companies.[2] The relationship between employers and insurers can take several forms. Large employers often self-insure, meaning that the firm pays all health care costs each year and hires insurers only to administer plans. For "fully-insured" employer groups, the insurance company both administers the plan and bears the financial risk.

About a fifth of health insurance policyholders cancel their policy in any given year.[3] When an employee leaves the employer group that purchased a policy on his or her behalf, the insurance relationship is typically severed. For employers offering multiple plan options, employees may opt out of one plan in favor of

---

1. Carmen Denavas-Walt, Bernadette D. Proctor, and Jessica Smith, 'Income, Poverty, and Health Insurance Coverage in the United States: 2006,' *Current Population Reports*, P60-233, *U.S. Census Bureau* (Washington, DC: U.S. Government Printing Office, 2007)., Table C-3.

2. Based on 2004 firm counts reported by the Census Bureau at http://www.census.gov/econ/susb/data/susb2004.html and The Kaiser Family Foundation and Health Retirement and Educational Trust, 'Employer Health Benefits Annual Survey,' (2006).

3. Randall Cebul, James B. Rebitzer, Lowell J. Taylor, Mark Votruba, 'Unhealthy Insurance Markets: Search Frictions and the Cost and Quality of Health Insurance,' *NBER Working Paper*, No. 14555, July 2009.

another, or employees may cancel their employer-based plan if they find more desirable insurance through a spouse's job or in the direct purchase market. Finally, 38 percent of the turnover in health insurance coverage is the result of employer groups canceling their existing policies, often as a prelude to selecting another insurer. Turnover rates are considerably higher for fully insured employers, a group largely made up of small and mid-sized employers who are typically less sophisticated about health insurance. Cebul et. al., report annual exit rates above 30 percent in this market, with roughly half the turnover due to employers exiting the insurance relationship.[4]

In an employer-based health insurance system, labor market mobility is clearly a major determinant of exit from insurance relationships, but why do so many employer groups switch their insurance carriers? A likely answer involves search frictions. In a competitive insurance market, the law of one price prevails and consequently there is little payoff for employer groups to switch insurers. In an insurance market with moderate search costs, however, insurers have some degree of market power and the law of one price does not hold. Instead, equilibrium is characterized by a distribution of prices supported on the low end by the marginal cost of insurance and on the high end by the purchaser's maximum willingness to pay.[5] Purchasers who find themselves in the expensive part of the premium distribution will have incentives to change insurers when a better offer arrives. Thus, the frequent exit of employer groups from their insurance relationship is quite natural in a search model, provided that search frictions are not too severe.[6]

---

4. Randall Cebul et al., 'Unhealthy Insurance Markets: Search Frictions and the Cost and Quality of Health Insurance,' (July 2009).

5. Kenneth Burdett and Dale T. Mortensen, 'Wage Differentials, Employer Size, and Unemployment,' *International Economic Review*, 39/2 (1998), 257–73; Mortensen, Dale T. Mortensen, *Wage Dispersion: Why Are Similar Workers Paid Differently* (Cambridge, Mass: MIT Press, 2003); Kevin Lang and Sumon Majumdar, 'The Pricing of Job Characteristics When Markets Do Not Clear: Theory and Policy Implications,' *International Economic Review*, 45/4 (2004), 1111–28; James D. Montgomery, 'Equilibrium Wage Dispersion and Interindustry Wage Differentials,' *Quarterly Journal of Economics*, 106/1 (1991), 163–79; Gerard R. Butters, 'Equilibrium Distributions of Sales and Advertising Prices,' *Review of Economic Studies*, 44/3 (1977), 465–91; and Alan Manning, *Monopsony in Motion: Imperfect Competition in Labor Markets* (Princeton, N.J.: Princeton University Press, 2003).

6. Cebul et al. provide estimates of the magnitude of search frictions in the U.S. health insurance market (Randall Cebul et al., 'Unhealthy Insurance Markets: Search Frictions and the Cost and Quality of Health Insurance,' (July 2009). The health insurance market in Switzerland exhibits considerable price dispersion, despite competition among insurers and a regulatory structure that supports a high degree of product uniformity (Frank, Richard G. and Karine Lamiraud. 2009. "Choice, Price Competition and Complexity in Markets for Health Insurance." *Journal of Economic Behavior and Organization*, 71:2, pp. 550–62). Switzerland requires all residents to purchase health insurance in a marketplace that features a large number of competing insurers. The government specifies a

Incentives to Invest in Future Health

Inadequate preventive care, especially for those with chronic disease, is one of the most important quality failures in the U.S. health care system.[7] McGlynn et al. estimate that only fifty-five percent of adults receive recommended levels of preventive care, while adults with a chronic illness—such as diabetes, asthma, coronary artery disease, chronic obstructed pulmonary disorders (COPD), and hypertension—receive only fifty-six percent of the chronic care recommended by clinical guidelines.[8] The care of patients with chronic diseases accounts for seventy-five percent of annual health care expenditures.[9] The complications associated with these conditions accumulate over time, so early interventions can improve patient care and reduce medical costs. The short expected duration of insurance relationships undermines insurers' incentives to invest in preventative care and disease management. Deficient incentives resulting from short-term insurance relationships are, we argue, an important contributor to these gaps in care.

Diabetes disease management offers a useful illustration of the sort of quality problems we have in mind.[10] Diabetes is a very important chronic disease. According to the Agency for Health Care Research and Quality seventeen million Americans have diabetes and one in seven either has the disease or is at risk for

---

uniform basic insurance package. Premiums, which are risk adjusted by location, gender and age, can differ between health plans, but within health plans an insurer must offer the same premium for individuals having the same age, gender and region of residence. In addition to this community rating feature, health insurers must accept every applicant for basic insurance, and individuals can switch insurance providers every six months. The differences between the maximum and minimum monthly premiums were 65.36 Euros in 1997 and 88.01 in 2004 (p. 38). The primary deterrent to switching in the Swiss context appears to have been psychological—either decision overload, under which the psychological costs of processing information as choice increases overwhelms individual's decision making capacity, or status quo bias. Also, Dormont et. al suggest that the "inertia" in the Swiss market is affected by the presence of supplemental policies (Brigitte Dormont, Pierre-Yves Geoffard, and Karine Lamiraud, 'The Influence of Supplementary Health Insurance on Switching Behaviour: Evidence on Swiss Data,' (Institute of Health Economics and Management: Universite de Lausanne, 2007). Switching costs may be high for these policies and insurers may use these supplemental policies as "risk selection" devices.

7. Institute of Medicine Committee on Quality of Health Care in America, *Crossing the Quality Chasm: A New Health Care System for the 20th Century* (Washington D.C: National Academy Press, 2001) at Table A1.

8. Elizabeth A. Mcglynn et al., 'The Quality of Health Care Delivered to Adults in the United States,' *New England Journal of Medicine*, 348/26 (2003), 2635–45.

9. National Center for Chronic Disease Prevention and Health Promotion 'Chronic Disease Overview,' <http://www.cdc.gov/nccdphp/overview.htm>

10. For an analogous discussion of bariatric surgery see Ronen Avraham and K. A. D. Camara, 'The Tragedy of the Human Commons,' *Cardozo Law Review*, 29/2 (2007), 479–511.

developing it.[11] Diabetes-related complications account for more than 200,000 deaths annually, 82,000 amputations, 38,000 new cases of end stage renal disease and 12,000 cases of blindness. Although there is no cure for diabetes, effective treatment and screening strategies exist to control co-morbid conditions and to extend the quality and length of life. Yet diabetes care in the United States has consistently failed to meet recommended quality standards and there are significant gaps in care.[12]

Diabetes disease management programs have emerged in the last decade as a strategy to slow the progression of the disease by aggressively monitoring and controlling blood levels of glycated hemoglobin (HbA1c) and low density lipoprotein (LDL). Implementing these programs is challenging because they require a combination of education efforts (aimed at patients and primary care providers) and sophisticated monitoring systems to track patient progress, assess physician performance, and coordinate information flows between pharmacies, labs, and the offices of various specialists and primary care providers. Insurers can also improve the patient adherence to disease management protocols by reducing prices and co-pays to encourage compliance.[13]

Clearly disease management involves up-front investments for payoffs later in time. Beaulieu et al. offer an analysis of the costs and benefits of diabetes disease management at a specific HMO, Health Partners.[14] They estimate that the program generated a positive social return that grew over time. The net private return, however, was negative in the first years and zero over the course of a decade. Policyholder turnover played a significant role in reducing private returns.[15]

Several indirect pieces of evidence also suggest that shortening the insurer-policy holder relationship may lead to fewer investments in future health. For example, one might expect that sectors of the labor market with high rates of job turnover should also have shorter insurer-policy holder relationships and therefore reduced incentives to invest in future health. Fang and Gavazza find that employees in industries with high turnover rates are less likely to be offered

11. Kaveh G. Shojania et al., 'Diabetes Mellitus Care,' in KG Shojania et al. (eds.), *Closing The Quality Gap: A Critical Analysis of Quality Improvement Strategies* (2; Rockville, MD: Agency for Healthcare Research and Quality, 2004).

12. Ibid.

13. Avi Dor and William Encinosa, 'Does Cost Sharing Affect Compliance? The Case of Prescription Drugs,' *National Bureau of Economic Research Working Paper Series*, No. 10738 (September 2004).

14. Nancy Beaulieu et al., 'The Business Case for Diabetes Disease Management for Managed Care Organizations,' *Forum for Health Economics & Policy*, 9/1 (2007), 1072.

15. *See also* Gertler and Simcoe's analysis of a different disease management program. (Paul J. Gertler and Tim S. Simcoe, 'Disease Management,' (SSRN, 2006).

health insurance from their employer.[16] Should health insurance be offered, employees in high turnover industries pay higher deductibles and a larger fraction of the insurance premium. As a result, these employees also spend less on health services and receive less preventative care. In retirement, however, employees who had worked in high turnover industries have higher medical expenditures—suggesting that attention to some health problems was postponed. Along similar lines, Herring finds that in cities with a high degree of employer-induced insurance turnover, there is a reduction in preventative care visits, but no reduction in acute care visits.[17]

If insurer-policy holder relationships are too short to sustain meaningful incentives for investments in disease management and preventative care, one might expect government mandates would help reduce the short-fall. Thus we find that twenty-seven states currently mandate coverage for diabetes self-management and education programs, though disease management mandates for other conditions remain rare.[18] The absence of long-term insurance relationships may also help explain the limited effects on health care costs of the managed care revolution of the 1990s, although other economic factors may also have played a role.[19]

Advocates for disease management often claim that the net savings from these programs generate a positive return for insurers who invest in them. If this "business case for quality" were to hold, then shouldn't insurers have appropriate incentives to invest in at least some kinds of disease management or other proactive health care? The presence of adverse selection and search frictions in insurance markets suggest that the answer to this question may be no. An insurer who offers excellent disease management programs must be concerned about attracting potentially expensive patients.[20] Search frictions create countervailing incentives for an insurance company. On one hand, imperfect competition allows insurers to capture a portion of the surplus generated by investments

16. Hanming Fang and Alessandro Gavazza, 'Dynamic Inefficiencies in Employment-Based Health Insurance System: Theory and Evidence,' *National Bureau of Economic Research Working Paper,* /No. 13371 (September 2007).

17. Bradley Herring, 'Suboptimal Coverage of Preventative Care Due to Expected Turnover among Private Insurers,' (Department of Health Policy & Management, Rollins School of Public Health, Emory University, 2006).

18. Victoria C. Bunce, J.P. Wieske, and Vlasta Prikazsky, 'Health Insurance Mandates in the States 2007,' (Council for Affordable Health Insurance, 2007).

19. David J. Cooper and James B. Rebitzer, 'Managed Care and Physician Incentives: The Effects of Competition on the Cost and Quality of Care,' *B.E. Journals in Economic Analysis and Policy: Contributions to Economic Analysis and Policy,* 5/1 (2006), 1–30.

20. Nancy Beaulieu et al., 'The Business Case for Diabetes Disease Management for Managed Care Organizations,' *Forum for Health Economics & Policy,* 9/1 (2007), 1072.

in future health, which should encourage investment.[21] On the other hand, search frictions discourage investment by increasing turnover—especially among fully insured employers.[22]

There is currently a heated debate about whether disease management programs yield monetary savings that more than offset their costs.[23] This focus on the "business case for quality" is incomplete, however, because it fails to consider the value to patients of improvements in future health and well being that result from these programs. In principle, insurers could capture some of this value in the form of higher premiums if they could count on long-term relationships with employer groups or individual policy holders. For example, policyholders might pay more in the present for an insurance policy that credibly promises to deliver these chronic disease management services should they be required in the future. But insurance companies cannot count on such long-term relationships with many or most insured individuals.

The problem of short- term insurance relationships is compounded by the near-universal movement of commercial insurance policyholders to Medicare at age sixty-five. Many chronic diseases are not manifest until late middle age so the movement to Medicare shortens private insurer's time horizon. For example, the lifetime risk of men developing diabetes in the United State is 32.8 percent. By age sixty, 18.09 percent of men will have developed the disease compared to 30.77 percent at age eighty.[24] The payoff to insurers for disease management of the many late developers of diabetes is obviously diminished when these policy holders switch to Medicare at sixty-five.

---

21. Randall Cebul et al., 'Unhealthy Insurance Markets: Search Frictions and the Cost and Quality of Health Insurance,' (July 2009).

22. Search frictions also enable insurers to capture returns from investments in future health made by individual policy holders or employer groups. Cebul et al. (Randall Cebul et al., 'Unhealthy Insurance Markets: Search Frictions and the Cost and Quality of Health Insurance,' (July 2009)); and Fang and Gavazza demonstrate that this will lead to additional under-investment (Hanming Fang and Alessandro Gavazza, 'Dynamic Inefficiencies in Employment-Based Health Insurance System: Theory and Evidence,' *National Bureau of Economic Research Working Paper,* /No. 13371 (September 2007)). The depressing effect of insurance market search frictions on investments in future health is analogous to the effect of labor market frictions on investments in general human capital as described in Acemoglu (Daron Acemoglu, 'Training and Innovation in an Imperfect Labour Market,' *Review of Economic Studies,* 64/3 (1997), 445–64) and Acemoglu and Pischke (Daron Acemoglu and Joern-Steffan Pischke, 'Beyond Becker: Training in Imperfect Labor Markets,' *The Economic Journal,* 109 (February 1999), F112–F42).

23. Congressional Budget Office, 'An Analysis of the Literature on Disease Management Programs,' (October 13th 2004).

24. K. M. Venkat Narayan et al., 'Lifetime Risk for Diabetes Mellitus in the United States,' *JAMA: Journal of the American Medical Association,* 290/14 (2003), 1884.

Administrative Costs

In his presidential address to the Econometric Society, Peter Diamond observed, "The administration of health insurance is expensive, and not adequately approached by a model of ideal insurance with no loading, i.e., with premiums equal to expected benefits."[25] Woolhandler, Campbell and Himmelstein calculated that the United States spends $1,059 per capita on the administration of its health care system, which amounts to thirty-one percent of total health care expenditures.[26] Canada, in contrast, spends $307 per capita on health care, which is 16.7 percent of its total health care expenditures (p. 768). Much of this difference is due to the relatively heavy reliance in the United State on private insurers, whose underwriting, billing, and marketing activities account for the bulk of overhead costs. If the complexity of insurance contracts and billing procedures cause hospitals, physicians, and employers to build bureaucracies to negotiate relationships with insurers, then the indirect effects of private insurance on administrative costs may be a good deal larger than the direct effects. For example, Woolhander et al. find that hospitals in the United States spend $315 per capita on administration, compared with $103 in Canada.[27] Similarly, the administrative costs of practitioners are $324 per capita in the U.S., versus $107 in Canada, while employers spend fifty seven dollars per capita in the United States, compared to eight dollars in Canada. Some have argued that these estimates may be too high, but even more modest alternative estimates yield substantial differences in administrative costs between Canada and the United States.[28] A recent Commonwealth Fund report found that if administrative expenditures in the United States were scaled back to the levels of Germany and Switzerland, the savings would be thirty-two to forty-six billion a year.[29] Germany and Switzerland have mixed private and public health insurance systems, so the implication is that substantial savings are possible even if the United States retained a mixed private and public system.

Fragmented insurance relationships contribute directly to high administrative costs because, as we learned from an insurance executive in charge of

---

25. Peter Diamond, 'Organizing the Health Insurance Market,' *Econometrica*, 60/6 (1992), 1233–54 at p. 1234.

26. Steffie Woolhandler, Terry Campbell, and David U. Himmelstein, 'Costs of Health Care Administration in the United States and Canada,' *New England Journal of Medicine*, 349/8 (August 21, 2003), 768–75.

27. Steffie Woolhandler, Terry Campbell, and David U. Himmelstein, 'Costs of Health Care Administration in the United States and Canada,' *New England Journal of Medicine*, 349/8 (August 21, 2003), 768–75.

28. Henry J. Aaron, 'The Costs of Health Care Administration in the United States and Canada—Questionable Answers to a Questionable Question,' *New England Journal of Medicine*, 349/8 (August 21, 2003).

29. Karen Davis et al., 'Slowing the Growth of U.S. Health Care Expenditures: What Are the Options?,' (The Commonwealth Fund, 2007)., p. 4.

managing insurance payment centers, the rapid churn in insurer-policy holder relationships adds an important additional complexity to the already difficult process of paying claims. Search frictions, which contribute significantly to high levels of insurance turnover especially in the fully-insured segment of the insurance market, also require that insurers devote considerable resources to marketing their products.

Search frictions may also increase administrative costs by increasing product variety and complexity. In a market with moderate frictions, insurers can benefit from complexity to the extent it limits product comparisons. Employer groups accept policies with high premiums and overly complex contracts, because the information about alternatives is sufficiently poor that the offer seems better than the available alternatives—at least for a time. There is considerable scope for product variety and complexity in insurance because of the large number of non-premium attributes of insurance policies. Products can have different co-pays, deductibles and caps for different types of services. The list of physicians in the network, the fees for out of network referrals, and the specific drugs in the formulary can vary as well. Hall describes how state insurance regulations for small employer groups further contribute to this complexity.[30] Woolhandler et al. note that Seattle alone had 757 distinct health insurance products.[31] Our own discussions with executives in the insurance industry suggest that this number is not atypical for metropolitan areas and may be conservative. To the extent that frictions lead to a proliferation of insurance products, they will also increase the resources required for marketing, claims processing and administration.[32]

---

30. Mark A. Hall, 'The Structure and Enforcement of Health Insurance Rating Reforms,' *Inquiry*, 37/4 (Winter 2000), 376.

31. Steffie Woolhandler, Terry Campbell, and David U. Himmelstein, 'Costs of Health Care Administration in the United States and Canada,' *New England Journal of Medicine*, 349/8 (August 21, 2003), 768–75.

32. The fact that search costs lead to an equilibrium distribution of premiums for identical policies also promotes product variety because at each point on the price distribution, insurers will offer a different mix of non-price insurance attributes. This argument is made formally in the context of labor markets and non-wage job attributes by Lang and Majumdar (Kevin Lang and Sumon Majumdar, 'The Pricing of Job Characteristics When Markets Do Not Clear: Theory and Policy Implications,' *International Economic Review*, 45/4 (2004), 1111–28). Some economists have pointed to adverse selection, rather than search frictions, as the cause of the high degree of product variation found in insurance (Peter Diamond, 'Organizing the Health Insurance Market,' *Econometrica*, 60/6 (1992), 1233–54). As Hall describes, even in states that attempt community rating, clever insurers do design policies and pricing strategies to deter bad risks (Mark A. Hall, 'The Structure and Enforcement of Health Insurance Rating Reforms,' *Inquiry*, 37/4 (Winter 2000), 376). These stratagems introduce an excessive number of insurance products and price variation into the small group market that further compound search frictions. At a theoretical level, the distinction between adverse selection and search frictions may be more

FRAGMENTATION IN HOSPITAL GOVERNANCE AND CARE

Medical care is delivered both in the hospital (in-patient care) and outside the hospital (out-patient or ambulatory care). Thirty-eight percent of all U.S. health care expenditures in 2004 were for hospital care.[33] There are over 5700 hospitals and approximately 19,000 physician practices in the United States.[34] Some hospitals are not-for-profit, others are for-profit; some hospitals have a research or teaching mission and close associations with research universities and medical schools, others focus on delivering care to particular communities, still others specialize in the treatment of specific diseases or conditions. The majority of physicians work in small single-specialty groups, although some large multi-specialty group practices do exist.[35] Some physicians may have "privileges" at more than one hospital and many more split their time and attention between hospital in-patient care and their office-based practices.[36]

Hospitals have a fragmented organizational structure because physicians are central to resource allocation and care processes in the hospital, yet they are largely independent of hospital management. The principle of physician autonomy is deeply embedded in the laws and regulations governing hospitals.[37] The doctor-patient relationship and the doctor's medical practice are usually separate and legally distinct from the rest of the hospital. Reimbursement for care that happens within hospitals is made separately to physicians and hospitals. As Harris put it in his seminal article on the internal organization of hospitals, "The net result is one organization split into two disjoint pieces, each with its own objectives, managers, pricing strategy and constraints."[38]

---

apparent than real (see Jin Li, 'Job Mobility, Wage Dispersion, and Asymmetric Information,' *Working paper Department of Economics, MIT*, (2007)).

33. Centers for Medicare and Medicaid Services and Office of the Actuary National Health Statistics Group, 2007 'Health Expenditure Data, Health Expenditures by State of Residence,' <http://www.cms.hhs.gov/NationalHealthExpendData/05_NationalHealthAccountsStateHealthAccounts.asp#TopOfPage.>

34. U.S. Centers for Disease Control and Prevention, National Center for Health Statistics, *Health, United States, 2006* (2006) and American Medical Association, 'Ama Physician Masterfile,' (2004).

35. Gail R. Wilensky, Nicholas Wolter, and Michelle M. Fischer, 'Gain Sharing: A Good Concept Getting a Bad Name?,' *Health Affairs*, 26 (2006-2007 Supplement 2006), w58–w67.

36. Elliott S. Fisher, Douglas O. Staiger, Julie P. W. Bynum, and Daniel J. Gottlieb, 'Creating Accountable Care Organizations: The Extended Hospital Medical Staff,' *Health Affairs*, 26 (2006-2007 Supplement 2006), w44–w57).

37. Mark A. Hall, 'Institutional Control of Physician Behavior: Legal Barriers to Health Care Cost Containment,' *University of Pennsylvania Law Review*, 137/2 (1988), 431–536.

38. Jeffrey E. Harris, 'The Internal Organization of Hospitals: Some Economic Implications,' *The Bell Journal of Economics*, 8/2 (Autumn 1977), 467–82, p. 468,

We argue below that fragmented organizational structures inhibit process improvement in hospitals leading to waste and inefficiency. The scope for process improvements in hospitals is hard to measure, but Medicare data on geographic variation in expenditures and outcomes suggests that inefficiencies may be large. Numerous studies find that expenditures for individuals in high cost areas are as much as 60 percent higher than health expenditures for similar individuals in low spending areas. Most of this geographic variation is unexplained by prices, demographics, or health status. Some regions seem prone to adopt inexpensive but effective care while other regions are prone to adopt high cost care that offers little or no measurable benefit.[39] For example in Knoxville, Tennessee, risk adjusted one year survival for a first heart-attack was 69.7 per 100 patients, with one-year spending of $20,720 compared to 65.6 per 100 patients $47,133 in New York.[40] Hospital expenditures are a major contributor to these geographic variations.[41]

Clinical Process Improvement and the Need for Close Coordination

The organizational independence and the clinical interdependence of physicians and hospitals can act as a drag on clinical process improvements. To illustrate this point, consider the process of sterilizing surgical instruments as described in a recent case study of the Stanford Hospital and Clinics.[42] Approximately fifty thousand instruments flowed through Stanford Hospital's operating rooms in 2004. Each instrument needs to be sterilized, processed, and delivered to the correct room at the correct time. As is typically the case, surgeons at Stanford Hospital were not hospital employees. Surgeons received a salary, as well as a fee for each surgery. In this case, they were members of Stanford Medical School faculty and they were free to practice at another facility should they choose to do so. If a surgeon chose to perform surgeries elsewhere, Stanford Hospital would lose that surgeon's expertise, patients, and revenues.

The process of providing instruments begins with a surgeon filling out a "preference card" that lists the supplies needed for a surgery. Technicians, who are hourly employees hired with only a few weeks of on-the-job training, then

---

39. Congressional Budget Office, 'Geographic Variation in Health Care Spending,' (2008).

40. Jonathan S. Skinner, Douglas O. Staiger, and Elliott S. Fisher, 'Is Technological Change in Medicine Always Worth It? The Case of Acute Myocardial Infarction,' *Health Affairs*, (2006) at W38.

41. Congressional Budget Office, 'Geographic Variation in Health Care Spending,' (2008).

42. Stefanos Zenios, Kate Surman, and Elena Pernas-Giz, 'Process Improvement in Stanford Hospital's Operation Room,' (Case: OIT-41: Stanford Graduate School of Business, 2004). We chose this study to illustrate the important role physicians play in process improvements in hospitals. The case, and our summary of it, is not intended to demonstrate either effective or ineffective handling of an administrative situation.

load the supplies onto a cart. Errors could occur for a variety of reasons: mistakes in filling out the preference card; technicians gathering incorrect instruments, perhaps because the bins in which the instruments sat were incorrectly labeled; or instruments that had not been reassembled properly after previous sterilization. The location of instruments in the hospital was supposed to be tracked by manual scanners, but employees frequently failed to scan. Emergencies and poor coordination meant that instruments were often needed again immediately after a previous use, making the preferred six-hour sterilization process impossible and forcing the use of less desirable "flash sterilization" with steam. Surgeons had no direct contact with the sterilization process or technicians, and held operating room nurses accountable for whether the desired instruments were available. Nurses were harshly blamed by surgeons for instrumentation failures, but nurses who delivered clean instruments on time achieved "star status" among surgeons. In this setting, some operating room staff shared instruments between surgical suites. Some nurses kept critical instruments in their personal lockers. Some surgeons also took instruments with them when they left the hospital.

Efficient use of surgical instruments requires coordination among a heterogeneous group that includes surgeons, nurses, anesthesiologists, sterilization technicians, and supply distribution staff. This sort of cross-functional coordination is generally accepted as crucial for providing high quality care in many areas. The Institute of Medicine's comprehensive study of health care quality, *Crossing the Quality Chasm*, lists the creation of effective work teams as one if its ten rules to redesign and improve care: "In the current system, care is taken to protect professional prerogatives and separate roles. The current system shows too little cooperation and teamwork. Instead, each discipline and type of organization tends to defend its authority at the expense of the total system's function."[43] The Institute of Medicine report (p. 83) also highlights surgical tray set-ups: "Suboptimization is seen, for example, in operating rooms that must maintain different surgical tray setups for different doctors performing the same procedure. Each doctor gets what he or she wants, but at the cost of introducing enormous complexity and possible error into the system. In the new system, people

43. Institute of Medicine Committee on Quality of Health Care in America, *Crossing the Quality Chasm: A New Health Care System for the 20th Century* (Washington D.C: National Academy Press, 2001), p. 83. For studies of the effect of team coordination on clinical outcomes see Jody Hoffer Gittell, 'Coordinating Mechanisms in Care Provider Groups: Relational Coordination as a Mediator and Input Uncertainty as a Moderator of Performance Effects,' *Management Science*, 48/11 (2002), 1408–26 and J. H. Gittell et al., 'Impact of Relational Coordination on Quality of Care, Postoperative Pain and Functioning, and Length of Stay: A Nine-Hospital Study of Surgical Patients,' *Medical Care*, 38/8 (2000), 807–19.

will understand the advantage of high levels of cooperation, coordination and standardization to guarantee excellence, continuity and reliability."[44]

The Institute of Medicine (2001 p. 83) traces the difficulty in forming work teams to the sociology of health care professions which focuses on "role definition, certification and licensure, or doing one's own work as the top priority. These attitudes are especially pronounced among physicians, and offer little training for work in collaborative settings." Audet, Doty, Shamasdin, and Schoenbaum, using the 2003 Commonwealth Fund National Survey of Physicians and Quality of Care, find that only one-third of physicians report participating in redesign efforts to improve the performance of the system of care in which they practice.[45]

Hospital Governance Structure

Although these sociological issues may indeed be impediments to quality improvement efforts, the fragmented governance structure of hospitals makes the problem worse. Physicians, as independent contractors, have high-powered incentives for devoting time and attention to their private practice, to other hospitals where they may have admitting privileges, or to research and teaching. Getting high levels of physician cooperation for addressing hospital-specific issues like the sterilization of instruments requires that the hospital offer equally high powered, countervailing incentives. Monetary incentives linked to the output of a team have been shown in other settings to be effective motivators, but these sorts of incentives are problematic in settings where the income and wealth of team members varies as dramatically as they do in a hospital setting.[46]

If physicians were employed directly by hospitals, then hospitals could structure their job responsibilities to address these issues.[47] A surgeon employed full-time at a hospital would certainly need compensation sufficient to offset lost income from outside activities, but once this participation constraint is achieved,

---

44. Institute of Medicine Committee on Quality of Health Care in America, *Crossing the Quality Chasm: A New Health Care System for the 20th Century* (Washington D.C: National Academy Press, 2001).

45. Anne-Marie J. Audet, Michelle M. Doty, Jamil Shamasdin, and Stephen C. Schoenbaum, 'Measure, Learn, and Improve: Physicians' Involvement in Quality Improvement,' *Health Affairs*, 24/3 (2005), 843–53, p. 847, Exhibit 2.

46. William E. Encinosa, III, Martin Gaynor, and James B. Rebitzer, 'The Sociology of Groups and the Economics of Incentives: Theory and Evidence on Compensation Systems,' *Journal of Economic Behavior and Organization*, 62/2 (2007), 187–214; Martin Gaynor, James B. Rebitzer, and Lowell J. Taylor, 'Physician Incentives in Health Maintenance Organizations,' *Journal of Political Economy*, 112/4 (2004), 915–31.

47. Bengt Holmstrom and Paul Milgrom, 'The Firm as an Incentive System,' *American Economic Review*, 84/4 (1994), 972–91; and Bengt Holmstrom, 'The Firm as a Subeconomy,' *Journal of Law, Economics, and Organization*, 15/1 (1999), 74–102; discuss these issues for employment relationships generally.

then more subtle and finely tuned non-pecuniary motivators can sustain a high commitment to broader hospital objectives. A substantial literature on high-commitment human resource systems establishes that employees can work hard in the interests of the employer in exchange for a combination of good pay, empowerment, trust, and interesting and fulfilling work.[48] In these human resource systems, employers do not provide high-powered monetary rewards for individual performance, but instead use a combination of screening, socialization, training in the objectives of the firm, and peer pressure to sustain high levels of motivation. Encinosa, Gaynor, and Rebitzer offer evidence on the presence of sociological and economic incentives within medical groups.[49]

Legal Doctrines Limiting Employment of Physicians by Hospitals

Given the advantages of close coordination, why don't hospitals evolve alternative governance structures that would integrate physicians more tightly? In many European health care systems—including Austria, Belgium, Denmark, Finland, France, Germany, Great Britain, Italy, the Netherlands, Norway, Spain, and Sweden—in-patient care is predominately or entirely overseen by salaried physicians employed by their hospital.[50] But in the United States, two long-standing legal doctrines have historically discouraged the employment of physicians by hospitals and tilted towards an independent contractor model: the "corporate practice of medicine doctrine" and the "doctrine of vicarious liability."

The "corporate practice of medicine" legal doctrine has its roots in state laws that prevent unlicensed entities from providing medical services. These statutes, which trace back to rules proposed by the American Medical Association in 1847, were motivated in part by a desire to protect the public from physicians with "divided loyalties," and in part by a desire to protect the professional autonomy of medical doctors from encroachments by corporations and hospitals.[51] The statutes and associated case law vary from state to state. Historically, the doctrine

---

48. John Roberts, *The Modern Firm: Organizational Design for Performance and Growth* (New York: Oxford University Press, 2004), p. 175.

49. William E. Encinosa, III, Martin Gaynor, and James B. Rebitzer, 'The Sociology of Groups and the Economics of Incentives: Theory and Evidence on Compensation Systems,' *Journal of Economic Behavior and Organization*, 62/2 (2007), 187–214.

50. European Observatory on Health Systems and Policies, 'Snapshots of Health Systems: The State of Affairs in 16 Countries in Summer 2004,' (Copenhagan: The World Health Organization Regional Office for Europe, 2004).

51. Mark A. Hall, 'Institutional Control of Physician Behavior: Legal Barriers to Health Care Cost Containment,' *University of Pennsylvania Law Review*, 137/2 (1988), 431–536, Nicole Huberfeld, 'Be Not Afraid of Change: Time to Eliminate the Corporate Practice of Medicine Doctrine,' *Health Matrix: Journal of Law Medicine*, 14/2 (Summer 2004), 243–91; Mark R. Yessian and Martha B. Kvall, 'State Prohibitions on Hospital Employment of Physicians,' *Department of Health and Human Services, Office of the Inspector General*, OEI-01-91-00770 (November 1991).

has effectively prohibited the employment of physicians by hospitals and other non-physician entities, but the current force of this prohibition is unclear.[52] Yessian and Kvell find that in 1991 only five states clearly prohibited hospitals from employing physicians, and even these states had exceptions for public hospitals, clinics operated by medical schools, and teaching hospitals. However, in many other states, some confusion still seems to exist about whether hospitals can employ physicians.[53]

According to the "doctrine of vicarious liability," principals are responsible for the consequences of actions taken by employees in the course of carrying out their duties. Thus, a hospital that hires physicians as employees accepts malpractice liability that the hospital wouldn't otherwise have to bear. Abraham and Weiler discuss the historical evolution of hospital liability.[54] Moreover, if the limits on malpractice insurance carried by physicians are lower than the limits for hospitals, and if the limit on the malpractice insurance acts as an effective cap on judgments—as Zeiler, Silver, Black, Hyman, and Sage find in a study of malpractice payments in Texas from 1990 through 2003—then having physicians rather than hospitals responsible for malpractice can lower overall malpractice payments.[55] Arlen and MacLeod present a theoretical analysis of this

---

52. James C. Robinson, *The Corporate Practice of Medicine: Competition and Innovation in Health Care* (Berkeley, Calif.: University of California Press, 1999) 261; and Nicole Huberfeld, 'Be Not Afraid of Change: Time to Eliminate the Corporate Practice of Medicine Doctrine,' *Health Matrix: Journal of Law Medicine*, 14/2 (Summer 2004), 243–91.

53. Mark R. Yessian and Martha B. Kvall, 'State Prohibitions on Hospital Employment of Physicians,' *Department of Health and Human Services, Office of the Inspector General*, OEI-OI-91-00770 (November 1991).

54. Kenneth S. Abraham and Paul C. Weiler, 'Enterprise Medical Liability and the Evolution of the American Health Care System,' *Harvard Law Review*, 108/2 (1994), 381. In a world of Coasian bargaining, the equilibrium expected costs of malpractice (and hence incentives to avoid malpractice) are not influenced by who is held liable for malpractice damages For example, a shift in liability from independent physicians with hospital privileges to hospitals would be compensated for by an offsetting reduction in the compensation of physician employees. Arlen and MacLeod make this point in the context of managed care organizations. See Jennifer Arlen and W. Bentley Macleod, 'Malpractice Liability for Physicians and Managed Care Organizations,' *2003 New York University Law Review New York University Law Review*, (December 2003), 1929-2006; Jennifer Arlen and W. Bentley Macleod, 'Beyond Master-Servant: A Critique of Vicarious Liability,' in M. Stuart Madden (ed.), *Exploring Tort Law* (Cambridge University Press, 2005b).; and Jennifer Arlen and W. Bentley Macleod, 'Torts, Expertise, and Authority: Liability of Physicians and Managed Care Organizations,' *RAND Journal of Economics*, 36/3 (Autumn 2005a), 494–519),

55. Kathryn Zeiler et al., 'Physicians' Insurance Limits and Malpractice Payments: Evidence from Texas Closed Claims, 1990-2003,' *Journal of Legal Studies*, (forthcoming).

issue in the context of managed care organizations.[56] Abraham and Weiler argue that the current system of vicarious liability offers insufficient incentives for hospitals to undertake the systematic process analysis and improvements required to improve patient safety.[57] For purposes of tort law, employment is defined by supervision and control. Thus, a hospital that relies largely on physicians as independent contractors would forgo some of the legal advantages of this set-up should it attempt to supervise, train, and otherwise exercise authority over physicians under its administrative control.

If the doctrine of vicarious liability was a powerful enough legal force to inhibit the integration of physicians with hospital operations, why did it not also inhibit the efforts of managed care organizations to regulate physician practice patterns? Part of the answer is that managed care organizations are covered under the federal Employee Retirement Security Act (ERISA), that restricts damages to the cost of denied coverage (and thus disallows compensatory or punitive damages) and preempts malpractice suits under state law.[58] To be clear, ERISA does not preclude malpractice suits under state law for negligent care delivered by physicians employed by managed care organization. Managed care organizations may, however, escape liability under state law if their physicians are independent contractors.[59]

Although legal doctrines and associated case law have created a legal landscape that has historically discouraged hospitals from employing physicians, hospitals and physicians are testing the boundaries of these rules and developing new professional practices and organizational forms that may integrate physicians more tightly into hospital operations and process improvement efforts.

Hospitalists

A particularly noteworthy innovation is the growing use of "hospitalists," a new medical specialty in which physicians, often internists, specialize in caring for patients who are in the hospital. Although there were only a few hundred such specialists in 1996, their number had risen to 8000 hospitalists by 2004 and

---

56. Jennifer Arlen and W. Bentley Macleod, 'Torts, Expertise, and Authority: Liability of Physicians and Managed Care Organizations,' *RAND Journal of Economics*, 36/3 (Autumn 2005a), 494–519. Outside of health care, Rebitzer found that safety problems at petrochemical plants were increased because of employers' attempts to evade vicarious liability through the use of independent contractors (James B. Rebitzer, 'Job Safety and Contract Workers in the Petrochemical Industry,' *Industrial Relations*, 34/1 (January 1995), 40–57).

57. Kenneth S. Abraham and Paul C. Weiler, 'Enterprise Medical Liability and the Evolution of the American Health Care System,' *Harvard Law Review*, 108/2 (1994), 381.

58. Jennifer Arlen and W. Bentley Macleod, 'Malpractice Liability for Physicians and Managed Care Organizations,' *2003 New York University Law Review*, (December 2003), 1929–2006.

59. Ibid.

rapid growth seems likely to continue.[60] Sometimes hospitalists are members of medical groups or managed care organizations; sometimes they are hospital employees.[61] With the shortening length of hospital stays and the higher level of complexity of care for hospital patients, it makes sense for office-based physicians to hand off responsibility to a physician stationed in and specializing in hospital care.[62]

Hospitalists would seem to be well-positioned to make investments in hospital specific human capital and also to participate in process improvements. However, evidence on the effects of hospitalists has been scarce. Meltzer discusses two studies that approximate a random design in that patients were allocated to a hospitalist or non-hospitalist based on who happened to be on call when the patient arrived. Both studies find that hospitalists modestly reduce length of stay and charges.[63]

Hospitalists do create some additional coordination costs, because office-based physicians hand their patients off to hospitalists when patients enter the hospital.[64] Ultimately, the effect of the hospitalist model of in-patient care quality will depend on the benefits from specialization exceeding the heightened coordination costs.

Integrating Hospitals and Physician Practices

Coordination of in-patient with out-patient treatment might also be facilitated by having hospitals integrate with physician practices. In some cases hospitals have acquired physician practices and placed doctors on salary. The motive for these purchases seems largely to be to lock-in profitable referrals and also to enhance hospital bargaining power.[65]

---

60. Robert M. Wachter, 'Hospitalists in the United States: Mission Accomplished or Work in Progress?,' *New England Journal of Medicine*, 2004 p. 1935–36.

61. James C. Robinson, *The Corporate Practice of Medicine: Competition and Innovation in Health Care* (Berkeley, Calif.: University of California Press, 1999) 261.

62. David Meltzer, 'Hospitalists and the Doctor Patient Relationships,' *Journal of Legal Studies*, 30 (June 2001).

63. Ibid.

64. David Meltzer, 'Hospitalists and the Doctor Patient Relationships,' *Journal of Legal Studies*, 30 (June 2001); and Robert M. Wachter, 'Hospitalists in the United States: Mission Accomplished or Work in Progress?,' *New England Journal of Medicine*, 2004 p. 1935-36.

65. David Dranove, *The Economic Evolution of American Health Care: From Marcus Welby to Managed Care* (Princeton, N.J.: Princeton University Press, 2000), p. 130; James C. Robinson, *The Corporate Practice of Medicine: Competition and Innovation in Health Care* (Berkeley, Calif.: University of California Press, 1999) 261; Lawrence Casalino and James C. Robinson, 'Alternative Models of Hospital-Physician Affiliation as the United States Moves Away from Tight Managed Care,' *Milbank Quarterly*, 81/2 (2003), 331–51; Lawton R. Burns and Mark V. Pauly, 'Integrated Delivery Networks: A Detour on the Road to

In other cases, hospitals construct alliances with physicians by forming "physician hospital organizations" or "management service organizations." A physician hospital organization is a joint venture between a hospital and physicians that serves as a single agent for managed care contracting and provides administrative services and utilization review; however, both the physicians and the hospital retain their identity as separate lines of business. A management service organization is a free-standing corporation. It provides services to medical practices, it may be the employer of the non-medical staff, and it may help coordinate planning and decision making.[66] These attempts at vertical integration have generally produced disappointing results. As Burns and Pauly put it, "The structures that were put in place to integrate hospitals, primary care providers, and specialists often failed to fundamentally alter the manner in which physicians practiced medicine and collaborated with other health care professionals (that is, 'clinical integration'). As a result, integrated structures rarely integrated the actual delivery of patient care."[67] Vertical integration between hospitals and physicians also poses practical difficulties. The arrangement is almost never exclusive; doctors and patients are constantly moving in and out of the system due to personal preferences and geographic convenience.[68] Indeed, the fraction of hospitals with physician hospital organizations and management service organizations peaked in 1996 and has been declining since.

To compensate for the lack of clinical integration, health care organizations have introduced a variety of clever incentive systems to motivate the physicians in the practices they acquire. These incentive experiments, however, have not met with much success, in part because many aspects of care integration are non-contractible and in part because incentive pay is too crude an instrument to achieve the multiple goals of efficiency in production, appropriate utilization and referrals, and delivery of high quality care.[69] Beaulieu and Barro offer a case study of one hospital system's attempt to introduce incentives into physician practices they purchased. The primary effect of increased incentive

Integrated Health Care?,' *Health Affairs*, 21/4 (2002); and Peter P. Budetti et al., 'Physician and Health System Integration,' *Health Affairs*, 21/1 (2002).

66. Lawton R. Burns, 'Models of Physician-Hospital Organization: Possibilities and Pitfalls,' *Leonard Davis Institute of Health Economics Issue Brief*, 2/7 (1995).

67. Lawton R. Burns and Mark V. Pauly, 'Integrated Delivery Networks: A Detour on the Road to Integrated Health Care?,' *Health Affairs*, 21/4 (2002), p. 134.

68. Robinson James C. Robinson, *The Corporate Practice of Medicine: Competition and Innovation in Health Care* (Berkeley, Calif.: University of California Press, 1999) 261, p. 192.

69. David Dranove, *The Economic Evolution of American Health Care: From Marcus Welby to Managed Care* (Princeton, N.J.: Princeton University Press, 2000), p. 135; James C. Robinson, *The Corporate Practice of Medicine: Competition and Innovation in Health Care* (Berkeley, Calif.: University of California Press, 1999) 261.

pay was to cause low performing physicians to leave the practices purchased by the hospital.[70]

ORGANIZATIONAL FRAGMENTATION AND INFORMATION TECHNOLOGY

In a fragmented health care delivery system, high quality care requires the smooth flow of information across diverse providers working within various organizations in both in-patient and out-patient settings. Pham, Schrag, O'Malley, Wu, and Bach provide some evidence on the scale of coordination required. They studied Medicare patients whose physicians were included in the Community Tracking Study physician survey. They report that patients with diabetes see a median of eight physicians in five distinct medical practices. Patients with coronary artery diseases see a median of ten physicians in six distinct practices. Moreover, the physician providing the most care is not constant from one year to the next.[71]

The large number of physicians and organizations involved in treatment clearly creates coordination challenges. There is some evidence suggesting that these challenges influence care outcomes. Skinner et. al. report an analysis of regional, risk-adjusted, one-year survival rates for Medicare patients following a first heart attack. After controlling for other aspects of the quality of care, the average number of different physicians involved in post-episode treatment in a hospital referral region was negatively associated with gains in regional one-year survival rates and positively associated with cost increases. In other words, regions that relied more heavily on coordination across more physicians were less adept at improving post-heart-attack care efficacy and efficiency.[72]

Modern information technology offers many tools to facilitate coordination and information flows, but the information technology revolution has been slow in coming to health care. Survey data collected in 2007–2008 reveals that only 4 percent of physicians have a fully functional electronic medical record system in their office and only 13 percent have a basic system.[73] Similarly low rates of IT adoption are reported for electronic medical records in hospital emergency

---

70. Jason Barro and Nancy Beaulieu, 'Selection and Improvement: Physician Responses to Financial Incentives,' *National Bureau of Economic Research Working Paper,* 10017 (2003).

71. Hoangmai H. Pham et al., 'Care Patterns in Medicare and Their Implications for Pay for Performance,' *New England Journal of Medicine,* 356/11 (March 15, 2007), 1130-9.

72. Jonathan S. Skinner, Douglas O. Staiger, and Elliott S. Fisher, 'Is Technological Change in Medicine Always Worth It? The Case of Acute Myocardial Infarction,' *Health Affairs,* (2006).

73. Catherine M. Desroches et al., 'Electronic Health Records in Ambulatory Care- a National Survey of Physicians,' *New England Journal of Medicine,* 359/1 (July 3, 2008), 10.

rooms and outpatient departments and physician order entry systems in hospitals.[74]

Part of the explanation for the slow implementation of modern information technology is the fragmented nature of the health care delivery system. As President Bush's Information Technology Advisory Committee concluded: [75]

"Unlike the nationalized health systems of many countries, however, the U.S. health care system is deliberately composed of private, independent hospitals, ambulatory care and long term care facilities, and private individual and group provider practices. While this arrangement has stimulated competition, maximized consumer choice, and provided ongoing incentives to excel and to innovate, the free market system does not inherently generate practical mechanisms for sharing information critical to patient care."

A report from the Institute of Medicine makes a similar point about the dearth of clinical decision support systems designed to help physicians avoid errors and implement evidence based treatment guidelines.[76]

To be effective, CDSS [clinical decision support systems] diagnostic systems require detailed, patient-specific clinical information (history, physical results, medications, laboratory test results), which in most health care settings resides in a variety of paper and automated datasets that cannot easily be integrated. Past efforts to develop automated medical record systems have not been very successful because of the lack of common standards for coding data, the absence of a data network connecting the many health care organizations and clinicians involved in patient care, and a number of other factors.

The obvious clinical value of sharing information across providers and the absence of standards for interoperable electronic medical records creates opportunities for insurers to act as information aggregators for their policy holders. Insurers can do this because all visits and procedures that require billing are coded into the records of the insurer. If the billing information is sufficiently complete, timely, and accurate, and if it can be integrated with pharmacy and laboratory information, it is possible to assemble something approximating a

---

74. Catherine Burt and Esther Hing, 'Use of Computerized Clinical Support Systems in Medical Settings: United States, 2001–03,' *Advance Data From Vital and Health Statistics* (Hyattsville, MD: National Center for Health Statistics, 2005).; and David M. Cutler, Naomi E. Feldman, and Jill R. Horwitz, 'U.S. Adoption of Computerized Physician Order Entry Systems,' *Health Affairs*, 24/6 (2005), 1654–63.

75. President's Information Technology Advisory Committee, 'Revolutionizing Health Care through Information Technology,' (Arlington, VA: Executive Office of the President of the United States, 2004). p. 7).

76. Institute of Medicine Committee on Quality of Health Care in America, *Crossing the Quality Chasm: A New Health Care System for the 20th Century* (Washington D.C: National Academy Press, 2001), p. 154.

comprehensive electronic medical record. Insurers are using such ersatz medical records to build clinical decision support systems to identify gaps in care. Javitt, Rebitzer, and Reisman report the results of a randomized trial of one such system.[77] Patients of physicians exposed to the system had reduced resource utilization (measured by total charges) and fewer unresolved gaps in care. Insurance-based systems are also being used to adjust co-pays and deductibles to encourage patient adherence to chronic disease treatment protocols.[78]

Insurance records, however, have important limitations as a source of clinical information. Claims data typically arrive slowly and contain far less clinical detail than true electronic medical records. Insurance-based records also do not follow employees when they change insurance companies. One insurance industry veteran with whom we spoke said it takes about a year for an insurance company to collect enough information about a patient to even know if they are eligible for a disease management program.

Some of the limitations of insurance-based data systems might be mitigated by a system of personal medical records that are the property of the individual. Companies such as WebMD work with employers and insurers to feed billing information, as well as pharmacy and lab data, into each individual's record. This information belongs to the individuals and stays with them. If, however, an individual's next job does not have a contract with WebMD, the flow of information from the insurer stops. Individuals can continue to add information to their personal medical record on their own, but this increases the likelihood of gaps and errors.

RESPONSES TO FRAGMENTATION

The organizational fragmentation of the U.S. health care system has its roots in important market forces (and failures), legal doctrine, government policy, and the state of information technology. Our analysis of fragmentation in insurance relationships suggests that disrupted insurer-policy holder relationships are likely to lead to insufficient investments in future health such as preventative care or disease management programs for chronic diseases. Our analysis of fragmented hospital governance emphasizes the difficulty of implementing important process improvements.

Some gains may result from changed government policy, but a good deal will depend on the development of improved organizational practices, legal doctrine

---

77. Jonathan C. Javitt, James B. Rebitzer, and Lonnie Reisman, 'Information Technology and Medical Missteps: Evidence from a Randomized Trial,' *Journal of Health Economics*, 27/23 (May 2008), 585–602.

78. Michael E. Chernew, Allison B. Rosen, and Mark A. Fendrick, 'Value-Based Insurance Design,' *Health Affairs: web exclusive*, 26/2 (2007), 8.

and information technology. In principle, policy makers could address short falls in investments in future health by mandating that insurers deliver the under-provided programs. Attempting to mandate precisely what care should be delivered is, however, unlikely to achieve fully satisfactory results. Unless the mandates are compatible with the incentives inherent in short insurer-policy-holder relationships, they are likely to lead to insufficient investments in perfunctory programs, which in extreme cases may become wasteful sham efforts. Mandates are further complicated by legal doctrines that dramatically limit the reach of any insurance mandate passed by an individual state.[79]

Policymakers could create incentives for process improvement by linking payments and care quality. Medicare will be attempting an approach along these lines when it introduces a policy in fiscal year 2009 that refuses additional payments to hospitals for preventable inpatient complications, errors, injuries, and infections that could have reasonably been prevented by good quality assurance processes.[80] But in clinical settings, performance measures are often imperfect. Linking high-powered incentives to these performance measures distorts incentives in ways leading to "cream skimming" and other undesirable provider behaviors.[81] Another important issue with pay-for-performance is that in a fragmented health care system, it is often unclear which provider should be held accountable for which outcomes. Pham, et al. investigated the ability of Medicare to "assign" a primary physician to a particular patient for the purpose of implementing pay for performance incentive systems. They conclude that it is often not possible to identify a single physician primarily responsible for care.[82]

An intriguing alternative approach put forward by Fischer et al., is to create "accountable care organizations" composed of hospitals and the physicians who treat or admit patients there.[83] Linking pay to the performance of these artificial entities would create incentives for improving the many clinical processes that span in-patient and out-patient settings, but implementing such a system will be

---

79. Ronen Avraham and K. A. D. Camara, 'The Tragedy of the Human Commons,' *Cardozo Law Review*, 29/2 (2007), 479–511.

80. Ellen T. Kurtzman, 'A Summary of the Impact of Reforms to the Hospital Inpatient Prospective Payment System (Ipps) on Nursing Services,' (The George Washington University, Department of Nursing Education, School of Medicine and Health Services, 2007).

81. David Dranove, David P. Kessler, Mark B. Mcclellan, and Mark Satterthwaite, 'Is More Information Better? The Effects of 'Report Cards" On Health Care Providers,' *Journal of Political Economy*, 111/3 (2003), 555–88.

82. Hoangmai H. Pham et al., 'Care Patterns in Medicare and Their Implications for Pay for Performance,' *New England Journal of Medicine*, 356/11 (March 15, 2007), 1130-90.

83. Elliott S. Fisher, Douglas O. Staiger, Julie P. W. Bynum, and Daniel J. Gottlieb, 'Creating Accountable Care Organizations: The Extended Hospital Medical Staff,' *Health Affairs*, 26 (2006-2007 Supplement 2006), w44--w57.

tricky. Free-riding issues will likely make it difficult to provide high-powered incentives across a large group of heterogeneous and loosely affiliated provider organizations.[84] Inducing physicians to form employment-like relationships with accountable care organizations may not be easier than employing them in hospitals. Introducing gain sharing among participants in these organizations will also require modification of federal laws. For example, Social Security Act Civil Monetary Penalties Law prohibits hospitals from making a payment to a physician as an inducement to limit services to Medicare or Medicaid patients under the physician's care. Similarly, an anti-kickback statute prohibits payments to reward referrals of patients participating in federal health care programs. The Stark laws prevent physicians from referring Medicare and Medicaid patients for health services from entities in which physicians have a financial relationship.[85]

If mandates and pay-for-performance are overly blunt policy instruments, perhaps more can be accomplished by reforming insurance markets.[86] Churn in insurance relationships results from labor market mobility, the switch to Medicare insurance at 65, and search frictions—with the latter being particularly important for the small employers in the fully-insured market segment. The easiest of these three causes to address are search frictions. Introducing a simple, extensively marketed, default insurance policy that employers could choose if no superior policy is offered will truncate the wide distribution of premiums and thus reduce turnover.

Our analysis of fragmentation in hospitals emphasized the legal barriers that discouraged the tight integration of physicians into quality improvement initiatives in hospitals. The legal system itself seems to be moving towards removing one of these obstacles—the corporate practice of medical doctrine. In our view, little would be lost and potentially much gained if courts and legislatures took action to accelerate this process. A good deal more might be gained if the rule of vicarious liability for malpractice would be replaced by an "enterprise liability rule," so that hospital liability for malpractice would not depend on whether the physician delivering care in the hospital was an independent contractor or employee. The hospitalist approach to in-patient care might also be a step forward in integrating physicians into hospital care improvement initiatives.

---

84. Martin Gaynor, James B. Rebitzer, and Lowell J. Taylor, 'Physician Incentives in Health Maintenance Organizations,' *Journal of Political Economy*, 112/4 (2004), 915–31; William E. Encinosa, III, Martin Gaynor, and James B. Rebitzer, 'The Sociology of Groups and the Economics of Incentives: Theory and Evidence on Compensation Systems,' *Journal of Economic Behavior and Organization*, 62/2 (2007), 187–14.

85. Gail R. Wilensky, Nicholas Wolter, and Michelle M. Fischer, 'Gain Sharing: A Good Concept Getting a Bad Name?,' *Health Affairs*, 26 (2006–2007 Supplement 2006), w58–w67.

86. Ronen Avraham and K. A. D. Camara, 'The Tragedy of the Human Commons,' *Cardozo Law Review*, 29/2 (2007), 479–511.

A final aspect of organizational fragmentation is the balkanized information technology infrastructure in the health care system. A first step in fixing the system would be the adoption of common electronic and linguistic communication standards.[87] These standards will lead to interoperable electronic medical records that should improve coordination among providers and reduce gaps in care. Analysis of the data in these electronic records will also help refine evidence-based treatment protocols and complementary clinical decision support tools will help disseminate best practice. In this way electronic medical records will allow health care to resemble other industries where continuous experimenting with standardized products and services are an important driver of efficiency gains.[88]

In the current fragmented system, patients must coordinate their own care across various providers. Coordination will be made easier by the development of portable patient health record systems. These records, although less detailed than electronic medical records, will help patients better manage their own medical affairs—especially when combined with electronic decision support tools. Many challenging care decisions, however, must be made when individuals are sick, anxious, financially taxed, and otherwise unable to act as effective decision makers. This fact will limit the degree to which coordination of care by patients can be an effective response to the organizational fragmentation of the U.S. health care system.

---

87. Katherine Swartz, 'Electronic Medical Records-Federal Standards Needed,' *Inquiry*, 43 (Winter 2006).

88. Ranga Ramanujam and Denise M. Rousseau, 'The Challenges Are Organizational Not Just Clinical,' *Journal of Organizational Behavior*, 27/7 (2006), 811–27.

4. CURING FRAGMENTATION WITH INTEGRATED DELIVERY SYSTEMS
What They Do, What Has Blocked Them, Why We Need Them, and How to Get There From Here*

ALAIN ENTHOVEN

WHAT DOES "FRAGMENTED" MEAN?

Fragmentation in our health care delivery occurs at two levels: with the individual patient, and at the community level.

The services provided to an individual patient are typically fragmented because the caregivers are usually not on the same team, especially if the patient has multiple coexisting conditions that require treatment by people from different disciplines. Typically, physicians are paid fees for services individually by their patients or insurers. If several physicians are involved in a case, they are probably economic rivals, not partners. Doctors and hospital personnel are not on the same team. In fact, doctors and hospitals often have conflicting economic interests, as when the doctors are paid fees for services while hospitals are paid by Medicare on the basis of fixed prospective payments per case. Recent news reports make it clear that more than a few doctors are receiving substantial amounts of money from device and drug manufacturers for using and recommending their products, which is a conflict of interest.[1] Typically, when several doctors are involved in a community hospital, the doctors and nurses are not following shared practice guidelines. The doctors and others may be sharing inpatient information, such as medical tests run in the hospital, but they are not

* The author gratefully acknowledges helpful criticisms and suggestions from Victor R. Fuchs, Patricia Mintz, Bruce Sams, MD, James A. Vohs, and Charles D. Weller. All errors of fact or interpretation are his own. Copyright© Alain Enthoven 2008.

1. For example, David Armstrong, *Doctors with Ties To Companies Push Aspirin Objections: Value of Daily Pill Questioned as Makers of Drugs, Tests Eye Lucrative New Market*, WALL STREET JOURNAL, April 24, 2006; Reed Ableson, *Financial Ties Cited as Issue In Spine Study*, N.Y. TIMES, January 30, 2008; Reed Ableson, *Drug Sales Bring Huge Profits, and Scrutiny, to Cancer Doctors*, N.Y. TIMES January 26, 2003; J. P. KASSIRER, MD, ON THE TAKE: HOW MEDICINE'S COMPLICITY WITH BIG BUSINESS CAN ENDANGER YOUR HEALTH, (2005). For additional references, *see* COMMITTEE FOR ECONOMIC DEVELOPMENT QUALITY, AFFORDABLE HEALTH CARE FOR ALL: MOVING BEYOND THE EMPLOYER-BASED HEALTH-INSURANCE SYSTEM, 101 n. 73.

sharing all information that is relevant to the patient's condition, such as tests done prior to hospitalization, or previous hospitalizations.

The costs of not sharing information, and of the lack of comprehensive longitudinal information on each patient, are illustrated by the case of an acquaintance who had been diagnosed with atrial fibrillation. The cardiologist prescribed warfarin to prevent blood clots causing strokes. Apparently, the cardiologist didn't know that the man had a history of bleeding ulcers, and that warfarin in his case was dangerous and harmful. The patient had to be hospitalized. I recounted this story to a physician who said "The cardiologist should have taken a compete history." Why didn't he take a history that revealed the potential problem? Possible answers illustrate some of the costs of fragmentation. Perhaps he was in a hurry, or he was aware of the limitations of taking histories from old men who may not remember things very well. In the fragmented financial system in which he worked, he would not be responsible for the negative consequences of his error, the costly hospitalization that followed it. The fee-for-service payment system actually rewarded him for his error (with more fees for visits to his hospitalized patient) and would not have paid him more for the time to take the history.

There is fragmentation in cases in which decision makers in one part of the non-system can make decisions that lay costs on other parts without accountability, as in the case of the presumably negligent cardiologist. There is similar fragmentation in a non-system in which physicians can write prescriptions with no responsibility for the cost consequences, and in which physicians can demand that hospitals deploy "the latest and greatest" technologies at the hospitals' and insurers' (therefore employers,' taxpayers' and consumers') expense, but in the absence of good evidence of value for money.

Fee-for-service payment is a centrifugal force that, if anything, punishes (with less revenue) coordination that saves resources. Fee-for-service works against multi-specialty group practice because it tells doctors that their money comes directly from their patients, not mediated by the group. If the physician sees that he or she is bringing in more revenue than the group is willing to pay, s/he has an incentive to leave the group and go into solo practice, or into single specialty group practice that can achieve a local monopoly in his/her specialty. Obviously, there are other incentives holding groups together, but some multi-specialty groups fall apart for this reason.

Fee-for-service payment can occur in several different ways. I am mainly referring here to the most problematic: fee-for-service payment by the patient or his insurer to the individual physician, which creates a conflict of interest at the individual level. There are arrangements like the Mayo Clinic in which patients and insurers pay the Clinic fees for services but the physicians are salaried. With a strong group culture, the fee-for-service incentives can be prevented from influencing physician behavior. In other cases, in other institutions, departmental budgets depend on fee-for-service revenues even though the physicians are salaried. In such cases, fee-for-service incentives may affect physicians.

Fragmentation is evident in the case of patients who fall into the cracks between institutions, as when inpatient medical records are not transferred to the ambulatory care sector, or chronic disease patients are not systematically helped to prevent the need for more hospitalization.

At the level of the whole community, there is fragmentation. Physicians often make specialty choices based on what insurers pay, which is often unrelated to community needs, or supply and demand. Medicare is an obvious case of this.[2] Hospitals build capacity and buy equipment that is often unrelated to population needs. This was the reason for Certificate of Need Laws. Some physicians are in conflict with hospitals when, responding to Medicare and other insurer pricing, they pick off the most lucrative services and take their patients to specialty hospitals in which they have a financial interest.[3] Fragmentation is evident when doctors and hospitals fail to collaborate in resource saving interventions for patients who "fall between the cracks."

The incentives in today's dominant fee-for-service system are often perverse. They punish (with less revenue) economizing behavior. Medicare pays the same amount regardless of quality. It rewards poor quality by paying doctors to treat complications caused by their own mistakes.[4] Fee-for-service also discourages teamwork, because it pays separately for the actions of individual providers. Health care systems could produce better care at less cost if provider incentives were aligned with the needs and wants of the American people for high quality *affordable* care.

INTEGRATION: THE OPPOSITE OF FRAGMENTATION

The meaning of "fragmented" may be clarified by contrasting it with its opposite, "integrated." The list of hallmarks of an integrated health care delivery system (IDS) includes the following

- Shared values and shared goals derived from those values.
- Alignment of the incentives of all providers and managers with each others' and with the interests of the patients in high-quality affordable care.

---

2. P.B. Ginsburg & J.M. Grossman, *When the Price Isn't Right: How Inadvertent Payment Incentives Drive Medical Care*, HEALTH AFF., WEB EXCLUSIVE W5–381, August 9, 2005. Political factors, considerations of equity, and the administrative complexity of adjusting prices to each local market, prevent Medicare prices from being based on local supply and demand.

3. *Id.*

4. Robert Pear, *Medicare, in a Different Tack, Moves to Link Doctors' Payments to Performance*, N.Y. TIMES, December 12, 2006, p. A27. Medicare has recently taken steps under administrative authority to cease reimbursing the extra costs for preventable errors. Robert Pear, *Medicare Says It Won't Cover Hospital Errors*, N.Y. TIMES, August 19, 2007, p. A1.

This is usually based on a common revenue stream shared by all providers. With this comes a culture of cost-consciousness. This supports one of the rules of process redesign recommended by the Institute of Medicine: "Continuous decrease in waste. The health system should not waste resources or patient time."[5] The common revenue stream facilitates smooth transfer of resources among components of the program so that savings in one part can be reinvested in another.

- Physician leadership: to be successful, an integrated delivery system must win the loyalty, commitment, and responsible participation of doctors.
- A culture of teamwork among providers, rather than the physician autonomy that dominates the culture of the fragmented system: doctors, nurses, and others working together to develop better rules and processes for how to do the work, in a culture of mutual trust and respect.
- A coordinating system or structure, usually a management hierarchy, to manage the operations of the system to maximize benefit to patients.
- Comprehensive, longitudinal medical records of each patient (preferably electronic), shared by all the providers caring for that patient, available, among other things, for tracking the experience of particular patients on a particular treatment (drug or device) to gather information for improvement.
- Shared practice guidelines, so that all providers are working on the same up to date understanding of what is best practice.
- "Patient-centered—providing care that is respectful of and responsive to individual patient preferences, needs, and values and ensuring that patient values guide all clinical decisions."[6]
- Integration across settings of care, inpatient, outpatient, doctor's office, home, so that patients are handed over systematically from one setting to another with appropriate transfer of information; location of care delivery in the least invasive and least costly appropriate setting.
- Matching of resources and services to the needs of the population served, including systematic application of preventive interventions to the enrolled population, for whom they will do the most good.

Another opposite to "fragmented" could be said to be "coordinated," that is harmonized in a common action or effort. Integration is one way of achieving coordination, but there are others, such as relational contracting between two or more separately owned entities. One example would be Toyota Motors and its suppliers, in which a high degree of incentives alignment and coordination of operations has been achieved without common ownership, as illustrated by "just

---

5. INSTITUTE OF MEDICINE, CROSSING THE QUALITY CHASM 9.
6. *Id.* at 6.

in time" delivery of parts.[7] Another would be the relationship between Kaiser Permanente and some of its suppliers of complex care, in which efforts are coordinated in the interest of patients. Indeed, Kaiser Permanente itself, which I am about to use as the epitome of integrated delivery system, is in fact a contractual partnership between Kaiser Foundation Health Plan and Hospitals, on one hand, and the Permanente Medical Groups on the other. Whether or not common ownership is best for coordination is a matter of circumstances and transactions costs. I use the term Integrated Delivery Systems (IDS) because that is the commonly used terminology for these systems.

In a paper attempting to explain why *systems* are needed, Laura Tollen and I wrote:

> There is more to safe, appropriate, affordable health care than what is evident to a patient in an encounter with an individual provider. We need systems to ensure that health care providers are carefully selected, trained, and proficient in the specific diagnosis and treatment needed by the patient; deployed in the appropriate numbers and specialties to meet a population's needs efficiently; current on evidence-based practice and supported by tools (such as monitoring and reminders) to overcome widespread practice variations and quality failures; supported by a complete up-to-date, and accurate medical history of each patient; supported by teams of colleagues sharing goals, work processes, and information and able to coordinate care across multiple settings; supported by a system that records test results, diagnoses, and treatments and transmits orders accurately; . . . and supported financially and logistically to participate in common efforts such as guideline development and pharmacy and therapeutics committees, which are important for evidence-based practice.[8]

In short, as the INSTITUTE OF MEDICINE (IOM) argued in CROSSING THE QUALITY CHASM, reform of U.S. health care needs to be based on redesigned *systems* of care.[9]

The most prominent and best integrated of the IDS are hospital-based, prepaid, multi-specialty group practices (PGP).[10] And the most prominent examples are the Kaiser Permanente programs in Northern and Southern California. These are, arguably, among the most efficient health care delivery systems

7. J.P. WOMACK, D.T. JONES, AND D. ROSS, THE MACHINE THAT CHANGED THE WORLD: THE STORY OF LEAN PRODUCTION, (1990).

8. A.C. Enthoven & L.A. Tollen, *Competition in Health Care: It Takes Systems to Pursue Quality and Efficiency*, HEALTH AFF., WEB EXCLUSIVE W5-420, September 7, 2005.

9. INSTITUTE OF MEDICINE, *supra* note 5, at 4.

10. A.C. ENTHOVEN & L.A. TOLLEN, TOWARD A 21ST CENTURY HEALTH SYSTEM: THE CONTRIBUTIONS AND PROMISE OF PREPAID GROUP PRACTICE (2004).

in the world.[11] PGPs provide care (or arrange and pay for, in the case of highly specialized care that needs to be referred out of the system), all paid for by the dues payments of voluntarily enrolled members or their employers. Incentives are aligned by the common source of funding for all elements of the system, and by the fact that the members are there by choice. Once a year, they can "vote with their feet" and switch to an alternative source of health care financing and delivery.[12] Physicians are paid salaries, not fee-for-service, salaries based on specialty and market requirements, plus bonuses based on quality indicators, measured patient satisfaction and teamwork, and overall financial success of the group. The medical groups have strong policies to prevent conflicts of interest.

In the fragmented non-system, insurers and providers are often adversaries that deal at arms length, and doctors and hospitals have divergent interests. There is often animosity in these relationships, as well as reluctance to do the other a favor. Kaiser Permanente is a tripartite organization: Medical Groups, Health Plan (the "insurance" arm that markets the service to members and employers), and Hospitals, linked by long-term relational contracts of mutual exclusivity. The three are integrated at the level of aligned incentives, shared revenue streams and shared values. The doctors cooperate with hospitals in many ways to improve quality and reduce cost. The doctors form teams to study the different medical devices on offer, including their performance over time (they keep registries), and they focus procurement on a few vendors with the best products with whom managers negotiate to maximize value for money for members. And in other ways they work with their hospitals to improve quality, efficiency, and to hold down costs.

The Medical Groups and the Health Plan are partners. Health Plan managers know that they will not prosper unless they have a good product—medical services—to sell. Therefore they need strong medical groups with physician incomes good enough to attract excellent doctors. The Medical Groups understand that they will not prosper unless Health Plan has an affordable product to sell.

There is a similar story in the case of Health Plan and Hospital relationships. Hospital goals are not to fill beds, to maximize net incomes, the apparent goal of some famous non-profit hospitals,[13] or buy more scanners than their enrolled population needs, but rather to be a part of an efficient delivery system that provides high quality care.

---

11. R.G.A. Feachem et al., *Getting More For Their Dollar: A Comparison of the NHS With California's Kaiser Permanente*, 324 BRITISH MEDICAL JOURNAL 135–141, 19 January 2002.

12. A.C. Enthoven AC Commentary: Competition made them do it. 324 BRITISH MEDICAL JOURNAL 143 19 January 2002.

13. John Carreyrou and Barbara Martinez, *Nonprofit Hospitals, Once For The Poor, Strike It Rich; With Tax Breaks, they Outperform For-Profit Rivals*, WALL STREET JOURNAL, April 4, 2008.

What about cost of care? In their Health Insurance Experiment, the RAND Corporation did a randomized controlled trial comparing "free choice" fee-for-service in Seattle and Group Health Cooperative of Puget Sound (GHC), a fully integrated PGP. RAND found that, when services in fee-for-service and Group Health were evaluated at common standard prices (to take price differences out of the comparison), that expenditures on the group randomized into GHC were twenty-eight percent less than expenditures on the group randomized into fee-for-service, for the same outcomes.[14] And this does not give GHC credit for ability to produce doctor visits at less cost by using doctor time more efficiently, or for ability to purchase drugs and devices more effectively.

This finding is important because it is the only randomized experiment measuring comparative costs. GHC accomplished this in a market in which most purchasers were not cost conscious (many unionized workers with employers paying one hundred percent of any premium) and in which they did not face competition in kind. It is likely that they could have done better if they had had incentives to do so. On the other hand, PGPs do not always cost 28 percent less than fee-for-service. Insurance companies have been trying to emulate the hospital use practices and other innovations of the PGPs with some success. And market conditions vary, with PGPs often operating in markets where there is not a great deal of cost-conscious choice (see below). So in actual practice, the cost difference might be less or more, depending on market conditions. But integrated systems surely have the potential and tools to cost much less than the fragmented non-system.

The cost difference would likely be more if competition over value for money were to motivate the kind of productivity improvement it has in other industries. As IDS apply technology to simplifying complex tasks that were formerly the province of highly trained specialists, those tasks can be managed by less expensive people, such as primary care physicians, and this will steadily make innovations in process improvements that get equal or better outcomes at less cost. The fragmented non-system has neither the capability nor the incentives to respond to such competition. The expensive specialists don't want process redesigns that reduce demand for their services. I think it is not unreasonable to believe that, over a decade or two, National Health Expenditures in a truly competitive market of IDS could be half what they will be if we stay with the fragmented non-system, unchallenged by competition to produce value for money.

Through incentives and organization, PGPs address many problems that have been of national concern at the level of public policy. There has been concern about hospitals building excess capacity, leading to the passage of Certificate of Need laws. The hospital-based PGPs have powerful incentives to match resources used to the needs of the population served. And they generally operate

---

14. J.P. NEWHOUSE, FREE FOR ALL? LESSONS FROM THE RAND HEALTH INSURANCE EXPERIMENT, (1993).

with lower bed-to-population ratios than are prevalent in the fragmented non-system. It takes an estimated seventeen years for new scientific discoveries to find their way into ordinary practice.[15] Kaiser Permanente has created a Care Management Institute in which teams of physicians, supported by health researchers, review the scientific literature and translate its implications into recommended practice guidelines that are transmitted promptly to physicians through their electronic information systems.[†] Continuing Medical Education requirements have reflected a concern that many doctors are not up to date. Practicing in a Permanente Medical Group must be like one continuing medical education program, supported by the above-mentioned information systems, peer reviews of ongoing medical records, and multi-specialty interactions between primary care physicians and specialists.

WHY DO WE HAVE THE FRAGMENTED NON-SYSTEM?

Where did fragmentation come from? Why does it persist and predominate over a superior alternative? *Basically, it is because that is the way the organized medical profession wanted it in the nineteenth and most of the twentieth centuries, as well as the lack of antitrust enforcement from World War II to the 1970s; the failure of antitrust enforcement in the 1980s-90s to block hospital mergers and consolidations, giving hospitals much greater negotiating leverage over payers (relieving them of the need to compete); and state insurance regulation (blocking selective provider contracting.)* Organized medicine—the American Medical Association and the affiliated county medical societies, doubtless representing the views and interests of their members—wanted the fragmented system because they saw it as in their economic interest.

In a brilliant article entitled *"Free choice" as a Restraint of Trade in American Health Care Delivery and Insurance*, Charles D. Weller characterized the traditional fragmented system as "Guild Free Choice."[16] The Guild model was based on the following principles:

- "Free choice of doctor" at all times. The insurer that pays the bills has no bargaining power with the doctor because it cannot influence whether or not the patient goes to any particular doctor.

---

† This is similar to the Institute for Clinical Systems Improvement created by Minnesota doctors in multi-specialty group practices, and to the Quality Enhancement Research Initiative (QUERI) created by the Veterans Health Administration.

15. Chassin MR, Is Health Care Ready for Six Sigma Quality? MILBANK QUARTERLY 76 (4) 1998 565–91.

16. C.D. Weller, 'Free Choice' as a Restraint of Trade in American Health Care Delivery and Insurance, 69 (5) IOWA LAW REVIEW (July 1984). Until the 1979 Federal Trade Commission ruling to the contrary, for many years antitrust was considered by many not to apply to medicine.

- "Free choice of treatment," i.e., nobody "interferes" with the doctor's treatment decisions and recommendations. This means no monitoring of compliance with established practice guidelines, no utilization management, no quality management, and no peer review. All these innovations have been resisted by organized medicine. In the past, when physicians talked about "necessary medical care," they meant care that is, *in the personal opinion of the individual doctor*, necessary for the patient's health. They did not accept that the payer, as the informed agent of the consumer/patient, has a legitimate right to question and review what they do.
- "Fee-for-service payment," which means that the doctor can always earn more by doing and prescribing more treatments (and more costly treatments) whether or not they would benefit the health of the patient. This creates a conflict of interest. More broadly, fee-for-service means freedom from accountability for the use of resources.
- "Direct doctor-patient negotiation of fees:" the patient is in a very weak position to bargain or shop because he depends on the good will of the doctor and lacks information about what others charge or how capable they are or how many visits or procedures they would take to solve a given problem. Insurers, on the other hand, have a great deal of such information and could use it in the patient's interest. But they are not allowed to do so in the Guild model.
- "Solo (or small single specialty group) practice." Doctors depend on other doctors for referrals. Organized medicine opposed multi-specialty group practices because within a multi-specialty group practice, primary care doctors can refer patients to their own specialist partners, thus preventing outside doctors from coercing them by threatening to deny them referrals.‡
- This model was accompanied by a culture of physician autonomy.

Together, these principles describe the foundations of the fragmented non-system. This model gives physicians an unusual degree of freedom to practice when and where they want, in patterns that may be poorly related to patient needs. Thus, we observe that there is unequal and often inappropriate distribution of physicians by specialty and geography, and this contributes to the wide variations in practices and frequencies of procedures described by Dr. Wennberg.[17]

Organized medicine fought, and objected strenuously to, practically every departure from that model, using political action, ostracism, boycotts, and other coercive tactics. The traditional Guild model for the organization of and payment

---

‡ In the 1920s, when Dr. Russell V. Lee founded the Palo Alto Medical Clinic, a multi-specialty group practice, he was expelled from the Santa Clara County Medical Society.

17. *See* Dartmouth Atlas, http://www.dartmouthatlas.org/.

for medical care maximized autonomy and economic benefits for physicians. Its performance should not be accepted as the standard for the health care system. It does not consider the important and legitimate need of patients for quality, affordable care, and insurance, and it does not consider the needs of taxpayers who are paying for their services.

The Guild model was established in the era when health insurance practically did not exist in this country. Fees and costs were restrained by limits on patients' willingness and ability to pay. The patients were using their own money and went without care they couldn't afford unless they were poor enough to be considered charity cases. During and after World War II, employment-based health insurance grew rapidly and became widespread. Most health insurance was based on Guild principles. Organized medicine and the hospital associations created Blue Shield and Blue Cross, offering "service benefit" insurance to assure payment on terms acceptable to them. (In that case, there were negotiated fees, but providers sat on both sides of the bargaining table where the fees were determined.)[18] For many years the hospital and medical associations granted lower prices to the Blues to assure their market positions and that their existence could be used to discipline all other kinds of health insurance and to be sure that all other insurers would fit into guild principles. Insurance companies set indemnity payments for particular services or groups of services that they would make to insured patients. Because of Guild principles, there was no contract between doctors and insurers.

Decisions about World War II wage and price controls, followed by exclusion of employer contributions to employee health insurance from the taxable income of employees in the Internal Revenue Code, as well as the fact that employment groups provided a logical basis for spreading of risks, put health insurance firmly in the hands of employers. But employment-based health insurance had and still has a strong bias toward fee-for-service medicine. Rather than fight the medical profession, employers fit in with the Guild model, with a few exceptions like Henry J. Kaiser. They were trying to buy insurance in the context of the model that existed, and not change the system. Employers often backed up indemnity insurance with "major medical insurance" that paid most of the patient's out-of-pocket cost not paid by indemnity insurance. Insurance left patients with little or no reason to care what services cost. The old restraint of the patient's ability and willingness to pay was removed or greatly attenuated by insurance.

The Guild model became untenable as costs soared. In the Guild model, the idea was that the doctor decides what he or she wants to do and what he or she wants to charge, and the patient's role is merely to pay and then seek

18. D.I. Kass & P.A. Pautler Staff Report on Physician Control of Blue Shield Plans, Bureau of Economics, Federal Trade Commission, Washington DC, November 1979.

reimbursement from his health plan or employer. This is a model that leaves employers and employees with minimal control over the costs of health care. In the 1980s, employers pressed for legislation to change state insurance laws to allow selective provider contracting. In a great irony, employers then found that they needed to include all the providers their employees might want, so they threw away the potential advantage of selective contracting. The Guild model had its last hurrah in the 1990s when state medical societies pressed legislatures successfully for "Any Willing Provider" laws.[19] Any Willing Provider is the antithesis of selective provider contracting. It says, in effect, that if a health insurer contracts with a provider, then "any willing provider" presumably of the same specialty, may also participate in that contract on the same terms. In that regime, no insurer can trade volume for price, and no provider has an incentive to be the low bidder.

The roots of prepaid group practice (PGP) go back to three movements in nineteenth century America. First, European immigrants created many fraternal organizations, mutual benefit societies, and workplace employee associations that contracted with physicians to care for dues-paying members. The second was the need to provide medical services for industrial workers in remote areas.[20] Industrial companies contracted for the care of employees and families. This was the origin of Kaiser Permanente. The third was the group practice of medicine, one of the leaders of which was the Mayo Clinic that evolved into group practice in the 1890s.

Organized medicine regularly condemned PGP as "contract medicine" and "unethical."[21] Historian Rickey Hendricks described the early days of a pioneer prepaid group practice:

> The Los Angeles County Medical Association (LACMA) made a bolder assault on a local prepaid group practice plan, also begun in 1929. Drs. Donald Ross and H. Clifford Loos established the Ross-Loos Clinic to serve 2,000 members of the Los Angeles County Employees Association of the Department of Water and Power. By the mid-1930s a group of about fifty doctors served approximately 40,000 people ... The Ross-Loos departure from solo fee-for-service practice alarmed local doctors now faced with hard economic times. Drs. Ross and Loos literally were cast out of the professional fraternity . . . In February 1934

---

19. A. Carroll & J.M. Ambrose, *Any Willing Provider Laws: Their Financial Effect on HMOs*, 27(6) JOURNAL OF HEALTH POL., POL'Y & L., 927–946.

20. Enthoven & Tollen, *supra* note 10; JON A. STEWART, APPENDIX: THE ORIGINS OF PREPAID GROUP PRACTICE IN THE UNITED STATES.

21. L.G. Goldberg and W. Greenberg, *The Emergence of Physician-Sponsored Health Insurance: a Historical Perspective, in* COMPETITION IN THE HEALTH CARE SECTOR, PAST, PRESENT, AND FUTURE, (W. Greenberg ed., 1978).

they were notified to appear before the LACMA Board of Councilors in ten days "to show cause' why they 'should not be censored and/or suspended, and/or expelled.' . . . They learned through a telephone inquiry that the charge was unethical advertising. Although they produced substantial evidence that they had not paid solicitors or for literature aimed at recruiting subscribers, the local association voted unanimously for expulsion. In a later report the AMA nevertheless alluded to the clinic group as if it was unethically financed. Since the real authority of the AMA was at the local level, the Ross-Loos physicians were, in effect, ostracized by their professional colleagues. The legal right to practice medicine was not contingent on membership in the county medical society, but doctors who were not members remained outside the professional referral network, were denied hospital privileges, and were unable to take specialty board examinations that became more important as specialization increased in the following decade.[22]

The term "unethical" as used by the AMA is not what a professor of ethics at a university might write about. These "medical ethics" referred to economic principles of the Guild model. Weller reported that

> In 1979 the Federal Trade Commission ruled that the "free choice" ethics of the American Medical Association (AMA) were a restraint of trade. The Commission found that the AMA's free choice ethics "impair[ed] competition from alternative providers by discouraging use of innovative arrangements that can deliver services at lower cost.[23]

Kaiser Permanente, now serving over eight million members, had its roots in the great construction projects of Henry J. Kaiser, including the California Aqueduct and the Grand Coulee Dam. Henry Kaiser contracted with Sidney Garfield, M.D., to provide medical services to construction workers and families for a fixed price per person per day for illness and injury not related to work.[24] During World War II, the same concept was extended to Kaiser's shipyards and steel mills. At the end of the war, the shipyards shut down. The doctors serving employees of the Kaiser enterprises decided to stay together and to offer their services to employees in the communities they served, still on the basis of per capita prepayment. These doctors and their program encountered considerable harassment from organized medicine in the State of California.[25]

Pulitzer Prize winning author Paul Starr recounted the experience with organized medicine of another nascent prepaid group practice.

---

22. R. HENDRICKS, A MODEL FOR NATIONAL HEALTH CARE: THE HISTORY OF KAISER PERMANENTE 16–18 (1993).
23. Weller, *supra* note 16.
24. Hendricks, *supra* note 22, at 26.
25. *Id.*

The whole question of "cooperative medicine" finally came to a head when the AMA was indicted on charges of violating the Sherman Anti Trust act in its efforts to suppress the Group Health Association (GHA) of Washington, D.C. GHA was organized in 1937 as a nonprofit cooperative by employees of the Federal Home Loan Bank. Even before the cooperative began service, the AMA called on legal authorities to take action against what it regarded as a form of "unlicensed, unregulated health insurance and the corporate practice of medicine." Unable to prevail on government, it undertook a full-scale campaign to put GHA out of business. As an appellate court later found, the AMA and local medical society threatened reprisals against any doctor who worked for the plan, prevented them from obtaining consultations and referrals, and succeeded in persuading every hospital in the District of Columbia to deny them admitting privileges, thereby cutting off members of the cooperative from hospital care. In December 1938 the Justice Department secured an indictment against the national and local medical organizations and their officers for conspiracy in restraint of trade to destroy the Group Health Association. In 1943 the Supreme Court upheld the conviction of the AMA on antitrust violations.[26]

This broad campaign against PGPs often descended to the level of abusive personal attacks by doctors against individual physicians and employees associated with PGPs. I personally witnessed some of them. A former CEO of Kaiser Permanente told me that at some social occasions where doctors were present, he was afraid to "admit" that he worked for Kaiser Permanente for fear of unleashing a torrent of invective.

This sustained attack has left its mark on our culture today. In the minds of many, there appears still to be something suspect or second-rate about doctors having incentives to make high quality health care affordable. The anti-PGP culture was reflected in the suspicion with which the Medicare program treated PGPs for many years. The effects of these historical attitudes persist today in the business models of the insurance companies, and in the practices of most employers. If our society persists in its negative attitude toward rewarding physicians for trying to make health care affordable, it is hard to see how we will be able to bring down the growth in National Health Expenditures to a sustainable rate.

Meanwhile, the Permanente Medical Groups retain the services of many excellent doctors, including graduates of the top medical schools, doctors whose main motivation is caring for patients, who would prefer to devote their time and energy to care of patients rather than running a small business, and who are not profit maximizers. A Permanente physician has recently served as President of the California Medical Association. Two surveys report that the Permanente

---

26. PAUL STARR, THE SOCIAL TRANSFORMATION OF AMERICAN MEDICINE 305 (1982).

physicians are the happiest doctors in California, doubtless in large part because they are self-governing, together they make all their own medical decisions without interference from insurance companies, and they work with only one insurance company, and that one is their responsible long-term partner.[27] The negative attitudes toward PGP are much less prevalent today among younger doctors who see the advantages of teamwork, physician leadership, and support systems, for quality of care and physician quality of life.

In other words, the fragmented non-system we have today is not the result of consumer choice in a free market. Rather, it is the consequence of the use of extra-market power by the organized medical profession to prevent a market outcome in which physicians might earn less or be held responsible for cost and outcomes. That set in place a model that has been reinforced by employers and insurance companies, each for their own reasons.

Few people realize how unfavorable today's market conditions are for the development and growth of integrated delivery systems. The employment-based health insurance market has two tiers: the employer and the employee. The first challenge is to overcome employers' preference to offer only one insurance carrier and the resulting lack of employee choice of delivery system. Most employers and insurers are oriented to the "single source" model. A 1997 survey found only twenty-three percent of insured employees were offered a choice of carrier.[28] There has not been a comparable survey since, but experienced industry observers tell me that the trend is toward "single source."

Health insurance, like all other forms of insurance, is regulated by the states—and was so even before the McCarran-Ferguson Act of 1946 codified their authority. Regulation by the states is costly, complex, and various. It is a barrier to firms entering new states, and a cause of conflict between federal and state laws. To market a new national insurance product, an insurer must go from state to state to secure approval. Most states regulate insurance rates, further delaying market entry. Contrast this with a federally chartered banking product or a mutual fund: once approved by a federal regulator, the new product can be marketed throughout the United States.

Both government and private employee health benefit programs that are self-funded are exempt from state insurance laws, including reserve requirements,

27. K. Grumbach et al. *California Physicians 2002: Practice and Perceptions.* San Francisco, CA: California Workforce Initiative at the UCSF Center for the Health Professions, December 2002. Also L. Chehab *et al., The Impact of Practice Setting on Physician Perceptions of the Quality of Practice and Patient Care in the Managed Care Era,* 161(2) ARCHIVES OF INTERNAL MEDICINE (2001).

28. S.H. Long & M.S. Marquis, TRENDS IN MANAGED CARE AND MANAGED COMPETITION, 18(6) HEALTH AFF. 133–139 (1999).

mandated benefits, premium taxes, and consumer protection regulations.[29] The Employee Retirement Income Security Act (ERISA) of 1974 does not apply to government programs, the majority of which are self funded.[30] ERISA preemption allows multi-state employers to offer the same package of covered benefits to all employees. Also, self-funding allows employers to hold onto their cash longer and keep the returns from investing it. From 1999 to 2007, the percentage of covered workers in partially or completely self-funded plans increased from 44 percent to 55 percent.[31] This makes it harder for risk-bearing prepaid group practices to compete in this market. Providers sharing the risks of the cost of care is an important part of the incentive structure of integrated delivery systems. To compete in the self-funded environment, they have to set up the costly apparatus of fee-for-service billing. If they do not fit in with self-funding, they are forced to offer coverages that include many costly state-mandated benefits that employers consider irrelevant for their employees.

Offering a choice of carriers can create costly administrative burdens for the employer. Many large employers are spread out over several or many geographical locations, sometimes with few employees at each site. Offering multiple choices of carriers at many locations would be very costly and complex. Integrated delivery systems are usually local entities; they are not built to handle the many sites of a large national employer.

Many insurance companies also avoid multiple-choice situations unless required to participate in them by large employers such as the Federal government, some state governments, and some large universities, or large pools of small employers, e.g., CalPERS. In fact, in Kaiser's early years, Blue Cross and Blue Shield threatened employment groups with cancellation if they offered Kaiser as an alternative choice plan, which was often successful in keeping Kaiser out of the group. They view choice as involving higher administrative costs (which it does), the risk of adverse selection (which it also does), and particularly competition, which they prefer to avoid. They offer employers lower premiums if they can cover their whole group. The technology to perform Risk Equalization, that is, to compensate health plans that enroll a more costly population at the expense of those plans that enroll less costly populations, and to do it prospectively, has only emerged in practical application in recent years. Medicare does it for participating Medicare Advantage plans. The Dutch are the first to do Risk

29. As a legal matter, this is fundamentally a matter of state insurance law. The leading case holding employer plans are not insurance under state law is State ex rel. Farmer v. Monsanto Co. 517 S.W.2d 129 (Mo. S.C. 1974).

30. The Kaiser Family Foundation and Health Research and Educational Trust, Employer Health Benefits 2007 Annual Survey 146.

31. *Id.* at 147.

Equalization on a national basis.[32] It would not be practical for most small or mid-sized employers.

Prepaid Group Practices are poor candidates for the single-source market because some people prefer not to be in one, find their locations inconvenient, or prefer to remain with their accustomed providers. For an employer to replace entirely a traditional "free choice" insurance plan with a PGP, employees would have to give up the doctors they know and like. For this reason, the Permanente Medical Groups from the beginning advocated for a "dual choice" requirement because the physicians understood that it would be difficult to form a good and trusting doctor-patient relationship with patients who were not free to choose them. Also, it was a response to organized medicine's charge of having "captive patients."

For PGPs to reach the employer group market, employers must be willing to offer multiple carriers and, in the case of new PGPs, be willing to incur the added administrative expense for what might be just a few employees at the outset. There are solutions to these problems which I will discuss below.

The problem of market access is further complicated by the fact that many of the choice-offering employers systematically subsidize more costly versus less costly delivery systems by contributing 80–100 percent of the premium of the plan of the employee's choice, thereby destroying the marketplace reward for offering a lower premium. A famous case of this is the Group Insurance Commission (GIC) of Massachusetts, which arranges health insurance for public employees. By law, the state pays 80 percent of the premium of the plan of the employee's choice. To understand what this does to incentives, suppose hypothetically, that Harvard Pilgrim Health Plan were to consider the possibility of lowering its premium by one dollar. Harvard Pilgrim management would know that when the premium difference was laundered through GIC and the Internal Revenue Code, the employee making the choice would get to save only twenty cents pre-tax, which in turn would mean about twleve cents after tax (assuming that, all taxes considered, the employee is in the 40 percent marginal tax bracket). It is likely that Harvard Pilgrim would be able to think of several ways of using that dollar in revenue to attract more members: better customer service, a wider network, less cost sharing, nicer facilities, etc. So GIC, as constituted by the legislature, promotes health care cost inflation in Massachusetts.

---

32. Gautam Naik, *Dutch Treatment: In Holland, Some See Model for U.S. Health-Care System*, WALL STREET JOURNAL, Sept 6, 2007. Also Wynand P.M.M. van de Ven, René C.J.A. van Vliet, and Leida M. Lamers, *Health-Adjusted Premium Subsidies in the Netherlands*, 23(3) HEALTH AFF., 45–55, May/June 2004, and Wynand P.P.M. van de Ven and Frederik Schut, *Universal Health Insurance in the Netherlands: A Model for the U.S.?* 27(3) HEALTH AFF. 771–781, May/June 2008. Also A.C. Enthoven, *A Living Example of Managed Competition: A Conversation with the Dutch Minister of Health, Ab Klink*, HEALTH AFF. Web Exclusive w196, April 8, 2008.

But it isn't the worst. Many unions have elevated 100 percent employer payment of premiums to the status of Holy Grail. A survey of the Fortune 500 by Maxwell and Temin published in 2002 reported that less than 10 percent of Fortune 500 employees had the combination of a choice of insurance carrier and a fixed dollar contribution from the employer so that they could keep the savings from choosing an economical health plan.[33] Moreover, a choice of just one fee-for-service plan and one PGP isn't good enough to create meaningful competition. For the market to work, there need to be several competitors, or better still, free entry by plans and delivery systems that would meet the standards of the market.

Why don't choice-offering employers paying 80–100 percent change to a fixed dollar contribution? Not without reason, they fear that, if they act alone, they would antagonize some employees while not getting the benefits of a competitive health care system. For the latter to happen, it would be necessary for most employers in the region to adopt the same policy.

GETTING THERE FROM HERE: CAN IT BE DONE?

Would it be possible for America to break out of the historical path that perpetuates the fragmented non-system? In 2004, I wrote the answer for Prepaid Group Practice would be to "open the markets and level the playing field."[34]

In concept, the answer is simple. But getting there from where we are today is very complex. The conceptually simple answer is to adopt a health care financing system in which every American has a wide, responsible, informed, individual, multiple choice of health plan, including group practice-based HMOs[35], as well as some PPOs, indemnity plans, and other plan designs, combined with a fixed dollar employer or government contribution, so that the chooser gets to keep all the savings generated by making an economical choice. The benefits covered by the competitors need to be similar, to mitigate risk selection and segmentation, and there needs to be Risk Equalization. The fine print exclusions

---

33. J. Maxwell and P. Temin, *Managed Competition Versus Industrial Purchasing of Health Care Among the Fortune 500*, 27(1) JOURNAL OF HEALTH POL., POL'Y & L. 5–30, February 2002.

34. Enthoven & Tollen, *supra* note 10, at 227–46.

35. Not all group practice-based HMOs are PGPs, but they are an approximation that allows them to compete with real PGPs. The difference in California is that the "California delegated model HMOs," as we call them, contract with multi-specialty group practices on the basis of per capita prepayment for professional services, with limited incentives to economize on institutional services. They differ from Kaiser in that the latter is fully at risk for all costs including hospital and pharmacy costs. I think it is likely that if market conditions forced it, most of these HMOs would migrate to becoming real PGPs. Their success is an indicator of what can be done in terms of market share for comparatively efficient plans.

need to be standardized so that the research costs of switching plans are minimized and people will be willing to switch plans on the basis of perceived value for money, without fear that they will be victims of some tricky fine-print exclusion.§** Principles like these describe what most people would recognize to be a normal competitive market. The model should also include regional pricing. I have called these principles "managed competition."[36] Like practically any other market in a developed economy, there need to be rules of the road, such as consumer protections, the law of contracts, information disclosure, etc. Such markets for health insurance are quite rare in the United States. But where they are present, and where group-practice-based HMOs exist, very high percentages of employees choose the HMOs.[37] It is 81 percent at Stanford and the University of California, and about 94 percent among Wisconsin public employees, 75 percent for Wells Fargo Bank in California.

These percents would likely never reach one hundred because there always will be people whose preferences and lifestyles do not fit with limiting their insured provider choices to those of one integrated delivery system. But that is not important as long as the standard for employer and government contributions is the premium of the most efficient system, and that system meets standards of high quality, and practically everyone has the option of joining an IDS if he or she wants to.

How could these principles be put into practice? One thing that would help would be if the federal and state governments put a limit on the amount of employer contribution that could be excluded from taxable income, as has been urged by economists over the years and even recommended by President Bush in his 2007 State of the Union Address. Economists would recommend that the limit be at the premium of the most efficient plan in each region.

---

§ One physician friend referred to "Swiss cheese insurance policies" because people would unexpectedly hit "air pockets" of exclusions in their coverage.

** Risk Equalization is a process in which the relative medical costs of each enrollee are predicted, based on statistical modeling using diagnostic history and other factors, the predicted costs for an enrolled population are added up for each insurer, and payments are made to compensate those insurers that enroll a more costly than average mix of patients. The purpose of this is to create incentives for insurers to attract and care for sick people, and not to avoid them as happens in competition without Risk Equalization.

36. A. Enthoven, *History and Principles of Managed Competition*, 12 (Supp.) HEALTH AFF. 24–48 (1993). Also *Theory and Practice of Managed Competition in Health Care Finance* Professor Dr. De Vries Lectures in Economics, North Holland, 1988.

37. The Federal Employees health benefits program is an imperfect realization of this model, yet in California in 2005, 58 percent of Federal employees chose HMOs. Cal PERS is also an imperfect realization of these principles, largely because it includes many local government agencies in which employee unions have achieved 100 percent employer payment of the premium of the plans of their choice. Yet, in the CalPERS population, about 70 percent have chosen HMOs.

As for offering choices, it is not impossible. The HMO Act of 1973 required employers of twenty-five or more to offer one group practice and one individual practice HMO to employees, as a choice, if such HMOs served the areas where employees lived and asked to be offered. Unfortunately, this did not come with a fixed dollar contribution requirement, so many employers continued to pay 80–100 percent of the premium of the employee's choice, with the consequences discussed above. And in the 1980s, the choice requirement was allowed to lapse.

There are at least two insurance brokerage firms in California that offer employees of contracting employers a choice among several delivery systems.[38] However, offering choices has not been a priority for employers, and the brokers have no control or influence over the contribution policies of the participating employers, many of whom continue with the 80–100 percent contribution policy.

In 2002, the Committee for Economic Development (CED), a business-supported, Washington-based, non-profit, non-partisan virtual public policy research organization that studies major issues bearing on public policy and economic growth issued a report on health expenditures, noting the lack of responsible consumer choice of integrated delivery systems and other models capable of managing quality and cost, published a report that recommended for employers:[39]

1. Demand transparent quality information and adherence to best medical practices; use comparative performance information to select plans and providers; incorporate accountability for cost and quality into contract specifications.
2. Offer wide, responsible health plan choices to employees in exchange for their greater financial responsibility. Such plans would incorporate contribution policies that encourage workers to choose efficient, high-quality plans . . . help to establish, operate, and manage regional purchasing cooperatives that offer affordable plans to small firms.[40]

In its 2007 report, CED noted "We have seen very little progress towards these recommendations." If anything, movement was in the wrong direction. A San Francisco-based purchasing cooperative offering multiple choices for employees of small employers went out of business. And the trend among large employers

---

38. *See* http://www.calchoice.com/AboutUs.aspx (last visited 4.25.08) Also http://www.keenan.com. Cal Choice focuses on the private sector, Keenan on public sector employers.

39. COMMITTEE FOR ECONOMIC DEVELOPMENT, A NEW VISION FOR HEALTH CARE; A LEADERSHIP ROLE FOR BUSINESS, (2002) (the summary of the 2002 report is taken from the Committee for Economic Development 2007 report).

40. *Id.* at 65.

appeared to be toward "full replacement" by a single carrier. The San Francisco experience showed that *voluntary* purchasing cooperatives were too vulnerable to adverse selection: the firms with the greatest difficulty finding affordable care (likely the sickest employees) were the first to join the pool. Thus, voluntary action not backed up by strong incentives to pool, is not likely to be viable.

Reflection on the many profound conflicts between the employer-based model of health insurance and the requirements of a rational market for health plans at the individual level suggests that the employment-based system is incompatible with an efficient, affordable, equitable health care system and needs to be replaced by a system of consumer-choice based universal health insurance. (A "single payer" system as in Medicare or Canada could address these problems also, but the Canadians and American Medicare have locked in fee-for-service and seem unable to change it.)

Here are some scenarios for getting to universal coverage with competition:

First, the Committee for Economic Development (CED) has offered a proposal to transform employer based health insurance along the following lines:

- Create an oversight agency modeled on the Federal Reserve, with its political independence and expertise, to be the regulator of health insurance for plans participating in the system, and to create and operate regional exchanges for health insurance. The "Health Fed" would get its revenues from a flat small percentage assessment on all insurance premiums so that it would not be dependent on annual Congressional appropriations. The reason for this is that the health services industry needs to be taken out of the realm of pork barrel politics. (Those who worry about another costly new bureaucracy should recognize that this would replace many costly and ineffective bureaucracies within employer groups.)[41]

- Regional exchanges would be institutions in which eligible persons could review price and quality information, execute their choice of plan, and make payment arrangements. Within the exchanges, there would be guaranteed issue for employees of covered firms and people subsidized by government programs, and community rating (i.e. same price for same product regardless of enrollee health status), and risk equalization.

- Create an alternative federal regulatory system that participating multi-state health insurers can choose. Designate the Health Fed as the regulatory agency. Health insurance is now a national industry, and public policy should encourage established health care financing and delivery systems to expand to other states in the interest of greater competition, by offering them an option of uniform national regulation—especially in a national system of health insurance.

---

41. This idea has been proposed by Senator Tom Daschle. *See* Tom Daschle, Critical: What We Can Do About The Health-Care Cost Crisis, (2008).

- The tax exclusion would be capped at the level of the low-priced plan in each region, and the savings would be applied to subsidies for people with low incomes. The employer tax deduction would be similarly capped.
- In the first phase, all employers of one hundred or fewer employees would be required to buy through the exchange as a requirement for continued access to the tax exclusion for their employees. Small employers are at the greatest disadvantage in the present system and the least likely to offer employees choices. This would give them advantages of economies of scale and economical choice. The tax incentive is needed to offset the danger of adverse selection against the exchange; without it, only the more costly groups would join. When this phase is completed successfully, the threshold for participation in the exchanges would be raised, progressively, until it includes all employers
- The principles of managed competition would apply, including a common minimum standard benefit package and Risk Equalization.
- A new, well and independently funded organization, an Institute for Medical Outcomes and Technology Assessment or Comparative Cost Effectiveness, would be created, possibly under the Health Fed, to provide badly needed independent assessments of comparative costs and effectiveness of medical technologies. The independence is needed to protect it from retaliation by members of Congress whose constituents are disappointed by the Institute's findings. It is essential for this Institute to have real credibility and freedom from sources of bias. Today, large amounts of money are wasted on technologies whose effectiveness and cost-effectiveness have not been properly evaluated, and which eventually turn out to be worthless or worse.[42]
- When this process is complete, and health expenditure growth moderated, and much of the delivery system transformed into various types of efficient integrated system, then, if the resources can be found and political support is there, employer contributions would be replaced by tax-financed fixed-dollar premium credits sufficient to buy everyone's way into membership in the least costly plan in their region, and universal health insurance will be achieved.[††] CED has recommended that we increase reliance on consumption taxes and reduce taxes on productive activities (working, saving

---

42. The idea for an Institute for Medical Outcomes and Technology Assessment comes from unpublished writings of Ezekiel Emanuel, Victor Fuchs and Alan Garber. For an example of a costly technology that, upon evaluation, was found to be worthless, that is High Dose Chemotherapy and Autologous Bone Marrow Transplant for metastatic breast cancer, *see* R.A. RETTIG ET AL., FALSE HOPE (2007).

†† Alternatively, the premium tax credits could be set at a lower amount, sufficient to insure that nobody's premium liability for the average-priced plan exceeds some target percentage of income, and combined with a mandate to buy health insurance.

and investing). A value added tax, as in Europe, or environment-friendly taxes such as a carbon tax, would fit this prescription.[43]

A similar proposal has been put forward by U.S. Senators Ron Wyden (D-Oregon) and Bob Bennett (R-Utah), called "The Healthy Americans Act," S.334. As of August 2008, it had sixteen bi-partisan cosponsors in the Senate, and a similar bill with bi-partisan support in the House. Some key features of this bill are:

- Universal, mandatory coverage based on individual price-sensitive choice of plan. People are required to enroll in the plan of their choice, with an enforcement mechanism.
- States create "Health Help Agencies" to perform the functions of exchanges described above.
- Guaranteed issue and community rating.
- Employers who have been insuring employees will translate their health insurance expenses for employees into cash equivalents and raise employee pay by those amounts. Employers will then be responsible for an "Employer Responsibility Payment" that looks like a payroll tax. This is used to fund subsidies for low income people.
- Health insurance payments will be collected through the income tax. The IRS could do the means testing.
- There will be a health care standard tax deduction for which itemization is not required.
- Premium subsidies for low-income families with a full subsidy for families at or below the Federal Poverty Line (FPL), phased out with income between one hundred percent and 400 percent of the FPL.
- Technology assessment would be done by existing institutions.
- The description suggests a leap from the present system without much focus on transitional steps.

The CED proposal can be understood as the Wyden-Bennett bill with five friendly amendments. The differences are less important than the similarities.

Another approach to expanding the scope for cost conscious consumer choice, but not universal health insurance, might be a generalization of a model developed by the startup company Extend Health.[44] Extend Health has insurance brokerage licenses in fifty states, web sites and call centers with trained personnel to assist clients, and contracts with General Motors, Ford, and Chrysler, and several

---

43. A dedicated value added tax has been recommended by Ezekiel Emanuel and Victor Fuchs. *See Health Care Vouchers—A Proposal for Universal Coverage*, 352(12) NEW ENG J. MED. March 24, 2005.

44. *See* http://www.extendhealth.com/. I am on the Advisory Board of this company. Our interests are aligned with what I perceive to be the public interest.

other large companies, to assist their retirees in obtaining health insurance. The companies make defined contributions on behalf of their salaried retirees, and then Extend Health facilitates their making and executing choices of plan. So far, they are working with Medicare-eligible retirees who are looking for Medicare Supplemental and Medicare Advantage policies. But Extend Health is now working with insurance carriers to develop fully insured coverage for pre-Medicare retirees which will be marketed in a similar way. There are complex issues of premium rating to be resolved. If this model works well, it would seem a natural extension to make it available for active employees whose employers are willing to give employees fixed dollar contributions and choices. This could be a natural fit, for example, for the car rental or fast food companies, with employees scattered in small units across America. It would let employees take advantage of local market conditions and get themselves the best deal available. This would not be universal health insurance. It would still be employment-based, but it could open up a great deal of that market to competition and an opportunity for IDS to grow.

How would health care delivery respond to a change to a fully competitive market at the individual level? The customers of insurers would become individuals, not employers, and insurers would compete to offer them value for money. Existing PGPs would expand. Existing IDS without their own health plans would create their own insurance arms, or partner with insurance companies. (There once was a Leahy Clinic-Blue Cross HMO.) Professor Stephen Shortell has identified 468 multi-specialty physician organizations with 100 or more MDs.[45] They might team up with insurers to offer "private label" products. Insurance companies could accelerate their efforts to create tiered high performance networks, or capitated primary care networks. New initiatives would doubtless emerge.

In all cases of such reforms of the market for people under age 65, *Medicare must also be reformed*, so that all people, or perhaps all people newly enrolling in Medicare, are presented with a fixed-dollar contribution by the government and a menu of competing alternative choices. One model of how this could be done was proposed by the National Bipartisan Commission on the Future of Medicare, also known as "Breaux-Thomas" for the bi-partisan co-chairs.[46] Breaux-Thomas proposed a Medicare Board to "direct and oversee periodic open enrollment periods; provide comparative information to beneficiaries regarding the plans in their areas; transmit information about beneficiaries' plan selections and corresponding premium obligations to the Social Security Administration to permit premium collection as occurs today with Medicare Part B premiums, enforce

---

45. *See* Stephen M. Shortell & Julie Schmittdiel, *Prepaid Groups and Organized Delivery Systems in* TOWARD A 21ST CENTURY HEALTH SYSTEM (Enthoven & Tollen eds.) (2004).

46. *See* National Bipartisan Commission on the Future of Medicare, http://thomas. loc.gov/medicare (last visited April 2, 2008).

financial and quality standards; review and approve benefit packages and service areas to ensure against the adverse selection that could be created through benefit design, delineation of service areas or other techniques; negotiate premiums with all health plans; and compute payments to plans (including risk and geographic adjustment)."[47] The Board would operate under a government charter that would describe its responsibilities and operating standards. A standard benefits package would be specified in law. There would be comprehensive coverage for low-income beneficiaries. On average, beneficiaries would be expected to pay twelve percent of the total cost of standard option plans. For plans that cost at or less than 85 percent of the national weighted average plan price, there would be no beneficiary premium. For plans with prices above the national weighted average, beneficiaries' premiums would include all costs above the national weighted average." This is called a "premium support payment" system.

Unfortunately, President Clinton "denounced its proposed report and said he would devise a plan of his own as an alternative."[48] He directed his appointees to vote against this proposal, so that of seventeen members, only ten voted for it, one vote short of the supermajority of eleven required for the report to be an official recommendation.

In closing, let me note that here is a special opportunity for lawyers and legislators. We must fix our fragmented health care system and move toward an efficient delivery system by re-aligning the perverse incentives so prevalent in our current fragmented non-system. Re-aligning the perverse incentives in health care to serve patients and the public has great potential value, brilliantly explained by Charles Schultze in the Godkin Lectures at Harvard University in 1976.[49] "Modifying the incentives of the private market" by "creating incentives so that public goals become private interests" is "perhaps *the* most important social invention mankind has yet achieved." Further, from a government regulation and legal point of view, Schultze also provides a breakthrough and new approach. He observes that governments "usually tend to see only one way of intervening," namely removing a set of the decisions from the decentralized and incentive-oriented private market and transferring them to the command-and-control techniques of government bureaucracy," completely ignoring the option of "modifying the incentives of the private market" to serve public goals. Unfortunately, he points out, modifying the incentives of the private market is "not considered a relevant alternative." Instead, "command-and-control techniques of government bureaucracy" are used, "specify[ing] in minute detail the particular actions that generate social efficiency and then command[ing] their

47. Final Breaux-Thomas Medicare Reform Proposal, http://medicare.commission. gov/medicare/index.html,.

48. Robert Pear, *Medicare Panel, Sharply Divided, Submits No Plan*, N.Y. TIMES, March 17, 1999.

49. CHARLES SCHULTZE, THE PUBLIC USE OF PRIVATE INTEREST (1977).

performance." Yet trying "to impose a solution without remedying the incentive structure," regularly fails, "consistently, the power of that structure defeats us." For example, "government attempts to deal with rapidly escalating health costs" [in Medicare and Medicaid] "have produced only burgeoning volumes of regulations and no results."

Thus, Schultze offers a breakthrough for government regulation and legal draftsmanship: "maximize the use of techniques that modify the structure of private incentives rather than those that rely on the command-and-control approach." This insight could be combined with the successful performance of Integrated Delivery Systems, especially in competitive environments, to lead us to comprehensive reform.

SUMMARY

Fragmentation of America's health care financing and delivery system is a major contributor to what ought to be considered unacceptably high rates of expenditure growth and medical errors. The opposite of fragmentation is integration. Integrated delivery systems do exist in the USA and care for some twelve million people or more, depending on definition. Through integration, these organizations have the power and tools to improve outcomes and mitigate expenditure growth, if they operate in an environment of cost conscious choice. They do what the Institute of Medicine recommends to *cross the quality chasm*.[50] Their growth has been blocked, in the past, by the concerted action of organized medicine. And now it is blocked by the employer-based system of health insurance because employers do not offer them as a choice in which the employees can keep the savings, and by insurance companies who want to be the sole source of health insurance for employers. America could move rapidly to integrated systems if we were to "open the markets and level the playing field" by adopting a reform model like the Wyden-Bennett Healthy Americans Act, the Dutch model, or the one proposed by the CED, in which everyone would have wide, responsible, individual and informed choice and multiple choices among alternative health care financing and delivery systems. Experience shows that when offered such a choice, great majorities of people choose integrated systems. The principles of such reforms are comparatively easy to state. The implementation is, unfortunately, extremely complex. But this country will not achieve a satisfactory health care system until it adopts the principles of universal coverage based on managed competition and allows Integrated Delivery Systems the opportunity to reach their full market potential.

---

50. Institute of Medicine, Crossing the Quality Chasm, *supra* note 5.

5. DEFRAGMENTING HEALTH CARE DELIVERY THROUGH QUALITY REPORTING

KRISTIN MADISON

I. INTRODUCTION: OUR FRAGMENTED HEALTH CARE SYSTEM

A common complaint about the American health care system is that it is not much of a system. A dictionary defines a system as "a regularly interacting or interdependent group of items forming a unified whole."[1] The American health care system may be comprised of many interacting and interdependent parts, but those who have come into contact with it are unlikely to label it a "unified whole." Rather than being unified or integrated or coordinated, the various actors within the system are fragmented. Payers, including government entities, private insurers, employers, and individual patients, use a variety of payment mechanisms to compensate service providers. Similarly, regulators, including state medical boards, other government entities, private accreditation organizations, and payers, focus on varying dimensions of provider performance and use varied tools to achieve varied goals.

Health care providers, too, are fragmented. This fragmentation takes numerous forms. Health care is provided by countless types of professionals and organizations, including physicians, nurses, technicians, other medical professionals, hospitals, surgery centers, outpatient clinics, urgent care centers, pharmacies, rehabilitation facilities, mental health facilities, and nursing homes. Coordination among providers both within and across these categories is often lacking. Although hospitals increasingly participate in multihospital systems, many hospitals remain independent.[2] And although physicians increasingly practice in larger groups, one-third of physicians still practice alone or with just

---

1. Merriam-Webster OnLine, *available at* http://www.merriam-webster.com/dictionary/system.

2. *See* Alison Evans Cuellar & Paul J. Gertler, *Trends in Hospital Consolidation: The Formation of Local Systems*, 22(6) HEALTH AFF. 77 (2003) (reporting increase in system membership among private hospitals between 1995 and 2000); Kristin Madison, *Multihospital System Membership and Patient Treatments, Expenditures, and Outcomes*, 39 HEALTH SERVICES RES. 749, 759 (reporting that system membership among nonpublic hospitals increased from about 48% in 1985 to 63% in 1998).

one other physician.[3] Less than a third of physicians work in medical school, HMO, or hospital practice settings.[4]

The fragmentation of actors within the health care system need not result in fragmentation of care delivery. A physician practicing alone may ensure continuity of care for his or her patients by directly providing a broad continuum of care. Alternatively, independent physicians, hospitals, and other suppliers of medical services can work together to ensure that even if they are fragmented, their services are sufficiently coordinated that they act as a "unified whole" in treating patients.

More generally, there is nothing inherently problematic about organizational fragmentation. If there are diseconomies of scale or scope in the production of health care services, then fragmentation might result in the delivery of higher quality, more efficient services. If coordination costs facing patients and providers are sufficiently low, or coordination is unnecessary, then patients may be able to obtain a desirable combination of services at reasonable cost, regardless of who delivers them.

In practice, however, fragmentation may be problematic, potentially contributing to both poor quality care and higher health care costs. Coordination costs in providing care for individual patients are not low. Patients face high coordination costs because of their lack of knowledge; physicians, because of the time and effort involved in sharing information about patients. Discontinuities in care may harm patients. In addition, fragmentation may prevent providers from realizing economies of scale and scope or taking advantage of complementarities in the production of health care services. For example, fragmentation may increase the costs of transmitting information about beneficial treatment options to all relevant providers. Fragmentation may also hinder efforts to implement monitoring and incentive mechanisms, a phenomenon illustrated by hospitals that have struggled to influence decision-making by members of their independent medical staffs.[5]

If fragmentation in health care delivery is undesirable because it worsens quality or raises costs, then why does it occur? Not surprisingly, just as there are many types of fragmentation, there are many potential contributors

---

3. *See* ALISON LIEBHABER & JOY M. GROSSMAN, PHYSICIANS MOVING TO MID-SIZED, SINGLE-SPECIALTY PRACTICES, RESULTS FROM THE COMMUNITY TRACKING STUDY NO. 18 (Aug. 2007), http://www.hschange.org/CONTENT/941/941.pdf (reporting that in 1996–97, 40.7% of surveyed physicians practiced in solo or two-physician practices, and 16% of physicians participated in groups with more than six physicians, while in 2004–05, comparable statistics were 32.5% and 21.8%).

4. *See id.* (reporting that in 2004–05, approximately 25.8% of physicians practiced in medical school, HMO, or hospital settings).

5. *See, e.g.,* James F. Blumstein, *Of Doctors and Hospitals: Setting the Analytical Framework for Managing and Regulating the Relationship,* 4 IND. HEALTH L. REV. 211, 222–25 (2007) (discussing relationships between hospitals and their medical staffs).

to fragmentation. Historical and cultural factors may dampen providers' enthusiasm to coordinate or consolidate. Financial considerations may undermine integration attempts. Fragmentation of one sort can encourage fragmentation of another; the fragmentation of payers, for example, increases the difficulty of offering providers sufficient incentives to undertake substantial coordination efforts.

Even where providers do seek stronger ties, they may face daunting regulatory roadblocks. As scholars have long recognized, public and private forms of regulation may constrain providers' interactions with one another, impeding contractual forms of coordination as well as full integration.[6] In order to promote competition, for example, antitrust law limits the options of hospitals, physicians, and other providers seeking to merge together or affiliate in other ways. Other regulatory limits on health care providers' ability to integrate share a different goal: to prevent providers from pursuing aims that diverge from those of their patients. These limits arise from many sources, including licensure laws, anti-kickback and self-referral laws, and medical staff bylaws.

This paper focuses on this last group of structural limits, those aimed at constraining the goals that providers may pursue, and their application to physicians. It argues that although these limits are important in a world in which patients and payers are unable to assess quality, their rationale weakens when health care quality measures are available.[7] Loosening these restrictions will permit more health care providers to pursue affiliations. At the same time, greater availability of health care quality measures will permit payers to implement incentives that encourage integration to the extent that it contributes to better outcomes.

---

6. Timothy Jost and Ezekiel Emanuel have cataloged many of the legal impediments to delivery system innovation, including the corporate practice of medicine doctrine, fraud and abuse laws, scope of practice limitations, certificate of need regulations, antitrust law, tax exempt organization laws, and Medicare payment rules. *See generally* Timothy Stoltzfus Jost & Ezekiel J. Emanuel, *Legal Reforms Necessary to Promote Delivery System Innovation,* 299 JAMA 2561 (2008). *See also* Stephen M. Shortell & Lawrence P. Casalino, *Health Care Reform Requires Accountable Care Systems,* 300 JAMA 95, 97 (2008) (noting that to implement accountable care systems, reforms of anti-kickback, fraud and abuse, antitrust, scope of practice, and corporate practice of medicine laws are necessary).

7. Michael Porter and Elizabeth Teisberg have similarly argued that some laws that hinder competition, such as the corporate practice of medicine doctrine and the Stark anti-self-referral statute, "were enacted in an effort to address abuses that occur when information on quality and cost is unavailable." *See* MICHAEL E. PORTER & ELIZABETH OLMSTED TEISBERG, REDEFINING HEALTH CARE: CREATING VALUE-BASED COMPETITION ON RESULTS 357 (2006). For an argument that the availability of quality measures may weaken the rationale for health care quality regulations more generally, see Kristin Madison, *Regulating Health Care Quality in an Information Age,* 40 U.C. DAVIS L. REV. 1577 (2007).

This chapter is organized as follows. Part II describes three regulatory contributors to fragmentation in health care delivery: the corporate practice of medicine doctrine, regulations that maintain a separation between hospitals and physicians, and anti-kickback and self-referral statutes. Part III examines the recent trend toward quality reporting and what it might mean for regulatory limits on health care providers' relationships. Part IV then considers how the health care system might be reshaped into more of a unified whole in light of the greater availability of health care quality measures.

II. THREE REGULATORY CONTRIBUTORS TO FRAGMENTATION

Although the legal and regulatory contributors to fragmentation among health care providers are numerous, this chapter focuses on just three, each of which reflects at least in part concerns about health care quality: the prohibition of the corporate practice of medicine, regulations requiring the independence of hospital medical staffs, and fraud and abuse laws.

A. Prohibition of Corporate Practice of Medicine

The corporate practice of medicine doctrine prohibits corporations from employing physicians to provide medical care.[8] Although a few states impose statutory restrictions on corporate practice, in other states the corporate practice prohibition arises from case law drawing upon statutory prohibitions on the unlicensed practice of medicine.[9] The doctrine's main effect is to prevent layperson owners and managers from controlling physicians' provision of care. Interpreted broadly, it would prevent a large company from directly hiring physicians to treat its employees; prohibit a non-physician entrepreneur from hiring physicians to deliver a full range of services to patients with a particular condition; and, in some cases, bar hospitals from employing physicians. The doctrine may not be as limiting as it first appears; some states have limited the doctrine's reach by finding that it does not apply to hospital employment of physicians,[10] for example, and entities may be able to form affiliations that fall outside its scope.[11]

---

8. *See generally* Nicole Huberfeld, *Be Not Afraid of Change: Time to Eliminate the Corporate Practice of Medicine Doctrine*, 14 HEALTH MATRIX 243 (2004), for a fuller discussion of the corporate practice of medicine doctrine and its prohibitions.

9. *See* BARRY R. FURROW ET AL., HEALTH LAW § 5–10 (2d ed. 2000).

10. *See, e.g.*, Berlin v. Sarah Bush Lincoln Health Ctr., 688 N.E.2d 106 (Ill. 1997); St. Francis Regional Medical Ctr., Inc., v. Weiss, 869 P.2d 606 (Kans. 1994).

11. Jost and Emanuel note that in many jurisdictions "the doctrine probably no longer applies," and "in others its status is unclear." *See* Jost & Emanuel, *supra* note 6, at 2561. They add that in some jurisdictions "it persists and must be evaded by organizational structures that confound incentives for coordination." *Id.*

Nonetheless, the doctrine restricts the ability of physicians to join with larger organizations that can play a role in integrating the provision of health care. By hindering integration, the corporate practice doctrine can stymie efforts to make structural reforms that would have the potential to reduce costs and improve quality.[12]

The typical justifications for the corporate practice doctrine are based on the implications of corporate practice for physicians and patients. One court explains that "[t]he prohibition on the corporate employment of physicians is invariably supported by several public policy arguments which espouse the dangers of lay control over professional judgment, the division of the physician's loyalty between his patient and his profitmaking employer, and the commercialization of the profession."[13] Lay control, loyalty to an employer, and commercialization all raise questions about physicians' status as members of a self-regulated profession. The uncharitable view of the corporate practice doctrine is that it facilitates physicians' efforts to establish full control over the delivery of care for their own sake, to increase the profession's power and profit.[14] An alternative, more charitable view is that it reflects an effort to protect patients by increasing the likelihood that physicians will act in patients' best interests.[15] After all, lay control, conflicted loyalties, and commercialization also raise questions about the integrity of the physician-patient relationship and the ability and incentives of physicians to serve patient needs, including through the delivery of high-quality care. Thus, one function the corporate practice doctrine might fulfill is protecting health care quality.

---

12. *See id.* (arguing that corporate practice doctrine limits delivery system reform). Respondents to a recent survey indicated that hospital employment of physicians led to "an increase in coordinated hospital-physician efforts to improve quality and control costs." To the extent that the corporate practice doctrine precludes such arrangements, these benefits would be more difficult to achieve. *See* Lawrence P. Casalino et al., *Hospital-Physician Relations: Two Tracks and the Decline of the Voluntary Medical Staff Model,* 27 HEALTH AFF. 1305, 1312 (2008). Another study finds that "anecdotal evidence from hospital systems reveals that once physicians achieve income security and stability through employment models, they turn their attention to patient care issues and demand clinical information technology to coordinate it." Lawton Robert Burns & Ralph W. Muller, *Hospital-Physician Collaboration: Landscape of Economic Integration and Impact on Clinical Integration,* 86 THE MILBANK QUARTERLY 375, 406 (2008).

13. *Berlin,* 688 N.E.2d at 110.

14. *See* Mark A. Hall, *Institutional Control of Physician Behavior: Legal Barriers to Health Care Cost Containment,* 137 U. PA. L. REV. 431, 515 (1988–1989) ("When courts enforce the corporate practice doctrine, they mistakenly suppose they are enforcing the legislature's *public* protection policies when in fact they are enforcing the profession's *economic* protection policies.").

15. *See* Huberfeld, *supra* note 8, at 245–49 (discussing physicians' historical concerns about quackery as well as loss of control).

B. Regulatorily-Reinforced Medical Staff Independence

The majority of physicians who work in hospitals are not hospital employees; rather, they are members of independent medical staffs.[16] Although the hospital administration is responsible for hospital operations as a whole, the medical staff typically is responsible for many of the quality oversight functions within the hospital setting.[17] Medical staff committees consider the applications of physicians seeking to join the staff, as well as reviewing the care provided by physicians within the facility. This division of duties is in part a consequence of hospitals' historically limited roles as providers of facilities and related administrative services. Hospitals served as physicians' workshops,[18] whereas physicians maintained primary responsibility for the delivery of care. Today hospitals take much more responsibility for the delivery of care within their facilities, but the split between hospitals and their medical staffs remains.[19]

One reason that medical staffs remain independent even as hospital responsibility for quality has increased is that both public and private regulation preserve the separation between hospital administration and the medical staff. State hospital licensure laws, for example, may mandate self-governance by medical staffs.[20] In addition, the Joint Commission, a private organization that accredits most hospitals, has created a number of standards that govern the relationship between hospitals and their medical staffs.[21] These public and private regulatory mechanisms reinforce the separation between hospitals and physicians.

---

16. *See* Hall, *supra* note 14, at 528–30 (discussing hospital medical staffs).

17. *See* John D. Blum, *Feng Shui and the Restructuring of the Hospital Corporation: A Call for Change in the Face of the Medical Error Epidemic*, 14 HEALTH MATRIX 5, 22 (2004) ("Under a delegated arrangement, the medical staff is largely responsible for clinical quality matters such as credentialing, quality improvement, utilization management, and infection control.").

18. *See* Mark Pauly & Michael Redisch, *The Not-for-Profit Hospital as a Physicians' Cooperative*, 63 AM. ECON. REV. 87 (1973) (modeling hospitals as physicians' cooperatives).

19. *See* Blumstein, *supra* note 5, at 225–28 (describing hospitals' independent interests in maintaining quality of care).

20. *See, e.g.*, CAL. BUS. & PROF. CODE § 2282.5(a) (West 2008) ("The medical staff's right of self-governance shall include, but not be limited to, all of the following: . . . (2) Establishing, in medical staff bylaws, rules, or regulations, clinical criteria and standards to oversee and manage quality assurance, utilization review, and other medical staff activities . . . ."). *See also* Hall, *supra* note 14, at 528–30 (discussing staff self-governance).

21. *See* FURROW ET AL., *supra* note 9, at §§ 1–4 (describing Joint Commission's accreditation process); Richard S. Saver, *Squandering the Gain: Gainsharing and the Continuing Dilemma of Physician Financial Incentives*, 98 Nw. U. L. REV. 145, 178 (2003) (explaining Joint Commission's role in preserving independence of medical staffs). Professor Saver provides several examples of relevant Joint Commission standards, such as § MS.1 (2002) ("One or more organized, self-governing medical staffs have overall responsibility for the

The independent status of hospital medical staffs serves some of the same functions as limitations on the corporate practice of medicine. By remaining independent and exercising control over physicians working within a hospital setting, medical staffs retain considerable autonomy, insulating to at least some extent their decision making processes from the demands of hospital administrators. Even in situations in which administrators or hospital boards retain final authority over hospital operations, the committees and processes established by organized medical staffs can greatly influence hospital operations, including operations related to quality oversight. The statutory provisions and accreditation standards preserving the divide between hospitals and medical staffs are thus consistent with physicians trying to expand their influence over the delivery of care.

If physicians act in the best interests of their patients, as is required by medical professionalism, the divide can help promote patient interests, including health care quality.[22] By retaining their independence, physicians preserve their ability to serve as patient advocates in circumstances in which hospital institutional objectives and individual patient objectives diverge.[23] Although hospitals may seek to increase their profits or decrease their costs, for example, physicians may seek to maximize the quality of care delivered to patients. Thus, health care quality is one concern that could at least arguably justify continued commitment to the bifurcated hospital organizational structure.

C. Fraud and Abuse Laws

A third type of regulatory barrier to integration among health care providers is fraud and abuse law. The anti-kickback statute prohibits individuals from knowingly and willfully soliciting or receiving remuneration in return for referrals or purchases for which payment may be made under a federal health care program, such as Medicare.[24] Most obviously, this statute prohibits coordination in the form of paying someone specifically to obtain a steady referral flow. Except under a narrow set of circumstances, these kickbacks are unlikely to have beneficial effects for patients. But the anti-kickback statute can also prohibit other forms of coordination for which only one purpose of the arrangement is

---

quality of professional services provided by individuals with clinical privileges . . . .") *Id.* at n.124.

22. *See, e.g.,* ABIM Foundation et al., *Medical Professionalism in the New Millennium: A Physician Charter,* 136 ANNALS INTERNAL MED. 243, 244 (2002) ("Professionalism is the basis of medicine's contract with society. It demands placing the interests of patients above those of the physician . . . .")

23. *See* Blumstein, *supra* note 5, at 223 ("The organization and structure of the hospital, therefore, seem to reflect an assumed need to insulate the members of the physician staff from the consideration of cost and other non-medical factors in their decision making.").

24. *See* 42 U.S.C. § 1320a-7b(b) (2000).

inducing referrals.[25] Moreover, the penalties under the anti-kickback statute are likely to chill the formation of structures in which money flows one way and referrals flow the other, even though the intent requirement is not satisfied, given the possibility that the structures could be mistaken as ones involving kickbacks. So, for example, if a hospital tries to build a stronger relationship with a referring physician that involves some form of payment—say, a consulting arrangement or an employment relationship—it would at least need to evaluate the arrangement under the anti-kickback statute.

Under the Stark statute, an anti-self-referral law, physicians cannot refer Medicare patients to an entity with which they have a financial relationship for the furnishing of designated health services, including clinical laboratory services, physical therapy services, and inpatient and outpatient hospital services, among others.[26] The Stark statute directly prohibits both ownership and compensation relationships between physicians and the entities to which they refer. Physicians wishing to provide continuity of care by referring a patient to a laboratory they own, for example, would have to first analyze whether their ownership would be consistent with the Stark statute. Similarly, a hospital wishing to employ a physician who refers patients to it must first consider the effects of the Stark statute.

The extent to which these statutes impede integration may not be as dramatic as they at first seem, given their numerous safe harbors and exceptions. The Stark statute, for example, contains an exception for physicians who provide in-office ancillary services, such as laboratory services, meeting certain requirements.[27] Both the anti-kickback and Stark statutes contain exceptions for employment arrangements meeting specified criteria.[28] In fact, in situations in which full integration through employment relationships is feasible, these exceptions may promote fuller integration rather than impede it.[29] In general, however, the anti-kickback and Stark statutes hinder efforts to establish financial relationships among health care providers.

Gainsharing programs offer one example of a type of provider relationship for which fraud and abuse law is an obstacle. Under these programs, hospitals agree

---

25. As the Office of the Inspector General of the Department of Health and Human Services ("OIG") often points out, under *United States v. Greber*, 760 F.2d 68 (3d Cir.), *cert denied*, 474 U.S. 988 (1985), the statute may be violated even if only one purpose of the remuneration was to induce referrals. *See, e.g.*, OIG, Advisory Opinion No. 06-22 (Nov. 9, 2006), *available at* http://www.oig.hhs.gov/fraud/docs/advisoryopinions/2006/AdvOpn06-22NewA.pdf.

26. 42 U.S.C. § 1395nn (2000).

27. 42 U.S.C. § 1395nn(b)(2) (2000).

28. 42 U.S.C. § 1320a-7b(b)(3)(B) (2000); 42 U.S.C. § 1395nn(e)(2) (2000).

29. *See* David M. Frankford, *Creating and Dividing the Fruits of Collective Economic Activity: Referrals Among Health Care Providers*, 89 COLUM. L. REV. 1861, 1911–18 (1989) (asserting that fraud and abuse regulations will tend to encourage full integration).

to pay physicians a portion of the savings achieved when physicians change their practices so as to deliver less costly care.[30] Because the hospital is paying physicians and the physicians are referring patients to the hospital, both the anti-kickback and Stark statutes are at least potentially implicated. Gainsharing programs also implicate another fraud and abuse statutory provision that subjects hospitals to monetary penalties if they knowingly make a payment to physicians to reduce or limit services provided to Medicare beneficiaries under the physicians' direct care.[31] Hospitals' ability to engage in such programs is therefore restricted.

Fraud and abuse laws have multiple objectives. They can protect competing health care providers by helping to ensure that patients are referred based on factors other than which entity is paying the highest kickbacks to referring physicians.[32] They can also protect payers by helping to control health care costs in a fee-for-service setting. Physicians paid kickbacks have a financial incentive to refer more often, which may mean that patients receive services that they otherwise would not have received. Physicians who own laboratories will receive more profits, the more tests they order, as long as reimbursements for lab tests exceed their costs. If physician-owners respond to this incentive, whoever pays for the tests will end up paying more. By eliminating these incentives, fraud and abuse laws can reduce health care costs.

At the same time, fraud and abuse laws can promote health care quality. Individuals receiving kickbacks for ordering tests may order unneeded tests, leaving patients to suffer any problematic health consequences associated with the tests without any corresponding possibility of health gain. Physicians whose patients need further health care services may refer on the basis of which provider promises the greatest financial reward, rather than on the basis of which provider is likely to deliver the best care for the patient. Physicians rewarded for reducing health care services may make decisions that ultimately harm patients.[33] Patients who suspect the presence of such problematic incentives may distrust their physicians, hindering the care process and ultimately reducing quality. Health care quality, then, is an important justification for maintaining fraud and abuse laws.

---

30. See generally Saver, supra note 21 (analyzing gainsharing programs).

31. 42 U.S.C. §1320a-7a(b)(1) (2000).

32. See, e.g., OIG, Advisory Opinion No. 01-1 (Jan. 11, 2001), available at http://www.oig.hhs.gov/fraud/docs/advisoryopinions/2001/a001-01.pdf (referring to concerns about "'cherry picking' healthy patients and steering sicker (and more costly) patients to hospitals that do not offer such arrangements" and "unfair competition (a 'race to the bottom') among hospitals offering cost sharing programs to foster physician loyalty and to attract more referrals").

33. See Saver, supra note 21 (referring to OIG's "fundamental concerns about gainsharing's threat to quality").

D. Costs of Regulatorily-Reinforced Fragmentation

The corporate practice of medicine doctrine, regulations protecting the independence of medical staffs, and fraud and abuse laws collectively reflect the interests of many parties—physicians, other health care providers, and payers, as well as patients—seeking to achieve disparate goals. One justification they all share, however, is that the structural restrictions they impose can help to improve health care quality. The corporate practice doctrine and self-governing staffs do so by ensuring the independence of physicians, who have an ethical duty to serve their patients' interests, including through the promotion of health care quality. The fraud and abuse statutes do so by prohibiting arrangements that give physicians financial incentives to depart from their ethical obligations.

Although these laws and regulations have the potential to benefit patients, this potential may not be realized. In fact, these organizational restrictions may even harm patients. Although the corporate practice limitation and the independence of medical staffs permit physicians to serve as patient advocates, they do not compel physicians to do so. Professional ethics may mandate that physicians deliver high-quality care, but physicians may choose to pursue other aims. Furthermore, to the extent that the institutions working with physicians can influence the care they deliver, the separation may impede initiatives that would improve quality or reduce costs.[34] The limitations threaten the ability of organizations to implement controls or other mechanisms that could alter care for the better. Similarly, although fraud and abuse laws constrain problematic incentives, they can also block relationships that could benefit patients, such as those established by gainsharing programs. In short, although these laws have the potential to enhance quality in a world in which quality is difficult to assess, they are also potentially problematic because they hinder efforts to find new ways to work together to deliver better, more efficient care.

III. QUALITY REPORTING AS A DEFRAGMENTING TOOL

A. Health Care Quality Measurement and Reporting

Structural regulations of health care organizations make sense in part because of the difficulty patients and payers face in assessing health care quality. If the quality of care provided by a hospital could be easily assessed by all, the hospital would have little to gain from exercising influence over physicians in ways that

---

34. For example, the corporate practice doctrine may hinder employment relationships that foster better care, including through adherence to clinical guidelines. *See, e.g.,* MEDICARE PAYMENT ADVISORY COMM'N, REFORMING THE DELIVERY SYSTEM 60 (June 2008) ("Hospitals find that employing physicians in leadership positions to interact with community physicians improves physician compliance with hospital initiatives and priorities, such as implementing clinical guidelines.").

would reduce quality below the level that patients and payers demand. Similarly, if patients and payers could acquire perfect information about patients' need for care and its quality, the incentives inherent in physicians' ownership of testing or treatment facilities would be less problematic. Patients could refuse recommended care or seek treatment elsewhere; payers could refuse to pay for unnecessary or substandard care. But, of course, perfect information is not available. Historically, it has been difficult to make any sort of meaningful assessment of quality. The prohibitive costs of evaluating quality have necessitated reliance on other approaches to ensure quality, or, more realistically, to reduce the likelihood of unacceptably low quality. Structural restrictions have served this need.

As a result of the information revolution, however, the costs of assessing quality have declined.[35] We have progressed from the stage where collecting and analyzing vast quantities of health-related data was merely possible to the stage where we are actually beginning to do it. The health care industry is in the midst of a performance measurement revolution.[36] Medical specialty societies and other entities are working to develop ways to measure quality using a combination of structural, process, and outcome criteria.[37] The National Quality Forum, a not-for-profit organization whose members include insurers, hospital systems, government agencies, consumer groups, and others, has endorsed more than two hundred consensus standards for health care quality measures that can be used in hospitals and other settings.[38] As part of their 2008 Physician Quality Reporting Initiative, the Centers for Medicare and Medicaid Services (CMS) are collecting data on physician performance on 119 quality measures, from blood sugar control in diabetes patients to weight screening.[39]

Many quality measures are publicly available. A federal compendium includes over two hundred sources of comparative quality information about health plans and various types of health care providers, including hospitals and physicians.[40]

---

35. For further discussion of the implications of the health information revolution for regulating quality, see generally Madison, *supra* note 7; *see also* Timothy S. Jost, *Oversight of the Quality of Medical Care: Regulation, Management, or the Market?*, 37 Ariz. L. Rev. 825 (1995).

36. *See generally* Inst. of Med., Performance Measurement: Accelerating Improvement (2006).

37. *See id. See also* Ronald M. Davis, *Autonomy v. Accountability: A Delicate Balance*, Am. Med. News (Aug. 20, 2007) (describing Physician Consortium for Performance Improvement, which contributed to development of CMS physician quality measures).

38. *See* National Quality Forum, http://www.qualityforum.org/ (last visited October 15, 2008).

39. *See* Ctrs. for Medicare & Medicaid Servs., Physician Quality Reporting Initiative, http://www.cms.hhs.gov/pqri/ (last visited October 15, 2008).

40. *See* U.S. Dep't of Health & Human Servs., Agency for Healthcare Research & Quality, Health Care Report Card Compendium, http://www.talkingquality.gov/compendium/ (last visited May 20, 2008).

One such source is Hospital Compare, a website maintained by the federal Department of Health and Human Services (HHS), which publishes hospital-specific measures of health care quality in the areas of cardiac care, pneumonia care, and the prevention of surgical infections.[41] States publish quality information too. Pennsylvania, for example, provides hospital-specific quality measures for cardiac bypass surgery and hip and knee replacement.[42] Numerous states have begun to publish hospital-specific data about infection rates.[43] The Joint Commission[44] and commercial information providers[45] also publish quality measures. Quality measures have become more widely available and broader in scope in recent years.

B. Why Quality Measurement Matters

One reason that quality measurement matters is that it can alleviate concerns about potential negative effects of provider integration. It may be true that even with quality measures, patients cannot determine whether they need a particular treatment, or whether they personally received high-quality care. Patients will not be able to determine, based on quality measures, whether the particular test they received at a physician-owned laboratory was performed properly. But patients can use aggregate data to make an assessment of the likely quality of a provider's care. For example, if the concern is that a hospital zealous about cost cutting might eschew costly but necessary infection control measures, ignoring the protests of its affiliated physicians, good scores on infection rate measures will likely assuage this concern.

Health plans can use aggregate health care quality measures in the process of network design. They can determine which physicians achieve desirable results

---

41. *See* U.S. Dep't of Health & Human Servs., Hospital Compare, http://www.hospitalcompare.hhs.gov/ (last visited May 26, 2008).

42. *See* PENNSYLVANIA HEALTH CARE COST CONTAINMENT COUNCIL ("PHC4"), PENNSYLVANIA'S GUIDE TO CORONARY ARTERY BYPASS GRAFT SURGERY 2004, 2–5 (Feb. 2006), http://www.phc4.org/reports/cabg/04/docs/cabg2004report.pdf; PHC4, TOTAL HIP AND KNEE REPLACEMENTS 7–23 (June 2005), http://www.phc4.org/reports/hipknee/02/docs/hipkneeFY2002report.pdf.

43. *See, e.g.*, State of Missouri, Dep't of Health & Human Servs., Missouri Healthcare-Associated Infection Reporting, http://www.dhss.mo.gov/HAI/ (last visited May 20, 2008); PHC4, Hospital-Acquired Infections in Pennsylvania 2005, http://www.phc4.org/hai/Default.aspx. *See also* CONSUMERS UNION, SUMMARY OF STATE ACTIVITY ON HOSPITAL ACQUIRED INFECTIONS, *available at* http://www.consumersunion.org/campaigns/stophospitalinfections/learn.html (last visited May 20, 2008) (reporting that twenty-two states require public reporting of hospital-acquired infections).

44. *See* The Joint Commission, Quality Check, http://www.qualitycheck.org/consumer/searchQCR.aspx (last visited May 26, 2008).

45. *See, e.g.*, HealthGrades, http://www.healthgrades.com/ (last visited May 26, 2008).

without regard to physician ownership of ancillary services. In addition, they can collect data about physicians' frequency of referrals for care, and through network design exclude or restrict patients' access to physicians with high rates of referrals. By doing so, health plans can blunt the incentives that physicians with ownership or compensation relationships with referral entities would otherwise have.

Drawing upon their health care expertise, health plans can also review the data available with respect to the treatment of individual members to determine whether care was appropriately provided. If a hospital took advantage of its relationship with physicians to reduce infection control efforts, or if integration resulted in less effective oversight mechanisms, patients might acquire more infections in the hospital. But given their increased ability to access the relevant information in the information age, health plans could then refuse to pay for treatment arising from infections. Indeed, both Medicare and private health care plans have begun to do this in some circumstances.[46] Similarly, if physicians make poor decisions about their patients' course of treatment because of the financial incentives they face, resulting in worse treatment processes or outcomes, a health plan could respond by withholding quality-based bonuses. Many payers are now paying for performance.[47]

The more widespread the development, collection, and dissemination of quality measures, the less need there is for laws restricting organizational structures that govern relationships among providers. The availability of quality measures supports an argument for dismantling or at least weakening laws related to corporate practice, medical staff independence, and fraud and abuse. If these regulatory measures are weakened, health care providers can engage in coordination and integration that the regulatory measures previously prohibited or chilled. Quality measures may also permit changes in the application and enforcement of other laws and regulations, such as antitrust laws, to accommodate more quality- and efficiency-enhancing integration.[48] In this way, quality reporting can promote the defragmentation of health care delivery.

---

46. *See* Changes to the Hospital Inpatient Prospective Payment Systems and Fiscal Year 2008 Rates, 72 Fed. Reg. 47,200 (Aug. 22, 2007); Press Release, BlueCross BlueShield Association, WellPoint Announces Initiative Aimed at Preventing Serious Medical Errors (April 2, 2008), *available at* http://www.bcbs.com/news/plans/wellpoint-announces-initiative.html.

47. On pay-for-performance programs generally, see Arnold M. Epstein et al., *Paying Physicians for High-Quality Care*, 350 NEW ENG. J. MED. 406 (2004) (describing pay-for-performance programs); Meredith B. Rosenthal et al., *Pay for Performance in Commercial HMOs*, 355 NEW ENG. J. MED. 1895 (2006) (describing HMOs' use of pay-for-performance programs to compensate physicians and hospitals).

48. For example, quality measures play an important role in the way the Federal Trade Commission applies the antitrust laws to physician networks. *See, e.g.*, Letter from David R. Pender, Acting Ass't Dir., Bureau of Competition, FTC, to Clifton E. Johnson & William H.

C. Three Caveats

The fact that quality reporting might promote defragmentation does not necessarily mean that it will do so. A gap between quality reporting's potential defragmenting power and its actual impact on defragmentation may arise for at least three reasons.

First, if quality measures are to reassure patients, payers, and policy makers that integration has not had unintended effects, the measures must be comprehensive and reliable and people must be willing and able to use them. Although new measures continue to be developed, they still do not measure every aspect of every type of care. The cost of collection of a truly comprehensive set of performance measures is simply too high, particularly in the absence of widespread electronic health records. There will likely always be unobserved quality differentials among providers. If the unobserved quality differentials in a given area are significant, then it may make sense to continue to rely on structural restrictions.

Relatedly, the quality measures that do exist must accurately reflect health care quality. The underlying data must be accurate, and so too must the measurement methodology. If an aggregate measure is not properly risk-adjusted, it will give a misleading picture of a particular provider's quality of care.

Finally, even if quality measures are both comprehensive and accurate, they do not justify weakening structural regulation if patients and payers are unable to use them. Quality measures cannot benefit those who are unaware of their existence, and may harm those who interpret them improperly. Patients who are very sick, are poorly educated, possess limited cognitive capacity, or have limited choice of providers are unlikely to be able to take full advantage of quality measures. Such patients may be better protected by traditional, market-displacing minimum quality regulations, or by payers or regulators who use quality measures on their behalf.[49]

A second reason that quality reporting's impact on fragmentation may be limited is the fact that quality is not the only concern underlying the regulations promoting fragmentation. Even if quality measures were nearly perfect in every way, for example, physicians may still wish to preserve the autonomy they gain by maintaining independent, self-governing medical staffs. If someone were to

---

Thompson (Mar. 28, 2006) (FTC Staff Advisory Opinion Concerning Suburban Health Org., Inc.); Lawrence P. Casalino, *The Federal Trade Commission, Clinical Integration, and the Organization of Physician Practice*, 31 J. HEALTH POL., POL'Y & L. 569 (2006) (analyzing FTC policy with respect to integrated practice associations and physician-hospital organizations). For a discussion of the role of quality measures in hospital merger cases, *see* Kristin Madison, *Hospital Mergers in an Era of Quality Improvement*, 7 HOUS. J. HEALTH L. & POL'Y 265 (2007).

49. *See* Madison, *supra* note 7, at 1617–24 (discussing how market-facilitating regulatory techniques such as report cards and market-channeling techniques such as pay-for-performance may differentially affect quality of care received by patients with different characteristics).

propose repealing licensure statutes or accreditation rules reinforcing staff independence, physicians would likely object. If physicians have sufficient influence over the rulemaking process, the regulations would not be weakened. To the extent that other concerns such as autonomy or cost control motivate these regulations, these concerns will need to be addressed before quality reporting can meaningfully contribute to defragmentation.

A third reason that quality reporting might not result in defragmentation is closely related to the second: The removal of legal barriers does not mean that providers will abandon fragmentation in favor of tightly integrated enterprises. Just as multiple factors contributed to the creation and preservation of fragmentation-promoting regulation, multiple factors hinder efforts to integrate. One possibility is that integration is simply not desirable. At some point, integrated organizations may become too large or complex to function well; moreover, direct coordination between providers may not always be necessary. Another possibility is that although patients, payers, or society as a whole would prefer greater coordination or integration among health care providers, the providers themselves may prefer to remain separate. If physicians have a strong preference for autonomy, they might not agree to integrate or coordinate with hospitals, even if legal limits on integration were removed. Physicians might refuse to work at hospitals that did not protect medical staff independence. Political, sociological, or financial factors, among others, could make the perceived or actual costs of integration higher than its benefits. For these reasons, removing legal barriers may help reduce fragmentation, but further steps may need to be taken.

IV. DEFRAGMENTING THE HEALTH CARE SYSTEM

A. Legal Reform Coupled with Quality Reporting

How should the health care system be reshaped in the aftermath of the quality measurement revolution? One potential answer is that the previously discussed restrictions on organizational form should simply be eliminated. The corporate practice of medicine doctrine would be a reasonable candidate for elimination.[50] As some scholars have noted, the legal reasoning often used to support it does not make much sense.[51] As others have noted, the doctrine does not seem to be a

---

50. Professors Porter and Teisberg similarly argue that the corporate practice of medicine doctrine should be phased out to permit value-creating integration. *See* PORTER & TEISBERG, *supra* note 7, at 358. As Jost and Emanuel note, "Many commentators have long called for the abolition of the corporate practice of medicine doctrine." Jost & Emanuel, *supra* note 6, at 2562.

51. *See, e.g.,* Hall, *supra* note 14, at 509–10 ("This puzzling doctrine is clouded with confused reasoning and is founded on an astounding series of logical fallacies."); *id.* at 511–14 (criticizing reasoning underlying corporate practice doctrine).

good fit for the modern health care system, in which outside influences on physician decision making abound.[52] Indeed, it has already begun to erode through the recognition of exceptions, such as the exception for hospital employment of physicians.[53] Laws and accreditation standards that dictate or reinforce the current medical staff structures within hospitals could also be repealed.

Given the multiple motivations behind these restrictions, however, their elimination may be difficult to achieve.[54] Moreover, given the current limitations on quality measures, the restrictions' elimination may sometimes be inadvisable. Intermediate approaches may fare better.[55] Mark Hall, for example, has suggested that courts should apply the corporate practice doctrine narrowly.[56] States could also impose disclosure requirements that would clarify the nature of the corporate relationship between an entity and individuals providing medical services. With respect to the independence of medical staff, states and regulators could limit the extent to which statutes dictate the rights and obligations of medical staff within private hospitals. Hospitals would then have more flexibility to implement reforms that would reduce the cost or improve the quality of care within their facilities. States could also limit the applicability of such statutes to hospitals that face little competition, such as critical access hospitals, where an independent physician voice arguably would have a more important role to play in serving the needs of patients.[57]

An intermediate approach may be especially appropriate in the area of fraud and abuse laws. Because the laws impede potentially cost-reducing and quality-enhancing integration, relaxing them may be beneficial. As discussed in Part III, however, patients' and payers' ability to monitor quality and cost may be

---

52. *See, e.g.*, Huberfeld, *supra* note 8, at 244–45 (describing why corporate practice doctrine should be eliminated, given nature of modern medical practice).

53. *See* FURROW ET AL., *supra* note 9, at § 5–10 (noting proliferation of exceptions to corporate practice doctrine).

54. Similarly, referring to laws impeding delivery system innovation, Jost and Emanuel argue that "[t]he wholesale repeal of these laws is neither possible nor advisable." Jost & Emanuel, *supra* note 6, at 2562. They support the creation of "a single governmental Commission for Innovation in Delivery Systems" that "would offer one-stop review to permit experimentation in delivery systems." *Id.* at 2563. They suggest that regulatory approvals be linked to formal evaluations "confirming that the innovations have lowered costs, improved quality, or both," and that successful experiments could then lead to proposals for legal reform. *Id.*

55. *Cf.* Blumstein, *supra* note 5, at 236–37 (arguing for regulatory flexibility for integrated delivery networks).

56. Hall argues that "judges should be circumspect" in applying the court-created branch of the corporate practice doctrine, *Hall, supra* note 14, at 514, and that courts should prohibit only arrangements that are demonstrably harmful. *Id.* at 517.

57. For a description of the criteria defining critical access hospitals, see http://www.cms.hhs.gov/Certificationandcomplianc/04_CAHs.asp (last visited May 23, 2008).

insufficient to ensure that financial relationships among providers do not produce undesirable results. An intermediate approach would generally preserve the fraud and abuse laws, at least for now, but include broad exceptions.

One possibility would be to maintain the current set of prohibitions, but to permit a necessity or quality defense. Michael Porter and Elizabeth Teisberg have suggested that a "results justification" should be added to the Stark laws.[58] For example, physicians could be permitted to refer patients to distant laboratories that they own as long as they could demonstrate the patients' need for testing and the quality of testing ultimately performed. Similarly, if a physician is accused of receiving kickbacks for referrals for testing, the physician could show that he or she adhered to accepted medical standards in ordering the test. The more cost, efficiency, and quality measures that are available both to characterize the individual's practice patterns and to illustrate the distribution of practices within the profession as a whole, the more workable such a defense would become.

For now, however, this defense is not likely to be an effective approach for encouraging meaningful integration. From the government's perspective, the problem would be that wide variation in accepted medical practice encompasses the costly, resource-intensive practice styles that referral incentives tend to create and that fraud and abuse laws are designed to combat.[59] In addition, physicians may be reluctant to take the legal risk associated with establishing such referral arrangements. Even if the eventual outcome would likely favor the physician, mounting a defense might be too time-consuming and expensive.

Another approach would be to expand fraud and abuse law exceptions or use the advisory opinion process to encourage forms of coordination likely to promote quality improvements or cost savings. One candidate for such an approach is gainsharing.

As explained in Part II.C, under a typical gainsharing program, a hospital would share with participating physicians a portion of the savings that result when physicians change their practices in such a way as to reduce hospital costs. Gainsharing potentially implicates the anti-kickback statute, the Stark statute, and a statutory prohibition of certain inducements to reduce care. In 1999, the HHS Office of the Inspector General (OIG) issued a bulletin announcing that gainsharing would violate this statutory prohibition and suggesting that OIG would "in the absence of any evidence that an arrangement has violated any

---

58. *See* PORTER & TEISBERG, *supra* note 7, at 358 (discussing the results justification, although not detailing the sorts of results physicians would need to disclose to adequately justify referral patterns). They also suggest that "[a]s results information becomes available, Stark law restrictions on coordination can be eliminated." *Id.*

59. In addition, if referral arrangements currently prohibited by fraud and abuse became widespread, they could alter the definition of accepted medical practice to include more resource-intensive approaches.

other statutes or adversely affected patient care, take into consideration in exercising its enforcement discretion whether a gainsharing arrangement was terminated expeditiously following publication of this Bulletin."[60]

Although gainsharing has risks, it also offers potentially significant benefits in the form of cost savings. By aligning physicians' incentives with those of hospitals, it can encourage physicians to adopt less costly and more efficient practices.[61] This potential was demonstrated in the early 1990s, when the Medicare Participating Heart Bypass Center Demonstration bundled payments to seven hospitals and affiliated physicians for their provision of services associated with coronary bypass surgery.[62] The hospitals and physicians were free to allocate the payment as they chose, including through gainsharing.[63] Three of four early participants in the demonstration were able to change operations in ways that generated cost savings, including for nursing expenses, pharmacy costs, and laboratory costs, without increasing mortality relative to the participants' competitors.[64] A study of more recent cardiac-related gainsharing programs showed a reduction of costs of over seven percent per patient.[65] Most of the savings resulted from negotiating lower prices with suppliers, but about nine percent resulted from reduced utilization.[66] Despite this reduction in resource use, quality did not appear to decline.[67]

These findings indicate that there may be reason to carve out legal exceptions to permit gainsharing programs. Academic commentators have suggested relaxing fraud and abuse laws to accommodate gainsharing.[68] Government actors have also increasingly shown support for the programs. OIG has proved to be more receptive to gainsharing programs in recent years than it was when it issued the 1999 bulletin. Since 2001 OIG has issued a series of advisory opinions stating that it would not impose sanctions on opinion requestors with respect to

---

60. *See* Special Advisory Bulletin on Gainsharing Arrangements and CMPs for Hospital Payments to Physicians to Reduce or Limit Services to Beneficiaries, 64 Fed. Reg. 37,985, 37,987 (July 14, 1999).

61. For a brief review of federally-sponsored gainsharing and pay-for-performance projects, see Revisions to Payment Policies Under the Physician Fee Schedule and Other Revisions, 73 Fed. Reg. 38,502, 38,550 (proposed July 7, 2008).

62. *See* Jerry Cromwell et al., *Medicare Participating Heart Bypass Center Demonstration, Executive Summary, Final Report* (July 24, 1998), *available at* http://www.cms.hhs.gov/DemoProjectsEvalRpts/downloads/Medicare_Heart_Bypass_Executive_Summary.pdf.

63. *See id. See also* Saver, *supra* note 21, at 204–06 (describing bypass demonstration).

64. *See* Cromwell et al., *supra* note 62, at ES-11–ES-15.

65. Jonathan D. Ketcham & Michael F. Furukawa, *Hospital-Physician Gainsharing in Cardiology*, 27 HEALTH AFF. 803, 803 (2008).

66. *Id.*

67. *Id.*

68. *See, e.g.,* Blumstein, *supra* note 5, at 234, 236 (suggesting that fraud and abuse laws should be revisited in light of gainsharing demonstration projects).

proposed gainsharing programs involving cardiac services.[69] In 2005, the Medicare Payment Assessment Commission (MedPAC) recommended that HHS be granted the authority to allow gainsharing arrangements between physicians and hospitals, and it has recently reiterated its support for relaxing legal restrictions to permit gainsharing.[70] Congress has also recently permitted a variety of demonstration programs involving gainsharing.[71]

The challenge in creating an exception to fraud and abuse laws for gainsharing programs is to separate beneficial financial incentives from problematic ones. The blanket prohibitions on gainsharing arise not from a conviction that every gainsharing program is bad, but instead from the difficulty in identifying promising ones. To be acceptable, gainsharing programs must include safeguards that reassure policy makers and others that the programs will not have undesirable results. Some of these safeguards are structural. The gainsharing programs currently permitted under the OIG advisory opinions, for example, include safeguards that restrict their scope by limiting aggregate payments to fifty percent of savings and limiting program duration to one year.[72]

Other safeguards focus more directly on quality. The OIG regularly notes that advisory opinion requestors' medical experts have determined that the specific changes proposed under the gainsharing programs would not negatively affect patient care; the OIG also highlights requestors' commitments to monitoring their programs' impact on quality in practice.[73] Outside organizations could also supply safeguards. In a comprehensive article examining the history and legal and policy implications of gainsharing, Richard Saver argues that Medicare's peer review bodies, Quality Improvement Organizations, should take a role in overseeing the quality of care delivered through gainsharing programs.[74]

---

69. See, e.g., OIG, Advisory Opinion No. 01-1 (Jan. 11, 2001), available at http://www.oig.hhs.gov/fraud/docs/advisoryopinions/2001/ao01-01.pdf; OIG, Advisory Opinion No. 05-02 (Feb. 10, 2005), available at http://www.oig.hhs.gov/fraud/docs/advisoryopinions/2005/ao0502.pdf; OIG, Advisory Opinion No. 06-22 (Nov. 9, 2006), available at http://www.oig.hhs.gov/fraud/docs/advisoryopinions/2006/AdvOpno6-22NewA.pdf.

70. Medicare Payment Advisory Comm'n, Physician-Owned Specialty Hospitals 44–47 (March 2005), available at http://www.medpac.gov/documents/Mar05_SpecHospitals.pdf ("The Commission believes that gainsharing arrangements have the potential to improve patient care and reduce hospital costs as long as safeguards are in place to minimize the undesirable incentives."); Glenn Hackbarth et al., *Collective Accountability for Medical Care—Toward Bundled Medicare Payments*, 359 NEW ENG. J. MED. 3, 5 (stating that MedPAC recommends that Congress ease restrictions on gainsharing).

71. See Ketcham & Furukawa, *supra* note 65, at 804 (describing history of gainsharing programs).

72. See, e.g., OIG, Advisory Opinion No. 06-22.

73. See, e.g., id.

74. Saver, *supra* note 21, at 232–34.

Both of these approaches to quality monitoring likely would involve scrutiny of some sort of quality indicators. The nature and extent of the quality measures that would be involved, however, are not clear. Although quality monitoring is key to these proposals, quality measurement and reporting do not seem to play a prominent role.

Attention to quality measures has increased in more recent years. In discussing the Medicare Health Care Quality Demonstration Program, which involves gainsharing, CMS recently emphasized its interest in program designs that "track patients well beyond a hospital episode to determine the impact of hospital-physician collaborations on preventing short and longer-term complications, duplication of services, and coordination of care across settings . . . ."[75] CMS also noted that in a series of demonstration projects authorized by the Deficit Reduction Act of 2005, each demonstration project "must also provide measures to monitor quality and efficiency in the participating project hospital(s)."[76]

Thus, although CMS has always been concerned about the quality of care associated with gainsharing programs, it appears to increasingly emphasize the role of quality measures as a safeguard. In the spring of 2008 CMS solicited comments about whether it should issue an exception for gainsharing from its rule prohibiting percentage-based compensation arrangements, and, if so, what safeguards to include.[77]

Objective quality measures could constitute one safeguard for such an exception. Programs could be required to specify quality measures in advance and to provide general information to patients about how quality would be monitored. Alternatively, hospitals could be required to make the quality measures involved publicly available. This could benefit patients by increasing provider accountability for the quality of care, while at the same time supplying a model for other providers seeking to measure their own quality, whether in connection with gainsharing or not. The main drawbacks associated with broader publication would be the likely greater costs associated with adequately explaining and publicizing the measures, as well as the concern that being forced to divulge potentially competitively sensitive information might discourage gainsharing participation.

In July 2008, CMS headed in the direction of requiring performance measure disclosure in connection with gainsharing-like programs when it issued a proposed rule that would create an exception to the Stark statute for "incentive payment and shared savings programs," a category that would include gainsharing programs.[78] It noted that "[s]uccessful programs often result in improved quality

75. Proposed Changes to the Hospital Inpatient Prospective Payment Systems and Fiscal Year 2009 Rates, 73 Fed. Reg. 23,528, 23,693 (April 30, 2008).

76. Proposed Changes, 73 Fed. Reg. at 23,693–94.

77. Proposed Changes, 73 Fed. Reg. at 23,694.

78. Revisions to Payment Policies Under the Physician Fee Schedule and Other Revisions, 73 Fed. Reg. 38,502, 38,548 (proposed July 7, 2008).

outcomes or cost savings (or both) for the hospital sponsoring the program," but also expressed concern about the possibility that some programs might become "potential vehicles for the unscrupulous to disguise payments for referrals or compromise quality of care for patients in the interest of maximizing revenues."[79] To prevent such abuses, the proposed rule included a number of requirements related to performance measures. For example, to qualify for an exception, a program must "identif[y] patient care quality measures or cost saving measures . . . or both that . . . [u]se an objective methodology, are verifiable, are supported by credible evidence, and are individually tracked."[80] The rule also requires that any patient care quality measures be included in CMS' Specification Manual for National Hospital Quality Measures.[81] In addition, it requires that hospitals provide "effective prior notice to patients affected by the incentive payment or shared savings program that . . . [d]escribes the performance measures in a manner reasonably designed to inform patients about the program."[82]

These requirements supply a potential template for use in designing broader gainsharing exceptions and safe harbors. Carefully identifying performance measures, for example, helps to ensure that they will incentivize behavior that actually improves quality or reduces costs. Requiring the use of quality measures listed in the CMS manual reinforces this result. Notice to patients can also serve as a safeguard; patients suspicious about the measure could go elsewhere.

At the same time, the proposed exception does not take full advantage of the safeguards that quality measures can offer. First, it does not appear to require that programs implementing cost saving measures *also* implement quality measures. Instead, the rule relies on other requirements to prevent quality degradation, such as a requirement for monitoring.[83] It would offer stronger safeguards to patients if it explicitly required the publication of relevant quality measures whenever shared savings programs are adopted.

Second, although disclosing the existence of a program to prospective patients may ensure some transparency, most patients would not be able to use this information in a meaningful way. Patients would likely find it difficult to predict how such programs would affect the quality of care. To address this problem, such disclosure could be supplemented with a requirement to disclose

---

79. Revisions to Payment Policies Under the Physician Fee Schedule and Other Revisions, 73 Fed. Reg. at 38,548.

80. Revisions to Payment Policies Under the Physician Fee Schedule and Other Revisions, 73 Fed. Reg. at 38,605 (to be codified at 42 C.F.R pt. 411) (proposed July 7, 2008).

81. Revisions to Payment Policies Under the Physician Fee Schedule and Other Revisions, 73 Fed. Reg. at 38,605.

82. Revisions to Payment Policies Under the Physician Fee Schedule and Other Revisions, 73 Fed. Reg. at 38,605.

83. Revisions to Payment Policies Under the Physician Fee Schedule and Other Revisions, 73 Fed. Reg. at 38,605.

performance measure *results* to patients. If they have already been compiled as part of a multiyear program, they could be disclosed to prospective patients; if not, they could be disclosed to former patients as a means of reassurance that their care was not jeopardized by the program. In addition, CMS might consider changing this requirement to mandate disclosure to others who might benefit from knowledge about the program. Payers, for example, may be well-positioned to act on patients' behalf; prospective patients who are searching for hospitals may be interested in learning of hospitals operating these programs. Although hospitals may already have incentives to disclose the existence and results of the programs to these additional audiences, a requirement to do so might promote broader dissemination of information about hospital quality issues.

Reforming fraud and abuse laws generally to permit gainsharing programs through exceptions or safe harbors could benefit patients, particularly if the safeguards included disclosure of quality measures. As quality and efficiency measures become more widely available, it may be possible to relax some of the arbitrary structural limitations OIG has looked favorably upon in gainsharing programs, such as limitations on amounts and program durations. However, one problem with the broad exception approach is the difficulty of ensuring that available quality measures are adequate in scope and well-tailored to capture any problematic effects of financial incentives. In discussing incentive programs in its recent proposed rule, CMS tackles this problem by requiring the use of quality measures in its own manual. This approach has the benefit of limiting the use of poor-quality quality measures, but at the cost of precluding the use of innovative quality measures that would meet the "credible medical evidence standard" but have not yet been added to the manual. In its discussion of this aspect of the rule, CMS suggested an alternative rule under which measures in the manual would be deemed to meet the standard.[84] They also solicited comments on whether to allow the measure requirements to be satisfied "by including criteria deemed by the Secretary in an advisory opinion to meet the requirement."[85] These alternative approaches are probably superior, since they provide reassurance for hospitals using the CMS manual measures while preserving the potential for the development of new types of measures.

Another approach would be to include among the exception or safe harbor requirements the submission of proposed quality measures to third parties for evaluation. Third parties are already involved in gainsharing projects; advisory opinion requestors, for example, already hire program administrators with

---

84. Revisions to Payment Policies Under the Physician Fee Schedule and Other Revisions, 73 Fed. Reg. at 38,553.

85. Revisions to Payment Policies Under the Physician Fee Schedule and Other Revisions, 73 Fed. Reg. at 38,553.

expertise in quality monitoring.[86] A number of health plans have recently agreed to submit their provider performance measures to third-party reviewers, demonstrating that this approach may be feasible.[87]

B. Financial Incentives Coupled with Quality Reporting

Financial incentives can play an important role in defragmenting the delivery of care. One reason that traditional gainsharing programs interest hospitals is that hospitals receive fixed payments per admission through Medicare's prospective payment system, which means that hospitals benefit if they find ways to reduce costs. But if Medicare or other payers were to adopt pay-for-performance systems, under which payment would be conditioned in part on quality, then hospitals might coordinate with physicians to improve hospital quality as well as to reduce hospital costs. Survey evidence suggests that some hospitals have already started down this path.[88]

One way to encourage quality-enhancing coordination is through a broader form of gainsharing program. Indeed, the Medicare Payment Advisory Commission has pointed out that such programs could be based in part on performance on quality measures.[89] The CMS proposed rule discussed previously referred to "incentive payment and shared savings programs," rather than just traditional gainsharing-like shared savings programs, in order to encompass programs harnessing the power of incentives to improve quality.[90] If legal reform allows gainsharing programs to flourish in a pay-for-performance environment,

---

86. *See, e.g.*, OIG, Advisory Opinion No. 06-22, *supra* note 69 (noting that Program Administrator had developed software that measured cost, quality, and utilization, and that these products were certified by American College of Cardiology and Society of Thoracic Surgery).

87. *See* Consumer-Purchaser Disclosure Project, Patient Charter for Physician Performance Measurement, Reporting and Tiering Programs: Ensuring Transparency, Fairness and Independent Review (April 1, 2008), http://healthcaredisclosure.org/docs/files/PatientCharter.pdf(charter endorsers will "[r]etain, at their own expense, the services of a nationally-recognized, independent health care quality standard-setting organization to review the plan's programs for consumers that measure, report, and tier physicians based on their performance").

88. Results from the Community Tracking Study suggest that "[h]ospitals employ physicians to gain cooperation with quality improvement efforts aimed at scoring well in pay-for-performance (P4P) and public reporting programs, which hospital executives anticipate will increase in importance." Casalino et al., *supra* note 12, at 1309. One hospital CEO stated that "[w]ith the increased emphasis on quality, public reporting, transparency, and having technology in place for evidence-based medicine, having closely aligned physicians is critical." *Id.*

89. MedPAC, *supra* note 70, at 46.

90. *See* Revisions to Payment Policies Under the Physician Fee Schedule and Other Revisions, 73 Fed. Reg. 38,502, 38,552 (proposed July 7, 2008) (discussing pay-for-performance programs and quality improvement objectives).

quality-enhancing as well as efficiency-enhancing coordination is likely to result.

Unfortunately, gainsharing programs of the sort historically pursued by providers have limited potential to ensure long-term coordination between hospitals and physicians. The programs finding their way into recent OIG advisory opinions and CMS demonstration projects are short-term and are structured around specific cost-saving measures that have already been identified. Reform of the laws relevant to gainsharing programs may incentivize attempts to identify and then engage in cost-saving improvements by permitting hospitals to compensate physicians using percentage-based arrangements in the short term. But such reform might not foster longer-term relationships among providers.

One way to encourage longer-term coordination is to alter payment methods. One payment approach that has attracted considerable attention among both government and private payers is the bundled payment. The heart bypass demonstration discussed previously was an early example of this approach; the Medicare program paid participating hospitals and physicians a bundled payment, leaving it to these entities to allocate the payment among themselves. If adopted as a permanent payment reform, this approach could generate long-term gains by aligning hospital and physician incentives on a long-term basis. The participating providers would have an incentive to work together to find ways to maximize their net revenues, whether through cost savings or other approaches. The precise nature of the ultimate incentives to alter the delivery of care would depend upon how hospitals and physicians allocate their joint revenues.

There has been a recent flurry of activity in the bundled payment area. For example, under the CMS Acute Care Episode demonstration, CMS will make a single payment for both hospital and physician services associated with a patient's stay in the hospital.[91] CMS noted that this demonstration would provide an opportunity for greater coordination and improvement in care, as well as efficiencies achieved through gainsharing.[92] In addition, MedPAC has been discussing a broader pilot program to study the viability of bundled payment for hospitals and physicians treating a patient for a particular condition.[93] Private payers, too, have announced similar plans to provide bundled payments, such as

---

91. *See* Press Release, Dep't of Health & Human Servs., Ctr. for Medicare & Medicaid Servs., CMS Announces Demonstration to Encourage Greater Collaboration and Improve Quality Using Bundled Hospital Payments (May 16, 2008).

92. CMS also noted that the some of the savings achieved as a result of the program may be passed along to beneficiaries receiving services under it.

93. *See* Medicare Payment Advisory Comm'n, Meeting Brief, April 9–10, 2008 (describing bundled payment plan), *available at* http://www.medpac.gov/transcripts/path to bundling.pdf.

age- and sickness-adjusted flat payments to physicians and hospitals, along with bonuses for quality improvement.[94]

One reason why a bundled payment approach may be particularly attractive now is the availability of quality measures that can facilitate monitoring of integrated organizations. Although many have stressed the potential benefits of bundled payment approaches, supporters of such approaches are also concerned about the potential for problematic effects.[95] In structuring the Acute Care Episode demonstration, for example, CMS chose to focus on cardiac and orthopedic care in part because quality measures were already available.[96] The availability of quality measures is obviously helpful if payers are studying the relationship between integration and quality improvement or if the bundled payment amount varies in accordance with measured quality. But quality measures are also important because they can help reassure patients and payers that providers' newly-aligned incentives do not lead them to jointly sacrifice quality in order to obtain lower costs. The use of quality measures in this way would mark a departure from the managed care era, when many were concerned that cost-cutting incentives inherent in capitation payments to physicians for bundled care would lead to deterioration in quality.[97]

C. Expanding and Improving Quality Measurement

As subpart B suggested, quality measures are important for fragmentation reduction efforts in at least two ways. First, they offer reassurance that potentially cost-reducing integration efforts have not degraded health care quality. Second, especially when coupled with pay-for-performance incentives or the incentives inherent in the competitive process, they can promote quality-improving integration. The ability of quality measures to serve these purposes well depends on their availability and design.

---

94. *See* Alice Dembner, *New Therapy for Old Woes*, BOSTON GLOBE, Jan. 22, 2008 (describing Blue Cross and Blue Shield of Massachusetts' proposed payment system).

95. *See, e.g.,* Hackbarth et al., *supra* note 70, at 4 (discussing possibility of bundled payment reform and asking whether Medicare can "protect against possible adverse effects of this policy, such as stinting on necessary care during an episode or increases in low-complexity admissions?")

96. *See* Press Release, Dep't of Health & Human Servs., *supra* note 91. *See also* Dep't of Health & Human Servs., Ctr. for Medicare & Medicaid Svcs., Anticipated ACE Demonstration Quality Monitoring Measures: Frequency of Reporting by Surgical Procedure, *available at* http://www.cms.hhs.gov/DemoProjectsEvalRpts/downloads/ACEQualityMeasures.pdf.

97. *See* Dembner, *supra* note 94 (noting similarities between insurer's bundled payment program and capitation programs as well as efforts to alleviate concerns through mechanisms such as public reporting of physician performance and pay-for-performance programs).

Many of the integration efforts between hospitals and physicians—including both private gainsharing efforts and federal demonstration projects—have focused on cardiac care. The main reason for this is most likely that cardiac care is a high volume, high revenue, and high cost area in which physicians have the potential to make decisions that reduce the costs of care. But cardiac care is also a promising area for demonstrations because it is well-suited for the development of easily calculable, reasonably reliable and informative quality measures. Similar quality measures are lacking for many other health care services. Although health care quality measures now exist in many more areas than ever before, health care experts will need to continue to develop and validate measures across many specialties in order to support broader integration efforts. It is important that the measures they develop be reliable. If based on incorrect data or improperly risk-adjusted, they will mislead anyone making decisions based on quality, including payers, patients, and providers themselves.

The scope of quality measures may also influence fragmentation. Some quality measures, especially process-based measures, are fairly narrow in scope and would not necessarily require coordination across provider types to achieve. A measure based on patient cholesterol testing, for example, might improve quality, but not necessarily by encouraging greater coordination or integration. A family practitioner is likely to be able to achieve good scores without coordinating with caregivers outside his or her own office. Providers often prefer this type of quality measure because it is more likely to be within their own control.

Other measures will be more likely to inspire coordination. One possibility is a measure that is based on coordination itself, as reported in patient surveys[98] or as indicated by objective data. But such measures are certainly not the only way or even necessarily the best way to promote coordination. Because hospitals depend on physicians, nurses, and others to ensure that patients receive the care they need, process-based quality measures can incentivize quality-enhancing coordination within the hospital setting. Outcome-based quality measures may provide even stronger incentives for coordination, regardless of setting. They incentivize coordination whenever multiple providers contribute to a patient outcome. Ideally, such measures would be attached to the individual or entity that faces the lowest costs or is otherwise best positioned to take a leadership role in integrating or coordinating with others.

The Institute of Medicine proposes the adoption of performance measures that hold all providers accountable for a patient's care across care settings, rather

---

98. *See, e.g.,* State of California, 2007 Health Care Quality Report Card, Medical Group Ratings, *available at* http://www.opa.ca.gov/report_card/medicalgroupmeasure.aspx ("Patients reported if someone from the doctor's office followed-up to give them their test results and if their doctor was up-to-date about any care the patient got from other doctors.").

than collecting only measures clearly attributable to a single provider's care.[99] These measures are aimed directly at the fragmentation problem. Although some providers may perceive quality or efficiency measures that depend partly on the work of others as unfair, such measures may better capture patient experience and would provide an incentive to work together when doing so would improve patient outcomes.

V. CONCLUSION

Fragmentation in the delivery of health care services has long concerned health care providers, administrators, commentators, and policy analysts. In the 1990s, there was considerable momentum toward integrated hospital and physician organizations,[100] spurred in part by a desire to respond to the rapid growth and bargaining strength of managed care organizations. However, as the managed care movement receded—due in part to patients' concerns about the quality of care—this momentum dissipated.[101] The impact of many of these integrated organizations on the delivery of care proved limited.[102]

Interest in mechanisms for integrating care is growing once again, but this time the results might be different. As providers begin to take advantage of the information that quality measures provide, they may begin to look for ways to increase quality. At the same time, as patients and payers become more aware of quality differentials, they will be more likely to demand higher quality. If they back their demand for quality with a willingness to pay for it, they supply an incentive for providers to pursue it. By bundling payments across multiple

---

99. *See* INST. OF MED., *supra* note 36, at 13, 89–90 ("measure sets should focus on measures of continuity and transitional care, as well as on longitudinal assessments of health outcomes and costs").

100. *See* Madison, *Hospital-Physician Affiliations and Patient Treatments, Expenditures, and Outcomes supra* note 2 (on growth of multihospital systems); Kristin Madison, *Hospital-Physician Affiliations and Patient Treatments, Expenditures, and Outcomes*, 39 HEALTH SERVICES RES. 257 (2004), and sources cited therein (documenting growth of various forms of hospital-physician affiliations).

101. *See* Thomas L. Greaney, *New Governance Norms and Quality of Care in Nonprofit Hospitals*, 14 ANNALS HEALTH L. 421, 431–32 (2005) (referring to link between managed care and integrated health systems).

102. *See* Madison, *Hospital-Physician Affiliations and Patient Treatments, Expenditures, and Outcomes, supra* note 100, at 257 and sources cited therein (finding little impact of hospital-physician affiliations on health outcomes). *See also* Blumstein, *supra* note 5, at 230–32 (reviewing literature on integrated delivery networks); Burns & Muller, *supra* note 12, at 378, 394, 402 (2008) (discussing the limited historical evidence of beneficial effects of hospital-physician collaborative arrangements). *Cf.* Peter P. Budetti et al., *Physician and Health System Integration*, 21(1) HEALTH AFF. 203 (2002) (in a study of fourteen organized delivery systems, finding that "many health systems did not align well with physicians").

service providers and varying payment according to the quality of services delivered, payers encourage cost-reducing and quality-enhancing integration.

Even if the main effect of increased integration were to encourage less costly modes of delivering care, quality measures can benefit patients by offering reassurance that new approaches to delivering care reduce costs by increasing efficiency, not reducing quality. This should help alleviate concerns that innovative payment mechanisms and increased integration might represent a return to the managed care systems that proved so unpopular in the 1990s.

Weakening laws and regulations that reinforce the fragmented structures of health care organizations, including the corporate practice doctrine, regulations aimed at hospital medical staffs, and fraud and abuse laws, would allow providers to engage in coordination and consolidation efforts that have the potential to benefit patients. Continuing to expand and improve quality measures would increase the likelihood that this potential is realized.

6. COMPETITION POLICY AND ORGANIZATIONAL FRAGMENTATION IN HEALTH CARE

THOMAS GREANEY

Once upon a time and a very good time it was, advocates for market-based approaches to health policy had a coherent story to tell. Cost and quality would remain suboptimal as long as fee-for-service medicine persisted and the myriad market imperfections that impede market efficiency went unchecked. Things could be righted, however, by adopting principles associated with managed care, together with pursuing sensible antitrust enforcement and government deregulation to clear away the private and regulatory underbrush obstructing market forces. Economic theorists and policy experts agreed that these steps would effectively address information, agency, and moral hazard problems and would begin to glue together the pieces of our fragmented delivery system. And, for a while, things seemed to work out as promised. Providers began to reorganize into firms and other integrating arrangements and health insurers adopted financial and contractual measures designed to align provider incentives with consumer needs. Regulators directed policies at removing obstacles to competition and antitrust enforcers sought to encourage efficient consolidation while blocking cartels and curbing development of provider oligopolies. Spiraling costs leveled off for a while and both payment systems and provider organizations began to adapt to market forces.

But things changed. A powerful backlash against managed care (precipitated in part by insurers' short-sighted and sometimes abusive tactics) gave rise to regulations that undermined some of the methods managed care had used effectively and payors gradually withdrew from active involvement in care management. Managed care and the competition-enhancing practices it had begun to spawn— integration and rivalry—unraveled. Several important lessons for competition policy emerged from the managed care era. First, a number of factors deeply embedded in the nation's health care apparatus encouraged resistance to competition. Even during the heyday of antitrust enforcement and market-favoring policies, many institutions and organizational structures changed little, as social norms and market imperfections proved to be powerful counterweights to conventional market incentives. In addition a host of statutes, judicial decisions, and governmental financing programs operated at cross purposes with the goals of competition policy. Nor are things likely to improve soon. Today's emerging market-oriented paradigm, "consumer directed health care"—which requires consumers to shoulder responsibility for making comparisons on the price, intensity, and quality of services they receive—threatens to increase fragmentation and does little to address the underlying imperfections of health care markets.

This chapter traces the path of competition law in health care and explains its chicken-and-egg relationship with provider organizational arrangements. It explores a central puzzle for future health care policy: Why have market forces failed to counteract organizational fragmentation? Answering this question requires an understanding of how competition policy is inexorably linked to the organizational architecture of health care and how the fragmentation that bedevils those arrangements has undermined its success. The chapter concludes with a negative assessment of recent consumer-driven approaches, finding them likely to increase fragmentation and incapable of delivering the benefits of competition.

HOW COMPETITION POLICY TRIED TO DEAL WITH FRAGMENTATION AND WHY IT FAILED

Antitrust Law's Two-Pronged Approach

Historically, much of what can be broadly classified as "competition policy" in health care is found in the application of antitrust principles to the conduct and structure of provider and payor organizations rather than in any sweeping statutory enactments. Although some landmark legislation, including the repeal of health planning statutes and adoption of the 1973 HMO law, ERISA, and laws enabling competitive contracting in federal and state-funded health programs, removed some important barriers to the growth of managed care, the task of dealing with unacceptable practices and problematic market structures was left to antitrust law. Antitrust law in the United States follows a common law approach, with courts applying broadly written statutes in individual cases brought by both government enforcers and aggrieved private parties.

For some thirty years, federal and state antitrust enforcement agencies (the Federal Trade Commission, the United States Department of Justice and state attorneys general) have employed antitrust law in federal court litigation to promote competition in health care. This battle has been fought on two fronts. First, applying standard principles of industrial organization economics, the agencies have devoted enormous resources to challenging cartels, professional restraints, mergers and anticompetitive joint ventures in the hospital, physician, pharmaceutical, and managed care sectors. Second, and less widely recognized, the agencies have engaged in extensive quasi-administrative efforts to encourage development of payment methods and organizations conducive to competition and efficiency. The latter, which has taken the form of advisory opinions, consent decrees, speeches, advice to legislatures, and statements of enforcement policy, has engendered controversy.[1] In litigating cases, the government's focus

---

1. See Thomas E. Kauper, *The Justice Department and the Antitrust Laws: Law Enforcer or Regulator?* 35 ANTITRUST BULL 83 (1990); Thomas L. Greaney, *Regulating for Efficiency in*

sometimes turned to engineering complex, conduct-oriented settlements rather than seeking structural or criminal remedies. In issuing policy statements or rendering advisory opinions the agencies have not hesitated to stress the desirability of preferred organizational forms, notably fully integrated, risk-sharing arrangements.[2] They have also tried to clear the way for joint ventures in purchasing, sharing information, and other forms of cooperation. Taken together, these efforts had a distinctly regulatory flavor, as the guidance provided often extended beyond generalities about enforcement priorities or assessments of the proper construction of precedent. In the case of physician networks, for example, the guidance regularly commended specific contractual arrangements and network operations that are likely to satisfy the agencies' interpretation of antitrust law. While prescriptive regulation and antitrust enforcement are usually seen as incompatible, in this case they were not. As argued below, the agencies' approach has been driven by an appropriate focus on mitigating market failure and was a necessary ingredient of sound competition policy.

Efforts to limit cartelization and provider monopolies in health care have been a staple of antitrust enforcement for almost thirty years. Following the Supreme Court's landmark decision in *Goldfarb v. Virginia State Bar*,[3] the Federal Trade Commission and Department of Justice embarked on a series of challenges to professional restraints of trade, including ethical codes prohibiting advertising, contracting, and affiliation with HMOs, and affiliation with alternative care providers. Since then, Federal and state enforcers also prosecuted nearly one hundred cases involving price-fixing cartels, physician boycotts that sought to deter innovative financing plans or block competition from alternative care providers, or to organize collective bidding.[4] Over the years, physician groups and associations have attempted to justify collective action on the basis of preserving professional sovereignty, "leveling the playing field" vis-à-vis insurers, assuring that efficient integration can take place, and protecting patients from

---

Health Care Through the Antitrust Laws, UTAH L. REV. 465 (1995); Thomas E. Sullivan, *The Antitrust Division as a RegulatoryAgency: Antitrust Policy in Transition*, 64 WASH U.Q. 997 (1986); Jon Leibowitz, Commissioner, Fed. Trade Comm'n, Health Care and the FTC: The Agency as Prosecutor and Policy Work, Remarks at the Antitrust in HealthCare Conference of the American Bar Association/American Health Lawyers Association (May 12, 2005) (transcript *available at* http://www.ftc.gov/speeches/leibowitz/050512healthcare.pdf).

2. *See* Lawrence Casalino, *The Federal Trade Commission, Clinical Integration, and the Organization of Physician Networks*, 31 J. HEALTH POL., POL'Y & L. 569 (2004).

3. Goldfarb v. Virginia State Bar, 421 U.S. 773 (1975).

4. *See, e.g.,* Am. Med. Ass'n, 94 F.T.C. 701 (1979), *aff'd as modified*, 638 F.2d 443 (2nd Cir. 1980), *aff'd by equally divided Court*, 452 U.S. 676 (1982); U.S. v. N.D. Hosp. Ass'n, 640 F. Supp. 1028 (D.N.D. 1986); Mich. State Med. Soc'y, 101 F.T.C. 191 (1983). *See generally* B. FURROW ET AL., HEALTH LAW §14-10, (2d ed. 2000) (1995). *See generally*, Thomas L. Greaney, *Whither Antitrust? The Uncertain Future of Competition Policy in Health Care*, 21 HEALTH AFF. 185 (March/April 2002).

low-quality care. On close inspection (by the antitrust agencies, courts, and Congress) these explanations have been found wanting. Even in cases in which legitimate concerns are raised, the mechanism sought—collective bargaining—was designed to shield physicians from market discipline with no guarantee that the promised benefits to the consumer would be realized. When plausible economic arguments supported factoring into the analysis other market conditions, such as quality of care, imperfect information, or the charitable mission of nonprofit hospitals, antitrust law turned a deaf ear.[5] Prompted by both pragmatic considerations and suggestive legal precedent, enforcers used standard microeconomic analysis, framing health care as functioning "like any other industry."

It should be noted that antitrust enforcement has been directed, with varying degrees of intensity and mixed success, at other sectors of the market. For example, enforcers have focused only sporadic efforts on dealing with problems in "upstream" markets, such as device and ancillary equipment suppliers and some sectors of the pharmaceutical market. In other areas aggressive enforcement has met with resistance from the courts. The FTC has devoted extensive resources in the past five years to dealing with abuses of intellectual property in the pharmaceutical industry, challenging agreements that kept generic drugs from entering the markets of brand name rivals and mergers and abuses of the patent system designed to improperly obtain or maintain monopoly power.[6] Finally, in several important areas, such as anticompetitive exclusion by group purchasing organizations and pharmaceutical benefit managers, in which conflicts of interest may cause serious impediments to market entry and innovation, governmental antitrust enforcers have been relatively quiescent.[7]

Provider market structure has also been a key target of antitrust enforcement efforts. Federal and state enforcers have litigated over thirty hospital merger cases and dozens more have been settled or abandoned. In addition, anticompetitive linkages between hospitals and physicians in physician hospital

---

5. See William Sage & Peter Hammer, *Antitrust Law, Healthcare Quality and the Courts,* 102 COLUM. L. REV. 545 (2002); Thomas L. Greaney, *Antitrust and Hospital Mergers: Does the Nonprofit Form Affect Competitive Substance?* 31 J. HEALTH POL., POL'Y & L. 511 (2006).

6. See, e.g. Schering-Plough Corp. v. FTC, 402 F.3d 1056 (11th Cir. 2005). The "reverse payments" cases have generated an enormous literature debating a host of economic and doctrinal issues. See e.g., Herbert Hovenkamp et al., *Anticompetitive Settlement of Intellectual Property Disputes,* 87 MINN. L. REV. 1719, 1720–21 (2003); Carl Shapiro, *Antitrust Limits to Patent Settlements,* 34 RAND J. ECON. 391, 391 (2003); James Langenfeld & Wenqing Li, *Intellectual Property and Agreements to Settle Patent Disputes: The Case of Settlement Agreements with Payments from Branded to Generic Drug Manufacturers,* 70 ANTITRUST L.J. 777 (2003).

7. See Letter from Senator Mark Montigny to FTC Chairman Deborah Platt Majoras (May 11, 2005) (letter from bipartisan group of state legislators urging investigation of PBM industry, noting that "numerous states are devoting considerable enforcement resources to combating fraudulent and anticompetitive conduct by PBMs").

organizations have been challenged and a few anticompetitive hospital networks have come under scrutiny. These cases were consistent with the view that the success of managed care competition hinged on the preservation of competitive provider markets. The theme of encouraging market structures in which managed care entities could successfully "play providers off" against each other through competitive bidding or negotiations was the hallmark of the federal antitrust strategy. At the same time, antitrust enforcers were inactive when confronted with vertical combinations and managed care mergers. Although a handful of cases were brought challenging monopsonistic ("buy side") abuses or monopoly-preserving ("sell-side") conduct by large health insurers and a few mergers involving large national firms resulted in spin-offs of a handful of contracts, little enforcement effort was directed at managed care companies.[8] As a general matter the agencies rejected the American Medical Association's repeated claims that oligopolistic managed care markets impeded competition, concluding instead that local insurance markets for the most part were competitively structured and lacked significant barriers to entry.[9]

Although initially successful in breaking down institutional barriers to competition and challenging hospital mergers, antitrust enforcement efforts have encountered a number of problems over the last decade. Most significantly, federal and state agencies experienced a series of seven consecutive defeats in federal court challenges to hospital mergers.[10] As discussed below, the decisions in those cases can be faulted on a number of grounds: failure to incorporate a sophisticated understanding of the market imperfection of health care markets, poor case selection by the government, and to some extend a judicial backlash against managed care.

The second prong of antitrust enforcement sought to focus the agencies' enforcement apparatus on creating an environment conducive to managed care

---

8. *See* United States v. UnitedHealth Group Inc., Case No. 1:05CV02436 (D.D.C. 2006), *available at* http://www.usdoj.gov/atr/cases/f216400/216423.htm (merger of UnitedHealth Group Inc. and PacifiCare Health Systems, Inc.) and United States v. UnitedHealth Group Inc., Case No. 1:08CV00322 (D.D.C. 2008), *available at* http://www.usdoj.gov/atr/cases/f237600/237613.htm (merger of UnitedHealth Group Inc. and Sierra Health Services, Inc.).

9. FEDERAL TRADE COMMISSION & U.S. DEPT. OF JUSTICE, IMPROVING HEALTH CARE: A DOSE OF COMPETITION, CH. 6 (2004)

10. *See* Thomas L. Greaney, *Chicago's Procrustean Bed: Applying Antitrust in Health Care*, 71 ANTITRUST L.J. 857, 917 (2004). Seeking to right their ship, the FTC challenged an already-consummated merger involving two nonprofit hospitals in Evanston Illinois. *See* In the Matter of Evanston Northwestern Hospital, FTC. Docket No. 9315 (Aug. 6, 2007), *available at* http://www.ftc.gov/os/adjpro/d9315/070806opinion.pdf. After finding the acquisition violated the Clayton Act, the Commission declined to require structural relief, instead ordering that the merged hospitals form separate and independent negotiating teams to contract with managed care organizations.

competition. The "apparatus" referred to here is a variety of formal and informal tools used by the agencies outside the narrow bounds of prosecuting antitrust abuses in judicial and administrative hearings. It includes settlements and consent decrees, speeches, advisory opinions, advice to legislators, and policy statements.[11] Because they encourage adoption of structures and arrangements that avoid antitrust risk, these tools have a distinctly prescriptive flavor. Although these undertakings controversially enmeshed the agencies in "regulation" (as opposed to seeking remedies by adjudication litigation), they also afforded an opportunity to direct providers and payors toward economically sound arrangements given the peculiarities of health care markets.

Countering fragmentation was a prominent objective of the government's regulatory agenda. In dispensing advice and negotiating settlements, the agencies stressed the desirability of integrating independent providers. The FTC and Department of Justice afforded safe harbor treatment for financial risk-sharing in their policy statements, and repeatedly signaled in speeches and advisory opinions that the agencies strongly favored integration via risk-sharing or formation of fully integrated firms and partnerships.[12] In eventually countenancing "clinical integration" as an alternative form of cooperation that could avoid summary condemnation, the agencies took pains to stipulate detailed conditions evidencing the sufficiency of integration and the necessity for price agreements.[13]

---

11. *See* Greaney *supra* note 1. *See also* Deborah Platt Majoras, Chairman, FTC, Remarks at the World Congress Leadership Summit: The Federal Trade Commission: Fostering a Competitive Health Care Environment That Benefits Patients (Feb. 28, 2005), *available at* http://www.ftc.gov/speeches/majoras/050301healthcare.pdf:

> [L]aw enforcement is not the only procedure we use to cure anticompetitive ailments. The FTC actively engages in advocacy before states and other federal Agencies, urging the adoption of pro competitive strategies for improving health care quality and bringing costs down . . . . [A]dvocacy can be very effective. Competition advocacy . . . can prevent legislation that might unintentionally injure competition—and raise patients' costs—from getting on the books in the first place.

12. *See* U.S. DEP'T OF JUSTICE & FED. TRADE COMM'N, STATEMENTS OF ANTITRUST ENFORCEMENT POLICY AND ANALYTICAL PRINCIPLES RELATING TO HEALTH CARE AND ANTITRUST, reprinted in 4 Trade Reg. Rep. (CCH) ¶ 13,152, at 20,788 (Sept. 30, 1994) (Eighth Statement) [hereinafter 1994 Policy Statements]; Letter from Jeffrey W. Brennan, Assistant Dir., Bureau of Competition, FTC, to Martin J. Thompson (Sept. 23, 2003) (Staff Advisory Opinion to Bay Area Preferred Physicians) [BAPP Advisory Opinion]; Letter from Jeffrey W. Brennan, Assistant Dir., Bureau of Competition, FTC, to Gregory G. Binford (Feb. 6, 2003) (Staff Advisory Opinion to PriMed Physicians).

13. Letter from Jeffrey W. Brennan, Assistant Dir., Bureau of Competition, FTC, to John J. Miles (Feb. 19, 2002) (Staff Advisory Opinion to MedSouth, Inc.) [MedSouth Advisory Opinion]. *See also*, Remarks of J. Thomas Rosch, Commissioner, Federal Trade

Though criticized as overly prescriptive,[14] the agencies' insistence on specific integrative activities was entirely appropriate in view of the market imperfections that plague the industry. Risk-sharing mechanisms, especially capitation and fee withholds, counteract the incentives of compensation systems to overprovide medical care. Without a strong commitment to the cooperative enterprise (such as mere physicians ownership in a network), incentives are lacking to counter the fee-for-service hydraulic for costly and excessive care. As Peter Hammer summarized the prevailing incentive structure, "[unintegrated] networks can be expected to maximize profits both by using whatever market power they possess to charge higher prices and by practicing medicine using traditional standards which are intrinsically biased in favor of over providing care."[15] Thus antitrust policy targeted fragmented systems and encouraged integration. However, for reasons discussed in the next section, neither the nudge of government advice nor the pressure of managed care bargaining proved sufficient to unseat entrenched provider organizational arrangements.

Antitrust as a (Mostly Unsuccessful) Antidote to Fragmentation
Superficially viewed, the antitrust agenda might seem to increase fragmentation as it prevents aggregation of providers into large entities or cooperation through alliances with competitors. However, the opposite is the case. Antitrust doctrine permits efficiency-enhancing integration, including mergers, joint ventures, and other forms of cooperation, between rivals and between entities in vertical relationships. Indeed, competitive markets should act to *stimulate* inter-firm cooperation through organizational structures and agreements that improve performance and lower costs. Properly applied, antitrust law promotes decentralized decision making by market participants, but encourages efficient combinations that serve consumer welfare.

Yet, in health care this rosy scenario was not realized, as antitrust enforcement had only modest success in encouraging efficient consolidation of providers. Multiple factors contributed to this outcome but it seems clear that the deeply entrenched norms, institutional structures, and legal regimes that have long supported fragmentation enabled providers to resist change. As a result, innovations in care delivery, organization, and financing that competition theorists thought inevitable did not spread. Providers remained content to

---

Commission, Clinical Integration in Antitrust: Prospects for the Future (Sept. 27, 2007), *available at* http://www.ftc.gov/speeches/rosch/070917clinic.pdf.

14. Clark C. Havighurst, *Are the Antitrust Agencies Overregulating Physician Networks?* 8 LOY. CONSUMER. L. REV. 78, (1995–96).

15. Peter J. Hammer, *Medical Antitrust Reform: Arrow, Coase, and the Changing Structure of the Firm, in* THE PRIVATIZATION OF HEALTH CARE REFORM 113, 115–16 (M. Gregg Bloche ed., 2003). *See also* Rosch *supra* note 13, at 19 ("financial incentives are safest way to proceed" given uncertainties about the incentives and implementation of clinical integration).

practice in silos, though some sectors, such as hospitals and certain physician specialties, formed local monopolies or oligopolies to further insulate themselves from rivalry. Questionable holdings in key cases and conflicting signals from other legal regimes legitimated these arrangements and ultimately the antitrust agenda did not generate the integrated systems or virtual networks needed for competition to have any serious bite.

Fragmentation at the provider level frustrated competition policy in a number of ways. For the large percentage of physicians practicing in small groups or single specialty practices, adapting to managed care's incentives for risk-sharing and economizing practices was extraordinarily difficult. Many physicians proved inept in assessing risk. In dealing with capitation, physician decisions seem subject to problems of over-optimism, endowment bias, and other departures from rational choice models identified by behavioral decision theorists.[16] At the same time, physicians jealously guarded their independence and were resistant to undertaking employment relationships or joining staff model HMOs or large practice groups. In the dozens of FTC cases challenging provider-sponsored networks, groups of physicians formed thinly-disguised cartels to gain market power to bargain with managed care companies. Elsewhere, physicians flocked to loosely structured PPOs that did little to promote price competition or instill incentives to change practice styles. Finally, the absence of vertical integration also frustrated managed care's performance. In hospital markets, in which most patients delegate hospital choice to their physicians, who do not internalize the costs of technology or excess capacity, hospitals benefited more from competing for physician affiliation (through various forms of non-price competition) than by economizing for the benefit of contracting. The net result was "networks" that did little to change practice patterns, and market structures that served as bulwarks against effective bargaining by managed care organizations.

Fragmentation arising out of health care financing exacerbated these problems and served to undermine managed care's incentives to promote development of efficient delivery organizations. With physicians typically contracting with multiple payors, incentives to change practice styles or adopt other methods for controlling cost or improving quality to conform to protocols of any single payor are attenuated. In addition, fee-for-service payment neglects many of the services key to developing integrated approaches to delivery. For example, it fails to pay for care coordination and information exchanges and undervalues other valuable services such as cognitive services and communications outside care encounters. With dominant payment methodologies rewarding physicians who do not integrate their practice arrangements, and given organized medicine's longstanding resistance to organizational hierarchies, it is not altogether surprising that managed care's competitive incentives failed to deliver change.

---

16. *See* Thomas L. Greaney, *Economic Regulation of Physicians: A Behavioral Economics Perspective*, 53 St. Louis U. L. J. 1189 (2009).

The antitrust agenda also encountered serious setbacks in court, as courts rejected a succession of FTC and Department of Justice challenges to hospital mergers and enforcers subsequently backed off monitoring the hospital sector. As a result (discussed in the following section) local hospital markets around the country became highly concentrated. Paradoxically, this consolidation also served to reinforce health sector fragmentation. It did so by strengthening hospitals' market power and hence their ability to resist managed care demands for economizing practices, such as forming integrated delivery system with physicians. Underlying these judicial decisions is a consistent failure to adapt legal analyses to the peculiar economics of competition in the health care sector. The principal shortcoming was the courts' tendency to oversimplify antitrust analysis by adopting plain vanilla, Chicago school assumptions about markets while failing to incorporate the effects of market imperfections in their analyses of health markets.[17] As a result, most of these hospital merger decisions found extraordinarily large geographic markets for basic acute care hospital services because they ignored the heterogeneity of demand for care and the fact that consumers exhibit different preferences for travel. Other cases refused to recognize supply side heterogeneity, failing to appreciate that mergers of "must have" hospitals may create risks of anticompetitive effects.[18] Health economists and commentators have roundly criticized these decisions as inconsistent with the economic realities of local competition and for misapprehending the interplay of managed care organizations (MCOs), employers, and insured persons in selecting hospitals.[19]

Legal analyses are not immune to the biases and preconceptions prevalent in the society at large. In rejecting hospital merger challenges and other antitrust challenges to provider market power, courts may have internalized skepticism about health care insurers popularly characterized as a "managed care backlash." Betraying a strong undercurrent of suspicion about the role of managed care and perhaps competition in general in health care markets, one federal Circuit decision quoted Judge Richard Posner's hyperbolic dictum that "the HMO's incentive is to keep you healthy if it can but if you get very sick, and are unlikely to recover to a healthy state involving few medical expenses, to let you die as quickly and cheaply as possible."[20] Other courts have gone further, explicitly

---

17. Thomas L. Greaney, *Chicago's Procrustean Bed: Applying Antitrust in Health Care*, 71 ANTITRUST L.J. 857 (2004).

18. United States v. Long Island Jewish Med. Ctr., 983 F. Supp. 121 (E.D.N.Y. 1997).

19. *See e.g.*, Kenneth L. Danger & H.E. Frech, *Critical Thinking About "Critical Loss" in Antitrust*, 46 ANTITRUST BULL. 339 (2001); James Langenfeld & Wenqing Li, *Critical Loss in Evaluating Mergers*, 46 ANTITRUST BULL. 299 (2001); Gregory Vistnes, *Hospitals, Mergers, and Two-Stage Hospital Competition*,67 ANTITRUST L.J. 671 (2000).

20. Federal Trade Commission v. Tenet Health Care Corp., 186 F.3d 1045, 1054 (8th Cir. 1999) (quoting Blue Cross & Blue Shield United v. Marshfield Clinic, 65 F.3d 1406, 1410 (7th Cir. 1995)).

downplaying testimony from managed care buyers or suggesting that competition resulting from rivalry among such entities was not in consumers' interest. Further, one federal court and some state attorneys general accepted consent decrees allowing mergers to proceed subject to regulatory controls on profits, price, and charitable care as a substitute for preserving market structures conducive to price competition.[21] Thus it is possible to discern in the case law an implicit suspicion of the very paradigm on which antitrust enforcement rested, namely vigorous bargaining by managed care organizations exerting pressure on providers to reorganize themselves to adopt more cost efficient arrangements.

Another factor contributing to the failure of competitive forces to encourage de-fragmentation of markets is the regulatory environment governing providers. Several significant legal regimes directly impede efficiency-enhancing cooperation among rivals. The federal anti-kickback and Stark laws bar many forms of vertical and horizontal cooperation that can improve efficiency. Together these two laws generally prohibit providers from receiving or paying for referrals and bar physician ownership and other financial relationships with entities to which they refer. Consequently, the fragmented community of physicians and hospitals is prevented from responding to competitive market incentives to integrate via joint ventures and contractual arrangements.[22] Perhaps more than any other regulatory obstacle, the inability of hospitals to share efficiency and cost effective improvements with physicians who order services impedes effective deployment of health resources.[23]

Another cluster of laws operate to impair the development of efficient "firms" or contractual arrangements that bridge traditional doctor-hospital boundaries. State certificate of need laws, for example, impair competition in acute care and some ambulatory services.[24] These laws, which create barriers to entry by rivals, especially physicians seeking to open specialty hospitals or ambulatory surgery centers, contribute indirectly to health sector fragmentation. They do so by institutionalizing existing physician-hospital relationships, essentially ossifying traditional, autonomous roles. For example, by erecting barriers for physicians wanting to operate ambulatory surgical facilities or acute care specialty hospitals,

---

21. FTC v. Butterworth Health Corp., 946 F. Supp. 1285, 1291 (W.D. Mich. 1996).

22. See James Blumstein, *The Fraud and Abuse Statute in an Evolving Healthcare Marketplace: Life in the Health Care Speakeasy*, 22 AM. J. L. & MED. 205 (1996); David Hyman, *Health Care Fraud and Abuse, Social Norms, and "The Trust Reposed in the Workmen."* J. LEGAL STUD. 531 (2001).

23. *See* Gail Wilensky, et al., *Gain Sharing: A Good Concept Getting a Bad Name?* 26 HEALTH AFF. 58 (2007).

24. *See* FEDERAL TRADE COMMISSION & U.S. DEPT. OF JUSTICE, IMPROVING HEALTH CARE: A DOSE OF COMPETITION 6 (2004) (summarizing evidence regarding the impact of CON laws on competition and cost control and urging states to reconsider whether CON laws are serving the public interest).

these laws significantly reduce opportunities for integrated service delivery. Adding to the problem is another body of law recognized in approximately a dozen states, the corporate practice of medicine doctrine, which inhibits medical professionals from working in employment relationships and prohibits corporate entities from assuming responsibility for the provision of services.[25] This doctrine prohibits (or imposes significant transaction costs on) arrangements between physicians and corporate entities that provide health care services. As such it operates to reduce opportunities establishing "firms" that can more efficiently organize care delivery. Finally, a network of other laws and regulations, including the Joint Commission (formerly, the Joint on the Accreditation of Healthcare Organizations) certification standards and those governing physician responsibilities and rights in hospital management, solidify professional autonomy within hospitals and reinforce barriers to hospitals asserting greater control to integrate their operations in a cost effective manner.[26]

The preceding catalogue of obstacles to integration should not be understood to suggest that competition theorists had everything right. Indeed, the brief that competition advocates presented for the capacity of managed care to address market failure overlooked several important obstacles.[27] For example, although it provided an effective mechanism for alleviating agency and information problems among providers, patients, and payors, managed care by itself could not address the serious information deficits with respect to quality and outcomes. As public goods, such information is under-produced in the market and requires government action though subsidy or direct provision. Paul Ginsburg summarized the need for public and private initiatives to improve technology assessment:

> Over the long haul, advancements in medical technology are far and away the biggest factor in rising costs. And our current financing system facilitates the rapid diffusion of expensive new technologies by paying most of their cost— even in the absence of careful consideration of their clinical effectiveness relative to existing treatments. Fundamental change in this dynamic would require support for improved and more frequent evaluation of new technologies prior to decisions about coverage, as well as carefully differentiated

---

25. *See e.g.*, Berlin v. Sarah Bush Lincoln Health Center, 688 N.E. 2d 106, (Ill. 1997); *see generally*, Mark A. Hall, *Institutional Control Of Physician Behavior*, 137 U. PA. L. REV. 431 (1988).

26. *See* John Blum, *Beyond the Bylaws: Hospital-Physician Relationships, Economics, And Conflicting Agendas*, 53 BUFF. L. REV. 459 (2005); *see also* John P. Marren et al., *Hospital Boards at Risk and the Need to Restructure the Relationship with the Medical Staff: Bylaws, Peer Review and Related Solutions*, 12 ANNALS HEALTH L. 179, 207-12(2003).

27. *See* Thomas L. Greaney, *Competitive Reform in Health Care: The Vulnerable Revolution*, 5 YALE. J. ON REG. 179, (1988) (predicting that competition in health care would not succeed if regulatory and infrastructure did not support it).

incentives built into the financing system that encourage both providers and patients to evaluate the clinical effectiveness of a given course of treatment against its cost.[28]

Although government policies in administering and financing public programs such as Medicare might have served this function, they did not. In recent years, the Centers for Medicare and Medicaid Services at the Department of Health and Human Services has, rather belatedly, undertaken initiatives encouraging "medical homes" and payments linked to performance. Moreover, a fact market proponents generally overlooked was that health care market failures may be exacerbated or perpetuated by "government failure," i.e., public policies that entrench market imperfections. To cite a few examples, federal tax policy has supported moral hazard in insurance; fee-for-service payment under Medicare reinforced physician agency problems and countenanced cost-ineffective practice styles; and licensure and accreditation have imposed entry and mobility barriers on providers.

The Aftermath: Market Concentration, Cartels, and Lax Antitrust Enforcement

Following the government's defeats in the hospital merger cases, an extraordinary consolidation occurred in hospital and insurance markets. Emboldened by the results in those cases and the government's reluctance to challenge mergers in court, concentration grew significantly in almost all sectors of health care delivery and payment. By one estimate over 900 hospital mergers occurred between 1994 and 2000, and by 2003 ninety-three percent of the nation's population lived in concentrated hospital markets.[29] In local acute care hospital markets the effects of concentration were striking. Research demonstrates that hospital consolidation in the 1990s raised overall inpatient prices by at least five percent and by forty percent or more when merging hospitals were closely located.[30] Anecdotal evidence confirms that payers in many local markets faced increased resistance to bargaining by hospitals and that this led to higher prices.[31] By some

---

28. Paul Ginsburg, Center for Studying Health System Change, statement before Subcommittee on Oversight, House Ways and Means Committee (June 22, 2004), *available at* http://waysandmeans.house.gov/hearings.asp?formmode=view&id=1687.

29. Claudie H. Williams et al., *How Has Hospital Consolidation Affected the Price and Quality of Hospital Care* 9 THE SYNTHESIS PROJECT 1,1 (Feb. 2006), *available at* http://www.rwjf.org/files/research/no9policybrief.pdf.

30. *See id.* (citing simulation studies show price increases of 53 percent; event studies indicating 40 percent increases and Structure-Conduct Performance studies showing 4–6 percent increases.). *See also* Robert Town et al., *The Welfare Consequences of Hospital Mergers* (Nat'l Bureau of Econ. Research, working paper 12233, 2006) (hospital mergers raised HMO premiums 3.2% and caused.3% decline in private insurance in 2001).

31. CENTER FOR STUDY OF HEALTH SYSTEMS CHANGE (periodic survey of competitive conditions in 12 markets), *available at* http://www.hschange.com/index.cgi?data=01.

accounts, a renewal of the "medical arms race" has occurred, as hospitals have undertaken significant expansions of capacity and accelerated technology acquisitions, in part owing to their capacity to induce demand following the demise of managed care.[32]

The consolidation that occurred in local hospital markets does not appear to have produced significant scale economies or other efficiencies that would benefit consumers. The literature on multihospital system performance shows little evidence of improvement in cost per admission, profitability or service provision to the community in the form of charity.[33] Likewise, hospital networks and alliances did not exhibit significant economies or other efficiencies.[34] The evidence on the effect of hospital mergers on quality is mixed: a recent summary of the literature concludes that the majority of studies find that hospital mergers lower quality, with that conclusion supported by the strongest studies.[35] In sum, the extensive hospital consolidation that occurred in the 1990s cannot be interpreted as a welfare-improving correction to market fragmentation. It also appears that many hospitals joined hospital "systems" which did not engage in meaningful integration or produce economic efficiencies. Instead, the merger wave appears to have been a successful effort to gain bargaining leverage, which hospitals used to deflect the price and volume discipline threatened by managed care contracting.

Competition in physician markets during the managed care era followed a somewhat different path. As discussed below, primary care physicians did not engage in widespread horizontal merger activity in the 1990s, and although the percentage of doctors in small practices declined, this market remained fragmented as multi-specialty practice did not increase significantly. Throughout that period and beyond, however, physicians engaged in extensive cartelization. Between 1976 and 1996, the FTC and Department of Justice initiated and settled by consent decrees approximately sixty five enforcement actions against hospital- and physician-contracting networks for jointly negotiating on behalf of their members with payors in a manner that constituted unlawful horizontal price-fixing agreements.[36] Remarkably, this vigorous record of prosecution did

---

32. *See* Robert A. Berenson et al., *Hospital-Physician Relations: Competition, Cooperation or Separation?*, HEALTH AFF. (2006).

33. *See* Lawton R. Burns & Mark V. Pauly, *Integrated Delivery Networks: A Detour on the Road to Integrated Health Care?*, 21 HEALTH AFF. 128 (July/Aug. 2002) (summarizing studies of horizontal hospital mergers).

34. *Id.; See also* Bazzoli, *The Financial Performance of Hospitals Belonging to Health Networks and Systems*, 37 INQUIRY 234 (2000).

35. Claudie H. Williams et al., *supra* note 29, at 1, 1. *See also* Vivian Ho & Barton Hamilton, *Hospital Mergers and Acquisitions: Does the Market Consolidation Harm Patients?*, 19 J. HEALTH ECON. 767 (2000).

36. *See* Thomas L. Greaney, *Thirty Years of Solicitude: Antitrust and Physician Cartels*, 7 HOUS. J. HEALTH L. & POL. 189, 189–91 (2007).

not deter the challenged conduct: since the beginning of this decade, the FTC has brought thirty-four such cases and the Antitrust Division of the DOJ challenged at least five similar arrangements as illegal horizontal restraints. The government's willingness to accept "wrist slap" consent decrees and employ administrative rather than prosecutorial approaches to the problem undoubtedly contributed to the widespread lack of compliance with antitrust norms.[37] Notably absent in the government's prosecutions were criminal and structural remedies or stringent civil remedies.

Finally, the health insurance market has undergone significant consolidation as there have been over 400 health insurer mergers in the past decade and virtually every major metropolitan market is highly concentrated. With premiums increasing almost nine percent per year between 2000 and 2007 (compared to workers' wages increasing only 3.4% per year), insurance market concentration has engendered considerable controversy.[38] However, antitrust challenges to insurer mergers or conduct have been few and far between. In the past seven years the DOJ has only required the restructuring of two proposed health insurance mergers, both with very modest divestitures. In the view of the federal agencies, insurer market power has not been significant, owing to perceived ease of entry and self insurance alternatives available to large employers. Though not expressly acknowledged, the agencies' lenient posture may reflect the view that managed care serves as an important counterweight to the power of providers. In essence, then, the government may have adopted a second-best strategy under which it is hoped that bilateral monopoly will achieve some measure of benefit to consumers.

In the end, competition policy failed to deliver competitively structured markets in large part because the delivery system failed to integrate. Bill Sage's epigram, "It's the delivery system, stupid" captures the obstacle that health reformers overlooked during the managed care era.[39] The aftermath—competition policy in contemporary health markets—is discussed in the following section.

COMPETITION AND FRAGMENTATION IN DISINTERMEDIATED (CONSUMER-DRIVEN) MARKETS

The preceding analysis suggests that managed care competition did not alleviate, and probably fell victim to, provider market fragmentation. Over the last ten

---

37. *See id* at 194.

38. Kaiser Family Foundation and Health Research and Education Trust, Employer Health Benefits: 2007 Annual Survey, *available at* http://www.kff.org/insurance/7672/upload/76723.pdf

39. William M. Sage, *Legislating Delivery System Reform: A 30,000-Foot View of the 800-Pound Gorilla*, 26 HEALTH AFF. 1553, 1553 (Nov./Dec. 2007) (noting the failure of the architects of the Clinton Health plan to encourage change in health delivery).

years health insurers have retreated from active management of care and a new market-oriented approach, "consumer-directed health care" (CDHC), has emerged. Although that phrase covers a lot of ground, as used here it reflects the broad shift of responsibility for choice and cost to consumers.[40] Relying increasingly on large co-payments, deductibles, and various benefit designs, insurance plans offer benefits packages that create incentives for consumers to take more responsibility to choose the nature and intensity of health services and providers who provide that care. Beyond the trend toward higher deductibles and co-payments, consumer-directed plans sometimes are linked with health reimbursement accounts which are dedicated funds supplied by employer and/or employee contributions that can be used to pay for certain medical expenses and services.[41] One rapidly growing variant, the health savings account (HSA), carries with it important tax benefits such as allowing taxpayers to exclude funds placed in an HSA from taxable income, provided that it is coupled with a high-deductible health plan.[42]

Provider Markets After Managed Care

For several reasons, the evolving "consumer directe health care"(CDHC) insurance market appears unlikely to reduce fragmentation. First, there are strong reasons to conclude that the competition-improving narrative that its proponents have advanced is seriously flawed.[43] America's experience with autonomous consumers shopping for health care services is certainly not encouraging. For example, uninsured consumers—who encounter the market for health services on a regular basis—face enormous difficulties in obtaining care at

---

40. *See* TIMOTHY STOLTZFUS JOST, HEALTH CARE AT RISK: A CRITIQUE OF THE CONSUMER DRIVEN MOVEMENT 119-45 (2007); John Jacobi, *After Managed Care: Gray Boxes, Tiers and Consumerism*, 47 ST. LOUIS U. L. J. 397 (2003).

41. *See* Paul Fronstin & Sara R. Collins, The 2nd Annual EBRI/Commonwealth Fund Consumerism in Health Survey 2006: Early Experience with High-Deductible and Consumer-Driven Plans, EBRI Issue Brief No. 300 (Dec. 2006), http://www.ebri.org/publications/ib/index.cfm?fa=ibDisp&content_id=3769. *See generally,* Wendy K. Mariner, *Can Consumer-Choice Plans Satisfy Patients? Problems with Theory and Practice in Health Insurance Contracts,* 69 BROOK. L. REV. 485 (2004) (describing consumer-driven plans and arguing that they effectively ask patients to ration their own care). *See also* Gary Claxton et al., *Health Benefits in 2006: Premium Increases Moderate, Enrollment in Consumer-Directed Health Plans Remains Modest,* 25 HEALTH AFF. (Sept. 26, 2006).

42. *See* Rev.RUI.2002-41, 2002-28 I.R.B. 75 (employer's contribution to HSA is not taxable if funds are used to pay certain medical expenses). *See also,* Melinda Beeuwkes Buntin et al., *Consumer-Directed Health Care: Early Evidence About Effects on Cost and Quality,* HEALTH AFF. (Oct. 24, 2006); Timothy S. Jost & Mark A. Hall, *The Role of State Regulation in Consumer-Driven Health Care,* 31 AM. J. L. & MED 395 (2005).

43. *See* Jost, *supra* note 40, at 119–45; Greaney, *supra* note 16.

reasonable costs.[44] In addition, prices are not readily available, or indeed knowable, ex ante.[45] More fundamentally, it should be clear that CDHC does little to counteract market failures other than moral hazard. Problems of agency, information deficits, and monopoly power in provider markets are left unchecked, and perhaps worsened, under a disintermediated insurance market.[46] Under these doubtful conditions, it is highly improbable that the market will transmit signals that will drive providers to reorganize into more efficient delivery systems.

Indeed, current trends in physician organization suggest that the structure of medical services delivery is moving in the wrong direction. There is considerable evidence that large multi-specialty groups offer clinically superior and seamless delivery of care and perform better in terms of collecting and distributing information, thereby improving quality.[47] A well-functioning financing system should encourage physicians to join such organizations in order to attract more patients by providing higher quality, cost-effective care. And indeed, during the managed care era, there was perceptible movement away from solo and small group physician practice, and in some markets, considerable growth among multi-specialty groups. However, as managed care receded, specialists began to move to mid-size, single-specialty groups, which provide less opportunity for quality improvement. As the Center for Studying Health System Change has concluded, financial incentives under the evolving insurance arrangements rewarded migration to inefficient organizational forms. Large single-specialty groups are able to gain market power to negotiate higher reimbursement without suffering penalties for higher costs or lower quality.[48] Further, these groups can assemble capital so that they can capitalize on flaws in the payment system, typically by moving into high reimbursement, capital-intensive services and opportunistically engaging in self-referral as permitted under exceptions to anti-self referral laws.[49]

---

44. *See* Mark A. Hall & Carl E. Schneider, *Patients as Consumers: Courts, Contracts, and the New Medical Marketplace*, 106 MICH. L. REV. 643, 645 (2008) (analyzing structure and outcome of health care markets for uninsured consumers and concluding, "The market for uninsured medical services is a calamity").

45. *See* Paul B. Ginsburg, *Shopping for Price in Medical Care*, HEALTH AFF. (Feb. 6, 2007), *available at* http://content.healthaffairs.org/cgi/content/full/26/2/w208.

46. *See* Bryan E. Dowd, *Coordinated Agency Versus Autonomous Consumers in Health Care Markets*, 24 Health Aff. 1501, 1502–1504(Nov/Dec 2006).

47. *See* TOWARD A 21ST CENTURY HEALTH SYSTEM: THE CONTRIBUTION AND PROMISE OF PREPAID GROUP PRACTICE (Alain Enthoven & Laura A. Tolen eds., 2004); STEVEN SHORTELL ET AL., REMAKING HEALTH CARE IN AMERICA: BUILDING ORGANIZED DELIVERY SYSTEMS (1996).

48. Hoangmai H. Pham & Paul B. Ginsburg, *Unhealthy Trends: The Future of Physician Services*, 26 HEALTH AFF. 1587 (Nov./Dec 2007).

49. *Id.*

Changes in financing have also altered the dynamics of competition in hospital markets. As noted earlier, concentration in many acute care hospital markets has given hospitals leverage to extract monopoly rents. In addition, the overall shift to passive contracting by insurers has undermined efficient resource allocation in hospital markets. Berenson, Bodenheimer, and Pham trace the impact of these changes:

> With the decline of risk contracting and a return to fee-for-service payment, hospitals were relieved of the need to manage costs for defined populations. They returned to the traditional business model of filling beds with well-insured patients. Faced with growing competition for patients, both from other hospitals and from ambulatory-based care, hospitals quickly adopted strategies dedicated to increasing the flow of patients into the hospital. In short, hospitals resumed what in the 1980s [was] described as a "medical arms race," a form of competition tending to increase, rather than reduce, costs.[50]

Further, physicians have seized upon emergent conditions to compete directly with hospitals, acquiring ownership interests in specialty hospitals, ambulatory surgery centers, diagnostic imaging facilities, and other ancillary service facilities. Anecdotal evidence, including interviews with employers and third-party payers, suggests that providers are able to exploit their agency relationship to induce demand and shift the locus of care to the facilities in which they have ownership interests.[51]

These developments have created new opportunities for both competition and collusion between hospitals and doctors.[52] In some cases, hospitals have established joint ventures with their physicians primarily as a defensive move, while in others they have acted to counter rivals using techniques ranging from vigorous competition to anticompetitive exclusionary tactics. From the perspective of competition policy, the import of emerging physician-hospital rivalry depends on the specifics of the markets involved.[53] In some cases

---

50. Robert A. Berenson et al., *Specialty-Service Lines: Salvos in the New Medical Arms Race*, HEALTH AFF. (July 25, 2006), *available at* http://content.healthaffairs.org/cgi/reprint/25/5/w337?maxtoshow=&HITS=10&hits=10&RESULTFORMAT=&author1=berenson&andorexactfulltext=and&searchid=1&FIRSTINDEX=0&resourcetype=HWCIT

51. *See* Berenson et. al., *Hospital-Physician Relations: Competition, Cooperation or Separation?*, HEALTH AFF. (Dec. 5, 2006),*available at.* http://content.healthaffairs.org/cgi/reprint/26/1/w31?maxtoshow=&HITS=10&hits=10&RESULTFORMAT=&author1=berenson&andorexactfulltext=and&searchid=1&FIRSTINDEX=0&resourcetype=HWCIT

52. *See e.g.*, Rome Ambulatory Surgery Center v. Rome Memorial Hospital, 330 F.Supp 2d 389 (N.D. N.Y. 2004); Gordon v. Lewiston Hospital, 272 F.Supp. 2d 393 (M.D. Pa. 2003). *See also*, Mahan v. Avera St. Luke's 621 N.W. 150 (S.D. 2000).

53. As a matter of economics, staff physicians and hospitals provide complementary products and each side benefits from free rider benefits of its association with the other. *See* David A. Argue, *An Economic Model of Competition Between General Hospitals and*

physician-owned entities may offer a valuable source of new competition in oli-gopolistically structured hospital markets; in others the physicians may be exter-nalizing costs on rival community hospitals. In the absence of the mediating influence of third-party payers, responsibility for sorting out the pro- and anti-competitive cases will fall on legislators, regulators, or antitrust enforcers.

Consumer-Driven Health Care: A Flawed Vehicle for Prompting Organizational Change

Will the new tools of the CDHC era counter fragmentation? Not likely, for several reasons. Insurers in the post-managed care era have largely turned to demand side incentives to assist consumers in making value-focused choices in health care. One tool, widely employed by insurers, is "tiering" which identifies provid-ers who charge lower fees and adjust practice styles to reduce marginally benefi-cial services and offers reduced cost sharing to beneficiaries who choose those providers. A related strategy that operates on the supply side, "pay for perfor-mance," rewards providers with higher reimbursement if they achieve specified cost and quality goals. Both of these approaches are even more vulnerable to the problems of market failure and fragmentation than the managed care methods that preceded them. Autonomous consumers face intractable problems of assembling accurate comparative information to make comparison among tiers and will still be subject to the compelling influence of their physician agents who recommend treatments and suggest referrals. With the bulk of the most costly care ordered by physicians but provided by others, and with many conditions requiring multiple care givers, it is often impossible to accurately target rewards (or penalties based on performance) in the absence of integrated systems.[54] Casting further doubt on the efficacy of these tools is the fact that the payment system rewards some less beneficial services (usually procedures and tests) more than others (such as cognitive services). This makes it hard to induce integrated practices to reduce lucrative services when they are underpaid for alternative services. In these instances, the integrated practice that "does the right thing" and in fact reduces costs may see reduced overall profits even if it is rewarded for its cost saving reductions.[55] Further, some research suggests that payors

---

Physician-Owned Specialty Practices, 20 ANTITRUST HEALTHCARE CHRON (July 2006) (Application of antitrust principles to acute care-specialty hospital disputes must closely evaluate the degree of complementarity in order to determine whether plausible efficien-cies justify challenged conduct).

54. *See* Michael F. Cannon, *Pay-For-Performance: Is Medicare a Good Candidate?* 7 YALE J. HEALTH POL. L.& ETHICS 1 (2007); James C. Robinson, *Managed Consumerism in Health Care*, 24 HEALTH AFF. 1478 (Nov/Dec 2005).

55. For an instructive example of the difficulties of constructing payment systems that reward high performing providers, *see* Hoangmai H. Pham et al., *Redesigning Care Delivery in Response to a High-Performance Network: The Virginia Mason Medical Center*, HEALTH

accounting for only a small fraction of their contracting physicians' patients may face difficulties in inducing physicians to change their practice style.[56]

Even if these cost containment strategies are widely adopted, they may ultimately prove insufficient given the design of CDHC plans. The incentives of consumer-directed plans are most likely to be effective with regard to routine care; for high-cost services, especially those occurring under emergent circumstances, financial incentives will have less impact, and in any event, CDHC plans offer full catastrophic coverage.[57] Further, fee-for-service reimbursement, employed by CDHC plans, focuses on episodes of care rather than treating chronic conditions or encouraging prevention, and thus operates at cross purposes with the cost containment strategies. More fundamentally, the vision of the competitive market constructed by CDHC tends to undermine risk pooling and shift financial burdens from the healthy to the sick and from the privileged to the underprivileged.[58] Ultimately, the "logic" of the CDHC market, which seems inexorable to its proponents, may not withstand political scrutiny, and a "CDHC backlash" seems likely to follow.

CONCLUSION

Viewed from the Panglossian perspective of some market advocates, competition inexorably drives suppliers to form firms or joint ventures and to adopt organizational forms that enable them to provide their services efficiently. But in health care, we have learned that market failure complicates things enormously. Agency issues, information deficits, and moral hazard alter incentives and interfere with rational choice. Managed care once seemed capable of helping to overcome those difficulties, and competition policymakers sought, sometimes quite explicitly, to aid that enterprise. For a variety of reasons antitrust came up short and managed care fell into disfavor. The lesson for policymakers and law enforcers is that the success of a competitive strategy in health care is highly contingent. Supportive measures in law and financing are required to create an organizational infrastructure that counters market failure and incentivizes the private sector to glue together its fragmented elements.

AFF. (July 10, 2007), *available at.* http://content.healthaffairs.org/cgi/reprint/26/1/w31? maxtoshow=&HITS=10&hits=10&RESULTFORMAT=&author1=berenson&andorexactfulltext =and&searchid=1&FIRSTINDEX=0&resourcetype=HWCIT. See also Paul B. Ginsburg & Joy M. Grossman, *When The Price Isn't Right: How Inadvertent Payment Incentives Drive Medical Care,* HEALTH AFF. (Aug. 9, 2005), *available at http://content.healthaffairs.org/cgi/ reprint/hlthaff.w5.376v1.*

56. See Sherry Glied & Joshua Graff Zivlin, *How Do Physicians Behave When Some (But Not All) Their Patients Are in Managed Care?* 21 J. Health Econ., 331 (2002).

57. *See* Jost, *supra* note 40.

58. *See* Robinson, *supra* note 54, at 1483.

7. OF DOCTORS AND HOSPITALS

Setting the Analytical Framework for Managing and Regulating the Relationship*

JAMES F. BLUMSTEIN**

I. INTRODUCTION

The issues surrounding the movement toward integration of physician services and the institutional and economic interests of hospitals raise some of the most critical, delicate, and longstanding health policy and law issues confronting analysts and policymakers.

1. How, and to what extent, should economic considerations factor into medical care decision making? That is, what is the proper relationship between technical medical/scientific factors and economic factors in the medical care decision making context? One traditional view—at one end of a continuum—suggests that the very introduction of economics into medical care decision making corrupts medical judgment and therefore should be avoided.[1] In that view, such conduct is sanctionable, even subject to punitive damages.[2] In some circles, this is still a prevalent point of view,[3] but some courts have recognized the inevitability of including economic factors in physician practice styles[4] while also recognizing that there are limits to the consideration of economics—a point beyond which

---

* This Article is derived from the McDonald-Merrill-Ketcham Lecture, delivered in February 2007 at Indiana University and appearing in the Indiana Health Law Review.

** The research assistance of Jeffrey Breen, class of 2007 at Vanderbilt Law School, is gratefully acknowledged

1. *See, e.g.*, Muse v. Charter Hosp. of Winston-Salem, Inc., 452 S.E.2d 589 (N.C. Ct. App. 1995), *aff'd per curiam*, 464 S.E.2d 44 (N.C. Sup. Ct. 1996).

2. *Id.*

3. For a general discussion of these issues, see James F. Blumstein, *Health Care Law and Policy: Whence and Whither?*, 14 HEALTH MATRIX 35 (2004).

4. *See, e.g.*, Pegram v. Herdrich, 530 U.S. 211 (2000) (recognizing the need to consider cost-benefit trade-offs in the managed care context); Sarka v. Regents of Univ. of Cal., 52 Cal. Rptr. 3d 810 (Cal. Ct. App. 2006) (allowing the student health service to terminate employment of a staff physician for relying too heavily on testing and too little on less expensive clinical medical judgment).

the compromising of professional standards can fairly be labeled as the corruption of medical judgment.[5]

2. What is the appropriate role of physicians, as expert autonomous professionals, in medical care decision making, and, correlatively, what are the appropriate legal, institutional, and regulatory structures to shape that role?[6] Dealing with that set of questions quickly turns to a consideration of different ways of thinking about medical care—about different paradigms or models—and their assumptions and implications.[7] The hospital formatively was structured in reliance on and in response to one way of thinking about medical care—the professional-scientific paradigm. Over time, legal obligations and financial responsibilities have redefined and reshaped the hospital. Hospitals now typically have independent duties to patients,[8] and responsibility for the quality of care that occurs within their walls. Hospitals also have a responsibility to manage within economic parameters and to take into consideration the hospital's institutional interest in quality assurance, marketing and patient flow, and cost containment.

These new environmental realities call into question the traditional "workshop" model[9], in which the hospital serves a role somewhat analogous to that of eBay, as a forum or catalyst for the practice of medicine and for the diagnosis and treatment of patients, but with few or no independent institutional interests at stake. New realities also call into question the tight regulatory vision of the hospital, with a separate medical staff

---

5. *See* Wickline v. State, 239 Cal. Rptr. 810, 820 (1986), *rev. dismissed*, 741 P.2d 613 (1987) (recognizing necessity for and validity of cost-containment programs, but noting that "it is essential that cost limitation programs not be permitted to corrupt medical judgment.").

6. For an important discussion of this issue, see M. Gregg Bloche, *Trust and Betrayal in the Medical Marketplace*, 55 STAN. L. REV. 919 (2002). For a different perspective, see Mark A. Hall, *Law, Medicine, and Trust*, 55 STAN. L. REV. 463 (2002).

7. *See, e.g.*, James F. Blumstein, *Health Care Reform and Competing Visions of Medical Care: Antitrust and State Provider Cooperation Legislation*, 79 CORNELL L. REV. 1459, 1459, 1463–86 (1994) (examining "the competing visions of medical care represented by the professional and the market-based economic paradigm" and "consider[ing] the implications of those visions for the development of public policy.") [hereinafter Blumstein, *Competing Visions*]. For a skeptical view of the market-based alternative to the traditional professional/scientific model, see M. Gregg Bloche, *The Invention of Health Law*, 91 CAL. L. REV. 247 (2003).

8. Sword v. NKC Hosps., Inc., 714 N.E.2d 142 (Ind. 1999) (adopting corporate negligence standard for hospital liability).

9. For a discussion of different models of the role of the hospital, *see* James F. Blumstein & Frank A. Sloan, *Antitrust and Hospital Peer Review*, 51 LAW & CONTEMP. PROBS. 7, 18–24 (Spring 1988); Philip C. Kissam et al., *Antitrust and Hospital Privileges: Testing the Conventional Wisdom*, 70 CAL. L. REV. 595 (1982); Mark V. Pauly & Martin Redisch, *The Not-for-Profit Hospital as a Physicians' Cooperative*, 63 AM. ECON. REV. 87 (1973).

with its own by-laws and, in some jurisdictions, independent legal status.[10] This traditional hospital structure has turned out to be ill-suited for certain new roles being thrust on hospitals. Integrated Delivery Networks (IDNs) (of which physician-hospital joint ventures are an example) have emerged over the past twenty years in part as a response to these new, largely economic, circumstances and in part as a result of the adaptivity constraints on hospitals that stem from a tight, one-size-fits-all regulatory structure that traditionally has defined the organization and governance of hospitals. Part of this Article will describe evidence of how these IDNs have emerged and how they have worked.

3. This Article will conclude that the regulatory flexibility that currently governs IDNs, as contrasted with hospitals, is desirable because it allows responsiveness to new circumstances in the marketplace, even though the evidence of IDN performance is not what some of its advocates might have hoped for to this point. Nevertheless, although overall regulatory rigidity towards IDNs is modest, IDNs still face regulatory landmines, such as the anti-kickback law,[11] which could adversely affect IDNs' ability to adapt and respond to changes in health care and the health care marketplace.[12]

A demonstration project to be initiated in 2007 and to run for several years is designed to determine the risks and benefits of gainsharing,[13] in which physicians and hospitals better align incentives to achieve quality assurance and cost containment objectives.[14] That demonstration should provide a vehicle for assessing, more broadly, the appropriate regulatory

---

10. *Compare* Lewisburg Cmty. Hosp., Inc. v. Alfredson, 805 S.W.2d 756 (Tenn. 1991) (holding medical staff by-laws to be a source of enforceable contract rights) *with* Mason v. Cent. Suffolk Hosp., 819 N.E.2d 1029 (N.Y. 2004) (holding that medical staff by-laws cannot serve as the basis for damages litigation).

11. For discussions of the landmines imposed on market-oriented approaches by the anti-kickback law, see James F. Blumstein, *The Fraud and Abuse Law in an Evolving Health Care Marketplace: Life in the Healthcare Speakeasy*, 22 AM. J. L. & MED. 205 (1996) [hereinafter Blumstein, *Speakeasy*]; James F. Blumstein, *Rationalizing the Fraud and Abuse Statute*, HEALTH AFF., Winter 1996, at 118.

12. For a discussion of general legal problems associated with different IDN forms, see Carl H. Hitchner et al., *Integrated Delivery Systems: A Survey of Organizational Models*, 29 WAKE FOREST L. REV. 273 (1994); *see also* John D. Blum, *Beyond the Bylaws: Hospital—Physician Relationships, Economics, and Conflicting Agendas*, 53 BUFFALO L. REV. 459 (2005) (exploring physician-hospital relations in the current marketplace context).

13. For a discussion of gainsharing and physician financial incentives, see Richard S. Saver, *Squandering the Gain: Gainsharing and the Continuing Dilemma of Physician Financial Incentives*, 98 Nw. U. L. REV. 145 (2003).

14. *See* Centers for Medicare & Medicaid Servs., U.S. Dep't of Health & Human Servs., "Physician-Hospital Collaboration Demonstration," http://www.cms.hhs.gov/DemoProjectsEvalRpts/downloads/PHCD_646_Solicitation.pdf(demonstration project description and request for proposal).

structure for IDNs and hospitals. The existing anti-kickback law may have ample flexibility through its safe harbor provisions and advisory opinion process to modify its unforeseen adverse impact on potentially constructive organizational restructuring in a changed, market-driven environment.

In general, this Article concludes that a regulatory regime should maintain flexibility and the ability to adapt to entrepreneurial opportunities. Regulatory strategy should reduce its emphasis (as in traditional hospital regulation) on micromanaging details of how organizations and institutions are structured. Greater emphasis should be placed on consequences to worry about, such as anti-competitive effects or poor-quality outcomes. The objective of regulatory policy should be to develop a regulatory regime that is neutral to organizational form and that allows institutions and physicians to cooperate or compete according to market conditions, provided that competitive conditions are maintained and quality outcomes are properly encouraged.

II. BACKGROUND AND OVERVIEW

1. **Considering Economics in Health Care Decisionmaking** Just over thirty years ago, Clark Havighurst and I made the case that economics had an important role to play in medical care decision making.[15] Trade-offs had to be made in the allocation of medical care resources, and institutional design was important in structuring decision making so that someone had an incentive to consider costs in resource allocation matters.[16]

The battle over the soul of Professional Standards Review Organizations (PSROs) was the context in which organized medicine attempted to tamp down the emerging policy concerns associated with rapidly escalating costs on public budgets as a result of Medicare and Medicaid. PSROs were designed as professionally-controlled peer review organization networks to help reduce the rate of increase in Medicare and Medicaid costs. Organized medicine aggressively sought to redirect the focus of the program to promotion of health care

---

15. Clark C. Havighurst & James F. Blumstein, *Coping with Quality/Cost Trade-offs in Medical Care: The Role of PSROs*, 70 Nw. U. L. Rev. 6 (1975).

16. *Id.* For other discussions of the importance of institutional structure and design, see James F. Blumstein, *Constitutional Perspectives on Governmental Decisions Affecting Human Life and Health*, 40 Law & Contemp. Probs. 231 (Autumn 1976); Clark C. Havighurst et al., *Strategies in Underwriting the Costs of Catastrophic Disease*, 40 Law & Contemp. Probs. 122 (Autumn 1976).

quality, resisting the cost-containment mission of PSRO originators.[17] Thirty-five years later that battle continues to rage; PSROs still exist, but the name of the organizations has morphed to Peer Review Organizations (PROs),[18] and, most recently, Quality Improvement Organizations (QIOs),[19] demonstrating that the naming and renaming of these entities reflect the agendas being pursued.[20]

A critical component of the Havighurst and Blumstein analysis was to draw a distinction between waste control and cost control. Waste control is the zero-benefit circumstance, what has come to be called "flat of the curve" medical care. Eliminating zero-benefit diagnoses and treatments is uncontroversial, and politicians love the discourse, because it seems that policy makers can achieve something for nothing—lower cost at no reduction in quality through the realization of true economies (i.e., improved efficiency). Undoubtedly, as John Wennberg and colleagues have shown, the opportunity for achievement of true economies—elimination of truly wasteful care—is available and should be pursued.[21] But, from an economics perspective, a more ambitious agenda is to challenge an incentive structure that results in high-cost care with small but only marginal benefits. The problem of cost control (as distinct from waste control) is "marginally productive, not unproductive, care."[22] Care deemed "unnecessary" is "neither wholly useless nor affirmatively harmful" but "could be rendered effectively and appropriately in a shorter time, in a less sophisticated facility, or

---

17. *See* Havighurst & Blumstein, *supra* note 15, at 42 n.123 (discussing organized medicine's efforts to reorient the PSRO program from cost containment to quality assurance).

18. The PSRO program became the PRO program in 1982. Timothy Stoltzfus Jost, *Administrative Law Issues Involving the Medicare Utilization and Quality Control Peer Review Organization (PRO) Program: Analysis and Recommendations*, 50 OHIO ST. L.J. 1, 5 (1989).

19. INST. OF MED., MEDICARE'S QUALITY IMPROVEMENT ORGANIZATION PROGRAM: MAXIMIZING POTENTIAL 19–32 (2006) (describing and providing an overview of QIO program).

20. For a proposal to use QIOs' authority to confer medical malpractice immunity in certain circumstances, *see* James F. Blumstein, *Medical Malpractice Standard-Setting: Developing Malpractice "Safe Harbors" As a New Role for QIOs?*, 59 VAND. L. REV. 1017 (2006).

21. *See, e.g.*, John E. Wennberg, *Variation in Use of Medicare Services Among Regions and Selected Academic Medical Centers: Is More Better?*, THE COMMONWEALTH FUND PUBLICATION NO. 874, Dec. 13, 2005, at 4 (noting "striking regional variations in the proportion of early stage breast cancer patients who undergo lumpectomy" and identifying "idiosyncratic practice style" as the "major source of such widely varying discretionary surgery rates.").

22. Mark A. Hall, *Institutional Control of Physician Behavior: Legal Barriers to Health Care Cost Containment*, 137 U. PA. L. REV. 431, 444 (1988).

on an outpatient basis."[23] In sum, a regime of cost control would result in some forgoing of marginally beneficial care as insufficiently justified based on an evaluation of costs and benefits. This idea later gained traction in managed care, although that movement was not forthright in adopting this analysis or explaining it to consumers.[24]

2. The Effect of Economics on Hospital Management Nearly twenty years ago, Mark Hall, a leading health law and policy commentator, noted that "[c]ost containment pressures will not relent until physicians have undergone a revolutionary change in behavior."[25] Changes in the health care environment, mostly from then-recently adopted prospective payment by Medicare (DRGs), created cost-based pressures on hospitals to manage within specified financial parameters.[26] However, while financial incentives such as prospective payment for hospitals create incentives for fiscal restraint and oversight, such payment-oriented initiatives often overlook the institutional and regulatory setting in which the incentives must be implemented.

Thus, cost-containment efforts such as prospective payment approaches are premised on an assumption that, through management intervention of some type, expensive physician behavior will change substantially.[27] This is the typical assumption of economically-focused, incentives-based interventions—that when incentives change, behavior changes. But, this general assumption, while often correct, can lead to unforeseen or unwanted consequences. If incentives are structured inappropriately, competition can have perverse consequences.[28] Therefore, attentiveness to institutional structure and design is critical in determining whether the outcomes that result from changed incentives are constructive or counter-productive.

---

23. Havighurst & Blumstein, *supra* note 15, at 32.

24. For a graphical depiction of the distinction between waste control and cost control, *see id.* at 17. In 2004, Tennessee adopted a statutory definition of medical necessity in its TennCare program (a Medicaid demonstration) that expressly includes economic factors in the determination of medical necessity and therefore in the scope of a beneficiary's entitlement to coverage. To qualify as medically necessary, a diagnosis or treatment (among other things) must be the "least costly alternative course of diagnosis or treatment that is adequate for the medical condition of the enrollee." TENN.CODE ANN. § 71-5-144(b) (3) (2004).

25. Hall, *supra* note 22, at 444.

26. Under the Medicare prospective payment system for inpatient care, a hospital is paid a certain sum for a patient's hospital stay based on a diagnostic category—a diagnosis-related group (DRG). In general, hospitals are at risk financially if the expenses associated with a hospital stay exceed the sum set prospectively by Medicare for the DRG.

27. Hall, *supra* note 22, at 448.

28. For a discussion of this issue, see Blumstein, *Competing Visions, supra* note 7, at 1494–95 & n.174.

In the hospital context, Hall demonstrated that traditional professional authority was reinforced by a "strong legal infrastructure" that created headwinds for management implementation of or inducement of changed physician behavior. The legal infrastructure insulated physicians from traditional management command-and-control techniques; in place of such direct controls, hospital managers were typically left with coax-and-cajole strategies, which made it particularly difficult for managers to effectuate counter-cultural behavior change in a professional setting.[29]

In the hospital setting, the organizational structure of the hospital, particularly the separate medical staff, supports and insulates professional autonomy of physicians who practice at a hospital.[30] A hospital's structure makes the initiation by management of behavioral change strategies of the medical staff a challenge for management and difficult to implement in a direct, authoritative way. The indirect management techniques characteristic of management of professionals are best suited to behavioral change consistent with the cultural norms of a profession. In the hospital management context, that means that quality improvement strategies, which are consistent with physicians' cultural norms, are likely to meet less resistance than cost-containment strategies, which tend to cut across the physicians' cultural grain. The introduction of economic considerations (e.g., cost containment) might well require structural changes in the institutional organization or design of the hospital, or both, which would better align the financial interests of the hospital and its physician staff.

Because of the primacy of the hospital in the health care arena at the time, Hall contended that the rigid, one-size-fits-all structure of the hospital had to be addressed if cost-containment initiatives were to succeed. Hall observed a

---

29. The cultures of physicians and hospital administrators often clash. *See* Donald E. L. Johnson, *Medical Group Cultures Pose Big Challenges*, HEALTH CARE STRATEGIC MGMT., Nov. 1997, at 2. Unlike managers, physicians tend to be narrowly focused on individual patients, view resources as unlimited (or should be), and have a highly developed professional identity. STEPHEN M. SHORTELL, EFFECTIVE HOSPITAL-PHYSICIAN RELATIONSHIPS 12 (1991). For a skeptical discussion of the effect of financial incentives in clinical decision-making, see David M. Frankford, *Managing Medical Clinicians' Work Through the Use of Financial Incentives*, 29 WAKE FOREST L. REV. 71, 79–83 (1994) (discussing the belief structure that underlies physicians' ways of thinking about medical care). Coax-and-cajole techniques are likely to be more effective in bringing about changes in behavior in the name of quality assurance because quality of care (unlike cost containment) is consistent with traditional physician cultural mores. *See* DONALD M. BERWICK ET AL., CURING HEALTH CARE 164 (1990) (suggesting the use of physician leadership, training, and education to bring about improved quality through coax-and-cajole not command-and-control techniques).

30. Maintenance of professional autonomy is a critical traditional value for physicians. *See* STEPHEN M. SHORTELL ET AL., REMAKING HEALTH CARE IN AMERICA 105–09 (1996); Blumstein & Sloan, *supra* note 9, at 22–24.

"critical need to integrate" the physician staff and hospital management "to bring physicians within the institution's economic framework."[31] Absent change, the prospective payment system potentially posed an "explosive" problem because physicians and hospitals faced "diametrically opposed incentives."[32] That is, physicians faced unconstrained fee-for-service incentives to use resources, while hospitals increasingly were "subject to fiscal restraint" through prospective payment, which placed hospitals at risk financially.[33] For Hall, through some form of integration of the physician staff and hospital management, the "profession's grip on the internal organization of hospitals must be broken in order for cost containment to succeed."[34]

IDNs and physician-hospital joint ventures must be seen in light of Hall's prediction. The struggle for primacy in these evolving organizations is a manifestation of the ongoing struggle for dominance in medical care decision making. An important issue is whether the organizational structure and control reflected in hospitals will be reproduced or varied in the evolving institutional and organizational environment, in which the regulatory structure does not command a predetermined outcome of the struggle.

3. Hospital Organizational Structure Ten years ago, economist Jamie Robinson noted that organizational form should be seen as the "outcome of a competitive process in which particular forms survive" where they best perform the functions that need to be performed.[35] Robinson viewed joint ventures between hospitals and physicians as having certain "advantages of coordination without the disadvantages of bureaucratization."[36] Stephen Shortell, a commentator on Robinson's article, recognized the advantages of institutional flexibility associated with specific organizational forms, but cautioned against "either-or" thinking that would embed a new institutional rigidity by creating "boxes of 'ideal types.'"[37] Shortell recommended maintenance of institutional flexibility and pluralism in institutional design.

---

31. Hall, *supra* note 22, at 505.

32. *Id.* at 507.

33. *Id.*

34. *Id.* This is the vision of the economist—use financial incentives to effect cultural change—but experts who study organizations and their structure tend to be pessimistic about the prospects for such substantial changes, especially among professionals such as physicians. Harrison Trice & Janice M. Beyer, The Cultures of Work Organizations 187 (1993); John G. Day, *Managed Care and the Medical Profession: Old Issues and Old Tensions The Building Blocks of Tomorrow's Health Care Delivery and Financing System*, 3 Conn. Ins. L.J. 1, 12 (1996); Frankford, *supra* note 29, at 80.

35. James C. Robinson, *Physician-Hospital Integration and the Economic Theory of the Firm*, 54 Med Care Res. Rev. 3, 12 (1997).

36. *Id.* at 21.

37. Stephen M. Shortell, Commentary, 54 Med Care Res. Rev. 25, 30 (1997).

As it has turned out, Shortell had good foresight. The IDNs of today come in many sizes, shapes, and structures. A critical benefit, which facilitates this type of pluralism in organizational form and design, is the lack of rigidity of organizational structure of the type that is imposed on hospitals by an entrenched and somewhat inflexible regulatory regime.[38] After two decades of integrated models of medical care, with physician-hospital joint ventures being significant examples,[39] experience suggests that the regulatory regime should, following the recommendation of Shortell, maintain institutional pluralism. No single model of organizational form or design should be locked in from a regulatory perspective, contrary to the approach that has been followed with respect to hospital structure and governance. The objective of regulatory policy in this field should be the promotion of regulatory flexibility and neutrality—a regulatory regime that focuses on results and outcomes, not on structure or governance.

The Gainsharing Demonstration, planned to commence in 2007,[40] should provide a vehicle for evaluating the benefits and identifying the risks of physician-hospital models of integration.[41] It also should suggest approaches for revising existing regulatory pitfalls that can confront physician-hospital relationships. The challenges raised by the federal anti-kickback law will likely be a central focus of the regulatory component of the demonstration. The extraordinary breadth of that statute, which prohibits the knowing and willful use of remuneration (conceived of broadly) to induce or solicit referrals, has placed limits on some potentially promising uses of gainsharing and can serve as a trip wire for institutional arrangements that constitute technical violations. However, the anti-kickback law itself contains two important self-corrective mechanisms that can allow regulatory accommodation without the need for legislative reform—regulatory safe harbors that can immunize constructive behavior that might otherwise run afoul of the broad proscriptions of the anti-kickback law, and advisory opinions, which are essentially case-specific safe harbors and which are legally binding in authorizing certain arrangements despite potential violations of the anti-kickback rules.[42]

---

38. The rigidity in hospital organization and structure stems from accreditation standards of the Joint Commission on Accreditation of Health Care Organizations (JCAHO), state licensure laws, and Medicare regulations. For a discussion of these regulatory rigidities, see Blum, *supra* note 12, at 461–64.

39. For a typology of organizational forms, see Carl H. Hitchner et al., *supra* note 12.

40. *See supra* note 14 and accompanying text.

41. *See* Gail R. Wilensky et al., *Gain Sharing: A Good Concept Getting a Bad Name?*, 26 HEALTH AFF. 58 (2007); *see supra* notes 12–13 and accompanying text.

42. *See* CLARK C. HAVIGHURST ET AL., HEALTH CARE LAW AND POLICY 462–63 (2d ed. 1998); Blumstein, *Speakeasy, supra* note 11; James F. Blumstein, *What Precisely Is "Fraud" in the Health Care Industry?*, WALL ST. J., Dec. 8, 1997, at A25.

III. WAYS OF THINKING ABOUT MEDICAL CARE:
THE DIFFERENT MODELS

As already alluded to in the first two Parts of this Article, there are several differ-ent approaches to thinking about medical care and their implications for public policy analysis. Specifically, these approaches include the professional/scientific model and the market-oriented model. At the threshold, however, it is important to recognize that these models are not intended to be exclusive or preclusive categories. Rather, elements of both models must exist side-by-side in the health care arena. The critical question for public policy is where to place the emphasis in any given set of circumstances—to determine where along a continuum public policy should be directed.

A. The Professional/Scientific Model: Its Assumptions and Implications

The professional/scientific model reflects a response to perceived market fail-ure.[43] It assumes a lack of knowledge on the part of patient-consumers and the scientific expertise of physicians—an asymmetry of information.[44] Patients are not knowledgeable and presumably incapable of becoming sufficiently informed so as to function as knowledgeable consumers in the medical care marketplace. In the face of consumer ignorance, the market cannot function well in the medical care arena.

The implication of this perception of market failure is that decision makers other than patients must be relied on. That is, professional providers, such as physicians, serve as substitute decision makers, displacing consumers. This vests tremendous authority in professionals, based on their scientific expertise, to make decisions that have not only scientific but also economic consequences. As substitute decision makers applying professionally-developed norms and practice standards, physicians under the professional/scientific model ultimately determine individual levels of quality and the volume of services for individuals (and ultimately aggregate levels of utilization and costs).

The professional/scientific model further assumes that diagnosis and treat-ment decisions are not influenced by financial incentives. Instead, such deci-sions are scientifically determined and are unrelated (or only marginally related) to financial incentives, as one would expect to be the case in a market-driven scenario. At one time, the claim that financial incentives do not matter was an

---

43. *See* PAUL STARR, THE SOCIAL TRANSFORMATION OF AMERICAN MEDICINE 226–27 (1982) (arguing that the professional/scientific model was not solely a response to market failure but a contributor to market failure in the service of professional dominance).

44. *See* Kenneth J. Arrow, *Uncertainty and the Welfare Economics of Medical Care*, 53 AM. ECON. REV. 941 (1963), *reprinted in* 26 J. HEALTH POL. POL'Y & L. 851, 871–72 (2001) (iden-tifying market failure in medical care and attributing it, in part, to an asymmetry of infor-mation between patients and physicians).

empirical one. In the last thirty years, however, analysts now realize that economic incentives shape individual and patient decision making and influence the levels of utilization as well as the location in which care is provided (e.g., inpatient vs. outpatient). The claim that financial incentives do not matter now rings more of a normative than an empirical bell; that is, consideration of economics is, or runs the risk of being, corrosive to medical practice and therefore is inappropriate.

B. The Market-oriented Model: Its Assumptions and Implications

The market-oriented response to market failure that stems from lack of consumer knowledge is to provide information and education. The objective of public policy under this view is to improve the flow of comprehensible information to consumers so that they can function better as consumers. One way to achieve this goal would be through the use of information intermediaries to help consumers understand and process unfamiliar information.

The market-oriented approach normatively relies on the importance of patient autonomy—the traditional authority of patients to understand the issues surrounding and to give consent to medical interventions.[45] The impetus for more involvement of patients in their own care responds, at least in part, to a bottom-up concern with patient empowerment.[46] The market-oriented approach also has gained momentum from patients who have shown a remarkable ability to learn about their own (often life-threatening) illnesses and, newly knowledgeable, are eager to participate with their physicians in decision making about their medical situations.

Expanded information flow to patients has been stimulated by the emergence of patient-centered rules of disclosure under the doctrine of informed consent.[47] The Internet and other technological advancements have led to the burgeoning of accessible, comprehensible information, which has resulted in the emergence of a more knowledgeable (and, therefore, empowered) patient. Such patient empowerment is manifested in the shared decision making movement, which is characterized by physicians and patients sharing more evenhandedly in a patient's medical diagnosis and treatment. These conversations between physicians and patients include medical and other (e.g., lifestyle and economic) factors that often inhere in a course of diagnosis and/or treatment.[48] Furthermore, evidence

---

45. "Common law principles recognize personal autonomy by requiring consent before a physician is authorized to touch a patient . . . . To be effective, consent must be 'informed.'" Blumstein, *Competing Visions, supra* note 7, at 1474. For a discussion of the informed consent doctrine, see Peter H. Schuck, *Rethinking Informed Consent*, 103 YALE L. J. 899 (1994).

46. *See* Blumstein, *Competing Visions, supra* note 7, at 1475 & n.66.

47. *See id.* at 1474–75 (discussing the doctrine of informed consent as an inroad on the traditional professional/scientific paradigm).

48. *See, e.g.,* Joseph F. Kasper et al., *Developing Shared Decision-Making Programs to Improve the Quality of Health Care*, 18 QUALITY REV. BULL. 183 (June 1992) (discussing

suggests that patients who participate in their own medical care decision making are more likely to adhere to appropriate courses of treatment.[49]

An important goal for advocates of a more market-oriented approach in health care is to develop an industry structured so that incentives are proper and private decision makers make both self-interested and socially appropriate decisions.

IV. THE HOSPITAL AS THE EMBODIMENT OF THE PROFESSIONAL/SCIENTIFIC MODEL

The organization and structure of the modern American hospital are driven by a regulatory regime that requires the existence of a separate medical staff within the hospital.[50] The separation between general administrative governance and medical staff governance within the hospital is a tool to ensure that professional autonomy in medical decision making will be free from lay influence or control[51] and has a rationale akin to that of the traditional doctrine that banned or restricted the corporate practice of medicine.[52] That is, physicians must be solely responsible for making scientifically-determined medical judgments without interference with those decisions by hospital administrative officials.[53] In some

---

risks of prostate surgery and choices of men about surgical and non-surgical treatment alternatives).

49. Blumstein, *Competing Visions, supra* note 7, at 1475.

50. *See* Blum, *supra* note 12, at 461–64; Hall, *supra* note 22, at 528–32 (providing a good background on the topic). The hospital structure has been referred to as "tripartite" because it contemplates a "board, medical staff, and administration." Blum, *supra* note 12, at 460. This structure is not happenstance but instead imposed by a universal regulatory regime that includes state licensure law, Medicare, and accreditation standards adopted and implemented by The Joint Commission. *Id.* at 461–63.

51. *See* Blumstein & Sloan, *supra* note 9, at 10–12 (discussing the historical evolution of the separate medical staff in the hospital setting).

52. *See* Arnold Rosoff, *The Business of Medicine: Problems with the Corporate Practice Doctrine*, 17 CUMB. L. REV. 485 (1987); Jeffrey F. Chase-Lubitz, Note, *The Corporate Practice of Medicine Doctrine: An Anachronism in the Modern Health Care Industry*, 40 VAND. L. REV. 445 (1987) (discussing the corporate practice of medicine doctrine). The corporate practice doctrine "prohibits corporations from providing professional medical services" and "is primarily inferred from state medical licensure acts, which regulate the profession of medicine and forbid its practice by unlicensed individuals." Berlin v. Sarah Bush Lincoln Health Ctr., 688 N.E.2d 106, 110 (Ill. 1997). One important underlying public policy concern is the "danger[] of lay control over professional judgment." *Id.*

53. *See* Beverly Cohen, *An Examination of the Right of Hospitals to Engage in Economic Credentialing*, 77 TEMP. L. REV. 705 (2004) (discussing the question of whether hospitals can make credentialing decisions on a basis other than professional competence). The JCAHO Accreditation Manual describes credentialing as follows: "Credentialing involves the collection, verification, and assessment of information regarding three critical

jurisdictions, the medical staff bylaws constitute binding and enforceable con-tractual obligations, which limit the authority of the hospital to make decisions about appointing or retaining its medical staff.[54]

The assumption underlying the regulatorily-imposed hospital structure is well-illustrated by *Muse v. Charter Hospital of Winston-Salem, Inc.*[55] *Muse* involved a mental health patient with thirty days of inpatient insurance coverage.[56] As the thirty days wound down, the hospital engaged in a process of discharge plan-ning, leading to the patient's discharge to a public mental health authority for outpatient treatment.[57]

Under conventional doctrine, hospitals are not permitted to abandon patients, but they may transfer patients to other suitable facilities. The question is whether the alternative facility is suitable to the needs of the patient.[58] Under the conven-tional doctrine, the abandonment inquiry in *Muse* would have focused on the suitability of the public mental health outpatient service to which the patient had been discharged. Instead, the court used a different analysis and held that a "hos-pital has the duty not to institute policies or practices which interfere with the doctor's medical judgment."[59] Although the doctor signed the patient's discharge papers, the hospital was found liable for wanton and willful conduct since it adopted a policy of discharge planning that seemed to the court to require patient discharge upon the expiration of the patient's insurance coverage.[60] Since the physician actually discharged the patient, the hospital was liable because it adopted a policy or practice that "interfered with the medical judgment" of the patient's attending physician.[61] One interpretation of what it meant for the hos-pital to "interfere" with the physician's medical judgment was that the hospital expected the physician to include in his decision making the consideration of the economic reality that the patient's insurance coverage was about to (and did) expire.

---

parameters: current licensure; education and relevant training; and experience, ability, and current competence to perform the requested privilege(s)." 2007 Comprehensive Accreditation Manual for Hospitals: The Official Handbook (CAMH) MS-15 (2007). Although these terms do not necessarily preclude the use of economic factors, they also do not explicitly include them. *Id.*

54. Lewisburg Cmty. Hosp., Inc. v. Alfredson, 805 S.W.2d 756, 759 (Tenn. 1991); *but see* Mason v. Cent. Suffolk Hosp., 819 N.E.2d 1029, 1030 (N.Y. 2004).

55. Muse v. Charter Hosp. of Winston-Salem, Inc., 452 S.E.2d 589 (N.C. Ct. App. 1995), *aff'd per curiam*, 464 S.E.2d 44 (N.C. Sup. Ct. 1996).

56. *Id.*, 452 S.E.2d at 593.

57. *Id.*

58. *See* Payton v. Weaver, 182 Cal. Rptr. 225 (1982).

59. *Muse*, 452 S.E.2d at 594.

60. *Id.*

61. *Id.*

The organization and structure of the hospital, therefore, seem to reflect an assumed need to insulate the members of the physician staff from the consideration of cost and other non-medical factors in their decision making. *Muse* shows a very low threshold for concluding that professional medical judgment is corrupted—encompassing, in the *Muse* case at least, the possibility that any consideration of economic factors in a physician's decision making process is an impermissible corruption of professional medical judgment.

The organization and structure of the hospital bear a certain resemblance to the structure of a university in which members of the faculty are autonomous on matters of educational decision making and protected under the norm of academic freedom from inappropriate administrative oversight. The separate medical staff contemplates a model of governance in which physicians enjoy medical governance prerogatives akin to the academic freedom of university faculty. This structure suggests very limited control by hospital administration and is consistent with viewing hospitals as a physicians' workshop. This traditional "workshop" vision of the hospital can be referred to as an eBay model of hospital governance and function.

In this vision, hospitals are not seen as having independent institutional interests; they are locations or forums in which patients receive care and physicians practice their profession. This structure, however, raises questions about routine management decisions that can affect the institutional interest of a hospital. For example, hospitals may seek to contract selectively or exclusively with certain physicians or physician groups for a variety of institutional reasons related to cost and/or quality issues. This raises the issue of economic credentialing—can hospitals base staff decisions on criteria other than physician competence?[62]

The question of economic credentialing demonstrates the tension between the traditional "workshop" or eBay vision of the hospital and the emerging reality that hospitals have their own institutional interests that need to be addressed and accommodated. Once it is recognized and acknowledged that hospitals have their own institutional interests, it becomes axiomatic that they will need to develop mechanisms by which they can attend to those interests.[63]

---

62. See Cohen, *supra* note 53, for a discussion of economic credentialing.

63. See Blumstein & Sloan, *supra* note 9, at 91, for an interesting discussion of how antitrust law can help to encourage hospital decision making more nearly to reflect the "mode of decisionmaking of more traditional economic entities such as firms." Blumstein and Sloan argue that "historically entrenched attitudes, professional prerogatives, economic dependence, institutional structural rigidities, and legal doctrines have created headwinds against the kind of hospital role" in which hospitals "will generally act in accordance with consumer interests to the extent that the external environment permits." *Id.* They advocate use of antitrust doctrine more aggressively "in compelling hospitals to act more like competitive economic entities." *Id.* Concentrating on "the most risky areas—physician cartel behavior," they recommend that "hospitals shoulder the burden of demonstrating the procompetitive character of decisions that, based on history

Physicians practicing within a hospital have a strong influence on the hospital's institutional interests related to such issues as medical errors, overall quality of care (and attendant concerns about reputation and liability), and cost of care (with hospitals often financially at risk for consistently above-average costs of services). Under such circumstances, it is important that medical practice in hospitals be brought in from the economic cold. Since hospitals have their own institutional interests, it is no longer desirable or probably even viable for medical practice within a hospital to remain outside the economics of the hospital or outside the authority structure of the management of the hospital.[64]

In a world where organizational form is the "outcome of a competitive process in which particular forms survive" because they best perform the functions that need to be performed,[65] it is not surprising that hospitals would seek to develop and embrace organizational forms and structures that better accommodate their own institutional interests and objectives. The built-in rigidity of the regulatory regime governing hospitals predictably led to the pursuit of other mechanisms that better perform certain functions that need to be performed—bringing economic and other non-medical factors into the decision making process and seeking greater hospital authority to assert quality-enhancement and cost-containment objectives.

V. THE EVOLVING EXTERNAL ENVIRONMENT AND ITS IMPACT

A conclusion in Part IV was that the traditional "workshop" or eBay model of the hospital is no longer appropriate because hospitals increasingly have independent institutional interests that need to be addressed and accommodated. This Part will identify and explain two of the most significant external factors that have led to the evolution of these independent institutional interests of hospitals.

A. Quality of Care
The first factor is a hospital's interest in promoting and managing the quality of care, including medical errors, that is provided in the hospital. This interest has both a positive and a negative component.

The positive component concerns a hospital's desire to promote its own reputation for quality and for managing effectively to assure quality[66] in a

---

and the insights of social science research, one can reasonably label prima facie anticompetitive." *Id.*

64. *See* Hall, *supra* note 22, at 507.

65. Robinson, *supra* note 35, at 21.

66. *See* William M. Sage & Peter J. Hammer, *A Copernican View of Health Care Antitrust,* 65 LAW & CONTEMP. PROBS. 241, 252–53 (Fall 2002), for a discussion of the

market-driven, competitive environment.[67] To achieve this objective, hospitals have an incentive to seek out organizational structures that allow hospital management more directly to design and implement quality-enhancement strategies that are consistent with the hospital's interest in promoting its reputation for quality. Pursuit of this institutional objective is particularly appropriate in light of the revelation by the Institute of Medicine of the degree to which medical errors occur in hospitals and of the systemic nature of those errors,[68] which not only lend themselves to an institutionally-oriented response but require it.[69]

The negative component of a hospital's interest in quality of care is that hospitals are increasingly responsible from a liability perspective for medical mal-occurrences that transpire within their four walls. The hospital's liability risk has grown along two related but distinct pathways—direct and vicarious liability.

Increasingly, there is a recognition that hospitals have a direct duty to their patients in the following four areas: (i) to maintain safe and adequate facilities and equipment; (ii) "to select and retain only competent physicians;" (iii) to oversee all persons who practice medicine and provide patient care within their walls; and (iv) to formulate, adopt, and enforce rules and policies to ensure quality of care for patients.[70] The breach of a direct duty to a patient can result in liability. Clearly, the hospital's direct duty to assure the provision of quality care to patients being treated within its walls places a managerial responsibility on the hospital as an institution. In turn, such responsibility leads hospital administrators to be concerned about how to implement that responsibility and to ensure compliance given the governance structure of hospitals. For example, the separate medical staff structure provides hospital managers with limited direct authority with respect to the selection or retention of physicians, even though the hospital

---

hospital's interest in promoting quality for its own institutional, competitive reasons in a managed care setting.

67. *See* Thomas E. Kauper, *The Role of Quality of Health Care Considerations in Antitrust Analysis*, 51 LAW & CONTEMP. PROBS. 273 (Spring 1988), for a discussion of the procompetitive aspects of promoting health care quality in a competitive, market-based environment.

68. *See* INSTITUTE OF MEDICINE, TO ERR IS HUMAN: BUILDING A SAFER HEALTH SYSTEM (1999).

69. *See* James F. Blumstein, *The Legal Liability Regime: How Well Is It Doing in Assuring Quality, Accounting for Costs, and Coping with an Evolving Reality in the Health Care Marketplace?*, 11 ANNALS HEALTH L. 125 (2002), for a discussion of the liability implications of the IOM findings.

70. *See, e.g.*, Thompson v. Nason Hosp., 591 A.2d 703, 707 (Pa. 1991) (describing the hospital's duties). *See generally* Sword v. NKC Hosp., Inc., 714 N.E.2d 142 (Ind. 1999) (adopting corporate negligence standard for hospital liability).

incurs liability for a failure to select and retain only competent physicians.[71] In sum, even though hospitals are typically left to manage by coax and cajole, not command and control, they are responsible, nevertheless, for assuring the non-negligent provision of quality care for patients.

Hospitals also have faced vicarious liability for negligence in patient care. For employees (e.g., physicians and nurses), the traditional doctrine of respondeat superior has been applied to hospitals.[72] In the hospital setting, even though most physicians with practice privileges are not hospital employees, courts increasingly have imposed vicarious liability on hospitals under principles of ostensible agency.[73] Under ostensible agency doctrine, a principal should be held liable for the negligent conduct of its agent if the person dealing with the agent had a reasonable belief (for which the principal can be held accountable) that the agent was authorized to act for its principal.[74]

One troubling concern with imputation of liability under ostensible agency is that the doctrine focuses analytically (in substantial part) (a) on the reasonableness of the patient's belief that the physician was the agent of the hospital and (b) on the conduct of the hospital in creating, reinforcing, or disabusing patients of that perception. The questions of patient perception and the reasonableness of the hospital's conduct in either reinforcing or offsetting that perception may not address the real underlying concern—finding a satisfying doctrinal substitute for respondeat superior in the absence of an employer-employee relationship. There is a considerable question of whether the application of the ostensible agency doctrine in the hospital context has intellectual integrity or whether it is an intellectual half-way house.

To have doctrinal integrity, the ostensible agency doctrine must allow a hospital to defend against liability by successfully challenging the reasonableness of a patient's belief that a physician is an agent of the hospital. Yet in *Grewe*, an ostensible agency case, the Michigan Supreme Court left open the question of

---

71. *See* Elam v. College Park Hosp., 183 Cal. Rptr. 156, 162–64 (Ct. App. 1982) (recognizing that although peer reviews for quality purposes are conducted by the independent medical staff, the hospital itself is ultimately responsible for assuring quality and failure in that process leads to liability under the doctrine of corporate negligence).

72. *See, e.g.,* McDonald v. Hampton Training Sch. for Nurses, 486 S.E.2d 299 (Va. 1997) (finding hospital liable for negligence of physician when physician is an employee of the hospital); Bernardi v. Cmty. Hosp. Ass'n, 443 P.2d 708, 713 (Colo. 1968) (applying respondeat superior principles to hospital liability for negligence of nurse employee).

73. *See, e.g.,* Grewe v. Mount Clemens Gen. Hosp., 273 N.W.2d 429, 434–35 (Mich. 1978)

74. *See, e.g., id.* at 434. Under *Grewe*, a plaintiff is obligated to establish (1) the patient had a reasonable belief in the agent's authority; (2) the patient's belief was generated by an act or the neglect of the hospital; and (3) the patient is not negligent—that is, the patient reasonably relied on his or her perception of the physician as the agent of the hospital. *Id.*

what the result would be "if plaintiff knew or should have known" that the relationship of the physician and the hospital was not that of agent and principal.[75] Given the nature of the doctrine and the elements of the doctrine, it is startling to have the *Grewe* court leave that issue open. Other courts applying ostensible agency or a variant (agency by estoppel)[76], however, have declined to give effect to obvious notices placed in an emergency room for the purpose of notifying the patient that the physicians practicing in the emergency room were independent contractors and not employees of the hospital.[77] This type of holding, which seems to challenge the doctrinal core of ostensible agency,[78] calls into question the integrity and viability of the doctrine in the hospital setting.

The doctrinal inadequacies of ostensible agency have led some courts to look for a more satisfying doctrine—one imposing on hospitals a non-delegable duty to assure non-negligent patient care within the hospital. Some courts have been reluctant to embrace the concept,[79] and even when embracing the concept in the context of an emergency room, courts accepting the doctrine have modified it. For example, in *Simmons v. Tuomey Regional Medical Center*, South Carolina purported to accept the non-delegation principle, imposing a non-delegable duty on hospitals to ensure the rendering of competent service to patients in the emergency room setting.[80] The *Simmons* court was critical of ostensible agency as a rationale for hospital liability because (i) it believed that requiring a finding that the hospital acted culpably in representing that it was the principal and the physicians were its agents was inappropriate and unnecessary and (ii) it believed that proof of the patient's reliance on the hospital's representation was also inappropriate and unnecessary.[81] Accordingly, the court imposed, as a matter of policy, a non-delegable duty on hospitals to render competent care to patients in its emergency room.[82] In describing the nature of the non-delegable duty, however, the *Simmons* court reintroduced many of the elements of ostensible agency such as the reasonableness of the patient's belief that the physician was a hospital employee.[83]

---

75. *Id.* at 435.

76. *See* Baptist Mem'l Hosp. Sys. v. Sampson, 969 S.W.2d 945, 947 n.2 (Tx. 1998) (noting that "[m]any courts use the terms ostensible agency, apparent agency, apparent authority, and agency by estoppel interchangeably" and that, "[a]s a practical matter, there is no distinction among them").

77. Clark v. Southview Hosp. & Family Health Ctr., 628 N.E.2d 47, 54 (Ohio 1994).

78. See *Baptist Mem'l Hosp. Sys.*, 969 S.W.2d at 950, for an example of a court giving effect under ostensible agency to hospital signage that informed emergency room patients of the physician-hospital relationship,

79. *See, e.g., id.* at 948–49.

80. Simmons v. Tuomey Reg'l Med. Ctr., 533 S.E.2d 312, 322 (S.C. 2000).

81. *See id.* at 320–21.

82. *Id.* at 322.

83. *Id.* at 323.

While the courts still struggle with the appropriate doctrinal formula for vicarious liability, the fact remains that courts have expanded hospitals' liability for the medical maloccurrences of their physicians and other medical care providers. Hospitals, regardless of whether they are positively seeking to advance quality as a reputation-based marketing plus or negatively concerned about the liability risks of poor quality and high error rates, are confronted with a situation in which hospital management needs to address and accommodate rationally the hospitals' own institutional interests. To the extent that the existing hospital organization and governance structure is not conducive to the pursuit of hospitals' own institutional interests regarding quality assurance, they are predictably going to seek out alternative arrangements and institutional structures that allow more direct hands-on management of the hospital for the achievement of quality-of-care objectives.

B. Cost Containment

The hospital's structure makes the introduction of economic considerations difficult. As noted previously, the hospital's structure is reflective of the professional/scientific model in which economic considerations are marginalized.[84] The structure of the hospital assumes that medical decision making is largely technical, exclusively a matter of scientific expertise, and entirely within the sphere of autonomous physician control. This rigid one-size-fits-all structure is an impediment to effective cost-containment initiatives implemented by hospitals. Because cost-containment is counter-cultural for physicians, and because the hospital governance structure compels reliance on coax-and-cajole techniques rather than command-and-control techniques of management, achieving hospitals' institutional cost-containment objectives is even more of a challenge than achieving a hospital's quality-of-care objectives.[85]

Yet, for hospitals, addressing and coping with cost-containment pressures have become more acute concerns. In his work on hospitals and cost containment, Mark Hall noted a "critical need to integrate" the physician staff and hospital management "to bring physicians within the institution's economic framework."[86] He also noted, however, the institutional constraints that impeded that development.[87]

---

84. *See supra* Parts III.A, IV.

85. See Frankford, *supra* note 29; Jonathan J. Frankel, Note, *Medical Malpractice Law and Health Care Cost Containment: Lessons for Reformers from the Clash of Cultures*, 103 YALE L.J. 1297 (1994), for a discussion of the problem of cost-containment from the perspective of a hostile physician culture.

86. Hall, *supra* note 22, at 505.

87. *Id.* at 505–07.

The shift in the way hospitals are paid—by Medicare and some private insurance carriers—has resulted in hospitals being expected to assume financial risk that they had not previously been expected to absorb. Previously, hospitals had been paid on a retrospective reimbursement basis, premised on cost reimbursement. If patients have insurance in such an environment, hospital finance is relatively straightforward. Hospitals spend money on patient care, and insurance carriers reimburse those expenditures. In such circumstances, hospitals have no substantial independent financial interests; they are not at risk financially.

When Medicare adopted a prospective payment system for inpatient hospital services in the 1980s, however, hospitals were expected to operate within pre-set fiscal parameters. If they did not manage their costs, they could no longer seek after-the-fact reimbursement for excess costs as they had done in the past. Instead, hospitals' revenues were limited to the amount of the prospective payment set by Medicare. A similar dynamic resulted from private insurers and health plans, which placed financial limits on hospitals through discounted pricing or capitation payment approaches. These tighter fiscal constraints imposed independent financial interests on hospitals, but the traditional hospital organizational and governance structure was premised on a model that assumed away the significance and even the legitimacy of cost considerations in medical care decision making.

The evolution of the health care marketplace allowed hospitals to pursue different roles, providing an opportunity for hospitals to reverse, to some extent, the power relationships with doctors—for example, by bidding for managed care contracts with health plans, thereby securing control of patient flow and channeling patients to physicians. The market and the confining structure of the hospital provided an incentive and an opportunity for hospitals to break out of the traditional "workshop" type of physician-hospital relationship. Sometimes, hospitals have incentives to cooperate with physicians, and sometimes they prefer strategically to compete with physicians. These new relationships, however, are occurring outside the traditional hospital-physician relationship structure.

The various models of physician-hospital relationships emerged in response to the reality that medical care is functioning in a market-based environment. They reflect a shift towards greater recognition and acceptance of market-based assumptions and realities. The traditional confining hospital structure was crafted under the controlling assumptions of the professional/scientific paradigm. The newer and still-emerging physician-hospital relationships that are developing outside the traditional hospital structure are entities and relationships that are premised on market-oriented principles and adaptive to the emergence of and legitimation of the market-oriented paradigm. IDNs, therefore, cannot be understood outside the need for physicians and hospitals to develop new structures to manage costs and promote quality (as good business practices).

VI. THE EVOLUTION OF INTEGRATED DELIVERY NETWORKS

As the above theoretical discussion suggests, there appears to be a consensus among empirical scholars who have studied the matter that physician-hospital integration "reflects providers' organizational responses to competitive pressures from rapidly expanding managed care health insurance."[88] That is, IDNs reflect the influence of and are a response to the emergence of the market model. They reflect no single prototype and can be led by hospitals or by physician groups.[89]

A. Competing Hypotheses and Rationales

The question has arisen as to the likely consequences of hospital-physician integration. Is such integration likely to result in efficiency gains? That is, do the more efficient integrated organizations offer *lower* prices to managed care plans through lower levels of utilization or other efficiencies in the production of medical care services? Or, alternatively, is integration really an attempt by providers to improve bargaining power (through enhanced market power) with managed care plans? Such a story would suggest *increased* prices instead of lower prices[90] and would also suggest that the IDNs were not designed or used for a fundamental restructuring of the physician dominance that characterized the traditional hospital structure and that had stemmed from a non-market-based premise.

B. The Evidence

Although the evidence is not uniform on the issues,[91] there is considerable evidence that hospitals with an integrated organizational structure do not have lower costs than unintegrated hospitals.[92] Hospital-physician integration seems to be a "strategic response to counter the rising monopsony power of managed care and is one of the sources of the recent increase in health care costs."[93]

---

88. Allison Evans Cuellar & Paul J. Gertler, *Strategic Integration of Hospitals and Physicians*, 25 J. HEALTH ECON. 1, 1 (2006).

89. For typologies of various forms of IDNs, *see id.* at 8–11; Hitchner et al., *supra* note 12.

90. This market-power scenario was a concern expressed by the recent report of the U.S. Department of Justice and the Federal Trade Commission. FED. TRADE COMM'N & DEP'T OF JUSTICE, IMPROVING HEALTH CARE: A DOSE OF COMPETITION 13 (2004) (Executive Summary).

91. *See, e.g.,* Federico Ciliberto & David Dranove, *The Effect of Physician-Hospital Affiliations on Hospital Prices in California*, 25 J. HEALTH ECON. 29, 37 (2006) (finding no evidence that vertical integration resulted in higher prices in California hospitals during the 1990s).

92. Cuellar & Gertler, *supra* note 88, at 11.

93. *Id.* at 26. The FTC and DOJ also expressed this concern in their joint report. *See* FED. TRADE COMM'N & DEP'T OF JUSTICE, *supra* note 90, at 13 (Executive Summary).

That is, much evidence seems to support the market-power explanation of IDNs, not the true efficiency explanation.[94] IDNs, in general, seem not to have been vehicles through which hospitals have asserted authority or developed pathways around traditional medical staff relationships to introduce cost-containment measures. "[I]ntegrated organizations have higher prices than stand-alone hospitals," with greater effects on exclusive arrangements and in less competitive markets.[95] In addition, at least in some studied areas, procedure rates seem to increase for hospitals with physician-hospital arrangements.[96] The result has been that expenditures in hospitals with physician-hospital organizations (PHOs) were three percent higher than expenditures of patients in non-PHO hospitals.[97]

In a survey of evidence, Lawton Burns and Mark Pauly confirmed the conclusion that "affiliating or linking outpatient care with a large and complex inpatient institution tends to raise the marginal and average cost of both inpatient and outpatient care."[98] IDNs have not, in general, achieved a high level of clinical integration, which could lead to efficiencies and higher quality. Overall, Burns and Pauly are pessimistic about the future of IDNs, observing that "[t]he proportion of hospitals with these types of alliances peaked in 1996 and has declined ever since."[99]

What conclusion, if any, can be drawn from this brief survey of evidence? It seems that IDNs have not fulfilled at least one aspiration—more efficient and lower cost delivery of medical care. It seems the objective that Mark Hall set out nearly twenty years ago—to change physician behavior and to reduce physician dominance[100]—has not (or at least has not yet) been achieved. But excessive pessimism also seems unwarranted. From a regulatory perspective, IDNs are not subject to the institutional or organizational rigidity of hospitals. Their organizational form can be flexible, driven by market realities, and unconstrained by the one-size-fits-all straitjacket of the hospital regulatory structure. This presents an opportunity for entrepreneurship and responsiveness to quality and cost challenges. IDNs have been and are likely to remain a battleground for the

---

94. *See, e.g.,* Alfredo G. Esposto, *Contractual Integration of Physician and Hospital Services,* 8 J. MGMT. & GOV'T 49 (2004) (concluding that cost-saving is not a basis for physician-hospital integration).

95. Cuellar & Gertler, *supra* note 88, at 26.

96. *See* Kristin Madison, *Hospital-Physician Affiliations and Patient Treatments, Expenditures, and Outcomes,* 39 HEALTH SERVICES RES. 257, 264–66 (2004) (studying certain cardiac procedures).

97. *Id.* at 272.

98. Lawton R. Burns & Mark V. Pauly, *Integrated Delivery Networks: A Detour on the Road to Integrated Health Care?,* 21 HEALTH AFF. 128, 130 (July/August 2002).

99. *Id.*

100. Hall, *supra* note 22, at 507.

maintenance of physician control and dominance, in partnership with provider hospitals that apparently would rather combine than combat.

Hospitals have real and justified fears of alienating physicians, who are the caregivers and can influence patients. IDNs allow for flexible ordering of physician relationships with hospitals and other types of organizational forms. They may not have fulfilled the objectives that many set for them, and regulatory vigilance of their potential for anticompetitive effects is certainly appropriate. But they remain an important organizational form—a potential vehicle for accommodating marketplace demands for cost sensitivity and quality assurance. The flexibility that still characterizes the regulatory regime for IDNs is an important plus; the strategic goal is to develop incentives appropriately so that IDNs can be used constructively to improve performance in containing costs and improving quality.

VII. PHYSICIAN-HOSPITAL INTERACTION: THE FUTURE

Recent survey evidence indicates that hospitals are increasingly fearful of competition from physicians and concerned about threats to "long-standing collaborative relationships between physicians and hospitals."[101] This includes a concern by hospital administrators that competition between physicians and hospitals could "threaten physicians' long-standing orientation toward supporting hospitals' social missions, including caring for the uninsured."[102]

From the perspective of traditional community hospitals, physician-owned specialty hospitals and other facilities (such as laboratories) pose a competitive threat. According to a 2005 survey, this threat has increased from that perceived by hospital administrators in the previous 2000 survey.[103] This increasingly significant marketplace phenomenon has meant that hospitals face "growing competition" with physicians "over services that had once been within the hospital domain."[104] Many times the hospital is competing with its own medical staff, who are "opening an ambulatory surgery center [or] diagnostic center" and

---

101. Robert A. Berenson et al., *Hospital-Physician Relations: Cooperation, Competition, or Separation?*, 26 HEALTH AFF. 31, 32 (2007).

102. *Id.* One surveyed hospital administrator expressed concern as follows: Doctors used to feel that in return for having the hospital as a place to care for their patients and earn income, they should contribute to the hospital, taking ED call, participating on committees, improving quality. Now they say to the hospital, screw you. . . . Many don't even come to the hospital any more." *Id.*

103. *Id.* at 33.

104. *Id.* at 34.

"shifting . . . services from hospital control to physician control."[105] This has led some surveyed hospital administrators to "consider[] the competition with physicians as actually more intense than with other hospitals in the community."[106]

This type of emerging competition between hospitals and physicians (including their own medical staff) highlights the point raised earlier—hospitals increasingly have their own independent institutional interests in the evolving health care marketplace. It reinforces the earlier critique of the traditional, rigid, one-size-fits-all regulatory regime of the modern American hospital. That traditional regulatory structure was a product of adherence to a vision—the professional/scientific paradigm—that no longer reflects the exclusive focus and function of the modern hospital. Hospitals are not merely workshops for physicians and do more than provide a forum or location in which physicians provide services to ignorant patients while the hospitals have no institutional interest in or accountability for what goes on within their four walls.

In response to growing physician competition, some hospitals will pursue cooperative or co-optative strategies, while others will seek to compete.[107] Cooperative or co-optative hospital strategies are often driven by a "'half a loaf is better than none'" rationale.[108] Facing a potential loss of revenues to a freestanding (typically physician-owned) entity, some hospitals will form a joint venture with physicians in order "to retain some of the revenues they otherwise might lose."[109] This may be driven by the rationale "that the collaboration will help assure continued physician referral of patients who need inpatient hospital services."[110] In general, hospital officials view joint ventures of this type with physicians as "a way to reduce potential lost revenues from outmigration of services to physicians."[111]

Physicians are attracted to this type of joint venture with hospitals "because of their capital, their management experience, and the broader pool of patients that might be attracted."[112] Such joint ventures may also be a "way to avoid risky, head-on competition with the hospital."[113] Some physicians, however, have sought to partner with independent companies that will "contribute capital and management expertise to a joint venture with a physician group."[114] By forming a joint venture with an independent company, physicians are indeed engaging in

---

105. *Id.* at 35.
106. *Id.*
107. *Id.* at 37.
108. *Id.* at 38.
109. *Id.*
110. *Id.*
111. *Id.*
112. *Id.*
113. *Id.*
114. *Id.* at 39.

direct competition with hospitals for services previously and historically provided by hospitals.

There is a concern that the legal regulatory regime may inhibit constructive cooperative arrangements. Relaxing restrictions on gainsharing might be an example of possible reform,[115] and the gainsharing demonstration should provide insight for consideration of regulatory reform in the anti-kickback and anti-self-referral arenas.[116]

Hospitals that might want to compete with, rather than cooperate with or co-opt, their staff physicians have traditionally faced an uncertain regulatory landscape. More recently (as described below), courts seem to recognize that hospitals have a legitimate interest in pursuing their own independent economic interests and have allowed hospitals to pursue policies designed to compete with physicians on their medical staffs.

The traditional hospital structure grants physicians control over medical staff competence through the credentialing process. The difficult issue arises when hospitals seek to incorporate criteria other than medical competence into the credentialing process. This is an understandable hospital response to competition from physicians, especially those on the hospital's medical staff.

As hospitals seek to compete on quality and price/cost, they seek greater control over decisions that affect their ability to manage quality and cost. Exclusive contracting with physicians or physician groups may be a way for hospitals to impose accountability for quality assurance on the medical staff, with a contractual means of enforcement. Similarly, a hospital may seek to impose conflict-of-interest rules, which, in other economic sectors, would be deemed conventional protections against the inappropriate appropriation of corporate opportunity. Because physicians have significant influence on referrals, hospitals may reasonably fear that physicians will direct well-insured patients to their own facilities while referring underinsured or uninsured patients to the hospitals for service. In most other sectors, such self-defensive measures would be self-evidently rational and legitimate, but there has been tremendous controversy in the hospital sector over whether such economic credentialing is appropriate or legal.[117]

Recent court decisions seem to show receptivity to hospital claims in this arena. Courts appear more comfortable with hospital initiatives that focus on the institutional interest of the hospital itself. For example, in *Baptist Health v. Murphy*,[118] a private nonprofit hospital excluded physicians from the medical

---

115. *See, e.g.,* Wilensky et al., *supra* note 41; *see also* MEDICARE PAYMENT ADVISORY COMMISSION, REPORT TO CONGRESS: PHYSICIAN-OWNED SPECIALTY HOSPITALS (March 2005), *available at* http://www.medpac.gov/documents/Mar05_SpecHospitals.pdf *See also* Saver, *supra* note 13.

116. *See supra* note 14.

117. For a recent consideration of these issues, see Cohen, *supra* note 53.

118. Baptist Health v. Murphy, 2006 Ark. LEXIS 58 (Ark. 2006).

staff if they acquired or held an ownership or investment interest in a competing hospital. The Arkansas Supreme Court rejected a challenge to the hospital's action.[119]

Analogously, in *City of Cookeville v. Humphrey*, the Tennessee Supreme Court allowed a public hospital to "close" its imaging department by entering into an exclusive contract with a radiology group.[120] The hospital faced competition from a physician-owned imaging facility and was concerned about losing business to it. The physicians who owned the imaging facility were members of the medical staff at the public hospital. Notably, the court held that no hearing under the medical staff bylaws was necessary since the purpose of the hearing procedure was to determine medical competency, and the decision to close the imaging department was based on non-medical considerations.[121] The hospital's "decision to close the staff of the Imaging Department is a business decision," so a "due process hearing would be purposeless."[122] No hearing is required as an abstract matter, but is required if relevant facts that can lead to a finding of liability and a remedy are placed in controversy.[123]

In *Mahan v. Avera St. Luke's*, the South Dakota Supreme Court similarly allowed a hospital to close its staff for certain procedures.[124] The court held that the hospital's medical staff bylaws did not apply because the hospital decision in question was "not about appointments or the assignment or curtailment of privileges."[125] Instead, the decision was "about an administrative decision to close [the hospital's] staff for certain procedures," so the medical staff by-laws "do not apply."[126] The South Dakota court was expressly solicitous of the hospital's interest in establishing "clear lines of management authority" and worried about the "confusion" that would ensue if the hospital's lay board had only a "minimal amount of control over its medical staff."[127]

---

119. *Id.* The Arkansas Supreme Court rejected a claim that the hospital's conduct violated the federal anti-kickback law. Had there been such a violation, the hospital's policy would have been invalid as a matter of public policy under state law. *See* Polk County v. Peters, 800 F. Supp. 1451, 1456 (D. Tex. 1992) (refusing to enforce a contract between a physician and a hospital in a claim for damages because the contract violated federal anti-kickback law and therefore was unenforceable under state law as against public policy).

120. City of Cookeville v. Humphrey, 126 S.W.3d 897, 907 (Tenn. 2004).

121. *Id.*

122. *Id.*

123. "[D]ue process protections are not triggered when the process would not serve any useful purpose or result in a remedy." *Id.* (citing Codd v. Velger, 429 U.S. 624, 627 (1977)).

124. Mahan v. Avera St. Luke's, 621 N.W.2d 150, 163 (S.D. 2001).

125. *Id.* at 157.

126. *Id.*

127. *Id.* at 159.

In *Radiation Therapy Oncology, P.C. v. Providence Hospital*,[128] a private non-profit hospital's board of directors decided to establish an "integrated and unified cancer-care center where both radiation-oncology and medical-oncology services would be delivered to patients from one location."[129] This transfer resulted from the "poor" relationships between the radiation oncologists and the medical oncologists practicing at the hospital.[130] Accordingly, the hospital transferred its oncology program to an office-based practice group owned by the hospital's non-profit parent institution. The radiation oncology group that had practiced at the hospital contested the transfer, as they would no longer see radiation oncology patients at the hospital. The radiation oncology group claimed that the transfer "was unrelated to quality-of-care concerns" and therefore impermissible.[131] In rejecting this position, the Alabama Supreme Court held that the hospital's decision to transfer oncology services "did not violate the medical-staff bylaws" because the transfer decision was a "business decision[]" that the hospital was permitted to make under its corporate bylaws independent of the medical staff bylaws.[132]

These four recent cases suggest that courts are increasingly sympathetic to hospitals' assertion of their own independent institutional interests and that as a result credentialing on grounds other than medical competence is gaining judicial assent. This is an especially important and positive development in circumstances in which hospitals are seeking and exercising authority to better achieve institutional objectives such as quality assurance, accountability, and cost containment.

These recent cases also are suggestive of a broader set of legal and regulatory objectives.

First, the legal and regulatory environment should not have a large impact on how physician-hospital relationships should be mediated. The lack of a rigid regulatory structure for IDNs should be retained; the existing regulatory approach for hospital governance should not be transferred to the IDN setting.

Second, regulatory flexibility and regulatory neutrality should be the guiding objectives of public policy in this arena.

Third, the Gainsharing Demonstration should provide an occasion and a vehicle for initiating a comprehensive review of existing doctrines (e.g., anti-kickback and anti-self-referral laws) so that the focus of regulation is on

---

128. Radiation Therapy Oncology, P.C. v. Providence Hosp., 906 So.2d 904 (Ala. 2005).

129. *Id.*

130. *Id.* at 908.

131. *Id.* at 909.

132. *Id.* at 910–11.

inappropriate outcomes (such as anti-competitive conditions or poor quality results) but is crafted to permit innovative structures.[133]

Finally, constraining the rate of growth of costs is now more than ever a quality-of-care issue[134] and an access-to-care issue. Broader and more affordable coverage for medical care is directly linked to the cost of care.[135] The need to deal with cost-of-care issues suggests rethinking the regulatory structure of hospitals, allowing a more direct mechanism for incorporating cost factors into medical care decision making,[136] while at the same time maintaining regulatory flexibility for non-hospital organizational forms of physician-hospital relationships.

In sum, incorporating economic considerations into medical care decision making is a critical policy objective. Physician-hospital arrangements outside the traditional hospital governance structure still can act as important tools for achieving this alignment of interests, and as a result, encourage physicians to take costs into account in their decision making process. Their form and structure should not be locked into a one-size-fits-all framework, and they should not receive *carte blanche* when concerns about quality or competition exist. Because they remain relatively free of built-in regulatory obstacles to an appropriate structure, the varied organizational forms should remain available as new ways to create appropriate incentives for cost containment and quality assurance. As Robinson argued ten years ago, the appropriate organizational form should be seen as the "outcome of a competitive process in which particular forms survive"

---

133. The enactment of the financial at-risk safe harbor under the anti-kickback law and the binding advisory opinion process under the anti-kickback and anti-self-referral laws are examples of this type of approach. *See* Havighurst et al., HEALTH CARE LAW AND POLICY, *supra* note 42, at 462–63, 495–96. In arrangements in which providers are financially at risk, for example, when managed care organizations receive capitated payments from Medicare, there is not a substantial risk of excess utilization, unlike the situation in which providers are paid on a fee-for-service basis. If there is a concern, it is with quality assurance not overutilization. *See* Timothy Stoltzfuss Jost & Sharon L. Davies, *The Empire Strikes Back: A Critique of the Backlash Against Fraud and Abuse Enforcement*, 51 ALA. L. REV. 239 (1999) (raising concern about quality-of-care considerations in capitated settings). Use of financial inducements should be less subject to scrutiny on cost-containment grounds in capitated situations. *See* Blumstein, *Speakeasy, supra* note 11. *See also* Blumstein & Sloan, *supra* note 9, at 78–82 (developing antitrust approach for specific contexts of antitrust risk).

134. *See, e.g.*, Radiation Therapy Oncology, P.C. v. Providence Hosp., 906 So.2d 904, 915–16 (Ala. 2005) (Harwood, J., concurring) (noting that a quality of care concept is "broad enough" to encompass cost-containment considerations).

135. The State of Tennessee has recognized this in its reform of TennCare, the state's Medicaid demonstration. *See supra* note 24 (outlining the TennCare definition of medical necessity that expressly incorporates cost considerations into the determination of medical necessity, which defines the scope of a public TennCare beneficiary's entitlement to medical care services).

136. *See* Blum, *supra* note 12; Hall, *supra* note 22.

where they best perform the functions that need to be performed.[137] And, in a regulatory-neutral environment, public policy attention should turn to creating a system of competition that incentivizes the provision of good quality care and appropriately incorporates economic considerations into the medical decision making process, while also providing appropriate disclosures to patients and involving patients in shared decision making.

---

137. Robinson, *supra* note 35, and accompanying text.

8. PROPERTY, PRIVACY, AND THE PURSUIT OF INTEGRATED ELECTRONIC MEDICAL RECORDS[1]

MARK A. HALL AND KEVIN A. SCHULMAN

[W]e have a twenty-first-century financial information infrastructure and a nineteenth-century health information infrastructure. Given what is at stake, health care should be the most IT-enabled of all our industries, not one of the least. Nonetheless, the "technologies" used to collect, manage, and distribute most of our medical information remain the pen, paper, telephone, fax, and Post-It note. Meanwhile, thousands of small organizations chew around the edges of the problem, spending hundreds of millions of dollars per year on proprietary clinical IT products that barely work and do not talk to each other. Health care organizations do not relish the problem, most vilify it, many are spending vast sums on proprietary products that do not coalesce into a systemwide solution, and the investment community has poured nearly a half-trillion dollars into failed HIT ["health information technology"] ventures that once claimed to be that solution. Nonetheless, no single health care organization or HIT venture has attained anything close to the critical mass necessary to effect such a fix. This is the textbook definition of a market failure.[2]

I. INTRODUCTION

A. The Stubborn Problem

Medical information is one of the most prominent, puzzling, frustrating and entrenched dimensions of fragmentation in U.S. health care finance and delivery. We each confront this reality every time we go to a new doctor. Each doctor starts a new medical relationship virtually from scratch, as if we've never been examined before. Unless our referring physician has dictated a personal note, the only convenient way to transmit information from our existing medical records is by the patient's own word of mouth, which the doctor enters by hand and then feels the need to painstakingly re-confirm by direct re-examination. Even basic patient identification and family history information is written out

---

1. This research was supported by a Robert Wood Johnson Foundation Investigator Award in Health Policy Research. We benefited greatly from conversations with and comments from Craig Richardson, Kristin Madison, Nicolas Terry, Brian Baum, and participants in the University of Minnesota Law School's Law and Economics colloquium.

2. J.D. Kleinke, *Dot-Gov: Market Failure and the Creation of a National Health Information Technology System*, 24(5) HEALTH AFF. 1246, 1247–48 (2005).

and re-entered for each new doctor—often even when they are practicing in the same medical system. And on, and on, throughout our kaleidoscopic medical system.[3]

The dystopia of health care information automation in the United States has frustrated the best and brightest minds for years, if not decades.[4] Widespread attention was first brought to the problem by an Institute of Medicine report in 1991.[5] Since then, an array of prominent organizations and individuals have made it their calling to overcome the barriers that keep health care providers from efficiently accessing and sharing a patient's complete medical record[6]— but so far to no avail. The costs are staggering—from 100 billion hard dollars each year driven by needless duplication of procedures to perhaps a half trillion softer dollars annually associated with medication errors, lost worker productivity, and, in the most extreme cases, loss of life.[7]

The vision of what IT could bring to health care is well-formed and has been discussed at length.[8] Agreement on where we need to go is universal—from the

---

3. For instance, frustration also extends to researchers who are forced to use primitive and cumbersome methods of primary data collection rather than being able to access consolidated information from existing medical records.

4. See Edward H. Shortliffe, Strategic *Action In Health Information Technology: Why The Obvious Has Taken So Long*, 24(5) HEALTH AFF. (2005) 1222–1233; Jeff Goldsmith et al., *Federal Health Information Policy: A Case Of Arrested Development*, 22(4) HEALTH AFF. 44 (2003); D.U. Himmelstein & S. Woolhandler, HOPE AND HYPE: PREDICTING THE IMPACT OF ELECTRONIC MEDICAL RECORDS, 24(5) HEALTH AFF. 1121 (2005).

5. Institute of Medicine, The Computer-Based Patient Record: An Essential Technology for Health Care (1991).

6. *See, e.g.*, Dept. Health and Human Services, Health Information Technology Home, http://www.hhs.gov/healthit/; National Committee on Vital and Health Statistics, Workgroup On National Health Information Infrastructure, http://www.ncvhs.hhs.gov/wg-nhii.htm; Markle Foundation, Connecting for Health, http://www.connectingforhealth.com/; Robert Wood Johnson Foundation, Project HealthDesign, http://www.projecthealthdesign.org/; California Healthcare Foundation, http://www.chcf.org/topics/index.cfm?topic=CL108; Paul M. Ellwood, Crossing the Health Policy Chasm (February 18, 2003), http://www.ppionline.org/ndol/print.cfm?contentid=251324.

7. These are "net" figures, that is, in excess of the costs of building and maintaining a comprehensive HIT system. FEDERICO GIROSI ET AL., EXTRAPOLATING EVIDENCE OF HEALTH INFORMATION TECHNOLOGY SAVINGS AND COSTS (2005), *available at* http://rand.org/pubs/monographs/MG410/; Jan Walker, et al., *The Value Of Health Care Information Exchange And Interoperability*, Health Affairs Web Exclusive, January 19, 2005, http://content.healthaffairs.org/cgi/content/full/hlthaff.w5.10/DC1; R. Hillestad, et al., *Can Electronic Medical Record Systems Transform Health Care? Potential Health Benefits, Savings, and Costs*, 24(5) HEALTH AFF. 1103 (2005). *See generally* Congressional Budget Office, Evidence on the Costs and Benefits of Health Information Technology (May 2008), *available at* http://www.cbo.gov/ftpdocs/91xx/doc9168/05-20-HealthIT.pdf

8. For the latest, *see* Rodney A. Hayward, *Access to Clinically-detailed Patient Information: a Fundamental Element for Improving the Efficiency and Quality of Healthcare*, 46(3) MED. CARE 229 (2008); K.D. Mandl & I.S. Kohane, *Tectonic Shifts in the Health Information*

President, to both Houses of Congress, to both major political parties, to hospitals, physicians, patients, payors, and the business community at large. Therefore, it is a puzzle why more progress has not been made. Only about a quarter of physicians use electronic medical records (EMRs) and fewer than 5% have fully functional systems.[9] Information technology (IT) is more prevalent in some hospital departments, such as radiology and laboratory testing, but fewer than 2% of hospitals have a comprehensive EMR system.[10]

Even though e-health is growing steadily and will soon exist in some form just about everywhere, the electronic systems that are in place rarely interconnect—a problem that is getting worse rather than better. The RAND Corporation summarizes that "the ability to share information from system to system is poor." This is because there "is no market pressure to develop HIT systems that can talk to each other." Instead, the "piecemeal implementation currently under way may actually create additional barriers to the development of a future standardized system because of the high costs of replacing or converting today's nonstandard systems."[11]

The challenge is how to move an enterprise representing one-sixth of U.S. GDP, with thirteen million employees and potentially almost three hundred million patients, from a decentralized, fragmented, paper-based world, to an integrated, automated, networked world where information follows the patient, information-based tools can aid in decision making and quality, and population health data can be mined to improve the quality and outcome of care for all.

The goal of integrated electronic medical records (I-EMRs) has unqualified support from all quarters, but every effort to achieve it seems to end up stalled at a tactical or practical level. The most well-intentioned individuals driven by a common commitment encounter an all too-consistent pattern. While starting with a grand vision, they invariably encounter resistance in the trenches:

this doctor doesn't support IT because he's concerned that automation of health information will de-value the his practice's resale value, . . . this hospital

---

Economy, 358 N ENG. J. MED. 1732 (2008); or any issue of these journals: INTERNATIONAL JOURNAL OF MEDICAL INFORMATICS, JOURNAL OF THE AMERICAN MEDICAL INFORMATICS ASSOCIATION, JOURNAL OF HEALTHCARE INFORMATION MANAGEMENT, METHODS OF INFORMATION IN MEDICINE; BMC MEDICAL INFORMATICS AND DECISION MAKING.

9. A.K. Jha, et al., *How Common are Electronic Health Records in the United States? A Summary of the Evidence*, 25(6) HEALTH AFF. w496 (2006), http://www.rwjf.org/pr/product.jsp?id=15315; Catherine M. DesRoches, et al., *Electronic Health Records in Ambulatory Care: A National Survey of Physicians*, 359 NEW ENG. J. MED. 50 (2008).

10. Ashish K. Jha, et al., *Use of Electronic Health Records in U.S. Hospitals*, 360 NEW ENGL. J. MED. 1628 (2009).

11. RAND Corporation, Health Information Technology: Can HIT Lower Costs and Improve Quality? (2005) http://www.rand.org/pubs/research_briefs/RB9136/index1.html; David J. Brailer, *Presidential Leadership and Health Information Technology*, 28(2) HEALTH AFF. w392 (April 2009).

won't allow access to their information, . . . these IT vendors won't interoperate, this business is concerned that its employees will be suspicious of any effort by the employer to encourage employee participation in electronic health systems, this hospital administrator does not believe there is any return on IT investment and therefore won't allocate the necessary funding to deploying the infrastructure.[12]

And so it goes—more money spent, more lives lost due to error, and more time gone by without making much progress toward the goal of interconnected electronic records for most patients and providers.

B. Private versus Public Solutions

Considering these failures, should the government intervene? Certainly, it should encourage and facilitate I-EMRs through various means,[13] as other countries have done, but in the United States, the many well-intentioned and amply-supported efforts to create interconnected EMRs through central community planning have failed miserably, owing to the difficulties in meeting all the concerns of all the various stakeholders.[14] If all else fails, perhaps the government will have no choice but to require EHR adoption and integration, but there would be huge opposition to a "command and control" approach.[15] To paraphrase,

---

12. Health Record Network, Response to Request for Information on CMS' Role in Personal Health Records (Aug. 31, 2005).

13. The strongest case is to encourage or require some degree of standardization of clinical and/or IT protocols. Discussing current options and proposals, see, e.g., 72 Fed. Reg. 30803 (Oct. 31, 2007); Rosenfeld S, Bernasek C, Mendelson D, *Medicare's Next Voyage: Encouraging Physicians to Adopt Health Information Technology*, 24(5) HEALTH AFF. 1138 (2005); Roger Taylor et al., *Promoting Health Information Technology: Is There A Case For More-Aggressive Government Action?*, 24(5) HEALTH AFF. 1234 (2005); David Brailer, *Action through Collaboration*, 24(5) HEALTH AFF. 1150 (2005); Jeff Goldsmith et al., *Federal Health Information Policy: A Case Of Arrested Development*, 22(4) HEALTH AFF. 44 (2003).

14. Exhaustively cataloguing the many failures, *see, e.g.*, Julia Adler-Milstein, et al., *The State Of Regional Health Information Organizations*, 27(1) HEALTH AFF. w60 (2007), *available at* http://content.healthaffairs.org/cgi/content/abstract/hlthaff.27.1.w60vi; Robert H. Miller and Bradley S. Miller, *The Santa Barbara County Care Data Exchange: What Happened?*, 26(5) HEALTH AFF. w568 2007; Jonah Frohlich, et al., *Lessons Learned From The Santa Barbara Project And Their Implications For Health Information Exchange*, 26(5) HEALTH AFF. w589 (2007), http://content.healthaffairs.org/cgi/content/full/26/5/w589; Bruce Merlin Fried, *Gauging the Progress of the National Health Information Technology Initiative: Perspectives from the Field* (2008) http://www.chcf.org/topics/view. cfm?itemid=133553; Joy M. Grossmanet al., *Creating Sustainable Local Health Information Exchanges: Can Barriers to Stakeholder Participation be Overcome?* (2008) http://www. hschange.org/CONTENT/970/;

15. *See, e.g.*, Kleinke, *supra* note 2, at 1250; *Summary of Responses to an Industry RFI Regarding a Role for CMS with Personal Health Records*, http://www.cms.hhs.gov/ PerHealthRecords/Downloads/SummaryofPersonalHealthRecord.pdf.

Americans usually resort to government mandates only after we've tried everything else first. This chapter explores whether there is still any hope for private initiative and market-driven innovation.

An analogy exists in the development of the Internet. Imagine that in 1990 a relatively small group of IT bureaucrats had sought to create the Internet of today. In a world in which personal computers in the home was uncommon and access was largely via slow-speed modems, when people still shopped only in stores and catalogues and used the public library for research, communicated only by letters, phones and faxes, etc., our clandestine team of IT bureaucrats would have had to anticipate every need, every implication and every cause and effect that occurs in something as massive and pervasive as the Internet we now know. This group would have needed to resolve every issue of deployment, standards, interoperability, new product design and new business model creation before the "product" was even introduced. Taken as a whole, these tasks would have led to the conclusion that "Internet 2010" could simply not be created. Yet every one of these actions did occur and coordinate, not by design but by market mechanisms, to create an environment that allowed the Internet to rapidly evolve to what we know it to be today.

Why is this spontaneous market development not happening for e-health? The primary barriers are not technological.[16] Instead, they are economic.[17] Realizing that the economics of e-health are shaped and driven by basic legal rights in networked medical information, this paper explores whether the law is responsible for, or might be a solution to, the balkanization of medical information.

II. THE STRUCTURE AND ECONOMICS OF ELECTRONIC MEDICAL RECORD NETWORKS

A. Network Economics

The economics of information networks reveal key reasons why many providers currently do not adopt Electronic Medical Record Networks (EMRs) and others do not interconnect the EMRs they have. The field of network economics has

---

16. Certainly, there are many practical issues that must be worked out, but they are solvable, at least in principle. *See, e.g.,* Pamela Hartzband & Jerome Groopman, *Off the Record: Avoiding the Pitfalls of Going Electronic,* 358 NEW ENG. J. MED. 1656 (2008); R.D. Kush, et al., *Electronic Health Records, Medical Research, And The Tower Of Babel,* 358 NEW ENG. J. MED. 1738 (2008); David Brailer, Action through Collaboration, 24(5) HEALTH AFF. 1150 (2005); W. Ed Hammond, *The Making and Adoption Of Health Data Standards,* 24(5) HEALTH AFF. 1205 (2005).

17. *Accord, see* Health Information Technology in the United States: *Where We Stand, 2008, available at* http://www.rwjf.org/files/research/062508.hit.exsummary.pdf.; CBO Report, *supra* note 7.

developed over the past generation to provide us with a much better understanding of the market dynamics for telecommunications, the Internet, credit cards, and other large and complex interconnected services.[18] The core economic characteristic of these networks is that the larger the network is, the more benefit there is to each user. Network effects exist whenever there are increasing returns to scale,[19] meaning that "the utility that a user derives from consumption of a good increases with the number of other agents consuming the good."[20]

There are obvious network economies in connecting electronic medical records.[21] The more providers who are connected, the more comprehensive and useful is the information for any single patient. And, the more patients that are included, the more likely that providers will agree to participate. More patients, providers and information make the network more useful not only for clinical work, but also for health services research and public health monitoring. If signing up more people produces more bang for the IT buck, why don't these win-win dynamics snowball into widespread EMR adoption and interconnection?

Network economics point to this answer: No one who is in a position to build the network can capture anywhere near its full social benefits.[22] In economic parlance, much of these benefits are externalized. Patients benefit from better

---

18. *See generally* Yochai Benkler, *The Wealth of Networks: How Social Production Transforms Markets and Freedom* (2006), http://www.benkler.org/wealth_of_networks/; Michael L. Katz & Carl Shapiro, *Network Externalities, Competition, and Compatibility*, 75 AM. ECON. REV. 424 (1985); S.J. Liebowitz & Stephen E. Margolis, *Network Effects and Externalities*, in THE NEW PALGRAVE DICTIONARY OF ECONOMICS AND THE LAW 671 (Peter Newman ed., 1998).

19. This sounds similar to "economies of scale," but those usually refer to decreasing costs. Networks may also have decreasing unit costs, but the term "network effects" refers to increasing benefits per user.

20. Mark A. Lemley & David McGowan, *Legal Implications of Network Economic Effects*, 86 CAL. L. REV. 479, 483 (1998).

21. Congressional Budget Office, Evidence on the Costs and Benefits of Health Information Technology, *supra* note 7.

22. *See generally id.;* P.G. Shekelle et al., *Costs and Benefits of Health Information Technology*, Evidence Report/Technology Assessment No. 132 (2006) at 12, http://www.ncbi.nlm.nih.gov/books/bv.fcgi?rid=hstat1b.chapter.6986 ("private return-on-investment (ROI) calculations can provide results that are quite different from those of societal cost-benefit analysis"); ANTHONY G. BOWER, THE DIFFUSION AND VALUE OF HEALTHCARE INFORMATION TECHNOLOGY 62–63 (2005), *available at* http://rand.org/pubs/monographs/MG272-1/ (stressing the "network externalities" that arise when each component of the system is under separate ownership).

Technically, it is not necessary for all of the networked benefits to be internalized, only a sufficient number to warrant the costs of building the network. *See* RUSSELL HARDIN, COLLECTIVE ACTION 41 (1982) (discussing so-called "k groups," which are subgroups who receive enough benefit from providing a collective good to be willing to do so for the benefit of a much larger group).

quality and the public at large benefits from research. Insurers (and other payors) benefit from lower costs, but only for the patients who are their subscribers. And each provider has a stake only in its treatments for its own patients.[23] None of these key actors benefits from all the gains that could be realized by the others, so none stands to accrue most of the rewards from the considerable costs of I-EMR development. (Estimates for a complete, nationwide system range from $100 billion to $300 billion.)[24]

Concretely illustrated, if a patient has seen four doctors already and is heading to a fifth, it is only the fifth who will benefit from the first four sharing their information in a useable form. A reciprocal network among them might make sense if they shared patients among each other in roughly equal proportions, but more likely some doctors tend to be senders and others receivers. Therefore, not everyone has the same incentive to invest in interconnected EMRs, and no one has sufficient incentive to pay the costs for the others. Because the networking costs are misaligned with the networking benefits, interconnection is rare or incomplete.

More or less the same is true among insurers (or the employers who pay them). Payors might have a greater and more direct economic stake in forcing providers to adopt I-EMRs, but their interest is only in their own subscribers or employees. Typically, each provider belongs to a dozen or more managed care networks. Therefore, it would be impractical for insurers or employers to insist on widespread adoption of a particular EMR system within their provider networks, regardless of who might foot the bill for doing so.

In addition, the particular institutional features of health care create negative economic incentives, that is, outright financial penalties, for networking. One benefit to patients of interconnecting is avoiding repeated testing to learn what other doctors already know. But, due to nearly ubiquitous fee-for-service reimbursement, from the doctor's perspective less testing means lost revenues. J.D. Kleinke astutely observes that, in "an industry rife with dirty little secrets, this is health care's dirtiest: . . . not knowing is good for business. . . . [T]he less the hospital knows about [a patient], the more services it can render, the more it

23. See CBO Report, *supra* note 7 ("doctors and hospitals would capture only a small fraction of HIT's potential economic benefits. It has been estimated that as much as 80 percent of the potential savings generated through HIT inure to insurers and health care group purchasers"); Shekelle, et al., *supra* note 22, at 13 ("it does not pay one insurer to subsidize HIT for an entire provider or organization because a substantial portion of the cost savings accrue to other payers").

24. Jan Walker et al., *The Value Of Health Care Information Exchange And Interoperability*, HEALTH AFFAIRS W5:10 (January 19, 2005) ($276 billion); Federico Girosi, et al., *supra* note 7 ($97 billion). *See generally* CBO Report, *supra* note 7 (surveying and critiquing studies).

can bill his health insurer, and the more it will collect."[25] This is why it is difficult or impossible to make a "business case" for providers' investment in I-EMRs, based only on the economic return on investment.

Doctors also fear that they will take on more liability exposure for knowing and managing information. The more information they have access to, the more they are potentially responsible for. Increased scope of responsibility with decreased compensation is a recipe for intransigence.

A straightforward remedy for the fragmentation of medical records is for providers to integrate into comprehensive delivery systems. It is no surprise that interconnected EMRs have arisen so far only in integrated systems that operate under fixed, global budgets.[26] The leading U.S. examples are Kaiser-Permanente and the Veterans Administration, which have had model EMRs in place for decades.[27] These delivery systems internalize most of the network benefits from adopting I-EMRs since they contain almost all of their patients' providers. Also, adopting EMRs does not cause negative economies for integrated systems. Reimbursement does not drop under global or capitated payments, and institutional liability does not expand.[28] Moreover, self-contained systems can interconnect EMRs more efficiently by adopting a single set of communications standards and protocols that apply to all of their physicians, who see only patients within the system.

So, clearly, the most effective solution to fragmentation is market or government integration of both health care delivery and financing. In fact, some analysts hope that the benefits of I-EMR will drive more systemic delivery-system integration, perhaps by pushing toward a single-payor system or back to something resembling staff and group model HMOs. But those much larger topics are fanciful hopes that wish away our problem. Certainly, if the lack of I-EMR diffusion is a symptom of our system's fragmentation, then curing the underlying disease

---

25. Kleinke, *supra* note 2, at 1250–51. *See also* Robert H. Miller and Christopher E. West, *The Value Of Electronic Health Records In Community Health Centers: Policy Implications*, HEALTH AFF. Jan/Feb 2007 26(1):206–214; Health Information Technology in the United States: The Information Base for Progress 43 (2006),http://www.rwjf.org/files/publications/other/EHRReport0609.pdf.

26. *See, e.g.*, D. Rotti, *A Comparison of Information Technology in General Practice in Ten Countries*, 10 HEALTHCARE Q. 107 (2007); Ashish K. Jha & David Blumenthal, *International Adoption of Electronic Health Records*, Chapter 7 in HEALTH INFORMATION TECHNOLOGY IN THE UNITED STATES: WHERE WE STAND, 2008, available at http://www.rwjf.org/files/research/062508.hit.exsummary.pdf.

27. P.G. Shekelle et al., *supra* note 22, at 13; GAO, HHS's Efforts to Promote Health Information Technology and Legal Barriers to Its Adoption, GAO-04-991R (Aug. 13, 2004), *supra* note 26; David Mechanic, *Rethinking Medical Professionalism: The Role of Information Technology and Practice Innovations*, 86 MILBANK Q. 327 (2008).

28. Furthermore, antitrust liability is not a concern for cooperation among providers within an integrated network.

would abate the ailment. But, we know that health care finance and delivery cannot be defragmented just by pressing a button. This book teaches us that fragmentation is chronic and deeply entrenched. Therefore, we need to search for effective ways to manage and mitigate its information management symptoms, along with all its other ills.

B. Partial Integration

Short of full integration, providers can attempt partial integration by forming a contractual network that shares resources such as medical records. Some hospitals, for instance, are willing to bear or defray IT costs for physicians who adopt their EMR systems. Hospitals' side payments to referring physicians are one way to overcome some of the network externalities that physicians face in providing hospitals treatment information about their patients. These side payments potentially run afoul, however, of Medicare and tax-exemption laws designed to insulate hospitals financially from their referring physicians.[29] This appears to be another instance of the more general phenomenon noted by professor Blumstein, that although these laws welcome or allow full integration among providers, they illogically threaten and therefore retard various contractual arrangements that are transitional states between no integration and complete integration.[30]

For hospital support of physician EMRs, this problem appears to be solved, at least for now. After lawyers and policy officials drew sufficient attention for Congress to mandate action, HHS and IRS responded with rulings that create protective safe-harbors for hospital support of EMR software and training (but not for hardware).[31] These rulings have addressed much of the legal uncertainty that made doctors and hospitals hesitant to share IT resources. However, they have not produced a groundswell of EMR interconnection. The fundamental reality still exists that, under prevailing reimbursement methods it is not in providers' economic interest to fully automate and interconnect medical information.

Even if providers were to integrate IT, Figure 1[32] depicts broader network externalities: information systems built around medical treatment needs may

---

29. GAO, HHS's Efforts to Promote Health Information Technology and Legal Barriers to Its Adoption, *supra* note 26; Sara Rosenbaum et al., Charting the Legal Environment of Health Information, George Washington University School of Public Health (May 2005),http://www.rwjf.org/files/research/Legal%20Environment%20 Long%20Version.pdf

30. James Blumstein, *The Fraud and Abuse Statute in an Evolving Healthcare Marketplace: Life in the Health Care Speakeasy*, 22 AM. J.L. & MED. 205 (1996).

31. 71 Fed. Reg. 45110, 45140 (Aug. 8, 2006); IRS Memorandum dated May 11, 2007, http://www.irs.gov/pub/irs-tege/ehrdirective.pdf.

32. From National Committee on Vital and Health Statistics, Personal Health Record Systems 12 (U.S. Department of Health and Human Services, 2006), http://www.ncvhs. hhs.gov/0602nhiirpt.pdf.

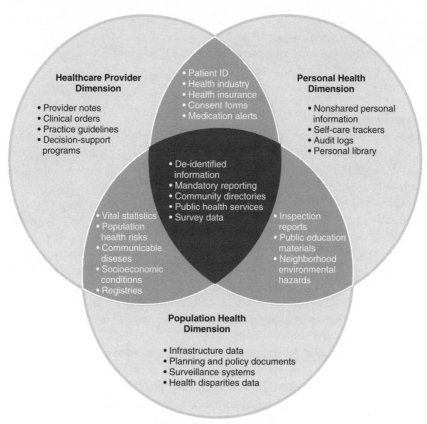

Healthcare Provider Dimension

• Provider notes
• Clinical orders
• Practice guidelines
• Decision-support programs

• Patient ID
• Health industry
• Health insurance
• Consent forms
• Medication alerts

Personal Health Dimension

• Nonshared personal information
• Self-care trackers
• Audit logs
• Personal library

• De-identified information
• Mandatory reporting
• Community directories
• Public health services
• Survey data

• Vital statistics
• Population health risks
• Communicable diseses
• Socioeconomic conditions
• Registries

• Inspection reports
• Public education materials
• Neighborhood environmental hazards

Population Health Dimension

• Infrastructure data
• Planning and policy documents
• Surveillance systems
• Health disparities data

FIGURE 1 SECTORS BENEFITING FROM NETWORKED EMRs

fail to take account of the larger set of concerns encompassed by patient health and population health.

The network externalities of provider-centric models have given rise to alternatives centered on insurers or employers,[33] but these too have their limitations. First, patients and providers may not trust payors sufficiently to contribute to and use their systems. Second, and more fundamentally, because most private doctors and almost all non-federal hospitals have patients from many different insurance plans, insurance-based models clearly fail to overcome fragmentation. Why should one insurer pay for an information system covering 10% of a doctor's patients that can be used for free on all patients? But, how is a doctor supposed to cope with a dozen different information systems? And why should

---

33. *See, e.g.*, K.D. Mandl & T.S. Kohane, *Tectonic Shifts in the Health Information Economy*, 358 NEW ENG. J. MED. 1732 (2008).

either doctor or insurer invest in providing information to other health plans and providers that patients switch to in the future.

In the end, both providers and payors face the fractured reality that an information system centered on a particular affinity group (providers, employers, or insurers) cannot efficiently interconnect all of a patient's relevant information over a lifetime. Therefore, we must look elsewhere for ways to structure electronic medical networks that will capture (or internalize) enough of the social benefits to warrant the private investments needed.[34]

C. Patient-Centered Models

One emerging model for I-EHRs is patient-centric.[35] Under this model, each patient will have a lifetime of digitized medical and health information at his fingertips, and those of his providers. Providers will contribute to and use this record, but it will be controlled by patients and maintained by third parties on behalf of patients.[36] At the moment, a widely-discussed development is the possibility of popular Internet portals such as Microsoft or Google hosting secure data repositories that patients control and providers use. Other options include

---

34. Outlining competing and overlapping models, see generally Connecting for Health, Financial, Legal and Organizational Approaches to Achieving Electronic Connectivity in Healthcare (Oct. 2004), http://www.connectingforhealth.org/assets/reports/flo_sustain_healtcare_rpt.pdf; David Blumenthal, *Expecting the Unexpected: Health Information Technology and Medical Professionalism, in* MEDICAL PROFESSIONALISM IN THE INFORMATION AGE, (D. Rothman & D. Blumenthal eds., 2009); Lisa Sprague, Personal Health Records: The People's Choice? (National Health Policy Forum, Nov. 2006), available at *www.nhpf. org/library/ forum-sessions/FS_PHRs_03-16-07.pdf;* Altarum, Environmental Scan of the Personal Health Record (PHR) Market (October 31, 2006), http://www.dhhs.gov/healthit/ahic/materials/meeting11/ce/EnvScan_PHRmarket.pdf; Nicolas P. Terry & Leslie P. Francis, *Ensuring the Privacy and Confidentiality of Electronic Health Records,* U. ILL. L. REV. 681 (2007); Nicolas P. Terry, *To HIPAA, a Son: Assessing the Technical, Conceptual, and Legal Frameworks for Patient Safety Information,* 12 WIDNER L. REV. 137 (2005); National Committee on Vital and Health Statistics, Personal Health Record Systems. U.S. Department of Health and Human Services (2006), http://www.ncvhs.hhs.gov/0602nhiirpt.pdf.

35. The seminal report is Connecting for Health, The Personal Health Working Group Final Report (Markle Foundation, June 2003) http://connectingforhealth.org/resources/final_phwg_report1.pdf. *See also* Robert Steinbrook, *Personally Controlled Online Health Data—the Next Big Thing in Medical Care?,* 358 NEW ENG. J. MED. 1653 (2008); Lisa Sprague, Personal Health Records: The People's Choice?, *supra* note 35. For a skeptical view, *see* Nicolas P. Terry, *Personal Health Records: Directing More Costs and Risks to Consumers?,* f1 Drexel L. Rev. 216 (2009).

36. For examples and detailed descriptions, *see* Carol Cronin, Personal Health Records: An Overview of What is Available to the Public, AARP Research Report (May 2006), http://www.aarp.org/research/health/carequality/2006_11_phr.html; Altarum, *supra* note 35.

memory cards or chips that patients carry with them (or perhaps even have implanted) for easy access and continual updating.

Aside from the technological challenges, these models raise practical concerns that are formidable.[37] Who has the "legal" version of the record that existed at any given point? Will patients trust the host institutions? Will doctors trust and use the information in records of uncertain provenance? Do privacy laws apply? To address these problems, others propose a trustee model that places a patient-controlled record in the hands of some type of trustworthy and expert "infomediary" or "records bank."[38]

We are not lacking for innovative ideas and alternative models. Which ones ultimately end up prevailing and in what forms will be determined not only by how well they work, but also by the basic legal framing of competing rights in and to medical information and its economic value. Some of these models assume that medical information is a public good. Others assume that patients have ultimate ownership and control. Some assume that medical information will change hands in exchange for money; others assume an admirable degree of non-remunerated cooperation, based on a variety of motives.

Increasingly, participants in and observers of the HIT sector recognize that monetizing access to medical information is necessary in order to align interests and overcome the economic barriers to forming I-EMRs. One leading group of diverse experts,[39] for instance, concluded that a "critical path to enabling a market" for I-EMRs is "[e]nabling consumers to monetize their medical data" by giving them "economic interests . . . from providing access to their data."[40]

---

37. *See* Sprague, *supra* note 36; Terry, *supra* note 36.

38. Agency for Healthcare Research and Quality, National Health Data Stewardship, 72 Fed. Reg. 30803 (Oct. 31, 2007); A. Shabo, *A Global Socio-Economic-Medico-Legal Model for the Sustainability of Longitudinal Electronic Health Records*, 45(3 & 5) METHODS INFO. MED. 240–5, 498–505 (2006); T.R. Knapp et al., *Property Rights and Privacy Principles*, 14(4) J HEALTHCARE INFO. MGMT. 83 (2000); Paul T. Kostyack, *The Emergence of the Healthcare Information Trust*, 12 HEALTH MATRIX 393 (2002); Judah Thornewill & Robert J. Esterhay, *Capitalizing the NHIN-A Strategy for Funding an Integrated Nationwide Network of Community HIEs*, 32(3) J. HEALTHCARE INFO. MGMT., 18 (2007); Edmund F. Haislmaier, Health Care Information Technology: Getting the Policy Right, Heritage Foundation WebMemo #1131 (June 16, 2006); http://www.heritage.org/Research/HealthCare/wm1131.cfm; Health Record Banking Alliance, http://www.healthbanking.org.

39. These were participants invited to a conference at Harvard Medical School, from academia, government, and industry. The conclusions described here were those of the business model discussion group at the conference.

40. PCHRI 2006, the Harvard Medical School Meeting on Personally Controlled Health Record Infrastructure, http://www.pchri.org/2006/presentations/pchri2006_track_output.pdf. *Accord*, Haislmaier, *supra* note 39 ("The best way to induce patients and providers to share the individual data they create is to help them unlock the value of that data and share in the benefits derived from letting others use it.").

But, is this allowed, and in what circumstances? Because the law's uncertainty over ownership and control of medical information is widely regarded as a major barrier to effective networking of EMRs, policy analysts consider the legal status of medical information to be a critical question at or near the top of issues needing resolution.[41] All parties are looking to the law to define the ownership, control, and commercialization potential of medical information. How these issues are resolved ultimately will determine which information network models are economically viable and what form they will take.

III. PROPERTY AND PRIVACY RIGHTS IN MEDICAL INFORMATION

Your original medical record is property of [the hospital], but the information in it belongs to you.[42]

The AMA [advocates] that physicians own [their electronic medical data] . . . . [William A. Hazel Jr., MD, a member of the AMA's Board of Trustees] said this is a concern because "there is tremendous economic value to the cumulative data in terms of analyzing patterns," and without clear physician ownership, third-party vendors could reap the profits.[43]

Because data is generated only by a patient-provider interaction, the most reasonable legal approach is to recognize both parties' claims to co-ownership of the resulting data. If other parties, such as a payer, are involved, then they too have a reasonable claim to ownership

---

41. Stressing the importance of legal resolution of property interests, *see, e.g.,* Haislmaier, *supra* note 39; Altarum, *supra* note 35 ("Ultimately, legal ownership of the PHR and its data is a core unresolved issue, and will likely require further clarification at the state and federal levels."); Marc A. Rodwin, *Patient Data: Professionalism, Property & Policy, in* MEDICAL PROFESSIONALISM IN THE INFORMATION AGE, David Rothman & David Blumenthal, eds. (2010); Rosenbaum et al., *supra* note 30, at 29 ("questions regarding ownership must be resolved at an extremely early stage of the process"); Nicolas P. Terry, *Legal Barriers to Realizing the Public Good in Clinical Data, in* INSTITUTE OF MEDICINE, CLINICAL DATA AS THE BASIC STAPLE OF HEALTH LEARNING (2009); Barbara Harty-Golder, *EMR Ownership Questions,* MEDICAL LABORATORY OBSERVER, July 2007; C. Safran, M. Bloomrosen, et al., *Toward a National Framework for the Secondary use of Health Data: an American Medical Informatics Association White Paper,* 14 J. AM. MED. INFO. ASSOC. 1 (2007), http://www.jamia.org/cgi/content/abstract/14/1/1.

42. www.bannerhealth.com. *See also* N.H. REV. STAT. ANN. x 332-I:1 ("All medical information contained in the medical records in the possession of any health care provider shall be deemed to be the property of the patient.").

43. Kevin B. O'Reilly, *AMA to Set Guidelines on Control of Record Data,* AM MED. NEWS, Nov. 28, 2005.

of that portion of the information that is generated by their involvement . . . . [The system] should be governed by a legal structure which recognizes that virtually all health system data is 'co-owned' by two or more parties.[44]

[A] serious impediment to a comprehensive approach in the U.S. is the lack of clarity in this country about the nature of the interest that individuals have in information about themselves: Is it a commodity interest, a consumer protection interest, a personal dignity interest, a civil right interest, all of the above, or no interest at all? . . . Without a coherent conception about the nature of a person's interest in personal data, it is difficult to design a legal regime to protect this interest appropriately.[45]

A. Legal Uncertainty as a Barrier

Who owns medical information? Patients, providers, both of the above, or no one? The law provides incomplete, unclear, and somewhat inconsistent answers. But does this matter? According to one version of the "Coase Theorem," which of two parties owns a resource does not necessarily affect social welfare as long as the transaction costs of trading the resource are roughly equivalent either way. [46] Regardless of how the law makes the initial assignment of ownership, the parties are free to reallocate their rights and responsibilities in whatever manner will best achieve their goals. But there is at least one important proviso to this Theorem: property rights must be clearly established so that the respective parties know their legal default positions.[47] As revealed by the preceding quotations, this condition clearly is not met here. The relevant parties are in a quandary over who owns or controls what and so they do not know for sure what needs to be done to construct any particular information network model.[48] Moreover, the initial assignment of rights determines *private* welfare to a great extent since these rights form the parties' initial endowments that confer bargaining power.

---

44. Haislmaier, *supra* note 39.

45. Pamela Samuelson, *Privacy as Intellectual Property?*, 52 STAN. L. REV. 1125, 1170–71 (2000).

46. Richard S. Murphy, *Property Rights In Personal Information: An Economic Defense Of Privacy*, 84 GEO. L.J. 2381, 2387, 2403, 2395, (1996) (applying Coase's theorem to property rights in personal information).

47. If legal positions are uncertain, parties can still attempt simply to stake a claim, forcing a negotiation toward a contractual settlement that determines respective rights, but such contracts bind only the immediate parties, and the process of negotiation is an expensive barrier. Establishing clear property rights a priori therefore greatly facilitates contractual transfer of these rights. Licensing of intellectual property rights is an obvious case in point.

48. Safran, *supra* note 41.

Accordingly, it matters a great deal to real-world actors who has exactly what rights in different aspects of medical record information.

Medical information, whether networked or not, has considerable commercial value. "[A] well-established multimillion-dollar business exists that utilizes secondary health data as its primary resource,"[49] for purposes such as marketing to physicians or conducting medical research.[50] Legal uncertainty or agnosticism over valuable property rights can spark a land grab that hoards rather than develops these productive assets. Once one party stakes its ownership claim, then so must all the other competing parties, for fear of being trumped. But, fencing off the terrain of medical information destroys the commons that might have supported valuable public goods. Witness the A.M.A.'s proclamation quoted above that physicians own the medical information they collect.[51] Likewise, the Center for Studying Health System Change observed that hospitals' greatest concern with I-EMRs is "losing competitive advantage by relinquishing control of 'their' data. They view[] clinical data as a key strategic asset, tying physicians and patients to their organization."[52]

Legal logjams arise also from privacy protections. Medical privacy is important, but we may be protecting it to a fault. The risk of infringing patients' privacy rights gives providers another reason to isolate their medical records.[53] In one empirical study, economists at the University of Virginia and M.I.T. found that state privacy laws make hospitals substantially less likely to choose HIT software that is easily compatible with neighboring hospitals.[54] Notably, the deterrence comes directly from dampening the network benefits of sharing electronic data among hospitals, which otherwise would have promoted hospital

---

49. *Id.* at 1.

50. Robert Steinbrook, *For Sale: Physicians' Prescribing Data*, 354 NEW ENG. J. MED.2745 (2006); Judah Thornewill & Robert J. Esterhay, *Capitalizing the NHIN-A Strategy for Funding an Integrated Nationwide Network of Community HIEs*, 32(3) J. HEALTHCARE INFO. MGMT., 18 (2007).

51. *Supra* note 44.

52. Grossman et al., *supra* note 14.

53. *See* HEALTH INFORMATION TECHNOLOGY IN THE UNITED STATES: THE INFORMATION BASE FOR PROGRESS (2006), at Chap. 5, p. 45; Bruce Merlin Fried, Gauging the Progress of the National Health Information Technology Initiative: Perspectives from the Field 12 (January 2008) http://www.chcf.org/topics/view.cfm?itemid=133553 (many leaders and experts in the HIT community "believe that the resulting series of state and federal privacy policies hinders the flow of personal health information."); Connecting for Health, Financial, Legal and Organizational Approaches to Achieving Electronic Connectivity in Healthcare (Oct. 2004), http://www.connectingforhealth.org/assets/reports/flo_sustain_healtcare_rpt.pdf; Grossman et al., *supra* note 14.

54. Amalia R. Miller & Catherine Tucker, Privacy Protection and Technology Diffusion: The Case of Electronic Medical Records 4 (February 5, 2008), *available at* http://ssrn.com/abstract=960233.

adoption of EMR.[55] The high prices paid for patient-anonymized data about physicians' prescribing behaviors demonstrates that, in the absence of privacy restrictions, vibrant markets in medical information can develop quickly and easily.

The legal threat from privacy laws may be based more on the perception of legal exposure than on its reality. A comprehensive analysis of all 113 relevant legal cases found no real cause for concern.[56] Nevertheless, the perception of legal risk appears to be genuine,[57] perhaps due simply to uncertainty over the possible effects of these complex laws. Uncertainty costs played a major role, for instance, in one of the most visible attempts and dramatic failures to establish an I-EMR system among local providers in Santa Barbara. There (according to the former National Coordinator for Health Information Technology), privacy laws "were major issues from the outset. More money was spent on attorneys' fees than on technology, consulting, or any other line item," because "[a]ny number of lawyers would draw different conclusions from the federal and state privacy rules that were spread across many chapters of code and among many agencies." Therefore, it was "difficult for fifteen provider-leaders of the Santa Barbara Project to understand or agree on what they could or should do under these rules."[58]

The oppressive aura of privacy laws is one reason that non-provider-based models for I-EMR networks are emerging so strongly (as noted above). If centralized medical records are maintained by someone who is not involved in health care finance or delivery, they are not subject to the same privacy strictures. Some analysts call for expanding the federal privacy rule to cover anyone who possesses identifiable patient information,[59] but the impact of existing privacy laws should be studied more carefully before making this potentially crippling jump.

From the economic perspective of investing in medical information, the lack of clear property rights plus the presence of strong privacy protections is the worst of both worlds. Privacy protections increase the costs of developing I-EMRs and uncertain property rights decrease the returns. How these barriers and

---

55. *Id.* at 21.

56. Sara Rosenbaum, et al., *Does HIPAA Preemption Pose a Legal Barrier To Health Information Transparency and Interoperability?*, 16(11) HEALTH L. REP. (BNA) 1 (2007).

57. The Georgetown study, *id.* at 2, for instance, concluded that "misunderstandings about the breadth, scope, and content of HIPAA's basic rules, and the flexibility that covered entities have to design their own privacy policies appear to contribute to the perception that HIPAA and its preemption provisions may impede the development of interoperable and transparent health care information systems."

58. David J. Brailer, *From Santa Barbara To Washington: A Person's And A Nation's Journey Toward Portable Health Information*, 26(5) HEALTH AFF., w581, w587 (2007).

59. *E.g.*, National Committee on Vital and Health Statistics, Personal Health Record Systems, *supra* note 35, at 21; Sharona Hoffman & Andy Podgurski, *In Sickness, Health, and Cyberspace: Protecting the Security of Electronic Private Health Information*, 48 B.U. L. REV. 331 (2007).

uncertainties are resolved could determine the kinds of networks that will emerge and how efficiently they can form. Accordingly, the next sections sort out who owns or controls exactly what, of both the pure information content of medical records and their physical embodiment. The tangible-intangible distinction is critical: the property regime that potentially applies to the paper or computer files that store medical records differs considerably from the intellectual property rights in their information content. We start with the latter.

B. Patients Lack Intellectual Property Rights in their Medical Information

People frequently ask: Is medical information the patient's property or the provider's? Framing the question this way fails to leave open the possibility that often no one owns information, even when it is important and valuable. According to intellectual property scholar Pam Samuelson, "the traditional view in American law has been that information as such cannot be owned by any person."[60] Statutorily created property rights in certain types of information (via patents or copyright) are exceptions to this general rule, created to induce the production of new information with the expectation that it will be freely available to all after ownership expires.

These general understandings about creative and technical ideas also apply to everyday information about people. Scholars have explained at length that people do not own the information they reveal about themselves when they shop in stores, browse the Internet, or set forth into other public arenas. Some analysts have argued for creating a species of intellectual property covering valuable information about ourselves, but courts and legislatures have not heeded these calls. One property law scholar explains that, "neither property nor torts theory recognizes individuals' rights in their [personal] information. At the heart of that nonrecognition is a view that personal information is no one's until collected. . . ." Instead, personal information is like a wild animal, "not owned by anyone until captured."[61]

These basic rules also govern medical information. As explained by the High Court of Australia in a case involving a patient's access to her own medical records, it "'is only in a loose metaphorical sense that any knowledge as such can be said to be property.'"[62] Privacy law gives patients the right to control access

---

60. Samuelson, *supra* note 46, at 1130–31.

61. Vera Bergelson, *It's Personal but Is It Mine? Toward Property Rights in Personal Information*, 37 U.C. DAVIS L. REV. 379, 403 (2003).

62. Breen v. Williams, 186 C.L.R. 71, 128 (per Gummow J.) (Australia 1996) (quoting Federal Commn'r of Taxation v. United Aircraft Corp., 68 C.L.R. 525, 534 (Australia 1943)). *See also* Rodwin, *supra* note 42 (the law "does not give patients exclusive ownership rights in this information, [n]or does the law grant exclusive property rights in patient data to other parties to have access to this information."); Mark A. Hall & Kevin A. Schulman, *Ownership of Medical Information*, 301 JAMA 1282 (2009).

to their medical information, and patients have rights to inspect, copy, and correct their medical records. Although these privacy and access rights can be enforced in ways similar to property rights, properly characterized they are not actually property rights that can readily be bought and sold.[63] Privacy and access rights arise out of the special relationship patients have with their providers and so they are enforceable only against those providers, not against the world at large.

For other types of personal information, lack of ownership leaves the information in the public domain where commercial or other productive uses can be made by anyone who cares to invest the resources in collecting and compiling it. (Witness phone books, for instance.) In contrast, because providers strongly guard the privacy of medical information, it remains out of circulation even though it is not, strictly speaking, owned. This combination of no ownership plus limited access leaves medical information lying dormant in an abandoned and fallow field (reminiscent of the former absence of phone books in the old Soviet bloc). Lacking any legal rights that clearly can be monetized, patients have no market mechanism for overcoming network externalities. Patients may control their medical information, but have no ready way to transfer their rights.[64]

As developed below, propertizing medical information could stimulate increased flow of medical information into more useful forms by giving the stakeholders rights of access and control they can buy and sell. But, we also must beware that expanding stakeholders' legally-protected economic rights could cause even more stultification. As we will learn shortly, there is a faint path between the extremes of too few and too many property rights in medical information. To see this more clearly, we next turn to providers' rights in their medical records.

C. Providers and Insurers Have Tangible Property Rights in Their Medical Records

Although medical information, per se, is not property, medical records are. The adage "possession is nine-tenths of the law" applies with full force to patients' records. Those who possess and compile medical records own their tangible

---

63. *See* Estate of Finkle, 90 Misc. 2d 550, 552, 395 N.Y.S.2d 343, 344 (N.Y.Sur. 1977).

64. Although there is no reason in legal theory that they could not transfer their rights, possible ways of doing so have not been tested in the market or in court, so we do not know for sure. One reason they have not been tried is the absence of any legal recognition on the part of third parties to further license or sell these rights. In other words, we might have some confidence that one-step transfers to an immediate party are permitted, but we have good reason to doubt or question whether downstream transfers and commercialization of patients' access rights would currently be allowed. This downstream uncertainty perhaps explains why this route has never been explored.

embodiment—whether paper or electronic.[65] Medical records in any form are recognized as key assets in a physician's practice, which can be assigned an express economic value and sold as part of the business.[66] This does not mean, however, that health care providers can own a patient's medical information per se. Owning a book does not equate with owning its intellectual content. A property interest in a patient's medical record means only that one owns the particular embodiment and not the pure information content.

This distinction is easy to obscure when medical records are in electronic rather than paper form, but the distinction is no more difficult to maintain than that between the copyright holder in music, art, literature, or software and the purchasers of digitized copies of each of these. Because information is intangible, a doctor's or hospital's ownership of medical records does not foreclose or interfere with others' ownership of different embodiments of the same information. The same is true for medical information that anyone else might lawfully compile.

Multiple ownership of different pieces of a patient's medical history, however, makes it difficult for anyone to assemble a complete record. Balkanization among providers and insurers creates what legal scholars have termed an "anti-commons" problem—one in which competing rights holders foreclose each other from productive use of a shared resource.[67] The term "anticommons" is meant to contrast with the more familiar "tragedy of the commons."[68] When no one owns a shared resource and there are competing uses—as when ranchers share a common pasture—then it frequently happens that the resource is depleted, to everyone's detriment (for instance, by overgrazing). Medical (or any other kind of) information does not present a commons problem because its use is nonrivalrous.[69] Multiple users do not deplete information; indeed, multiple users may enhance the information's value. But instead, overlapping interests in

---

65. *Finkle*, 90 Misc.2d at 552, ("the vast majority of states hold 'that medical records are the property of the physician or the hospital and not the property of the patient.'") (quoting Gotkin v. Miller, 379 F.Supp. 859, 866–867 (E.D.N.Y.1974), aff'd. 514 F.2d 125 (2d Cir. 1975)); Terry, *supra* note 35, at 709 ("It is generally accepted that doctors own the medical records they keep about patients."); Paul V. Stearns, *Access to and Cost of Reproduction of Patient Medical Records: A Comparison of State laws*, 21 J. LEGAL MED. 79, 98 (2000).

66. *See* Grossman et al., *supra* note 14, at 11 ("Institutions and provider practices treat health data as a business asset over which these organizations can exert property rights"). *Cf.* Bergelson, *supra* note 62, at 404, 411 (in variety of legal and business contexts, courts and commercial practices consistently regard customer lists as property).

67. *See* Rodwin, *supra* note 42.

68. The seminal article is Michael Heller, *The Tragedy of the Anticommons: Property in Transition from Marx to Markets*, 111 HARV. L. REV. 621 (1998).

69. Richard A. Posner, *The Right of Privacy*, 12 GEORGIA LAW REV. 393 (1978).

a patient's medical information creates the opposite problem: the inability of anyone to compile and use a complete record.

More than one stakeholder having the right to block or exclude others from using or developing a good is a classic anticommons situation. Each of a patient's health care providers and insurers control a piece of the patient's complete medical treatment and health history and therefore each has the ability to exclude others from forming or using the complete record. Because the complete record has greater value than the sum of its parts, there is value to be gained in gathering all the pieces together, but no single provider or insurer can accomplish this.

Conceivably, an organizer could pay all necessary providers and insurers to induce their cooperation, but this would raise significant issues under the state and federal privacy laws addressed above. Patients can give permission to reveal or release medical information, but privacy laws deter using this legal authority to build repositories that can be shared with others for a fee. These laws make it cumbersome to share medical information with others. They also cloud whether a patient's permission can include selling access to medical information. Even if law does not strictly prohibit this, it does not clearly allow it, and public policy advocates often disfavor commodifying or monetizing medical information.[70]

If these uncertainties could be resolved, we would still face a more fundamental problem. Multiple stakeholders in a single prize creates problems of coordination and strategic behavior that are difficult to solve through private ordering.[71] Where the prize is a network benefit—one whose value depends on the number of joiners—later joiners sometimes obtain or confer more value than early ones, creating an obvious disincentive to join at all.[72] Real estate developers know this as the hold-out problem. In HIT, one form of this dynamic is the reluctance to join until technology standards are settled, for fear the early systems will soon become outmoded. Elsewhere, we can see other analogies in the "thickets" or "stacking" of multiple intellectual property interests in different aspects of a complex new technology or an entertainment production.[73] In these various situations, divided ownership or control of a common good makes it extremely difficult to assemble the pieces of the pie even though the collective benefits would be well worth the costs.

---

70. *See, e.g.*, National Committee on Vital and Health Statistics, *supra* note 35, at 19(expressing concern that "relying entirely on market forces to determine the nature and direction of PHR systems could cause personal health information to be exploited for its economic value without adequate consumer controls.").

71. F. Scott Kieff & Troy A. Paredes, *Engineering a Deal: Toward a Private Ordering Solution to the Anticommons Problem*, 48 B.C. L. Rev. 111 (2007).

72. Mark A. Lemley, *Private Property*, 52 Stan. L. Rev. 1545, 1553 (2000).

73. Kieff & Paredes, *supra* note 72; Michael A. Heller & Rebecca S. Eisenberg, *Can Patents Deter Innovation? The Anticommons in Biomedical Research*, 280 Science 698 (1998); Mark A. Lemley & Carl Shapiro, *Patient Holdup and Royalty Stacking*, 85 Tex. L. Rev. 1991 (2007).

This tragedy of the anticommons explains, for instance, the lack of interoperability among EMRs even when they do exist. A comprehensive survey by the influential Markle Foundation concluded that providers' ownership of medical records is a barrier to I-EHRs because "providers treat patient information as a highly proprietary asset that serves as a means of differentiation from the competition . . . . As a result, IT vendors compete without data standards and healthcare data becomes institution-based and compartmentalized."[74] According to another report, "the momentum [toward electronic records] is so great that the effort could be at risk of fragmenting, with companies and institutions producing a dizzying array of personally controlled health records. 'The danger is that they each create their own system and every American now has the opportunity to have 17 personally controlled records rather than one.'"[75]

Overcoming fractured ownership is critical to constructing a functioning I-EMR system. Imagine, for instance, that the country had tried in the 1950s to assemble its current interstate highway system out of thousands of separate segments that were privately owned. The coordination problems would be immense, and the holdout problems insurmountable. Imagine also if local nuisance ordinances gave any neighboring resident a right to object if traffic noise or pollution were a bother. Obviously, a smooth flowing, interconnected highway system could never form under these legal and economic conditions, yet these essentially are the conditions that afflict medical information. Health care providers and payors own each local segment of the envisioned information highway, and patients are the affected parties whose permission is needed for access. The resulting anticommons phenomena for I-EMRs are severe.

D. Patients' Rights of Access Are Necessary but Not Sufficient

Can private law loosen this logjam? Property theorists warn that, once anticommons conditions are created, they can be very difficult to undo. One possible solution is a hierarchy of rights, whereby providers' interests are subsidiary to a patient's. If a patient could command his providers to cooperate with a medical record compiler, then a well motivated and informed patient might be able to break through the thicket of providers' and insurers' competing interests.

A blunt way to confer this authority would be to declare that patients have ultimate ownership of their medical records and that providers' interests are merely "custodial," holding them in trust for the benefit of their patients. Trusteeships and bailments are certainly well known in law, and this is essentially the legal

---

74. Connecting for Health, Financial, Legal and Organizational Approaches to Achieving Electronic Connectivity in Healthcare *supra* note 54.

75. Personally Controlled Health Records: Are They the Next Big Thing?, Focus: News from Harvard Medical, Dental, and Public Health Schools (Oct. 27, 2006), http://focus.hms.harvard.edu/2006/102706/information_technology.shtml (quoting a Harvard professor who is an expert on HIT).

characterization being adopted by non-health care hosts of patient-controlled personal health records (such as Microsoft and Google). However, mere custodianship does not fit the law's current understanding of providers' true ownership of their medical records.[76] The next section explores whether patients *should* be given an intellectual property interest in their medical information, but presently the law decidedly does *not* do so.

Short of ownership, though, the law does give patients a right to inspect, copy, and correct their medical information. (In other words, a provider's property right to exclude others is good against all the world except the patient.) Prior to HIPAA, this access right was (and still is) embodied in a host of state statutes,[77] and it is part of providers' common law fiduciary duties arising from their professional relationships with patients.[78] The federal privacy rule makes this right to access medical records universal, including the right to receive medical information in electronic form or in any other format requested if that is "readily" done.[79]

A patient's access right to information is very useful for our purposes. It could accomplish what needs to happen in order to create a consolidated medical

---

76. Perhaps providers were legal custodians in an earlier time. *See, e.g.,* Pyramid Life Ins. Co. v. Masonic Hospital Ass'n of Payne County, Okl., 191 F.Supp. 51, 54 D.C.Okl. (1961) ("the keeper of the records is only the custodian and not the owner of that information constituting the medical records of the patient. The patient has a property right in the information appearing or portrayed on the records . . . "). Custodianship fit the practice, prior to photocopy machines, of transferring the original record rather than a copy whenever it was needed for legal or other medical purposes. "Medical Records," in Encyclopedia of Everyday Law, www.enotes.com/everyday-law-encyclopedia/medical-records. Once photocopying became the norm, however, providers insisted on retaining the original— consistent with their claim of its ownership. This history suggests the possibility of returning to a concept of custodianship once medical records become primarily electronic and therefore no special legal importance is attached to possession of the "original." See Shabo, *supra* note 39.

77. *See generally* Comment, *Patient Access To Medical Records In Washington,* 57 WASH. L. REV. 697 (1983); Paul V. Stearns, *Access To And Cost of Reproduction Of Patient Medical Records: A Comparison of State Laws,* 21 J LEG MED. 79 (2000); Center on Medical Records Right and Privacy, Georgetown University, http://ihcrp.georgetown.edu/privacy/publications.html.

78. *See* Cannell v. Medical and Surgical Clinic, S.C., 21 Ill.App.3d 383, 315 N.E.2d 278 (Ill.App. 1974) ("the fiducial qualities of the patient-physician relationship require disclosure of medical data to a patient or his agent on request"). Similarly, Murphy v. Godwin, 303 A.2d 668 (Del. Super. 1973) held that a physician has a legal duty to assist a patient with completing insurance application forms, based on "recognized incidents of the doctor-patient relationship."

79. *See* American Recovery and Reinvestment Act of 2009 (ARRA), P.L. 111-5, section 13405(e); Joy Pritts, *Altered States: State Health Privacy Laws and the Impact of the Federal Health Privacy Rule,* YALE J. HEALTH POL'Y, L. & ETHICS, (2002).

record, and it can be exercised by a patient's representative. One major hitch is the cost of exercising this right. The Privacy Rule permits providers to charge reasonable fees for the costs of copying (including labor) and for preparing a summary or explanation.[80] One study found that hospitals' fees "range very widely, from $2–$55 for short records of fifteen pages to $15–$585 for long ones of 500 pages."[81] A potential solution for the fee problem is insurance reimbursement.[82] Health plans that sponsor I-EMRs could require provider cooperation as a condition of membership in the network, or they could pay a modest fee or supplement for doing so voluntarily, recapturing some or all of any net costs through supplemental premiums.[83]

Assisting patients and providers in compiling a comprehensive medical record does not solve all of our problems, however. It is not possible to capture many of the social or network benefits of this compilation unless the complier or custodian has the right to sell access to their information under terms controlled by the patient. Patients can allow a compiler to exercise their access and control rights on their behalf, but these custodial rights are personal and fiduciary; therefore patients cannot obviously transfer them in a form that can be easily retransferred or monetized. As developed more below, we are not contemplating irrevocable or absolute transfers, only transfers in a form similar to a license for use that the patient can revoke at any time, but even this limited license for non-exclusive and temporary use cannot clearly be put into the stream of commerce under current law.

Thus, we return to the issue of network externalities discussed above: optimal incentives for I-EMRs will not exist unless an entity (or person) can capture and distribute much[84] of the economic value for a group of providers, insurers, and patients.[85] Law can facilitate the compilation of a patient's entire medical

---

80. 45 CFR 164.524. However, the fee may not include costs associated with searching for and retrieving the requested information.

81. G. Fioriglio & P. Szolovits, *Copy Fees And Patients' Rights To Obtain A Copy Of Their Medical Records: From Law To Reality*, AMIA ANNU SYMP PROC. 251 (2005).

82. *See generally* Kleinke, *supra* note 2, at 1258 ("The government has the ability to catalyze the creation and deployment of an HIT infrastructure by wedding that infrastructure to all of its reimbursement policies"); Dave Hansen, Rise of the e-mandates: Soon, You May Not Have a Choice, AM. MED. NEWS, Dec. 17, 2007.

83. One analysis estimates the annual costs for providers' assistance would be less than $50 per subscriber. Thornewill & Esterhay, *supra* note 51, at 21.

84. We say "much" rather than "most" or "all" because the compiler need only capture its costs plus a reasonable profit margin, which might be considerably less than the full economic value if an I-EMR creates a large consumer surplus, as many analysts believe it would. *See* Brett M. Frischmann & Mark A. Lemley, *Spillovers*, 107 COLUM. L. REV. 257, 300 (2007).

85. We mean to leave open the very real possibility that several or many different I-EMR networks could co-exist.

treatment and health history from among multiple independent records holders, and can reward doctors for using consolidated records—if only someone is willing to pay the costs of doing this. These costs can be considerable, however,[86] which means that the compiler must be in a position to reap and distribute some economic reward from this endeavor by sublicensing or reselling its limited rights. Thus, Heritage Foundation scholar Edmund F. Haislmaier has it right, that "an explicit mechanism for monetizing the value of medical information and passing that value back to the data owners is a major advantage. . . . The best way to induce patients and providers to share the individual data they create is to help them unlock the value of that data and share in the benefits derived from letting others use it."[87] Currently, law either prohibits this, or it does not clearly permit this, for any of the existing permutations of property and privacy rights.

Property rights are one (but not the only) means to monetize access to information. In other arenas of intellectual property law, it is naive to think that enough people will invest enough of their creative talents and scientific ingenuity primarily for public good, so we give them patents and copyrights. Similarly, if patients were given ownership of their complete medical treatment and health histories, they could license to compilers their rights to that information in a propertized form that could be more fully developed and commercialized. These third parties could then form contracts or partnerships with others who use or contribute to the databases (including doctors and insurers).

Locating these initial rights with patients in no way determines the eventual locus or form of ensuing medical records networks. Instead, the idea is to create a market mechanism for rewarding those who control access to medical information, in order to place those rights in a stream of commerce that can carry them to their highest and best use. In a proper legal environment, these blood vessels will grow where they need to go. The following section explores this idea. It draws from the vigorous academic debate over whether personal information collected through commercial transactions or Internet browsing should be protected by either property law or privacy law regimes.

IV. SHOULD PATIENTS HAVE PROPERTY RIGHTS?

There is nothing which so generally strikes the imagination, and engages the affection of mankind, as the right of property.—Sir William Blackstone[88]

---

86. Estimates for a complete, nationwide I-EMR system range from $100 billion to $300 billion. *Supra* note 24.

87. Haislmaier, *supra* note 39.

88. 2 COMMENTARIES ON THE LAWS OF ENGLAND 1–2 (1978).

Entrenched and competing property rights by health care providers and insurers, coupled with patients' privacy rights, have locked out much of the potential value of networked medical information. We have described this architectural fragmentation in the economic terms of network externalities and the tragedy of the anticommons. Those who own this information are not in a position to capture its full value, and those who are in such a position are not clearly permitted to purchase and sell rights to the information.

Absent outright government compulsion, the fluidity needed to efficiently assemble countless scattered pieces of medical information into an I-EMR could be achieved in a variety of ways. Here, we focus on giving patients either property rights or other legal rights to all of their medical information in a form that they can transfer to a data assembler, for deployment into various productive uses. There are numerous variations on the precise institutional arrangements that could accomplish this transfer and deployment.[89] Rather than obsessing over particular institutional arrangements, here we focus on the core rights that patients should possess in order to enable their participation in the necessary financial rewards.

Our analysis is drawn primarily from the vigorous debate among legal scholars over ownership and protection of personal information revealed through consumer transactions or Internet browsing. The explosive growth of technologies for capturing this information, and in hidden markets for trading it, brought anxious attention to how and whether consumers should be given more control over their personal information.[90] The issues we face here, though, differ in at least one critical respect. Personal information in non-medical settings is not protected by any existing privacy laws, whereas medical information is. Therefore, the legal policy problem for non-medical information is how to restrict the otherwise free flow and use of such information. Our problem is just the opposite: the privacy of medical information is amply protected when in the hands of care providers and insurers. Property or other legal rights are needed to dislodge that information into more productive circulation, while keeping in place appropriate safeguards. Needing only to protect information puts the property debate in a much different light than also needing to produce more value from it. Nevertheless, the fully developed scholarly debate over property rights in general personal information sheds considerable light on the competing arguments for "propertizing" medical information.

---

89. See *supra* note 35.

90. *See generally* Symposium, 32 CONN. L. REV. 809–948 (2000); Symposium, 52 STAN. L. REV. 987 (2000); Paul M. Schwartz, *Property, Privacy, and Personal Data*, 117 HARV. L. REV. 2055 (2004); Bergelson, *supra* note 62, at 414–19 (2003).

A. Arguments In Favor of Property

When law has confronted similar issues, legislatures have created intellectual property rights such as copyright and patents, as exceptions to the general rule that information is in the public domain. These legal rights serve the focused instrumental goal of generating private incentives to invest time, energy and resources into creating, discovering, and/or developing valuable information.[91] Should a similar approach be used for medical information?[92] Even though incentives are not needed to create it (since it is created when patients seek treatment),[93] financial rewards are needed to compile and transform it into useful forms. Property rights are an ideal way to bundle patients' rights into a legal form that can be monetized and put into a stream of commerce. Fully realizing the economic potential of valuable assets is, in modern times, property law's primary purpose. "We deem something property in order to facilitate its transfer."[94]

Even when non-economic values loom large, some civil rights advocates favor property protections because of their strength and resonance in our legal system.[95] For instance, civil libertarian George Annas advocates giving people property rights in their own DNA in order to protect infringements from commercial interests.[96] Propertization opponent Sonia Suter concedes that property "has always been a powerful tool to protect important interests because it is familiar and effective. Property has teeth and 'symbolic force.'"[97]

The other extreme to propertization is depropertization—that is, placing such information in the public domain. That route is unappealing for a variety of reasons. Providers' and insurers' existing property rights would be eliminated. That might pose significant constitutional issues and would spark strong political opposition. Moreover, since privacy protections would remain, public domain access would still be very limited. And, any economic benefits derived from this information would not flow back to patients. Conferring additional and superior property rights to patients appears to be a more feasible and appropriate route.

---

91. See Samuelson, *supra* note 46, at 1140.

92. Analogously, some states (OR, FL, CO, GA) have given people property rights in their genetic information, to serve the instrumental goal of preventing others from capitalizing on and exploiting this information. Sonia Suter, *Disentangling Privacy from Property: Toward a Deeper Understanding of Genetic Privacy*, 72 GEORGE WASHINGTON LAW REV. 737, 747 (2004).

93. Rodwin, *supra* note 42.

94. Jessica Litman, *Information Privacy/Information Property*, 52 STAN. L. REV. 1283, 1296 (2000).

95. *Id.* at 1290.

96. George J. Annas et al., *Drafting the Genetic Privacy Act: Science, Policy and Practical Considerations*, 23 J. LAW, MED. & ETHICS 360–66 (1995).

97. Suter, *supra* note 93, at 751.

This route is also supported by the seminal economic theory developed by Calebresi and Melamed.[98] Their classic article[99] outlines the general criteria by which society should prefer a property regime over a liability (or, in our case, regulatory) regime for determining access to and use of valuable resources. In general, property rules are preferable when markets determine best uses more efficiently than courts (or, in our case, regulatory agencies). Markets are generally preferred in economic arenas unless "market valuation of the entitlement is deemed inefficient," or when a liability (or regulatory) rule "facilitates a combination of efficiency and distributive results which would be difficult to achieve under a property rule."[100]

In medical settings, these obviously are large questions that demand wide-ranging analysis, but much of that can be short-circuited by observing that we do not face an all-or-nothing choice. Medical privacy law already contains much (and perhaps too much) of the normative content missing from property law. The issue, then, is whether this field should be overwhelmingly normative— under a legal regime that specifies most of the allowable and unallowable uses—or instead should have a less-normative zone that permits individuals more leeway to decide what uses to make of their medical information and what value those uses should have. Adding property rights to privacy protections would move us in that direction.

Privacy laws are concerned mainly with controlling access to information rather than putting medical information to innovative uses. Therefore, they do not embrace a set of norms and practices that countenance financial transactions. Privacy laws facilitate the ready release of information only for narrow and specific treatment purposes. Thus, they primarily express negative liberties—the rights to exclude, limit, and refuse. Property law, in contrast, embraces a broader set of positive liberties: the rights to use, transfer, develop, etc.

Also, privacy rights grow out of the special nature of the relationships in medical care delivery between patient and care providers.[101] Therefore, they are enforceable only against the particular providers who generate and possess this information. It is difficult to anticipate and specify all the conditions that would be needed to allow the free flow of medical information since this depends on

---

98. We owe this insight to Bergelson, *supra* note 62, at 417. See also Thomas W. Merrill & Henry E. Smith, *The Property/Contract Interface*, 101 COLUM. L. REV. 773 (2001).

99. Guido Calabresi & Douglas Melamed, *Property Rules, Liability Rules, and Inalienability: One View of the Cathedral*, 85 HARV. L. REV. 1089 (1972).

100. *Id.* at 1110.

101. Suter, *supra* note 93, at 773. Stressing the relational (as opposed to transactional) basis of health care law generally, *see* Mark A. Hall & Carl E. Schneider, *Where is the "There" in Health Law? Can It Become a Coherent Field?* 14 HEALTH MATRIX 101 (2004); Wm. M. Sage, *Some Principles Require Principals: Why Banning "Conflicts of Interest" Won't Solve Incentive Problems in Biomedical Research*, 85 TX. L. REV. 1413 (2007).

who possesses and controls the information and on its variety of potential uses. The same is true for specifying necessary protections. Building these rights and protections into the legal status of the information itself is therefore an advantage. The other option is for freedoms and protections to derive only from the origins or location of the information—that is, a patient's particular relationship with the person who holds the information.

Property law addresses these enforcement concerns by creating rights that tend to "run with the chattel," in other words, that are enforceable against the world at large and not just against particular parties based on their relationship with the patient.[102] Also, property law provides a strong legal basis for seeking injunctive remedies against infringements.[103] To these extents, property law might confer more extensive rights than privacy law alone.

Finally, property law invokes a fairly standard bundle of protections that are well-established and understood in the law, rather than requiring specification and interpretation of each stick in the bundle. This relative simplicity and ease of recognition facilitates productive development. Using examples from the former Soviet bloc, property law scholar Michael Heller concludes that productive use "emerges more successfully in resources that begin transition [into a newly created market economy] with a single owner holding a near-standard bundle of market legal rights."[104] It is always possible to craft more tailored legal specifications that fit a particular subject area more exactly, but perfection should not be pursued to the detriment of workable improvements. Property law theorist Henry Smith explains that using existing legal bundles can ultimately be more efficient because they are recognizable and so conserve on information costs: legal "lumpiness has its advantages" because "the on/off quality of [property law] allows complexity to be managed through modularity."[105]

B. Arguments Against Property

There are several substantial arguments against giving patients property rights in their medical information. Many privacy advocates view propertization of personal information as "morally obnoxious . . . anathema" because of the law's expressive or symbolic function.[106] They feel that property law connotes a crass commercial attitude about information that inherently has deeply emotional and existential human significance. Sonia Suter articulates this position most

---

102. Explaining this "in rem" character of property rights, see Henry Hansmann and Reinier Kraakman, *Property, Contract and Verification*, 31 J. Leg. Stud. 373 (2002).

103. Samuelson, *supra* note 46, at 1149.

104. Heller, *supra* note 69, at 631.

105. Henry E. Smith, *Intellectual Property as Property: Delineating Entitlements in Information*, 116 Yale L.J. 1742 (2007). *See also* Thomas W. Merrill & Henry E. Smith, *Optimal Standardization in the Law of Property*, 110 Yale L.J. 1 (2000).

106. *See* Samuelson, *supra* note 46, at 1143 (reviewing, but not embracing, this position).

forcefully. In her view, medical information is "integral to the self" because it "is about us in very central and personal ways."[107] Rather than protecting "the wholeness of the self and of relationships through which the self flourishes," property "by definition, commodifies and disaggregates the parts from the self." Therefore, "conceptualizing [medical] information as property distorts and impoverishes our understanding of the dignitary, personhood interests we have in this information and the nature of relationships we hope will be built around and through its disclosure."[108]

Those who stress the special significance of personal medical information are adamantly opposed to governing its use primarily through marketplace norms. Intellectual property scholars are rightly concerned that reducing the exchange of information to purely transactional legal analysis will produce commercial practices that give people little or no choice over what becomes of their vital information. According to Jessica Litman, the assumption "that initial legal ownership of [information] would enable individuals to restrain their downstream use by negotiating conditions of use before disclosing them . . . seems to be inspired by a fairy-tale picture of easy bargaining in cyberspace through the use of intelligent agents. . . . That's nonsense."[109] Mark Lemley agrees that, "from a privacy perspective, an intellectual property right that is regularly signed away may turn out to be less protection than we want to give individuals. To do any good, the right might have to be inalienable and waivable only in certain limited circumstances."[110]

These concerns have pressing salience for access to and control of medical information, but the default rules of property law strongly favor allowing property owners to permanently relinquish all of their rights to a purchaser. Alienability is the "raison d'etre of property" rights[111] because this is the legal characteristic that makes valuable assets easily exchangeable. Although actual commercial practices embrace many less absolute transactional forms such as leasing and licensing, property law strongly disfavors mandatory restraints on full alienation.[112]

Full alienability conflicts sharply with the values we associate with personal medical information. It is inconceivable that we would embrace a legal regime allowing patients to forever relinquish rights to access and control their medical information, yet this is one of the core elements in property law's classic bundle

---

107. Suter, *supra* note 93, at 773.

108. *Id.* at 749, 798.

109. Litman, *supra* note 95, at 1297.

110. Mark A. Lemley, *supra* note 73, at 1551 (2000). *Accord* Murphy, *supra* note 47, at 2413; Paul M. Schwartz, *Property, Privacy, and Personal Data*, 117 HARV. L. REV. 2055, 2077 (2004).

111. Litman, *supra* note 95, at 1295.

112. Samuelson, *supra* note 46, at 1145.

of rights. In general, medical information law should have a strong normative content—specifying permitted and impermissible uses and modes of obtaining consent. Privacy law does this to a considerable extent, but property law is adamantly neutral (for the most part).

This clash could be avoided by constructing a more limited bundle of property rights—as intellectual property law does generally (for instance, by limiting the length of those rights), or as patent law specially does (in a variety of ways) to take account of the importance of medical uses.[113] But, the more sticks that are removed or shortened, the less compelling becomes the argument for pursing a bundling approach to begin with. As Mark Lemley observes, "a properly designed right would look rather more like a system of regulation than a system of property rights."[114]

HIT system architecture could be designed creatively to reduce the complexity of a non-bundled regulatory regime.[115] The detailed limits required by regulators or desired by contracting parties could be specified and enforced efficiently by embedding them in the software that operates I-EMRs. The technological sophistication of electronic systems makes it possible to protect individual rights at a much more granular level than traditional regulatory or contracting systems. Thus, according to Jonathan Zittrain, the "expression of rights through a trusted system may allow for 'baby-splitting' among interests that is not feasible in more traditional regimes. For example, in place of the stalemate over who should 'own' a record, a well-defined self-enforcing rights architecture could allow information sharing without having to ultimately resolve matters in as coarse a way as 'owner' or 'non-owner.'"[116]

Still, if any kind of property regime were adopted for medical information, additional lines would need to be drawn between this type of information and

---

113. For instance, patents on medical procedures cannot be enforced against physicians, Aaron Kesselheim & Michelle Mello, *Medical-Process Patents: Monopolizing the Delivery of Health Care*, 355 NEW ENG. J. MED. 2036 (2006), and the government can issue "compulsory licenses" for patented drugs during medical emergencies. Simone A. Rose, *On Purple Pills, Stem Cells, and Other Market Failures: A Case for a Limited Compulsory Licensing Scheme for Patent Property*, 48 HOW. L.J. 579 (2005). Also, drug developers receive extensions of their patent periods to account for the delay in FDA review prior to marketing, and they may infringe the patents of their competitors in order to pursue testing needed for FDA review.

114. Lemley, *supra* note 73, at 1556. For instance, Vera Bergelson, *supra* note 62, at 439, proposes and explicates a complicated scheme for personal information generally under which people would "would own this information during their lifetime, subject to a (i) non-exclusive automatic inalienable license to the original collector and (ii) limited non-exclusive automatic license to the general public."

115. Jonathan Zittrain, *What the Publisher Can Teach the Patient: Intellectual Property and Privacy in an Era of Trusted Privication*, 52 STANFORD LAW REV. 1201 (2000).

116. *Id.* at 1246.

other personal information, over which there are no property rights. The balance of opinion among property scholars opposes propertizing personal information generally, and the arguments of the minority so far have not convinced lawmakers to the contrary. For medical information, there are good reasons to find the propertization arguments more compelling, but if we accepted those arguments we would then need to differentiate the two realms of personal information, which adds an additional element of complexity.

However, much the same is true for any type of intellectual property regime. Because property is not inherent in information, when creating intellectual property it is always necessary to define, justify and distinguish what is protected from what is not. In part, we have undertaken this chore already for medical information by defining special privacy protections. Similar definitions could also describe the scope of patients' property rights. However, property law definitions would likely differ from those in existing privacy law because, as noted above, the latter arise from special fiduciary responsibilities of health care providers and they have somewhat different aims. Having to carefully excavate these additional layers is another reason to pause before planting oneself firmly in a property regime.

Finally, property rights might frustrate the very goals they seek, by inhibiting the public goods value of medical information. Creating more property rights may not be the best solution to an anti-commons problem that was created in part by too many property rights in the first place. "An intellectual property law governing personal data would result in the creation of literally billions of new intellectual property rights every day; economics wisely counsels us not to expect frictionless licensing in this circumstance."[117] The Internet, for instance, owes its spectacular success to the fact that its basic structure and elements are all in the public domain.[118] Imagine how its development might have stalled or been severely stunted if key elements were protected by copyrights or patents.

For medical information, Professor Marc Rodwin makes an impressive argument that conferring property rights would interfere with important public goods, such as assembling research databases and engaging in public health monitoring.[119] His focus is primarily on de-identified data rather than the personalized medical records we consider here, but his objections must be considered carefully. If patients had property rights, would the government have to pay them "just compensation" for any "taking" of medical information for public

---

117. Lemley, *supra* note 73, at 1553.

118. Lemley & McGowan, *supra* note 20, at 540.

119. Rodwin, *supra* note 42; Marc A. Rodwin, *The Case for Public Ownership of Patient Data*, 302 JAMA 86 (2009); *see also* Litman, *supra* note 95, at 1294 ("When we recognize property rights in facts, we endorse the idea that facts may be privately owned and that the owner of a fact is entitled to restrict the uses to which that fact may be put. That notion is radical.").

purposes? We are not constitutional scholars, but we presume not if the information is not identifiable to the patient, since any property interest resides in patient-specific information. Government presumably would not take identifiable information except for public health purposes under its police power, as now happens without constitutional objection. Any newly created or expanded property rights would be against the backdrop of these long-standing government practices and polices and therefore could be made subject to them. Still, creating new property rights might give patients more legal power than they currently possess to refuse uses (or demand payments) for either public or private purposes.

C. Common Ground

Whichever route we pursue, it will not result in a pure legal regime. As with any other type of intellectual property, because these legal rules are specially constructed to serve an instrumental purpose, we cannot avoid a fairly sui generis set of rules, especially considering the unique importance attached to medical information. Therefore, in the end it may not matter a great deal whether the bundle of rights in medical information is built stick by stick, starting with simple contract and privacy rights, or reconstructed from a larger existing set of property rights. This can be seen in the broader debate over personal information generally. Some scholars favor a special bundle of property rights,[120] others favor a special set of tort rules,[121] and still others feel that contract rights are sufficient if properly enforced.[122] Despite these differences, what is common (albeit far from identical) among them is a set of shared concerns about the important interests that require legal protection and facilitation.

Drawing from this common ground, we suggest the following principles to guide construction of patients' rights to license access to their own medical information:

1. People should be able themselves, or through their agents, to authorize access to and use of their medical information for financial rewards, and these licenses should be transferable.

   Without clear recognition of this core entitlement, network benefits will not be captured (or "internalized") sufficient to give anyone in the health care finance and delivery system (as it is currently structured) enough incentive to invest in the construction of I-EMRs. Conferring rights of access and use should not be demandable as an absolute condition of

---

120. E.g., Bergelson, *supra* note 62; Schwartz, *supra* note 111 (advocating a "hybrid inalienability regime" that allows sale of personal info but only if there is a default rule (with opt-out) that restricts further transfers).

121. *E.g.*, Samuelson, *supra* note 46; Litman, *supra* note 95.

122. *E.g.*, Zittrain, *supra* note 116; Lemley, *supra* note 73.

providing or insuring health care services. However, positive or negative incentives can be offered as long as they are not unconscionable.[123]

2. Default rules should be set with some degree of paternalism toward protecting patients' interests, in order to take account of the cognitive and other limitations on consent involving vital medical information.

For instance, default rules can be set in a way that forces more choice and more information. Usually, to minimize transaction costs, legal default rules are set in an "opt-out" fashion according to what most parties would accept when fully informed, so that these rules apply unless otherwise specified. However, if a substantial minority strongly dislikes the majority option, there may be good reason to adopt a more protective default rule that requires parties to affirmatively opt in to the majority position. Otherwise, the net social condition might be suboptimal if the default position is offered only on a take-it-or-leave-it basis, with no real choice or with a technical choice but inadequate notice.[124]

3. Some rights or protections should be nonwaivable (or inalienable) and should follow the information, regardless of agreement or provenance.

For instance, patients should always retain their basic rights to inspect, copy and correct medical records, and patients should have a nonwaivable right to revoke any permissions they give for access or use. Being able to back out of an improvident bargain helps to correct for market flaws by preventing initial mistakes from having long-term consequences.[125] This power also gives market participants a strong incentive to conform their behavior to patients' expectations. Further protections can be had by overseeing the "infomediaries" that assemble and process medical information and by embedding safeguards in the software architecture of the system. These protective mechanisms can originate either from regulators or entrepreneurs.

4. Patients' rights to control or sell access to their medical information should be limited to data that can be linked to them personally.

If information is anonymized (or "deidentified") so that it cannot reasonably be connected to anyone in particular, the individual's claim to the value of the information ceases, as does the need for strong legal protections. Recognizing this limit will foster more public benefits from medical research and public health monitoring.

V. SUMMARY AND CONCLUSION

Because information by its nature can be used by many people at once without depletion, it does not suffer from the same "tragedy of the commons" problems

---

123. *Accord*, Bergelson, *supra* note 62, at 447.
124. Murphy, *supra* note 47, at 2412–16.
125. Schwartz, *supra* note 111, at 2105–06.

as does tangible property.[126] Therefore, property rights are not needed to allocate access. Instead, conferring ownership or control of information can block its beneficial use. Thus, information, generally speaking, is usually regarded as being in the public domain unless there are good reasons in public policy to propertize it. In other areas of intellectual property, that reason is to provide an economic incentive to discover or create information that otherwise might not exist.[127] For medical information, there is quite a distinct reason: overcoming system fragmentation.

Deeply fractured health care finance and delivery presents two daunting economic challenges that must be solved to fashion the interconnected electronic information systems missing from most other important social arenas. Fragmentation creates *network externalities* that prevent any one actor from realizing much of the social benefits to be derived from I-EMRs. No actor—including government insurers—has sufficient incentives to make the necessary investments. Solutions to the network economics problems can be imagined, but they are barred by a patchwork of laws that either frustrate well-intentioned efforts to integrate information, or that give individual stakeholders the power and incentive to block integration. Medical care providers, for instance, have inherent control of medical information owing to their ownership of the tangible embodiment of medical records and their legal obligations to protect its privacy. Also, owing to reimbursement systems and legal uncertainties, doctors and hospitals lack sufficient incentives or authority to share their records with each other. These phenomena can be usefully thought of as examples of a "tragedy of the *anti-commons*."

Absent government mandates or actual integration of our kaleidoscopic finance and delivery system, the only way to loosen this economic and legal stultification is to permit transfer payments among the various stakeholders that control access to valuable medical information. This can be accomplished in a variety of ways, such as through reimbursement systems and the reform of "fraud and abuse" laws. Here, though, we focus principally on ordinary property and contract laws that would allow patients to license their rights of access and use, under appropriately protective rules and institutions. These rules can be constructed either as a newly-designed form of intellectual property, or as a specially-crafted set of contractual and privacy rights.

The previous section outlines the pros and cons of the two general approaches and describes the common ground between them. Property rights are bundled, powerful, recognizable, and market-enabling, but they also are coarse, crass, greed-inducing, and possibly obstructive. Contract rights coupled with regulatory protections are malleable, fine-grained, situational, and normative, but they

---

126. Litman, *supra* note 95, at 1294.
127. *See* Samuelson, *supra* note 46, at 1140.

also are complex and potentially oppressive, and they tend to be enforceable only against particular parties based on their relationship with patients.

Common ground between these approaches can be formed by agreeing that patients' rights to medical information should be tradable in some form that can be monetized, but that special protections and institutions are needed to prevent marketplace abuses. These include giving patients a nonwaivable right to terminate permission to access and use their information, and making their rights to inspect, copy, and correct medical information inalienable. A public or private coordinating institution is needed to protect patients and ensure adequate market conditions, but the choice of that institution should not dictate the ultimate structure of medical information networks.

In all of this, we are informed by certain basic lessons that can be learned from a review of the academic literature on property rights generally. Economic and social rights can suffer from too little or too much legal protection, creating either insufficient or excessive incentives for investment, leading to suboptimal development or social harms from excess development. Also, legal protections can exist in a variety of different forms. Thus, for property rights in medical information, we can think of legal protections being arrayed on a spectrum from strong to nonexistent, for each of a variety of stakeholders and potential uses. Rights to medical information can be overlapping (or nonexclusive) as long as there is a clear hierarchy of rights that gives one party ultimate control.

The problem broadly conceived, then, is to find the right mix and forms of property rights among patients, providers, researchers, and compilers to maximize the social benefits of I-EMRs while minimizing social or individual harms—but to do this without making the rules so complex that they are unmanageable, unintelligible, or unreliable. Clear but adaptable rules are needed so that stakeholders can make heterogeneous decisions that sort out which of several competing models for I-EMRs works best, and in what combination. This is a tall order, but it must be filled since legal uncertainty is itself a major deterrent to more productive use of medical information.

9. VALUE-BASED PURCHASING OPPORTUNITIES IN TRADITIONAL MEDICARE
A Proposal and Legal Evaluation

TIMOTHY STOLTZFUS JOST

LAWRENCE P. CASALINO

I. INTRODUCTION

> We should recognize that the scientific side of medicine is up to date and in full synchronization with the peaks of human achievement, while for the most part the social side and the economic . . . are often archaic and ineffective in operation . . .
>
> We find ourselves . . . with a splendid body of trained men and women . . . but without an administrative or economic system which will give all members of our society an even or an adequate opportunity to profit by them.[1]

This description of the U.S. health care system was written in 1932 by Ray Lyman Wilbur, chairman of the Committee on the Costs of Medical Care. Much has changed since the Committee's report. Our physicians wield powers through technologies and medications that could scarcely be imagined in Dr. Wilbur's time. Medicare, Medicaid, and commercial health insurers pump thousands of billions of dollars into the system every year. But much has remained the same. The quality of health care in the United States is highly variable, and overall falls far short of what it could be, given our knowledge and technical capacity.[2] This quality gap—along with the highest-in-the-world costs of the U.S. system—is attributable in large part to the fragmented "archaic and ineffective" organization and operation of our delivery system and to the structure of Medicare.

Medicare could use its position as by far the largest payor for health care to take the lead in trying to induce the delivery system to focus on providing high quality care consistently and efficiently.[3] However, although CMS has recently

---

1. Ray Lyman Wilbur, *The High Points in the Recommendations of the Committee on the Costs of Medical Care*, 207 NEW ENG. J.MED. 1073, 1073, 1074 (1932).

2. INSTITUTE OF MEDICINE, TO ERR IS HUMAN: BUILDING A SAFER HEALTH SYSTEM (2000); Elizabeth A. McGlynn et al., *The Quality of Health Care Delivered to Adults in the United States*, 348 NEW ENG.J.MED. 2635 (2003).

3. Robert A. Berenson, *Why and How Traditional Medicare Should be Permitted to More Aggressively Address Excessive Health Care Spending*, (Discussion Paper for the Center for

implemented numerous initiatives aimed at increasing quality and/or control-ling costs, Medicare for the most part still follows its traditional model: providers submit claims and Medicare pays them. High quality, efficient physicians and hospitals are not rewarded for investments of time and money that they make to provide better care. In fact, the opposite is the case: to the extent that these invest-ments keep patients healthier and reduce their need for medical care, hospitals, and physicians that invest in improving care are actually paid less. Meanwhile, physicians and hospitals that provide more services—even if these services are unnecessary—are paid for each of these services.

Some analysts believe that the traditional Medicare system is incapable of forming the centerpiece of an effective, modern health care system. They urge reliance on private health insurance plans and on the Medicare Advantage pro-gram. Our purpose in this paper is not to consider the advantages and disadvan-tages of private health insurers or of Medicare Advantage. Rather, we suggest that there are many actions that traditional Medicare could and should take to become a "value-based purchaser," and that, because of Medicare's size, such actions would go far toward improving the quality and controlling the costs of U.S. health care.[4]

This paper is a combination of two papers that we wrote for a project spon-sored by the Urban Institute and New America Foundation under the oversight of Robert Berenson and Len Nichols. Lawrence Casalino contributed a paper proposing a restructuring of traditional Medicare payment to achieve value-based purchasing. Timothy Jost's paper examined the legal changes that Congress and the Department of Health and Human Services would need to make to accomplish this goal. This paper combines both in a greatly abbreviated version.

II. THE PROPOSALS

As a value-based purchaser, traditional Medicare would seek "to obtain the right kind and mix of services, of acceptable quality, at a reasonable cost."[5] The proposals made by Dr. Casalino follow. They are founded primarily on two concepts as explained further below, the Accountable Care System (ACS) and the medical home:

Advanced Studies in Behavior Sciences Project on *Creating an Equitable, Efficient, and Sustainable Medicare for the 21st Century* 2007) (Hereinafter, "Berenson, Traditional Medicare"); Robert A. Berenson, *Getting Serious About Excessive Medicare Spending: A Purchasing Model*, HEALTH AFF. WEB EXCL., W586-02 (2003).

4. Robert A. Berenson & Dean M. Harris, *Using Managed Care Tools in Traditional Medicare: Should We? Could We?* 65 LAW & CONTEMP. PROBS. 139 (2002).

5. Berenson, *Traditional Medicare, supra* note 3.

Make Conditions for Participation in Medicare More Stringent

1. Medicare would maintain a census of U.S. physicians, medical practices, and ACSs, which would be updated annually. Each physician, each medical practice/group, and each ACS would be required to report a limited amount of pertinent information annually.[6]

2. Medicare would set a date by which each physician and hospital would be required to submit electronically a limited amount of information useful for quality and cost analyses. The amount of information required would be increased over time as information systems and physicians' and hospitals' ability to use them are enhanced.

3. For a limited number of services—notably imaging, surgical, and endoscopic procedures performed within physicians' offices—Medicare would require physicians to meet explicit standards for their equipment and record-keeping, and for the training of the involved physicians and staff.

4. Individual hospitals would be excluded from participation in Medicare if they failed to meet minimum—quite low—quality standards for four years in a row. Reinstatement would be possible if certain criteria were met. ACSs would be stripped of their ACS status if they failed to meet minimum quality standards for two years in a row. Again, reinstatement would be possible if certain criteria were met.

5. For a very limited number of highly complex procedures—e.g. transplants—only designated Centers of Excellence would be permitted to participate in Medicare.

Encourage Beneficiaries to Choose a Medical Home

Medicare would encourage, but not require, beneficiaries to choose a medical practice as their medical home. Beneficiaries who chose a medical home would be permitted to see physicians outside their medical home practice without a referral. Beneficiaries would be permitted to change their medical home choice twice within a year, or to cease having a medical home.

Change Payment Methods to Reward Quality and Efficiency

1. Medicare would pay hospitals using an inpatient and outpatient prospective payment system with relative payment rates revised so that some

---

6. There is a dual rationale for this proposal: first, having an up-to-date census of medical practices is essential for measuring, for rewarding, and for improving quality and cost-effectiveness and for understanding which types of practices provide better care; second, such a census is not likely to exist unless supported by government—i.e., it is a public good.

services are not significantly more profitable than others. In addition, bonuses for quality and patient satisfaction would be available (See Table 1).

2. Medicare's payment and bonus system would differ between hospitals that are part of an ACS and hospitals that are not. Non-ACS hospitals would continue to receive the national annual payment update and would be eligible for bonuses based on measures of the hospital's quality of care and of patient satisfaction with the hospital. ACS hospitals would receive an annual payment update based on the overall cost to Medicare for all services for patients assigned to the ACS and would be eligible for bonuses based on patient satisfaction and for large quality bonuses; quality bonuses would be based on an extended set of measures of the ACS's quality of care.

3. Medicare would pay physicians based on a revised Resource Based Relative Value Scale (RBRVS) system and a revised system for annual payment rate updates. In addition, bonuses for quality and for patient satisfaction, and a monthly medical home fee would be available (See Table 2).

4. Medicare would pay a substantial risk-adjusted monthly medical home fee to eligible practices for each beneficiary who chose a practice as a medical home. Face-to-face cognitive (evaluation and management, E&M) services provided to a patient by any physician within his/her medical home practice would be reimbursed at a lower fee-for-service rate than cognitive services provided for non-medical home patients. The cognitive services fee-for-service rate for medical home patients would be set at a level intended to make it neither profitable nor unprofitable for a physician to see the patient face-to-face. Preventive services and procedures would be reimbursed at the same fee-for-service rates for medical home and non-medical home patients.

TABLE 1 PAYMENT METHODS AND PUBLIC REPORTING FOR HOSPITALS

	DRG-based Payment	Quality Bonus	Patient Satisfaction Bonus	Payment for Avoidable Complications	Public Reporting
Not part of an ACS	National update annually	Hospital inpatient and outpatient care	Hospital inpatient and outpatient care	Denied	Hospital quality and patient satisfaction
Part of an ACS	Annual update specific to that ACS	Care provided by the ACS	Same as above	Not used	Same as above

TABLE 2 PAYMENT METHODS AND PUBLIC REPORTING FOR PHYSICIANS

	Cognitive Services	Preventive Services	Procedures	Quality Bonus	Patient Satisfaction Bonus	Public Reporting of Quality	Public Reporting of Patient Satisfaction
Not ACS member; not member of a medical home practice	Fee-for-service; annual national rate update	Fee-for-service; annual national rate update	Fee-for-service; annual national rate update	?*	Based on the individual physician**	No	Based on the individual physician
Not ACS member; member of a medical home practice	Discounted fee-for-service + medical home payment; national rate update***	Same as in the row above.					
ACS member	Discounted fee-for-service + medical home payment; annual update specific to that ACS***	Fee-for-service; annual update specific to that ACS	Fee-for-service; annual update specific to that ACS	Quality of care of the ACS	Based on individual physician**	ACS quality would be reported	Based on the individual physician

* Small amounts would be paid to individual physicians to the extent that reliable and valid risk-adjusted measurement can be done.

** Would include questions about the practice, if any, of which the physician is a member.

*** Reimbursement for non-medical home patients would be at the full fee-for-service rate.

5. Medicare would pay physicians in different ways, depending on whether they were members of an ACS or not and on whether their practice was accredited as a medical home or not. Non-ACS physicians would continue to be paid on a fee-for-service basis via the RBRVS system, would receive the national annual payment update, and would be eligible for bonuses based on patient satisfaction and possibly on measures of the quality of care they provide. ACS physicians would be paid on a fee-for-service basis via the RBRVS system, would receive an annual payment update inversely related to the overall cost to Medicare for all services for patients assigned to the ACS in the previous year, and would be eligible for bonuses based on patient satisfaction and for quality bonuses based on an extended set of measures of the ACS's quality of care. The quality bonus money would be paid to the ACS, which would divide it among physicians and hospitals according to its own internal policies. ACSs and non-ACS medical practices accredited as medical homes would receive a risk-adjusted monthly medical home fee, and would be paid at a discounted fee-for-service rate for cognitive/E&M services and at the full fee-for-service rate for preventive care and procedural services.

6. Medicare would not make additional payments for such things as care coordination or e-mail or phone communication with patients. These would be compensated indirectly through the medical home fee, quality and patient satisfaction bonuses, and, for ACSs, though higher annual payment updates (to the extent, if any, that these activities reduce the overall costs of patients' care).

7. The payment systems proposed in this paper would be implemented in a way that is budget neutral.

Provide Public Information on Quality Performance

Medicare would issue annual public reports on provider quality and on patients' experience with providers. Public reporting of patient experience with individual physicians could also be done, although it would be excessively expensive to survey patients of each physician in the U.S. annually. Public reporting of quality measure scores for individual physicians should not be done unless it is becomes possible to obtain, at the individual physician level, statistically reliable and valid measurements, risk-adjusted when necessary, of important elements of quality.

Explicitly Design Incentive Programs to Avoid Unintended Consequences

Programs for rewarding quality and efficiency can have unintended and undesirable consequences, such as increasing disparities in health care delivery and/or reducing providers' attention to important but unmeasured areas of quality. Medicare's programs would incorporate design features explicitly intended to minimize or eliminate these undesirable consequences and would incorporate ongoing evaluation explicitly intended to identify them if they occur.

Provide Services to Help Improve Quality and Control Costs

1. If strong evidence established that disease management was able to reduce costs while improving quality, Medicare would contract with organizations to have disease management services provided to the beneficiaries most likely to benefit from these services.
2. Medicare Quality Improvement Organizations (QIOs) would work to support provider organizations in the activities encouraged by these proposals.

Transform Medicare into a Learning System

1. Medicare should build evaluation activities into each important new program and program change.
2. Medicare should make data available to researchers without undue obstacles or delays.

Do Not Be Penny-Wise and Pound-Foolish: Fund Medicare Administrative Functions Adequately

CMS should receive adequate funding to effectively carry out the activities necessary to being a value-based purchaser.

III. THE MEDICAL HOME

The concept of the "medical home" has received increasing attention during the past few years.[7] Although it is central to the medical home concept that "each patient has an ongoing relationship with a personal physician trained to provide first contact, continuous, and comprehensive care," the medical home should be conceived as the medical practice—consisting of physicians and other staff—and not as an individual physician. The personal physician who attends to the patient within the medical home will usually be a primary care physician, but for certain patients with chronic illnesses, a specialist could function as the personal physician to the extent that he or she is willing and able to provide first contact,

---

7. Leigh A. Backer, *The Medical Home: An Idea Whose Time Has Come . . . Again*, 14(8) FAM. PRAC. MANAG. 38 (2007); AMERICAN ACADEMY OF FAMILY PHYSICIANS (AAFP), THE AMERICAN ACADEMY OF PEDIATRICS (AAP), THE AMERICAN COLLEGE OF PHYSICIANS (ACP) AND THE AMERICAN OSTEOPATHIC ASSOCIATION (AOA), JOINT PRINCIPLES OF THE PATIENT-CENTERED MEDICAL HOME (2007).

continuous, and comprehensive care. The personal physician and staff of a medical home would take responsibility for coordinating a patient's care both among physicians within the home practice and across all elements of the health care system (e.g., hospitals, specialist physicians outside the home practice, and rehabilitation facilities).

The medical home would make face-to-face visits available for patients on the day that the patient wants to be seen. The staff of the medical home would rely on increased use of e-mail and the telephone to communicate with patients. The medical home staff would work proactively to provide care to its population of patients between face-to-face visits, using registries and organized care management processes to provide appropriate screening, preventive, and follow-up care to their patients—both those who are healthy and those who suffer from chronic illness.

Medicare should encourage, but not require, beneficiaries to choose a medical practice as their medical home. Beneficiaries who choose a medical home should be permitted to see physicians outside their medical home practice without a referral and to change their medical home choice twice within a year, or to drop out of having a medical home at all.

Medicare should require that medical practices that request designation as medical homes demonstrate that they have the requisite characteristics. Medicare would deem that a practice or ACS qualifies as a medical home if it is certified by an outside organization, possibly the National Committee for Quality Assurance (NCQA), which has recently begun a medical home certification program. Medicare would also require that this organization conduct random on-site audits of certified practices to verify that they actually are providing medical home services. In addition, patient satisfaction surveys would include questions relevant to medical homes; if medical home patients did not report receiving appropriate services, an on-site audit would be triggered.

Medicare would pay medical homes for cognitive/E&M services on a discounted fee-for-service rate. The medical home fee and fee-for-service payment rates would be set so that the amount that Medicare would spend annually for both combined would not exceed the amount Medicare would have paid if it had simply paid full fee-for-service rates for E&M services for these beneficiaries.

What would prevent practices from simply pocketing medical home payments and doing little or nothing to provide medical home services? First, practices that do so would have to be less than candid when describing their services to accreditation organizations. Second, they would lose their medical home patients, and thus their payments, as patients discover that they are not receiving services. Third, they would lose their medical home designation from Medicare, either because of a random audit by the organization that accredits medical homes, or because patient responses on patient experience surveys trigger an audit because they suggest that medical home services are not being provided. Fourth, insofar as practices receive bonuses for quality, for patient satisfaction, and for cost control, these bonuses would afford an incentive to provide medical home services. Fifth, practices that provide attentive medical home services will likely look better in the public reports of patient satisfaction that Medicare will publish.

IV. ACCOUNTABLE CARE SYSTEMS

For decades, many—though by no means all—policy analysts have argued that large multi-specialty group practices can provide better care at lower cost than the small practices in which most U.S. physicians work.[8] However, such organizations remain the exception rather than the rule in U.S. health care. New ones are very difficult and expensive to create. Many physicians prefer the autonomy and the "human scale" offered by the small practice setting. Medicare and private health insurance plans traditionally have not rewarded organizations that provide higher quality or lower costs: a physician churning patients rapidly through his or her own practice has been able to enjoy both autonomy and a high income.

This paper does not argue that Medicare should adopt policies aimed, in effect, at forcing physicians (and hospitals) into large, integrated organizations. Medicare should, however, structure incentives in such a way that organizations that provide better care will be rewarded for doing so. It is difficult to provide desirable incentives in the fragmented, small practice system that is prevalent in the U.S.[9] Moreover, it is possible to measure and reward performance on much broader areas of quality and cost-control in large organizations than it is in small physician practices.

Medicare should designate a type of organization—to be called an Accountable Care System (ACS)—that is better able to serve as a unit of accountability for costs and quality. ACSs could be the large, integrated organizations long envisaged by reformers, and epitomized by Kaiser, or could be "virtual organizations" linking small practices and hospitals,[10] for example, Independent Practice Associations (IPAs) or Physician Hospital Organizations (PHOs). IPAs and PHOs—with a few notable exceptions—have not been very effective vehicles for

---

8. TOWARD A 21ST CENTURY HEALTH SYSTEM: THE CONTRIBUTIONS AND PROMISE OF PREPAID GROUP PRACTICE (Alain C. Enthoven & Laura A. Tolen eds., 2004); Alain C. Enthoven & Laura A. Tolen, *Competition in Health Care: It Takes Systems to Pursue Quality and Efficiency*, HEALTH AFF. WEB. EXCL., Sept. 7, 2005 at W5-420; STEPHEN M. SHORTELL, ROBIN R. GILLIES, DAVID A. ANDERSON, ET AL., REMAKING HEALTH CARE IN AMERICA: BUILDING ORGANIZED DELIVERY SYSTEMS (1996); ARNOLD S. RELMAN, A SECOND OPINION: RESCUING AMERICA'S HEALTH CARE (2007).

9. John E. Wennberg et al., *Extending the P4P Agenda, Part 2: How Medicare Can Reduce Waste and Improve the Care of the Chronically Ill*, 26 HEALTH AFF. 1574 (2007).

10. Stephen M. Shortell & Lawrence P. Casalino, *Healthcare Reform Requires Accountable Care Systems*, 300(1) JAMA 95–97 (July 2, 2008).

improving medical care, but if quality and cost-effectiveness really were rewarded, this might change. Physicians would not be required to affiliate with an ACS, but, if ACSs perform well, it might be to their advantage to do so.

To achieve ACS Medicare status, organizations would have to meet three requirements. First, the organization must be willing to take responsibility for the overall cost and quality of care for a population of patients. Second, the organization must have the size and scope to fulfill this responsibility. Third, the organization must be accredited as a medical home.

The population of patients for whom the ACS is held responsible would consist of (1) beneficiaries who voluntarily choose to designate the ACS as their medical home for seven months or more in a given year and (2) beneficiaries who do not choose an ACS as their medical home, but who receive most of their care there. Each year, such beneficiaries would be retroactively assigned to the ACS for purposes of quality and cost measurement based on algorithms analyzing Medicare claims. Beneficiaries could be assigned to an ACS, for example, if they had more than sixty percent of their outpatient and inpatient visits with the ACS's physicians in a given year.

For its population of beneficiaries, an ACS would be responsible for all Medicare costs incurred for those beneficiaries and for the quality of care they receive. Though beneficiaries would be free to seek services from any provider included in Medicare, the ACS would be responsible for services provided within the organization as well as for those provided outside the organization. This would give the ACS a strong incentive to be attractive as a medical home to which patients want to turn first when seeking care; to refer patients to high quality, efficient providers when outside services are needed; and to coordinate care whether it is provided inside or outside the ACS.

Because an ACS would be a relatively large organization, and because it would be responsible for the full range of costs and quality for its patients, it would be possible for Medicare to use a broader and deeper set of measures, including outcome measures, to reward high quality, cost-effective care than is possible for individual physicians, medical groups, or hospitals. Further, payment would flow to the ACS through the prospective payment system for hospitals and through medical home payments and fee-for-service for physicians, *not* through capitation. Capitation for the entire projected cost of patient care, or for a large part of it, is not desirable because it requires patient lock-in, because it may provide an incentive to control costs that may be too strong, and because it puts an organization at major financial risk (therefore requiring deep financial reserves, limiting the types of organization that can be designated as an ACS, and raising problematic regulatory issues).

Medicare would designate an organization as an ACS based on its request to be so designated and on simple structural criteria indicating that (1) the organization has a central office to receive and distribute Medicare payments,

(2) the organization qualifies as a medical home, and (3) the organization has sufficient size and scope to:

a) provide primary care and most specialty care physician services;
b) have sufficient capital and economies of scale to implement organized processes to improve the quality and control the costs of care; and
c) have the ability to sustain financial reverses if the organization performs poorly in caring for its population of Medicare beneficiaries.

The minimum number of physicians required for an organization to be classified as an ACS could plausibly be defined as one hundred physicians, although some ACSs would likely be much larger. An ACS might or might not include one or more hospitals or other providers, such as rehabilitation facilities and home health services.

All ACSs would be medical homes, but not all medical homes would be part of an ACS. A medical home practice could be quite small and still meet the accreditation standards to be designated as a medical home. Medicare should structure its incentives in accordance with the proposals offered above so that ACSs can be attractive to many physicians and hospitals, but should not structure them in such a way that providers feel that they have little choice but to join an ACS.

As beneficiaries become familiar with the advantages of designating a medical home—and realize that these advantages come with no cost—it is likely that most would choose medical homes. This would prompt more practices to reorganize so that they can provide medical home services (and be designated by Medicare as eligible to be a medical home). It might lead more practices to join ACSs, if, as seems likely, ACSs can make resources available to assist practices in providing medical home services. If increasing numbers of patients designate medical homes, it would become progressively easier for Medicare to assign patients to practices (should Medicare decide to measure quality and/or costs at the practice level) and to ACSs.

V. LEGAL ISSUES RAISED BY VALUE-BASED MEDICARE PURCHASING: INTRODUCTION

Any change in the health care delivery system is bound to present knotty legal issues. Our proposals raise potential issues under a host of legal authorities, including the United States Constitution, Medicare law, the Federal Acquisition Regulations, the Privacy Act, the Freedom of Information Act, the Health Insurance Portability and Accountability Act Privacy Regulations, the antitrust laws, the bribe and kickback prohibition, the self-referral prohibition, and state laws regulating physician practices and managed care. Each of these issues is discussed in detail in our papers, and not all of them can be touched on here.

Most of our proposals described above cannot be implemented without changes in one or more federal statutes. In many instances, it might be possible to rely on current demonstration or pilot project authority to implement a proposal on a trial basis: 2006 amendments to the Social Security Act, for example, established a Medicare medical home demonstration project that could be used to test out the medical home concept, which was expanded by 2008 amendments.[11] But permanent changes will require amendment to Title XVIII of the Social Security Act. Any statutory changes, of course, must be consistent with the Constitution.

VI. CONSTITUTIONAL CONSTRAINTS

The Fifth Amendment provides: "No person shall be . . . deprived of life, liberty, or property, without due process of law; nor shall private property be taken for public use, without just compensation." The explicit just compensation and implicit equal protection provisions of the Fifth Amendment would not seem to stand in the way of value purchasing. The Supreme Court long ago decided that Social Security Act entitlements do not create vested property rights and can be changed at the will of Congress. Although providers often complain that Medicare (or Medicaid) payment levels are inadequate, and thus take their property without just compensation, no provider is compelled to participate in Medicare and a provider dissatisfied with payment levels can simply withdraw.[12] Challenges to prospective changes in payment levels or methods have uniformly been rejected on this basis. Equal protection claims have also been generally rejected under a rational basis test, and since the 1970s, substantive due process challenges to Medicare program provisions have consistently failed.

Procedural due process claims, on the other hand, have more potential. Courts have generally rejected claims that providers have a property interest in Medicare participation, reasoning that the Medicare program exists for the benefit of beneficiaries, not providers. This may change in light of the Supreme Court's 2000 decision in *United States v. Fischer*, recognizing that providers are also beneficiaries of the program, but the change is not yet apparent.[13] A more plausible argument is that providers have a liberty interest in not having their reputations impugned by Medicare without an opportunity to respond.

---

11. Pub. L. 109–432, Div. B, Title II, §204, Dec. 20, 2006; Pub. L. 110–275, § 133.

12. Garelick v. Sullivan, 987 F.2d 913 (2d Cir.1993); Whitney v. Heckler, 780 F.2d 963 (11th Cir.), *cert. denied* 479 U.S. 813 (1986); St. Francis Hosp. Ctr. v. Heckler, 714 F2d 872 (7th Cir. 1983); Metrolina Family Practice Group, P.A. v. Sullivan, 767 F.Supp. 1314 (W.D.N.C. 1989), *aff'd* 929 F.2d 693 (4th Cir. 1991); Pharmacist Political Action Committee of Maryland v. Harris, 502 F.Supp. 1235 (D.C. Md. 1980).

13. Fischer v. United States, 529 U.S. 667 (2000).

A provider excluded from a Centers of Excellence program, or even a provider given a low quality rating or denied a quality bonus, might be able to press a claim for some sort of due process based on reputational injury resulting in financial loss.

Of course, under the *Mathews v. Eldridge* calculus, the process required might be quite summary if the court viewed the provider's right to be insubstantial or the issue at stake relatively clear. Congress can, for example, provide that some legislative-type decisions were non-reviewable, as it has routinely done in the Medicare program. But Congress will probably have to provide at least some informal opportunity to resolve factual disputes in value-based purchasing programs. The AMA Guidelines for Pay-for-Performance Programs, for example, call for: 1) physician access to data and analysis used to construct performance ratings prior to use; 2) physician access to preliminary ratings and an opportunity to improve performance before performance is reported or used for payment; 3) an opportunity to review and appeal ratings before they are released; and 4) an opportunity to include physician responses adjacent to ratings.[14] This level of procedural protections is not required by due process, but lesser protections will be resisted by at least some providers.

VII. CONSTRAINTS IMPOSED BY THE MEDICARE STATUTE

The ability of the traditional Medicare program to move to value purchasing is greatly limited by the nature, structure, and terms of the Medicare statute, Title XVIII of the Social Security Act. Although several strategies proposed in our paper could be implemented without statutory amendment, the comprehensiveness of the Medicare statute's treatment of service coverage and provider payment makes it unlikely that recommendations that affect these issues could be implemented without changes in the Medicare law.

Title XVIII begins with eight introductory sections, followed in turn by five parts each of which contains numerous sections. Section 1801 (42 U.S.C. § 1395), which begins the Act, states:

> Nothing in this subchapter shall be construed to authorize any Federal officer or employee to exercise any supervision or control over the practice of medicine or the manner in which medical services are provided, . . .

---

14. AMA, Guidelines for Pay-for-Performance Programs, 3–4 (June 21, 2005). *See also* Sara Rosenbaum et al., *An Assessment of Legal Issues Raised in "High Performing" Health Plan Quality and Efficiency Tiering Arrangements: Can the Patient Be Saved?* 15(39) BNA's Health Care Policy Report 1 (Oct. 8, 2007) (recommending procedural protections for rating programs in private health plans).

The initial subsection of section 1802, which follows, continues:

Any individual entitled to insurance benefits under this subchapter may obtain health services from any institution, agency, or person qualified to participate under this subchapter if such institution, agency, or person undertakes to provide him such services.

Parts A, B, C, D, and E of the statute which follow establish the familiar elements of the Medicare Program.

Both Part A and Part B begin with a specific and closed-ended "scope of benefits" section listing what each part covers.[15] Both also define the cost-sharing obligations imposed on beneficiaries. Both parts describe methods of payment for Medicare services, indeed most of the remaining sections of both parts as well as a number of sections of Part E, deal with payment. Historically Part A payments were based on reasonable costs or charges and Part B on reasonable charges. Both Parts still retain these forms of payment as the default mode.[16] But in fact, virtually every item and service currently covered by Part A or B is now paid for through a prospective payment system or fee schedule. These provisions describe with great specificity how payments are to be made, and leave little room for flexibility. 42 U.S.C. § 1395w-4, which establishes the resource-based relative value scale (RBRVS) physician fee schedule extends to over 23,000 words and 3600 sentences, while 42 U.S.C. § 1395ww, which establishes inpatient hospital diagnosis-related group (DRG) PPS system includes almost 92,000 words and over 13,000 sentences.

Parts A and B also specify procedures that providers must follow to get paid. Providers, professionals, and suppliers must meet participation requirements and in many cases must sign a participation agreement.[17] A physician must initially certify and periodically recertify the need for many Part A and B services.[18] Claims for physician or practitioner services must be properly coded for diagnosis.[19] Payments must generally be made directly to a provider, professional, or supplier, and can only be made by assignment to a third party under limited and specific circumstances.[20] Finally, relationships among Medicare providers, professionals, and suppliers are closely regulated by the bribe and kickback and self-referral statutes, discussed below.[21]

All of this makes a Procrustean bed for value-based purchasing strategies. Several of the strategies proposed by our paper including the use of payment

---

15. 42 U.S.C. §§ 1395c, 1395d, 1395k.
16. 42 U.S.C. §§ 1395ff(b); 1395l(a)(1).
17. 42 U.S.C. §§ 1395u(h), 1395cc.
18. 42 U.S.C. §§ 1395f(a)(2); 1395cc.
19. 42 U.S.C. § 1395u(p).
20. 42 U.S.C. §§ 1395g(c), 1395u(b)(3), (6).
21. 42 U.S.C. §§ 1320a-7b, 1395nn.

bonuses or penalties to encourage higher quality and lower cost services and the use of differential payment updates to encourage better cost and quality performance or selective contracting with particular providers are starkly inconsistent with statutory requirements and to that extent prohibited without statutory amendment.

Whether or not a court would block CMS from implementing a value purchasing program inconsistent with the statute is, of course, another question. The "supervision or control of the practice of medicine" prohibition of Title XVIII's first section is unlikely to prove a substantial barrier. The courts have long recognized that it does not limit the ability of CMS to regulate Medicare payment methods.[22] Were CMS to establish a value-based purchasing program by regulation, however, and were that program ultimately to be challenged in court by a disappointed beneficiary or provider, a court would likely strike down the program under section 706 of the Administrative Procedures Act as violating a specific payment statutory provision. Although the courts have generously applied the deference to administrative agencies recognized in *Chevron U.S.A., Inc. v. Natural Resources Defense Council, Inc.*[23] in reviewing Medicare program decisions, there are limits to how far it can stretch.

Health reform legislation pending in Congress at this writing includes proposals for medical home and accountable care pilot programs. If this legislation is adopted, it would largely obviate these problems.

VIII. PROVIDER QUALITY AND COST REPORTING INITIATIVES

One of our recommendations explicitly calls for reporting of quality data to the public, whereas others seem to assume that such information would be available. CMS currently collects and disseminates some quality data. But CMS data collection efforts must not only find their authority somewhere in the Medicare statute, but also triangulate between three other laws: the Privacy Act, the Freedom of Information Act, and the Health Insurance Portability and Accountability Act. First, the Privacy Act of 1974, 5 U.S.C. § 552a, limits the ability of the federal government to disclose records that pertain to an "individual" and that are kept in systems of records without prior written consent.[24] The Privacy Act does not protect health care institutions, but does cover physicians, other practitioners, and patients. It imposes a number of obligations on an

---

22. *See* American Academy of Ophthalmology, Inc. v. Sullivan, 998 F.2d 377, 387 (6th Cir. 1993); Home Health Care v. Heckler, 717 F.2d 587 (D.C.Cir. 1983); Portland Adventist Med. Ctr. v. Heckler, 561 F.Supp. 1092 (D.D.C. 1983).

23. 467 U.S. 837 (1984).

24. 5 U.S.C. § 552a(b). CMS, as well as its contractors, are further governed by the DHHS Privacy Rule, 45 C.F.R. § 5b.2(b).

agency, including 1) keeping an accounting of disclosures made; 2) maintaining accurate and secure records; 3) permitting a person with respect to whom records are kept to review and copy the records, request a correction of the record if the individual believes it to be inaccurate, and obtain a review if a request for correction is denied; and 4) disclosing a statement of disagreement with the contents of a record together with the record when a contested record is disclosed.[25] The statute also allows an individual who was denied a request for correction to sue in federal court, and to recover attorney fees if the individual prevails.[26] The Privacy Act may, therefore, afford physicians and other practitioners a means to challenge the publication of quality information they consider to be incorrect. This is another reason to proceed cautiously in making physician-specific information publicly available.

The Freedom of Information Act requires a federal agency like CMS to make available upon request any records within its possession reasonably described in the request unless the records are exempt from disclosure.[27] Any provider-specific information collected by HHS may be subject to a FOIA request, a consideration CMS must take into account as it collects quality or patient satisfaction data.[28]

Third, identifiable health information is protected by the Health Insurance Portability and Accountability Act (HIPAA) privacy standards. The HIPAA regulations do not govern HHS, as they only apply to health providers, health plans, health care clearinghouses, and business associates of health plans, providers, or clearinghouses.[29] They also only apply to individually-identifiable health information.[30] Current CMS quality information disclosure initiatives are directed at disclosing provider or practitioner-specific information, but not individually-identifiable patient information. However, insofar as the HIPAA regulations articulate a commitment to health information privacy, and patients rely on that commitment, some quality information disclosures could be problematic.

---

25. 5 U.S.C. § 552a(c), (d), and (e). Curiously, the DHHS Rule does not specify to whom appeals can be made from CMS, although it does for most other DHHS units. *See* 45 C.F.R. § 5b.8(a).

26. 5 U.S.C. § 552a(g).

27. 5 U.S.C. § 552(a)(3).

28. A recent federal court of appeals case rejected a FOIA request for disclosure of the total payments received by doctors in several locations from Medicare. The court recognized that the doctors had a substantial privacy interest in this information, and that disclosure would not serve the public interest. Similarly, other information collected on doctors may be protected from disclosure under FOIA, but it would depend on the relative strength of the provider's privacy interest and the public interest in disclosure. Consumers' Checkbook v. United States Department of Health and Human Services, 554 F.3d. 1046 (D.C. Cir. 2009).

29. 42 U.S.C. § 17394; 45 C.F.R. § 164.104(a).

30. 45 C.F.R. § 164.502(a), incorporating definitions found in 45 C.F.R. § 160.103.

If physician-specific quality information were released, for example, for treatment of diabetes patients, and a particular doctor only had a handful of such patients, the privacy of information regarding those patients would be at risk.

IX. LEGAL ISSUES AFFECTING ACCOUNTABLE CARE SYSTEMS

Although the most important legal issues facing the establishment of a value purchasing programs for traditional Medicare will probably involve the authority of HHS to pay such programs, a wholly separate but also important set of legal issues is presented by the recommendations involving ACSs and other organizations that would actually provide the services.

There are at least five bodies of law that are relevant to ACS proposals: the antitrust laws, the self-referral laws and regulations, the bribe and kickback prohibition, the prohibition against incentives for reducing services for Medicare beneficiaries, and state regulation of physician groups and associations.

The Sherman Antitrust Act prohibits "every contract, combination, . . . or conspiracy in restraint of trade," and also prohibits "monopolization."[31] Fully integrated medical practice groups and integrated delivery systems are not combinations in restraint of trade, because they are single entities. ACSs formed from non-integrated group medical practices or from loose alliances of other entities are likely to be treated as "combinations," however. The key question with respect to these entities will be whether they are "in restraint of trade." It is clear that physician organizations formed for the purposes of bargaining with payors can be "in restraint of trade"—indeed they can be in per se violation of the antitrust laws.[32]

The ACSs formed under our proposal would not be in violation of the antitrust laws in their dealings with Medicare because they would be receiving administered prices rather than engaging in negotiations. It is very likely, however, that once a network of physicians (and other providers) had gone to the trouble of setting up the administrative structure of an ACS, there would be a real temptation to use the ACS structure to negotiate with private managed care organizations or Medicaid. If such uses of an ACS were prohibited, moreover, it is likely that physicians and providers would have less incentive to organize an ACS.

The Federal Trade Commission and Department of Justice statements on enforcement policy with respect to the antitrust laws in health care establish "safe harbors" within which health care providers can operate without fear of antitrust sanctions. The physician network joint ventures guideline would apply to many ACSs. Under this safe harbor, several factors are relevant, including the percentage of physicians (in each relevant specialty who have active hospital staff

---

31. 15 U.S.C. § 1.
32. Arizona v. Maricopa County Medical Society, 457 U.S. 332 (1982).

privileges) in a geographic market that participate in the joint venture, whether the network joint venture is exclusive or non-exclusive, and whether the entity is financially integrated or not. Some ACSs may be sufficiently financially integrated to fit within this safe harbor, but some may not. Entities that do not meet the requirements of the guidelines are reviewed under the rule of reason, and may pass scrutiny on the basis of procompetitive efficiencies achieved through clinical integration—that is, a high level of collaboration toward efficiency and quality. Most ACSs will probably pass muster under the financial or clinical integration tests, but if an ACS attempted to negotiate with payors lacking both, it would be at risk for antitrust sanctions.

The implications of the federal self-referral prohibition and "bribe and kickback" laws for ACSs will also need to be explored. The Stark self-referral laws prohibit physicians who have (or whose immediate family members have) a "financial relationship" with a provider from referring Medicare or Medicaid patients to that provider for "designated health services."[33] The problem posed by the self-referral laws for ACSs is that some ACSs may provide designated health services in addition to physician services. Our proposal, for example, recognizes that ACSs may include both physicians and hospitals and should decide how to allocate pay-for-performance bonuses among both physicians and hospitals.

The self-referral issue will vary depending on whether the payment is made through a physician group (which qualified as an ACS or provided medical home services, for example) or through an ACS that is not a single physician group. Payment through a physician group is the least problematic approach, since the self-referral statute and regulations specifically address issues raised by group practices. The group practice exceptions are complicated,[34] but if all their requirements are met, groups can pay their members "productivity bonuses and profit shares," based on services personally performed or supervised by the member (but not based on referred services), which should allow distribution of value purchasing payments.

If payments are made to a physician through an ACS that is not a single physician group, the self-referral laws may not be implicated as long as the payments are for the physician's own services or for services supervised by the physician under Medicare's "incident to" rules. Nonetheless, given the complexity of the prohibition, it would be best if Congress or HHS promulgated a specific exception to the self-referral prohibition for ACSs.

The anti-kickback law prohibits "knowingly and willfully" paying or receiving, offering or soliciting remuneration in return for referring a patient or for arranging or furnishing a service paid for by a federal health care program.[35] Here, as with the self-referral statute, the concern is that an ACS would "remunerate" a

---

33. 42 U.S.C. § 1395nn(a).
34. 42 U.S.C. § 1395nn(b)(1) & (2); (h)(4); 42 C.F.R. §§ 411.351, 411.352, 411.355(a), (b).
35. 42 U.S.C. § 1320a-7b.

physician while at the same time the physician would be referring patients to the physicians, hospitals, or other providers affiliated with the ACS. The statutory and regulatory exceptions and safe harbors under the bribe and kickback law are less numerous and comprehensive than those under the self-referral law, and would not necessarily cover ACS arrangements. But violation of the bribe and kickback statute requires intent, and if an entity implemented a statutorily authorized value-based purchasing arrangement, it could hardly be accused of having done so with intent to violate the anti-kickback statute.[36] Again, the simplest thing would be for Congress or the Office of Inspector General to recognize an explicit exception or establish a safe harbor for value purchasing.

A fourth statute of concern is 42 U.S.C. § 1320a-7a(b)(1) & (2), which prohibits hospitals from knowingly paying and physicians from knowingly receiving payments as an inducement to reduce or limit services to Medicare or Medicaid beneficiaries. This statute, together with the anti-kickback statute, has driven the concern that the HHS Office of Inspector General has had with "gainsharing" arrangements, under which hospitals reward physicians for reducing hospital costs by giving the physicians a share in cost reductions. One of the purposes of value purchasing, of course, is to constrain Medicare costs, so it is to some extent at cross-purposes with the reduction of services prohibition. "Black box" gainsharing arrangements, under which hospitals pay physicians for overall cost reduction without attributing specific payments to specific savings, were disapproved by an OIG Special Advisory Opinion on gainsharing in 1999.[37] Since that time, however, the OIG has issued a half dozen advisory opinions approving specific gainsharing arrangements that included precautions against abuse. Congress also adopted a provision authorizing a gainsharing demonstration project late in 2006.[38] It would probably be wise for Congress to adopt an exception to the inducement statute for ACSs, although the OIG could perhaps issue an advisory bulletin authorizing value purchasing arrangements as permissible under the statute without further authority.

The final issue is state regulation of medical groups or ACSs that would participate in a value-based purchasing program. Across the fifty states, there are literally hundreds of state statutes that mention medical groups, independent practice organizations, physician hospital organizations, integrated delivery systems, and provider-sponsored organizations.[39] These statutes address a wide

---

36. *See* United States v. Starks, 157 F.3d 833 (11th Cir. 1998) (upholding jury instruction that violation of the law requires "a bad purpose, either to disobey or disregard the law").

37. Gainsharing Arrangements and CMPs for Hospital Payments to Physicians to Reduce or Limit Services to Beneficiaries http://oig.hhs.gov/fraud/docs/alertsandbulletins/gainsh.htm

38. Pub. L. 109–171, Title V, § 5007, Feb. 8, 2006, 120 Stat. 34.

39. *See, e.g.,* Cal. Civ. Code §§ 56.05, 56.10 (governing confidentiality of medical records); Cal. Health & Safety Code § 1367.10 (disclosure of provider incentive payments); Cal.

variety of topics, from liability, to quality assurance, to utilization review, to claims payment, to solvency for downstream risk-bearing organizations. Some of these statutes will in all likelihood limit the flexibility, or even the formation, of entities through which Medicare will pay physicians under the proposed value purchasing arrangements.

Congress could, of course, preempt state laws that apply to ACSs and Medical Homes, as it does with respect to regulation of Medicare Advantage plans. Current Medicare law preempts all state laws governing Medicare Advantage plans except laws relating to licensure and solvency.[40] If value-based purchasing organizations used their structures to pursue private business, of course, they would not be protected by federal preemption and would be subject to state regulation. The organizational forms and procedures that entities adopted to comply with state regulation would undoubtedly affect their participation in Medicare as well. This may not be a problem that the federal government can fix. Each organization will have to decide whether to use the ACS form to seek business with payors other than Medicare, to figure out what this will mean for state law compliance, and to weigh whether it is worth organizing to pursue Medicare business if state law precludes seeking business with other payors.

XI. CONCLUSION

Traditional Medicare should move forward in implementing value-based purchasing arrangements based on the Accountable Care System and medical home concepts. Congress should remove legal barriers to allowing this to happen.

Health & Safety Code § 1375.7 (health care providers' bill of rights governing contacts between health plans and provider groups); 215 Ill.Comp.Stat.Ann. 5/386b (governing contracts between IPAs and PHOs and physicians and providers); 410 Ill.Comp.Stat. Ann.§ 517/5 (collection of credentials data on physicians); New York McKinney's Public Health Law § 4406-c (gag clause prohibition and requirements for provider contracts); and Oregon Rev. Stat. Ann. § 743.801 (defining "independent practice association" as a corporation of providers formed to contract with health plans or employers, and subjecting IPAs to certain regulatory requirements)

40. 42 U.S.C. § 1395w-26(b)(3). Prior to 2003, this section only preempted state laws relating to benefit requirements, provider inclusion and treatment, coverage determinations, and marketing.

10. A MORE EQUITABLE AND EFFICIENT APPROACH TO INSURING THE UNINSURABLE

ERIC HELLAND AND JONATHAN KLICK

1. INTRODUCTION

Employer provided health insurance is largely the result of historical accident in the United States. In the face of wage and price controls enforced by the government during World War II, employers used health care coverage (among other in-kind benefits) as a second-best channel to attract workers in a particularly tight labor market. This vestige of government intervention likely endures due to health insurance's favorable tax treatment, as it remains one of the few benefits that goes untaxed for the employee and serves as a deduction for the employer.

This tying of insurance to employment generates a number of distortions in the labor market. However, it does provide an especially valuable benefit to individuals with conditions that generate relatively high expected health costs. By pooling these individuals with other employees facing relatively low expected costs, the high-cost individuals are cross-subsidized by their fellow workers. Although such a scenario generates efficiency distortions, other normative considerations, such as fairness or some other element of social justice, may lead society to decide that the efficiency losses are worth bearing. Policy makers may decide that it is reasonable to induce the relatively healthy to pick up some of the tab for the relatively unhealthy as part of the social safety net. Further, on pragmatic grounds, a policy decision may be made that it is better to make it easier for the high-cost individuals to obtain coverage; this would avoid situations in which these individuals would forego early health care, which ultimately would lead to larger costs, likely to be borne by the public, in the future, when the high-cost individuals would qualify for Medicare.

In this paper, we argue that although concern for individuals with relatively high expected health care costs may justify significant cross-subsidization on normative grounds, it makes sense as a matter of fairness and in terms of minimizing attendant efficiency losses to sever the employment link, enacting a program through which cross-subsidization occurs within society more generally.

Although we provide more detail below, our proposal is fairly simple. Policy makers determine the baseline level of coverage to be required as well as some income-based affordability metric. Individuals would then be required to demonstrate that they have coverage meeting or exceeding the chosen baseline or else provide evidence that they obtained multiple price quotes from different insurers that exceed the affordability index implied by their income level. Individuals doing the latter would receive federally provided insurance for the appropriate income-adjusted price. Competition among insurers in such a system is likely to push toward accurate pricing of an individual's risk, and it allows for a broadening of the risk pool. Further, it spreads the burden of cross-subsidization more equally across taxpayers and rids the system of the labor market inefficiencies created through tax advantaged employer provided health insurance.

In Section 2, we briefly review the literature on labor market distortions related to health insurance benefits. In Section 3, we provide a short discussion of how many individuals are likely to be "uninsurable" in an insurance market in which coverage is not tied to a person's employer. Section 4 lays out our proposal, including a discussion of the determinants of health insurance affordability and our pricing mechanism. Section 5 discusses the necessary federalization of Medicaid and the abolishment of state-level insurance mandates that accompanies our proposal. Section 6 examines the experience of other countries to shed light on the efficacy of our proposal, and Section 7 concludes.

2. DISTORTIONS IN THE EMPLOYER BASED SYSTEM

Tying health insurance to employment has the potential to generate multiple distortions in the labor market. Gruber and Madrian review the empirical literature on these distortions. They find that there is almost unanimous agreement across studies using different identification strategies and different data that the bundling of health insurance with employment leads individuals to delay their retirement on average. Namely, individuals whose employers provide insurance during the term of employment but not after retirement continue working longer than those whose employers continue coverage into retirement. This effect is statistically and economically significant, with some estimates suggesting a differential as large as two years.[1]

There is also some evidence that employment-based insurance reduces job mobility as individuals who otherwise may wish to change employers are reluctant to do so for fear of not being able to secure comparable coverage from a new employer. Various identification strategies have been employed to examine this issue, and while the evidence is mixed, the studies employing more credible identification strategies show that the lock-in effect may be substantial. Several studies published after the Gruber and Madrian review, including Adams[2] and

---

1. Gruber, Jonathan, and Brigitte Madrian. 2002. "Health Insurance, Labor Supply, and Job Mobility: A Critical Review of the Literature." *NBER Working Paper:* 8817.

2. Adams, Scott. 2004. "Employer-Provided Health Insurance and Job Change." *Contemporary Economic Policy,* 22(3): 357–369.

Bansak and Raphael[3] continue to find at least some evidence of health insurance related job lock in.

Gruber and Madrian note that there are very few estimates of the welfare effects of these labor market distortions in the literature. Examining various approaches, they place the upper bound of the welfare costs of decreased mobility at somewhere between nine and thirty billion annually, but they suggest these estimates are very crude. Essentially no work has been done on the welfare effects of insurance induced labor market distortions other than the lock in effects.[4]

3. INSURABILITY IN THE INDIVIDUAL MARKET

Despite the distortions discussed above, a number of individuals have pointed out that tying insurance to employment has the benefit of limiting adverse selection problems, as relatively healthy individuals are not generally induced to drop out of the risk pool when they effectively cross-subsidize their relatively unhealthy co-workers. These commentators suggest that because job choice is multi-dimensional and individual employees likely enjoy some surplus along those various dimensions, the relatively small cost of the cross-subsidy does not appear to induce individuals to sort very strongly along health cost dimensions across firms. Further, the tax subsidy might mitigate the incentive for healthy individuals to switch or decline coverage in the face of this cross subsidy. Although there are some partial counter-examples[5], this view is fairly prominent among health economists.

The presumption behind this view is that if this employer-based pooling did not exist, high-cost individuals would have difficulty obtaining insurance in the non-group market. Although historical estimates place the fraction of Americans who are "uninsurable" around 1 percent[6], subsequent investigation suggests

---

3. Bansak, Cynthia, and Steven Raphael. 2005. "The State Children's Health Insurance Program and Job Mobility." Working paper.

4. Note that at the upper end of this estimate, the improvement in welfare from eliminating just this lock-in effect is comparable to at least some estimates of the cost of insuring the uninsured. *See*, for example, Hadley, Jack, and John Holahan. 2003. "Covering The Uninsured: How Much Would It Cost?" *Health Affairs*, Jan-Jun;Suppl Web Exclusives:W3-250-65.

5. See, for example, Altman, Daniel, David Cutler, and Richard Zeckhauser. 1998. "Adverse Selection and Adverse Retention." *American Economic Review*, 88(2): 122–126 and Cutler, David, and Richard Zeckhauser. 1998. "Adverse Selection in Health Insurance." *Frontiers in Health Policy Research*, vol. 1, Alan Garber, ed., MIT Press: 1-31.

6. Laudicina, Susan. 1988. "State Health Risk Pools: Insuring the 'Uninsurable.'" *Health Affairs*, 7(4): 97–104.

that the actual number is much higher[7]. Further, even if some moderate to high-cost individuals are not uninsurable in a formal sense, they may be able to acquire coverage in the non-group market that is deemed inadequate or too expensive according to a social or political consensus. A number of states have adopted community rating laws and/or guaranteed issue and renewal laws in an effort to avoid these problems in the non-group market, but many of these attempts have not been successful in generating a robust individual market. Arguably, the presence of better employer-based insurance options can lead to an adverse retention problem for individual plans in states with these laws[8], although evidence on this is mixed[9].

However, even if these kinds of policies could be effective in bolstering the non-group insurance market, the mobility distortions discussed above might simply be moved to the residence, as opposed to the employer level. Further, there is a distinct possibility that state-to-state heterogeneity in terms of these policies could generate adverse selection/retention problems as well.

Further, from a normative stand point, if society determines that high-cost individuals deserve assistance, either directly through tax credits or state-provided subsidies or indirectly through state-wide cross subsidies among insured individuals, there is no particularly good reason to restrict this subsidization to occurring within the state's boundaries (much less within a firm's boundaries). It is not clear why it should be the case that low-cost individuals (or taxpayers generally) should subsidize a high-cost individual in their state, but low-cost individuals in a bordering state have no obligation to subsidize that individual.

Standard principles of federalism fall short of justifying this state-based subsidization. Given the common view of health care as a primary good, there is little reason to be concerned with heterogeneity in voter preferences across state lines regarding what should and should not be covered. Basing coverage decisions on these divergent preferences is likely to worsen the geographic health disparities many people already find lamentable. Further, differential provision across states could affect residential choices in a way that is problematic with relatively generous states attracting a disproportionate number of high-cost individuals. Lastly, as discussed more fully below, perverse incentives are generated by a fragmented system in which early life health care for those receiving subsidies, when health capital is built up and when preventive care may have the

7. Pollitz, Karen, and Richard Sorian. 2002. "Ensuring Health Security: Is the Individual Market Ready for Prime Time?" *Health Affairs*, W372–376.

8. See, for example, Monheit, Alan, Joel Cantor, Margaret Koller, and Kimberly Fox. 2004. "Community Rating and Sustainable Individual Health Insurance Markets: Trends in the New Jersey Individual Health Coverage Program." *Health Affairs*, 23(4): 167–175.

9. See, for example, Buchmueller, Thomas, and John DiNardo. 2002. "Did Community Rating Induce an Adverse Selection Death Spiral?" *American Economic Review*, 92(1): 280–294.

most efficacy, is governed by state interests, whereas the benefits of that care accrue to the federal Medicare system.

4. EXPANDING THE POOL

It makes little sense on efficiency or equity grounds to maintain the tax distortions that support the employer based health insurance system in the United States. If it is desirable to cross-subsidize high-cost individuals, there is no strong reason to operationalize those subsidies through the employment channel. Our proposal is to move individuals requiring these subsidies to a broad-based pool financed through the federal tax system. Such a program would eliminate the labor market distortions discussed above, and carrying out the program at the federal level avoids the problems associated with state-based policies. Our proposal differs from a fully nationalized health insurance program in that it only includes individuals who cannot find affordable coverage in the private market. A hybrid system like this at least partially retains the positive aspects of competition among insurers, allowing for innovation in the market, and, as described below, it harnesses the market's pricing mechanism to determine who needs the public insurance.

4.a Means Tested Care

Defining affordability with respect to heath insurance is largely a normative or political question. Bundorf and Pauly examine a number of different potential standards for affordability and provide estimates of how many individuals would be unable to afford coverage under each definition.[10] Determining what constitutes requisite coverage is likewise outside of the analytical sphere. However, once those normative issues are decided, presumably through political means, taking into account the relative value of preventive care and taking the current commitments to fund coverage for the elderly as given, federal legislators and regulators can develop a schedule of income-adjusted thresholds above which coverage will be deemed as unaffordable for the individual. The individual, as described below, will then be required to either procure private coverage meeting or exceeding the set minimum or, in the event he or she is unable to find private coverage for less than the threshold cost (and unwilling to pay the above-threshold prices he or she is quoted), the individual will enter the public insurance program, paying (presumably through the existing tax system) a sum equal to the threshold amount.

---

10. Bundorf, Kate, and Mark Pauly. 2006. "Is Health Insurance Affordable for the Uninsured?" *Journal of Health Economics*, 25(4): 650–673.

4.b Ensuring Correct Pricing

To qualify for the public coverage, an individual would need to provide evidence that he or she received multiple quotes from private insurers for the minimum coverage that exceeded his or her threshold. Market forces would induce insurers to compete both on the margins of administrative costs and pricing accuracy. Maintaining this reliance on market pricing mechanisms relieves the federal program from making individual decisions regarding who receives public coverage. Further, relative to a fully public insurance system, the potential remains for private innovations in terms of administrative practices, pricing models, and customer service. Additionally, relative to the fully public system, individuals in the private system retain a large degree of choice across insurers.

If there are concerns that insurance markets might collectively over-price individuals representing negligible profit margins to avoid covering these individuals, federal regulators could monitor insurer pricing decisions using cost data from the public program. Namely, by comparing actual expenditures for individuals priced out of the private market with the price quotes they procured from private insurers, federal regulators could identify insurers that systematically misprice certain types of individuals at the aggregate level in order to remove them from the private risk pools. By using fines and other sanctions, federal regulators could mitigate the potential for this possibility.

4.c Other Strategic Concerns

Another concern with respect to our proposal is that insurers will forego preventive treatments that could be cost justified over the patient's (non-Medicare) life horizon but are not profitable on a short term basis. In such a situation, the insurer will have an incentive to quote a relatively low current premium that does not reflect the cost of the preventive care only to raise the cost once the subsequent health problem develops. At this point the customer is more likely to fall under the public system as the price rises above the government set income threshold.

There exist both market and mandate-based solutions to this strategic concern. From the market perspective, if the public system is made to be undesirable along amenity/luxury dimensions (e.g., limited provider choice, longer wait times, less attractive hospital facilities such as non-private rooms, etc.), consumers will prefer to remain in the private system, making insurers who provide preventive care more attractive. To remedy the short-term vs. long-term incongruity of preventive care, insurers would find it profitable to enter into long-term policies with their customers, in much the same way that the term life insurance market operates today.[11]

---

11. Presumably, like in the term life insurance market, providers would perform examinations of customers before entering into the contract, allowing for more accurate pricing.

Alternately, the government could simply include the cost-justified preventive treatments in the baseline coverage it requires. For cost-effective preventive care that only generates health improvements in old age, after Medicare kicks in, this option becomes especially important. As discussed below, this concern arises even among those individuals currently enrolled in Medicaid.

5. GAINS FROM UN-FRAGMENTING PUBLIC HEALTH INSURANCE

Insurers in the current U.S. system potentially face large difficulties in terms of internalizing the benefits of preventive care.[12] For many maladies, the benefits of prevention only occur fairly late in life when Medicare would reap the reduced costs due to measures undertaken years before. Further, even in those instances where cost savings arise before the individual becomes Medicare-eligible, an insurer faces uncertainty as to whether the individual will still be a customer or not. Both of these forces push against insurers investing in preventive care on the margin.

Especially in the case of diabetes, but perhaps more generally as well, these issues may be even more acute among the poor who potentially have the weakest incentives to engage in prevention on their own due to high subjective discount rates, health knowledge deficits, or other obstacles to successful health management. However, because of the fragmented public health insurance system in this country, state Medicaid programs have little incentive to invest in preventive care when the benefits of that care are likely to accrue to the federal Medicare program. Although perhaps some of these incentive problems can be mitigated through federal directives and differential matching formulas within the Medicaid system, these seem like relatively poor policy tools relative to an un-fragmented/integrated public insurance program. Perhaps this is why state Medicaid programs fare relatively poorly in studies examining the degree to which enrollees receive preventive care.[13]

As implied above, integrating the poor and elderly public health systems will require standardizing what counts as standard or covered care. This would represent a departure from the current Medicaid system which can (and does)

With the rapidly declining costs of DNA mapping (see Pollack 2008), such examinations will become increasingly cost-effective.

12. See the discussion in the context of diabetes coverage in Klick, Jonathan, and Thomas Stratmann. 2007. "Diabetes Treatments and Moral Hazard." *Journal of Law and Economics*, 50(3): 519–538 or more generally in Avraham, Ronen, and K.A.D. Camara. 2007. "The Tragedy of the Human Commons." *Cardozo Law Review*, 29(2): 479–511.

13. See, for example, Armour, Brian, and Melinda Pitts. 2005. "The Quality of Preventive and Diagnostic Medical Care: Why Do Southern States Underperform?" *Federal Reserve Bank of Atlanta Economic Review*, 90(1): 59–67.

provide very divergent coverage from state to state.[14] Such standardization may improve social welfare as care dollars can be moved from relatively low marginal benefit uses to higher marginal benefit uses. Further, it almost surely would represent an improvement in equity, as the location of an individual is presumably morally irrelevant to the question of how much care he or she should receive. This standardization is also a practical requirement for the program as laid out above, given the requirement that a standard coverage package be defined. Eliminating the patchwork of state-level care mandates could also generate savings for private insurers as well as they would no longer need to master fifty different sets of regulations regarding what must be covered and at what terms.

6. EVIDENCE FROM OTHER COUNTRIES

Countries' methods of providing health care services differ in a myriad of ways. Governments often run hospitals and clinics and employ health care providers within the civil service. Often there is a "private" sector operating parallel to the government system. In other countries the hospitals and providers are private in the sense that they are not part of the civil service paid by the government directly. Yet even in these systems the government's role in financing the health care system is large. Given the role governments generally play in financing health care, even in those countries in which the provision of health care is ostensibly private, it is misleading in the extreme to speak of a "free market" in heath care.

Even with that important caveat there are important differences in the way countries finance health care that provide some insights into our proposal. In essence most countries with a private provision of health care services have some sort of mandate that individuals purchase insurance. They further provide a subsidy of some sort to individuals who are unable to pay for the mandated coverage. Interestingly, the subsidy is typically linked to an income or age threshold. In a typical scheme those individuals with income below a certain level are eligible for government assistance in purchasing health insurance, as are retired persons. Rarely is the subsidy tied to health risk. Although the price of private insurance is often risk-rated, governments rarely provide a larger subsidy to those who have greater risk of costly medical care.

The heart of our proposal is to shift the means test for public assistance away from an income-means test and toward a health-risk test. One might argue that the public subsidy systems currently have such a test. Age and income are important predictors of health risk. In the United States Medicaid provides insurance for low-income individuals whereas Medicare provides it for the elderly.

---

14. *See*, for example, Greve, Michael, and Jinney Smith. 2003. "What Goes Up May Not Go Down: State Medicaid Decisions in Times of Plenty." AEI Papers and Studies.

The problem is that age and income are imperfect predictors of health costs.[15] Some individuals with relatively high income but chronic conditions do not receive health insurance in the United States whereas those with very low health risk but low income are covered. Aside from the obvious equity considerations of such an arrangement, it creates a system in which private health insurance providers will compete on price, benefits, and the composition of the risk pool. With a regulated price and a requirement to offer the same benefits to all policy holders, removing high-risk individuals is perhaps the lowest cost margin on which to compete.

This problem has been addressed is several different ways in different countries. In particular we focus on three systems: the Netherlands, Chile, and Germany. The Netherlands and Germany have public funding for private health insurance. Although both have extensive public clinics and hospitals, there is a large private sector providing health services. Chile, by contrast, has a public health insurance system operating parallel to a smaller private health care system. In all three cases, risk of the insurance pool for the public system is determined by income and age. Importantly, all three mandate coverage. In particular we are interested in how these systems manage to include all individuals in the system of insurance, the adverse selection problems they face, and the lessons offered to the United States by each.

6.a Germany

Health care in Germany is financed by a combination of required health insurance, contributions for general tax revenues, private health insurance, and co-payments by the individual. The financing of health care in Germany begins with a mandated membership in one of the "sickness funds." Contributions to these funds are required for those earning below a certain level. The sickness funds system is financed by employee and employer contributions and the contribution rate is determined only by income and is not risk adjusted. Although, in theory, sickness funds can set their own contribution rates, there appears to be very little difference in contribution rates. In addition, the funds are open to all and all offer similar benefits. Contribution level to a sickness fund does not determine benefits.

The ability of German health care consumers to choose a sickness fund is relatively recent. Since 1995, Germans can choose from over four hundred sickness funds and all must accept any application. Consumers have the freedom to change once a year or when they move to a new employer. Even this level of choice has produced different cost levels. It is clear, according to the Organisation for Economic Co-operation and Development (OECD) that some funds have

---

15. *See* Newhouse, J. P., 1994 "Patients at Risk: Health Reform and Risk Adjustment," *Health Affairs*, Spring: 132–146.

attracted higher risk populations given different costs associated with funds. The use of co-payments has risen recently as well. A number of Germans buy supplementary health insurance to cover these co-payments, dental visits, and to receive treatment in greater privacy.

Most relevant to our proposal, Germany allows high-income earners to opt out of the sickness fund by purchasing private insurance. About one in three eligible for private insurance opts out.[16] In general, these individuals are treated in the same hospitals and clinics as those on the public system, and private insurance seems largely to provide access to top specialists as well as coverage for those who work or travel extensively outside of German.

6.b The Netherlands

Provision of health care in the Netherlands is closer to our proposal. The OECD describes Holland as one of the few countries where private health insurance plays a significant role in principal coverage. In the Netherlands, as in Germany and Chile, everyone is covered by a mandate to buy insurance and those earning less than a certain threshold must purchase it from the government. There is no opt in or out except that people in the Dutch public insurance system (sickness funds) can buy supplemental insurance. Prior to the late 1980s, sickness fund participation was voluntary, which resulted in healthy individuals departing the sickness funds for private insurance. This adverse selection led the Dutch government to end the voluntary opt-out for those earning less than a specified income level.

Currently about thirty one percent of the population is covered by private insurance and is not eligible for public insurance. As in Germany, contracts with private insurance are annual and must be renewed if the enrollee wishes to continue coverage. Employers in the Netherlands also play a significant role in offering private health insurance and financing it for employees by providing contributions on behalf of employees.

Almost everyone in the public system (ninety three percent in 2000) purchases supplemental coverage. Although there is no opting out of the sickness fund coverage, the vast majority of the Dutch have some form of private insurance. These insurers, whether offering supplemental or full private coverage, are generally not-for-profit companies and are fewer in number than the German system.[17]

The proportion of the population in sickness funds, and hence private insurance, has been extremely stable for a number of years with two-thirds of the population (those with the lowest income) insured by the sickness funds. In part this is because the government provision of a subsidy and the mandate to be in

---

16. In 2000 about 7.4 million Germans had private insurance.

17. In 2002, forty-seven companies offered coverage with the largest controlling 15 percent of market.

the sickness fund are tied to an income threshold designed to keep the proportions constant. Everyone in the sickness fund receives a subsidy toward their compulsory health insurance premium. The subsidy is paid by mandatory income-dependent contributions collected as taxes. The subsidies are to some extent risk adjusted. Specifically the subsidy is designed to equal the risk of the person's "risk group" minus approximately ten percent, which the individual pays to the sickness fund of his or her choice.

6.c Chile

Prior to 1981, all workers in Chile contributed to a compulsory public health system—Fonasa. The system was publicly administered, and the care was provided by government employees. The system was not typically used by high-income individuals. After 1981, Chile instituted a health care mandate under which anyone who opted for the private system—Isapres—was exempt from the requirement to pay into the public system. Currently all workers must contribute seven percent of their wage or pension (although, in the case of the Isapres, they can contribute more) to either the Fonasa or Isapres. In the case of the public system, there is a maximum compulsory contribution. Workers who opt out of the public system can choose one of ten plans but most purchase health insurance. Currently, the private system covers sixteen percent of the population, although that number has been falling in recent years. One important difference between the Chilean and the German or Dutch models discussed above is that opting out in Chile is not directly tied to income.

Even within the public system there is some choice. The public system offers two options. The first allows patients to choose their provider with the patient paying a co-payment. Alternatively, patients can choose to use the state-owned hospital system where there is no co-pay. The public system is not fully funded by contributions for workers. Fisher (2004) suggests that this is largely due to the system's coverage of the indigent population. In 2003 it received fifty four percent of its revenues for the government.

The private system, by contrast, risk-rates the price charged to participants. Fisher reports that these premiums are typically greater than the seven percent contribution for the private system. Like the public system, the private plans also have HMOs and choice options and typically both have a co-payment or, more typically, reimbursement does not cover the full cost of treatment. In total, a participant in a private plan typically has about sixty eight percent of his or her medical bills covered (Fisher, 2004). One further important difference between the Chilean model and the Dutch and German models is that private health insurers are typically for-profit.

Although opting out of the public system is not specifically tied to income in Chile, the private system is typically too expensive for low-income Chileans. Fisher finds that 3.1 percent of the lowest income quartile is in the private system, while fifty four percent of highest income quartile is in the private system.

% of population in private health insurance system

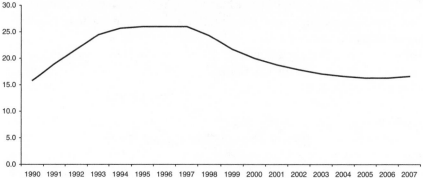

FIGURE 1 PRIVATE INSURANCE SHARE IN CHILE

Another difference between the Chilean system and those of the Dutch and Germans is that the number of enrollees has been declining since 1997. As the figure below shows, the percentage of the population in the private system has stabilized in recent years but has fallen from its high of twenty five percent.

The exact reasons for the decline are unclear, but Fisher and others posit that it is due to increased unemployment in Chile as well as increased funding for the public system. In addition, rising health care costs, caused by increasing cost of treatment, have made the public system, with its flat premium, based on seven percent of income, more attractive. A final reason appears to be a reduction in adverse selection. In recent years, the Chilean government has made it more difficult to switch into the public system if an individual becomes ill. This has reduced the number of private policies without catastrophic coverage and raised the price of private insurance. There is some evidence that private plans without catastrophic coverage were purchased by individuals who intended to use the public system if they became gravely ill.[18]

Cream skimming by private insurers and adverse selection by participants still remains. The price structure of the private plans also contributes to the problem. When an individual becomes ill, the private premium can rise while the public premium remains constant or may even fall if the illness reduces income. Currently, private plans must offer a policy renewal to an existing member, but price is unregulated. Sapelli and Torche find that private insurance is more likely for younger individuals, those with higher income and poorer health status but

---

18. *See* Fisher, Ronald, Pablo Gonzalez and Pablo Serra (2006) "Does Competition in Privatized Social Services Work? The Chilean Experience." *World Development*, 34(4): 647–664.

lower risk based on public information.[19] This suggests that there is adverse selection in both directions. Private plans want to get rid of high-risk individuals, and those with poor health, who can afford it, are opting into the private system.

One of the main criticisms of the Chilean model is that it is not equitable. The private system is much more expensive than the public system, with per beneficiary cost almost 60 percent greater than public care. It is unclear why. One possibility is that the public system may be more efficient, but, given that the public system provides very different types of treatment than the private system, it is hard to draw any conclusions. For example, Fisher notes that 65 percent of all births in the private system are cesarean sections, whereas the corresponding rate is far lower in the public system.

Aggregate level evidence suggests that inequality as measured by the relationship between income and contact with the health system is far smaller than many allege.[20] Consider a simple regression that estimates the relationship between income and contact with the health system. A larger positive coefficient on income in this regression indicates that higher-income individuals are more likely to have contact with the health system controlling for a variety of other factors such as age, sex, and health status. In Chile, Sapelli and Sapelli and Torche find a negative coefficient on income indicating that lower-income individuals are more likely to have contact with the health system (either public or private).[21] Only at the highest quartile of income does access and expenditure diverge. How much inequality does this generate? Sapelli find that the Chilean system is about as equal as the typical European system.[22] He concludes that the system has less inequality than the Netherlands, Spain, and the UK.

19. Sapelli, Claudio (2004) "Risk segmentation and equity in the Chilean mandatory health insurance system," *Social Science and Medicine*, 58:259–265. Sapelli, C. and A. Torche (2000) The Mandatory Health Insurance System in Chile: Explaining the Choice between Public and Private Insurance. *International Journal of Health Economics and Finance*.

20. *See*, for example, Wagstaff, A. and E. Van Doorslaer (1993). "Equity in the finance of health care: methods and findings." *Equity in the Finance and Delivery of Health Care: An International Perspective. Commission of the European Communities Health Service Research Series*, 8:20–48.

21. Sapelli, Claudio (2004) "Risk segmentation and equity in the Chilean mandatory health insurance system," *Social Science and Medicine*, 58:259–265 and Sapelli, C. and A. Torche (2000) The Mandatory Health Insurance System in Chile: Explaining the Choice between Public and Private Insurance. *International Journal of Health Economics and Finance*.

22. Sapelli, Claudio (2004) "Risk segmentation and equity in the Chilean mandatory health insurance system," *Social Science and Medicine*, 58:259–265

7. CONCLUSION

In this short proposal, we lay out an argument for providing an alternative to employer-based health insurance pooling for high-cost individuals. By developing a federal-level program for individuals deemed to not be able to afford standard care in the private non-group market, the burden of cross-subsidizing these individuals will be borne for broadly leading to a more equitable system. From a cost perspective, unbundling employment and health care insurance may generate efficiency gains as labor market distortions arising from the current system are remedied. Also, un-fragmenting the state and federal level Medicaid and Medicare systems could potentially allow for the better internalization of the benefits from preventive care among the relatively poor and unhealthy.

11. ENDING THE SPECIALTY HOSPITAL WARS
A Plea for Pilot Programs as Information-Forcing Regulatory Design

FRANK PASQUALE[*]

I. INTRODUCTION

Niche providers, including single-specialty hospitals (SSHs)[1] and ambulatory surgical centers (ASCs),[2] provide important health care options for many patients.[3] ASCs developed in the 1970s in order to provide locations for procedures that did not require overnight stays. Specialty hospitals offered more complex procedures in ASC-like settings. General hospitals at first "made their peace" with ASCs because they did not pose too great a competitive threat, and because they themselves could enter the ASC market. But as niche providers grow in number and size, the centripetal forces driving more lucrative procedures away from the general hospital have become a controversial issue in US health care policy.

By diverting away the best-insured patients from general hospitals, specialty hospitals threaten to further undermine the already fading patterns of

* Loftus Professor of Law, Seton Hall University School of Law; Associate Director of the Center for Health and Pharmaceutical Law and Policy, Seton Hall University.

1. Federal law defines single specialty hospitals as hospitals that are primarily and exclusively engaged in the care and treatment of one of the following: patients with cardiac conditions, patients with orthopedic conditions, patients receiving surgical procedures, or any other specialized category of patients or cases that the Secretary designates as inconsistent with the purpose of permitting physician ownership and investment interest in a hospital. *See* U.S. General Accounting Office, *Specialty Hospitals: Information on National Market Share, Physician Ownership, and Patients Serviced*, GA00030683R, 1 (Apr. 2003).

2. The current federal definition of an Ambulatory Surgical Center (ASC) is any distinct entity that operates exclusively for the purpose of providing surgical services to patients not requiring hospitalization, and has an agreement with CMS to participate in Medicare. *Id.*, at 12.

3. The AHA broadly defines niche providers to include "heart hospitals, orthopedic hospitals, surgical hospitals, ASCs, cancer hospitals and centers, dialysis clinics, pain centers, imaging centers, mammography centers, and a host of other narrowly focused providers." American Hospital Association, *Promises Under Pressure, available at* http://www.aha.org/aha/content/2003/pdf/annualmeetinghipaa03.pdf (last accessed Feb. 27, 2008). The term "niche providers" in this article primarily refers to specialty hospitals and ambulatory surgery centers.

cross-subsidization that have aided un- and under-insured Americans. A general hospital will often cross-subsidize vital public services (like emergency departments or uncompensated care) from the margins achieved by its cardiac or orthopedics department. When such profitable departments migrate away from the general hospital, it is not easy to find alternative funding for such services. The resulting specialty hospitals often do not provide the type of community benefits—including emergency rooms, unsponsored care, or medical education—offered by many competing general hospitals. Both they and ASCs can more easily avoid serving Medicaid patients, costly Medicare patients, and the uninsured than similarly situated general community hospitals can.

Defenders of cross-subsidization have used many tactics to stem the flow of dollars and entrepreneurial doctors to niche providers. After convincing Congress to put a temporary moratorium on specialty hospital participation in the Medicare program, general hospitals focused on lobbying the executive branch (and state governments) to stymie their spread.[4] They also used Certificate of Need (CON) laws and other state level regulations to deter entry of niche competitors.

Though they may protect access to care for the nonwealthy, these tactics have a cost. An on-again, off-again moratorium on specialty hospitals has generated legal uncertainty about their viability. Even their staunchest critics admit that something like the Shouldice Hernia Hospital in Canada does provide a model of innovation in health care.[5] Moreover, critics of CON laws are legion. Other regulatory moves, such as state self-referral laws or an elimination of the Stark Law's whole-hospital exception, might distract from gainsharing opportunities and pay-for-performance measures that many hope will increase efficiency in the health care system.

In response to these perceived shortcomings of regulation, a coalescing consensus of scholars and policymakers has begun supporting alterations in tax law

---

4. John Iglehart, *The Emergence of Physician-Owned Specialty Hospitals*, 352 NEW ENG. J. MED. 78 (1/6/2005) ("The American Hospital Association (AHA) and the Federation of American Hospitals (FAH) have begun an aggressive effort to thwart the development of more specialty hospitals. They combined forces for many reasons, not the least of which was that the largest member of both organizations, the HCA, attributed one third of its lower-than-expected earnings per share in its first-quarter financial report for 2003 to the increase in competition from physician-owned specialty hospitals and ambulatory-surgery centers.)"; Anne S. Kimbol, *The Debate Over Specialty Hospitals: How Physician-Hospital Relationships Have Reached a New Fault Line Over These "Focused Factories,"* 38 J. HEALTH L. 633 (2005).

5. Regina Herzlinger has written business school case studies that identify a similar level of efficiency at one U.S. specialty heart hospital. Regina Herzlinger and Peter Stavros, "MedCath Corporation (A)," Harvard Business School Case No. 303-041, rev. August 2006, p. 10; Regina Herzlinger and Peter Stavros, "MedCath Corporation (C)," Harvard Business School Case No. 305-097, rev. May 2006. Herzlinger has been one of the main proponents of specialty hospitals as "focused factories."

or payment levels to supplant these complex regulatory responses to niche providers. If specialty hospitals are "cherrypicking" the healthiest Medicare patients and most lucrative DRGs, then reimbursements should be altered to better reflect the true cost of care. If they are eroding an infrastructure of emergent or indigent care, state authorities can tax them in order to directly subsidize these services. Such payment system changes appear to many commentators to be more efficient, calibrated, and transparent than regulatory requirements.

Unfortunately, the monetary carrots and sticks of tax and payment adjustments may themselves be insufficiently calibrated to provide a just response to niche providers. First, a federal system-level change may be insensitive to variations in states' and localities' treatments of niche providers. It may make sense to reduce reimbursement in general for certain services, but if a state is already imposing a tax on them, should the federal "clawback" be adjusted in that state? If California were to require specialty hospitals to maintain some emergency facilities, would these, more community-oriented, specialty hospitals suffer the same DRG cutbacks as facilities in other states that did not face the same burdens?

Second, even if niche providers' contributions were adequately acknowledged by payment and tax systems, they can play very different roles in different communities. For example, after the specialized Black Hills Surgery Center opened in Rapid City, South Dakota, a nearby general hospital "posted an $8.3 million [annual] operating loss and [saw] its debt rating downgraded."[6] But in some markets, general hospitals may peacefully coexist with specialty hospitals.[7] Specialty hospitals also interact with one another. One specialty hospital in an area may provide a "focused factory" that creates opportunities for developing expertise, but a surfeit of such hospitals in the same place may dissipate these

---

6. David Armstrong, *A Surgeon Earns Riches, Enmity By Plucking Profitable Patients,* WALL ST. J., Aug. 2, 2005, excerpted in http://www.thehealthcareblog.com/the_health_care_blog/2005/08/wsjcom_a_surgeo.html. One of the founders of the Black Hills Surgery Center made $9 million when he sold off his share of the hospital. *Id.*

7. Ann Tynan et al., *General Hospitals, Specialty Hospitals, and Financially Vulnerable Patients,* CENTER FOR STUDYING HEALTH SYSTEM CHANGE RESEARCH BRIEF, Apr. 2009 ("safety net hospitals [in three markets] . . . . reported limited impact from specialty hospitals since safety net hospitals generally do not compete for insured patients."); Medicare Payment Advisory Comm'n, Report to Congress: *Physician-Owned Specialty Hospitals Revisited,* Executive Summary, vi-vii. (Aug. 2006) ("While specialty hospitals may often take profitable surgical patients from the competitor community hospitals, most competitor community hospitals appeared to compensate for this lost revenue. In addition, based on a longitudinal study of general hospital profit margins in markets with and without specialty hospitals, studies found that the most important predictor of general hospital profitability was the extent of competition from other *general* hospitals in the same market area."); John E. Schneider, et al., *Economic and Policy Analysis of Specialty Hospitals,* Health Economics Consulting Group report, Feb. 4, 2005, available at http://www.heartland.org/custom/semod_policybot/pdf/17229.pdf.

efficiencies by assuring that no particular institution has enough surgeries to assure an experienced staff.[8]

All of these possibilities create difficult challenges for efforts to treat niche providers fairly. Like some of my previous work in intellectual property and health law, this piece is designed primarily to alert policymakers to the need for more targeted assessment of the impact of market forces on communities. Taxation (and reduction of payments to) niche providers should be based on their real effects in particular markets, not generalized assumptions about their role.

In a debate that has become increasingly complex and controversial, it is essential to focus on the central normative claim behind general hospitals' resistance to competition from specialty hospitals: these niche providers' threat to cross-subsidization of care for the indigent and uninsured. To the extent specialty hospitals undermine that cross-subsidization, we can frame the moral options available here economically: to try to recover the lost cross-subsidy from specialty hospitals themselves, or to provide direct state subsidy to general hospitals. Specialty hospital advocates may call the former strategy "robbing Peter to pay Paul," and object to the "cannibalization" of health care funding for one segment of the population from another's spending. However, such penalties are appropriate to the extent the specialty hospital's competitive strategy consists in the avoidance of the sickest and least insured patients. Such cream-skimming "competition" is worse than no competition at all.

Unfortunately, the data necessary to make the distinctions crucial to this theoretical model of optimal specialty hospital entry are not yet developed. There have been many studies of specialty hospitals, but they have not yet given us an accurate picture of the exact contours of their competitive strategies. We have some idea of the extent of patient selection at hospitals responding to a MedPac survey, but little sense of the efficiencies pursued at these institutions. The robustness of cross-subsidization at general hospitals is also under dispute, with some actually facing lawsuits seeking to revoke their tax-exempt status because of alleged shirking of community service obligations.

Given this paucity of data, and the variability of specialty hospitals' impact on given communities, policy makers should take a new approach to these entities. Pilot programs would encourage experimentation in the delivery system without risking widespread disruption of care for the uninsured and emergency services. The Centers for Medicare & Medicaid Services (CMS) has already embraced the idea of pilot programs in other contexts, and they could be especially appropriate here if specialty hospitals were permitted in markets where general hospitals

---

8. MAGGIE MAHAR, MONEY-DRIVEN MEDICINE 41–44 (2002) (noting that "a competitive threat works to improve care only if the added capacity is needed. Facilities that siphon dollars from general care hospitals by replicating existing services while offering only minor improvements in the quality of care (more convenient parking, for example, or larger rooms for patients) serve only to weaken a community's total health system.")

had a demonstrably poor record of community service. In such markets, cross-subsidization is probably already low, and specialty hospital threats to it are not as much of a concern as they are in areas where general hospitals consistently serve a substantial base of indigent and uninsured patients.

Part II begins making the case for pilot programs by laying out basic facts about the current performance of specialty hospitals. Part III describes the increasingly complex legal landscape surrounding them—including directly applicable provisions of state and federal laws, and incumbent hospitals' strategies to deploy other regulations, statutes, and common law to gain competitive advantage. After briefly describing the drawbacks of all these strategies, Part IV advances the positive contribution of this chapter—a turn to pilot programs that would promote an evidence-based response to the rise of specialty hospitals.

II. ASSESSING THE IMPACT OF SPECIALTY HOSPITALS

The Medicare Modernization and Prescription Drug Act of 2003 included several provisions designed to offset the cost of the Medicare Part D's prescription drug benefit. Congress ordered both the GAO and CMS to scrutinize niche providers' payment levels. ASC reimbursement rates went through some major changes, but revisions were developed in relatively routine administrative proceedings. Specialty hospitals have been caught up in deeper controversies. Many legal commentators and health policy experts have proposed model responses to the issue, ranging from flat bans on specialty hospitals to encouragement of them. Each side can draw on a substantial literature assessing the costs and benefits of niche providers.

In order to sort through this literature, it is important to clarify exactly how specialty hospitals threaten to undermine extant models of health system finance. Next, the benefits of specialty hospitals must be weighed against these costs. After surveying the literature on the effects of specialty hospitals on health care and health finance generally, this chapter will explore regulatory responses to niche providers, critiques of these regulatory responses, and the emerging consensus focusing on tax and payment system adjustments as a response to specialty hospitals' rise.[9]

---

9. Representative publications in this vein include Richard S. Saver, *Squandering the Gain: Gainsharing and the Continuing Dilemma of Physician Financial Incentives*, 98 Nw. U. L. Rev. 145, 151 (2003); David N. Heard, Student Comment, *The Specialty Hospital Debate: The Difficulty of Promoting Fair Competition Without Stifling Efficiency*, 6 Hous. J. Health L. & Pol'y 215, 235 (2005); Suzanne Strothkamp, Note and Comment, *Understanding the Physician-Owned Specialty Hospital Phenomenon: The Confluence of DRG Payment Methodology and Physician Self-Referral Laws*, 38 J. Health L. 673, 693 (2005).

A. The Development of Niche Providers

Health law has long regulated the struggle between physicians, hospitals, and third–party payors for profit and autonomy.[10] When doctors are frustrated by the policies or revenue opportunities at a particular general hospital, they can be tempted to break away from it to form a separate entity designed to cater more directly to their (and their patients') needs. Ambulatory surgical centers (ASCs) arose in the 1970s and 1980s in order to give particular groups of physicians the opportunity to manage their own affairs in a setting dedicated to their own narrow specialization.[11] Because these centers were more spread out geographically, hospital services were also more conveniently located for many lucrative demographics. ASC's primarily provide services similar to those offered by hospital outpatient surgery departments.[12] ASCs are very common and now directly rival the number of hospital-owned outpatient surgery departments.[13]

In the wake of managed care cost-containment, many cardiac and orthopedic surgeons began to look for new sources of revenue.[14] The ASC model appeared promising, but given the recovery times involved in their practice areas, cardiac and orthopedic surgeons could not start their own ASCs; these tended to be licensed only for "23-hour" beds, a period of recovery often too short for the most lucrative procedures performed in their specialties. Yet once many states did away with their CON laws and the whole-hospital exception to the Stark Laws became clear,[15] another path to autonomy and profits manifest: the specialty hospital, devoted entirely to procedures its physician-owners specialized in.[16] Of course, children's hospitals and women's hospitals long predated these institutions, and "eye and ear" infirmaries and cancer centers also focus on particular

---

10. Paul Starr, *Transformation of American Medicine* Symposium, *Transforming American Medicine: A Twenty-Year Retrospective on The Social Transformation of American Medicine*, 29 J. HEALTH, POL. & L. 557 (2004); Paul Starr, Response, *Transforming American Medicine: A Twenty-Year Retrospective on The Social Transformation of American Medicine*, 29 J. HEALTH, POL. & L. 1005 (2004).

11. *See* American Hospital Association, *supra* note 3, at 3.

12. *Id.*

13. *Id.* There are about 4200 ASCs in the US. For the purposes of this paper ASCs and specialty hospitals will be referred collectively as "niche providers."

14. See generally H.H. Pham et al., *Financial Pressures Spur Physician Entrepreneurialism*, HEALTH AFFAIRS 23, no. 2 (2004): 70–81, available at http://content.healthaffairs.org/cgi/content/full/23/2/70.

15. While a doctor may not refer patients to an ancillary unit in which the doctors owns an interest, self-referral is permitted for a whole hospital in which the physician has an interest.

16. A specialty hospital focuses on one area, such as cardiac procedures, surgery, or orthopedics. U.S. Gen. Acct. Office, *Specialty Hospitals: Information on National Market Share, Physician Ownership, and Patients Served* 1 (Apr. 2003), http://www.gao.gov/new.items/do3683r.pdf (last visited Feb. 28, 2006).

diagnoses and treatments.[17] But the new breed of cardiac, orthopedic, and surgical hospitals eventually attracted the attention of the Department of Health and Human Services (and Congress) because some suspected they were driven more by financial than medical reasons.[18]

Physician-owners of these institutions claim that they are freer to spend time on patient care and medical innovation once they can avoid the administrative work common at general hospitals. However, they are focusing their services on a group that is, by and large, either more prosperous than the average American, less sick than the average patient, or both. The poor and the very sick can be shut out of these new care options, and left with a medical system from which many dynamic and innovative practitioners have exited.

Charitable exemptions offer favorable tax status to many nonprofit hospitals because they are presumed to be providing valuable community services. The Emergency Medical Treatment and Active Labor Act (EMTALA) requires most nonprofit hospitals to provide "screening" and "stabilization" for anyone with an emergency condition.[19] Teaching hospitals provide postgraduate medical education for medical staff, and are only incompletely compensated for this training by the government.[20] A safety net of "hospitals of last resort" care for millions of

---

17. "Limited-service providers, also known as 'niche' or specialty providers, are not new, but the nature and pace of their growth is." American Hospital Association, *Limited Service—Niche Providers* (2005), http://www.aha.org/aha/issues/LSP/(Accessed Feb. 27, 2008) 178.

18. Iglehart, *supra* note 4; Kelly J. Devers, *Specialty Hospitals: Focused Factories or Cream Skimmers?*, Health System Change Issue Brief, Vol. 62, (April 2003), available at http://www.hschange.com/CONTENT/552/ ("The reasons for specialty hospital development are complex and vary across markets, but analysis suggests that three factors are important drivers of this trend nationally: relatively high reimbursements for certain procedures, physicians' desire for greater control over management decisions affecting productivity and quality and specialists' desire to increase their income in the face of reduced reimbursement for professional services.").

19. Emergency Medical Treatment and Active Labor Act, 42 U.S.C. § 1395dd(b) (2007); Memorandum from Thomas E. Hamilton, Dir., Survey and Certification Group, Ctrs. for Medicare & Medicaid Servs. to State Survey Agency Dirs., 1 (Apr. 26, 2007) (EMTALA requirements apply to all hospital facilities with the exception of so-called "critical access hospitals"); *Physician-Owned Specialty Hospitals: Hearing Before the S. Comm on Finance*, 109th Cong. 11 (2006) (statement of Mark B. McClellan, Administrator, Ctrs. for Medicare & Medicaid Servs.) (Proposing a rule that would require specialty hospitals to be able to treat reasonably foreseeable emergencies that arise at their facilities and take emergency transfers from other hospitals where appropriate).

20. Marie Price, *OSU Medical Center Sues Oklahoma Health Care Authority over Medicaid Issue*, J. Rec. Legis. Rep. (Oklahoma City, OK), Jun. 19, 2007; Linda Aiken & Marni Gwyhter, *Medicare Funding for Nursing Education-Case for Policy Change*, 273 JAMA 1528–1532 (1995).

uninsured individuals.[21] Though some nonprofits are prospering, many of those which do the most to care for the un- and under-insured are being squeezed by declining government reimbursement rates,[22] rising personnel costs,[23] and the market power of insurers.[24]

General hospitals have many strategies for responding to these cost pressures and third-party payor-enforced price cuts. They can demand higher reimbursement rates from private insurers than from government insurance programs. They can charge uninsured patients far more than the insured, potentially generating comparative windfalls from those few uninsured wealthy enough to pay for undiscounted services.[25] They can lobby Medicare to adjust payments for certain DRGs to better reflect the cost of services provided to individuals.[26] They can also apply for disproportionate share payments, which "preserve access to

21. *See* National Association for Public Hospitals, America's Public Hospitals and Health Systems, 2007—Results of the Annual NAPH Hospital Characteristics Survey, at 15 *available at* http://www.naph.org/Publications/Characteristics-2007.aspx (last accessed Sep. 23, 2009) (noting that in 2007, NAPH members served 8.3 million primary and specialty care visits and 2.5 million emergency department visits). .

22. Lynne Fagnani, *Testimony at Congressional Hearing National Public Hospital Safety-Net in Crisis: D.C. General Hospital in Focus* (Mar. 22, 2001) transcript *available at* http://www.dcwatch.com/issues/pbc010322d.htm—oral.

23. For one example, *see* Shaila Dewan & Kevin Sack, *A Safety-Net Hospital Falls into Financial Crisis*, N.Y TIMES, Jan. 8, 2008, *available at* http://www.nytimes.com/2008/01/08/us/08grady.html?scp=2&sq=paying±Training±hospitals&st=nyt.

24. *See* National Association for Public Hospitals, *supra* note 22 at 14 (explaining that the funding of care to the uninsured and underserved is often the target of government budget cuts which makes care delivery and innovation difficult).

25. Mark S. Hall, Price-Gouging by Doctors and Hospitals, available at http://www.healthreformwatch.com/2009/07/19/price-gouging-by-doctors-and-hospitals/comment-page-1/ ("A comprehensive analysis of data hospitals report to Medicare shows that, on average, hospitals charge uninsured patients two-and-a-half times more than they charge insured patients and three times more than their actual costs. In some states mark-ups average four-fold."); Johns Hopkins Bloomberg School of Public Health, *Hospitals Charge Uninsured and "Self Pay" Patients more than Double What Insured Patients Pay*, May 8, 2007, *available at http://www.jhsph.edu/publichealthnews/press_releases/2007/anderson_hospital_charges.html;* Reed Abelson & Jonathon M. Glater, *Suits Challenge Hospitals Bills of Uninsured*, N.Y. TIMES, Jun.17, 2004, *available at* http://www.nytimes.com/2004/06/17/business/suits-challenge-hospital-bills-of-uninsured.html.

26. "Diagnosis Related Group:" a feature of the Medicare Prospective Payment System (PPS) that classifies hospital cases into one of approximately 500 groups for payment to providers based on a combination of factors such as diagnosis, age, sex, and complications; Tax Equity and Fiscal Responsibility Act of 1982, Pub. L. No. 97-248 §101, 96 Stat. 33–36 (codified as amended at 42 U.S.C. §1395ww(a)-(c) (Supp. 1985)).

care for Medicare and low-income populations by financially assisting the hospitals they use."[27]

The American Hospital Association (AHA) claims that physician-owned limited-service hospitals raise other hospitals' costs and lead to utilization of unnecessary services because of physician self-referrals.[28] One trade association estimates that there were 263 physician-owned hospitals in the United States in 2008.[29] Although this is a very small number when compared to the number of hospitals in general (which number about 5000 as of 2008), the compelling business model behind many specialty hospitals makes their rapid spread a distinct possibility—especially if cost containment pressures elsewhere lead specialists to seek new sources of revenue.

Since physician investors and owners of specialty hospitals actively self-refer, the AHA claims that they divert market share from community hospitals.[30] The AHA also claims that niche providers reduce quality, undermine equal access to facilities, and jeopardize patient safety.[31] They are not subject to the same quality inspections as community hospitals, are not equipped to deal with emergency situations, and are able to "cherry pick" the most lucrative patients based on favorable DRGs, health status, and insurance status.[32] This leaves many community hospitals with the burden of treating uninsured patients with complex medical conditions. The AHA claims that the presence of physician-owned specialty hospitals will damage the United States health care system by increasing cost and weakening the "safety net" that community hospitals can provide. It has called for physician-owned specialty hospitals to be heavily regulated on the

27. http://www.aamc.org/advocacy/library/teachhosp/hosp0003.htm. Medicare makes a DSH adjustment for hospital inpatient services to assist in offsetting uncompensated care, whether from the uninsured, underinsured, or indigent. The amount of adjustment "is based on the disproportionate patient percentage (DPP), which is equal to the sum of the percentage of Medicare inpatient days (including Medicare Advantage inpatient days) attributable to patients entitled to both Medicare Part A and Supplemental Security Income (SSI) and the percentage of total patient days attributable to patients eligible for Medicaid but not eligible for Medicare Part A." Centers for Medicare and Medicaid Services, *Fact Sheet: Medicare Disproportionate Share Hospital*, at 1 (April 2008), *available at* http://www.cms.hhs.gov/MLNProducts/downloads/2009_mdsh.pdf.

28. American Hospital Association, *Stat: Tackling Today's Challenges: Limited Service Providers, available at* http://www.ifasc.com/documents/AHA2004Paper-LimitedServiceProviders.pdf, (2004).

29. *See* American Hospital Association analysis of state surveys of CMS data, *available at http://www.aha.org/aha/trendwatch/2008/twapr2008selfreferral.ppt* (2007).

30. *Id.* For the purposes of this paper, "community" or "general" hospital will refer both to for-profit and nonprofit entities that offer the full range of services normally associated with hospitals.

31. *Id.*

32. *Id.*

federal and state level, and claims that Medicare authorities need to take a much closer look at reimbursement rates for ASCs.

The AHA's influence and disturbing projections about the financial health of general hospitals led to a moratorium on Medicare payments to specialty hospitals in 2003.[33] When the moratorium expired, there was a flurry of interest in administrative action designed to address specialty hospitals.[34] Reports from the GAO and the Medicare Payment Advisory Commission have investigated the impact of specialty hospitals, whereas CMS rulemakings have focused on re-assessing payment levels for ASC procedures.

B. Evaluating Niche Providers

Advocates believe that specialty hospitals and ASCs provide new incentives for doctors to control costs and increase competition in the health care market.[35] They also see the "spinning off" of these facilities as a step toward increased specialization and expertise, ultimately leading to quality increases at more accessible facilities. To advocates, niche providers are promoting advances in cost-containment, quality, and access.

Critics tell a diametrically opposed story. In her *Money Driven Medicine*, Maggie Mahar argues that untrammeled growth of specialty hospitals can lead to a misallocation of a community's health resources. Other commentators see self-referral at the root of both overspending and unnecessary procedures. Specialty hospitals can be extremely capital-intensive, and doctor-owners are under great pressure to earn back that investment.[36]

---

33. 42 U.S.C. 1395nn(a)(1)–(d)(3), banning new Medicare 855A applications by specialty hospitals for 18 months.

34. David Glendinning, *Moratorium for Doctor-owned Hospitals Now Over*, AMA NEWS, Aug. 28, 2006, *available at* http://www.ama-assn.org/amednews/2006/08/28/gvsa0828.htm.

35. *See* Herzlinger, *Focused Factories*; parallel arguments from the AAASC website include: "a) ASCs are often more conveniently located for patients. Because ASCs tend to be much smaller, and have more convenient parking, they also tend to be more easily accessible to patients than hospital settings; b) ASCs are able to improve efficiencies, which minimizes patient waiting times; c) ASCs offer superior outcomes, in part because of staff specialization; d) ASCs are more patient-focused, and strive for 100 percent patient satisfaction; e) ASCs are more affordable for patients. (*Ambulatory Surgery Centers: A Positive Trend in Health Care. available at* http://www.ascassociation.org/advocacy/AmbulatorySurgeryCentersPositiveTrendHealthCare.pdf).

36. Rebecca Bethard, *Physician Self-Referral: Beyond Stark II*, 43 BRANDEIS L.J. 465, 478–479 (2005) ("As full-service public hospitals watch funds divert to specialty facilities, their ability to provide needed services is placed at risk. Further restriction of physician self-referral is an important component for both the federal and state governments. The most effective course is for the prohibition of physician referral of patients to any entity in which they have a financial interest for both public funds and private pay sources.")

Whatever the motivations of those backing niche providers, their services should be judged on the classic axes of evaluation for health care: cost, quality, and access. Although data on the first two elements is mixed, it is increasingly clear that specialty hospitals (and some smaller niche providers) can contribute to trends that have long undermined the cross-subsidization that has aided America's un- and under-insured.

1. **Cost** Specialty hospitals claim that they provide services at less cost than their general hospital competitors. For example, the specialty hospital need not buy supplies in the wide range of areas that a full service hospital has to plan for. There are many basic services that specialty hospitals usually do not provide, allowing them to focus on cutting costs within their specialty.[37]

The AHA claims that, physician investment in niche providers ultimately drives medical costs higher.[38] One recent study indicates that "orthopedic and surgical specialty hospitals appear to have significantly levels of cost-inefficiency.[39] Physician investors self-refer, a practice that can generate conflicts of interest.[40] Patients must worry that physicians' advice is biased toward options that maximize their compensation. Physician-investors may also feel pressure to perform a higher number of procedures to increase the specialty hospital's profitability.[41] According to the AHA, the higher utilization causes increased costs for both the individual patients (in the form of higher procedure prices at physician-owned specialty hospital) and can increase rates for the entire community.[42]

---

37. Katherine E. Ericksen, Statute Note, *Prescribing the Best Facilities for Our Nation's Health Care: Physician-Owned Facilities vs. Community Hospitals*, 8 J. L. & FAM. STUD. 449, 456–57 (2006).

38. *See* American Hospital Association, *supra* note 3, at 6.

39. Kathleen Carey, et al., *Specialty and Full-Service Hospitals: A Comparative Cost Analysis*, 43(5) HEALTH SERVICES RESEARCH (Oct. 2008), at 1879.

40. *Id. See also* MedPAC Report *supra*, note 7, which described in detail the financial incentives for surgeon-owners to self-refer:

Although the incremental income from ownership may not be large relative to each physician's annual income, the incentive for a group of physician-investors to increase admissions can be substantially larger than specialty hospital advocates suggest. Specialty hospital advocates omit two key factors when discussing the profits associated with increasing admissions. First, a large share of hospital costs are fixed over the short run—that is, they do not increase when an additional patient is admitted to a hospital with excess capacity. By filling an empty bed with a patient, the hospital's additional expense will be limited to the costs that vary with the admission, such as supplies, devices, and additional nursing hours to care for the patient. . . . Second, physicians together own at least a 30 percent interest in most physician-owned specialty hospitals. By being part of a group of physicians that admit most of their patients to the specialty hospital, each physician receives not only the profits from his own patients but also a share of the profits from the other physicians' patients.

41. American Hospital Association, *supra* note 3, at 6.

42. *Id.*

Physicians that refer patients to niche providers in which they have invested receive a share in the earnings of the niche provider as well as their own professional fees.[43] Some studies have confirmed a correlation between a physician's referral rate to such facilities and the value of the physician's investment in the facility.[44] The correlation is related to the type of the specialty hospital; it is stronger in orthopedic than in cardiac hospitals.[45] The likelihood of physician self-referral is also related to the size of the physician's interest in the hospitals.[46] Cardiac hospitals that are less than fifty percent owned by physicians only receive ten percent more referrals than average, whereas hospitals in which physicians own a majority interest receive fifty percent more referrals.[47]

Some other studies conclude that niche providers increase the volume of health care spending in the community. The Congressional Budget Office estimates that fewer procedures, services and products are used when physician have no financial incentive in the care they provide.[48] The opening of specialty hospitals can cause more utilization in communities, and that increasing demand can lead to increasing costs. A recent study of orthopedic niche providers found that orthopedic specialty hospitals drove up the cost of spinal fusion surgical procedures in some markets by 121 percent between 1999 and 2004; ninety one percent of the surgeries were performed at the orthopedic physician-owned specialty hospital.[49] In a study of Medicare beneficiaries from 1995 through 2003, the rates for revascularization were higher in hospital referral regions where new cardiac programs opened at cardiac niche providers when compared with regions in which new cardiac programs opened at general hospitals.[50] Additionally, a Medicare cost report found that fifty-seven percent of niche providers had profit margins above ten percent, whereas only seventeen percent of community hospitals in the United States had profit margins over ten percent.[51] Overall, the financial gains for owners of specialty hospitals may be

---

43. Leslie Greenwald, et al, *Specialty Versus Community Hospitals: Referrals, Quality, And Community Benefits*, 25(1) HEALTH AFF. 106, 109 (2006).

44. *Id.*

45. *Id.*

46. *Id.*

47. *Id.*

48. *See* American Hospital Association, *supra* note 3, *citing* Peter Orzsag, Letter to the Hon. Sam Johnson (Congressional Budget Office 2007).

49. J.M. Mitchell, *Utilization Changes Following Market Entry by Niche Providers*, 64(3) MED. CARE RES. & REV. 395, 410 (2007).

50. Nallamothu Brahmajee, et al, *Opening of Specialty Hospital Cardiac Hospitals and Use of Coronary Revascularization in Medicare Beneficiaries*, 297(9) JAMA 962, 966 (2007).

51. *See* American Hospital Association, *supra* note 3, at 6.

causing increased utilization that generally drives increases in the cost of health care.[52]

The Medicare Payment Advisory Commission ("MedPAC") also studied specialty hospital performance in the context of particular cases. According to MedPAC, "After controlling for [some] potential sources of variation, including patient severity, we found that both the aggregate mean and median values for costs at physician-owned specialty hospitals are higher than the corresponding values for peer, competitor, and community hospitals."[53] But due to small sample size and the failure of several surveyed hospitals to respond, it was unwilling to find these differences were statistically significant.[54]

2. Quality Proponents of specialty hospitals claim that, even if they do drive up costs, there are good medical reasons for developing "focused factories" of medical expertise.[55] After third-party payors and managers began increasingly affecting the medical decision making process, physicians fought back for greater autonomy.[56] Physician owners of these hospitals claim that they provide more efficient care because they only have to be concerned with supplies and personnel in their area of expertise.[57] In some instances, physicians may themselves specialize, each performing one small role in, say, a knee surgery. Some international

52. *See* SHANNON BROWNLEE, OVERTREATED (2007); MAGGIE MAHAR, MONEY-DRIVEN MEDICINE.

53. MedPAC Report, *supra* note 7, at 14–15 ("Actual lengths of stay were 17 percent to 31 percent lower than regional averages, depending on the type of specialty hospital. Moreover, specialty hospitals' lengths of stay were often significantly shorter, relative to the expected average, than those for peer hospitals.").

54. *Id.* at 13 ("The data available to make this comparison are limited. Data are available for only a small number of specialty hospitals, and those hospitals have not been operating for long. Over time, as the hospitals establish themselves and expand their market share, their relative costs could change.").

55. Kelly J. Devers, et al, *Specialty Hospitals: Focused Factories or Cream Skimmers?*, Issue Brief, Center for Studying Health System Change, Apr. 2003, at 2; REGINA HERZLINGER, MARKET-DRIVEN HEALTH CARE: WHO WINS, WHO LOSES IN THE TRANSFORMATION OF AMERICA'S LARGEST SERVICE INDUSTRY, (1997); *see also* Maureen Kwiecinski, *Limiting Conflicts of Interest Arising From Physician Investment in Specialty Hospitals*" 88 MARQ. L. REV., 418 (2004) (citing U.S. General Accounting Office, Specialty Hospitals: Geographic Location, Services Provided, and Financial Performance, GAO-04-167, p. 3–4 (Oct. 2003)).

56. Steven D. Wales, *The Stark Law: Boon or Boondoggle? An Analysis of the Prohibition on Physician Self-Referrals*, 27 L. & PSYCH. REV. 1, 28 (2003).

57. ROBERT JAMES CIMASI, HEALTH CAPITAL CONSULTANTS, THE ATTACK ON SPECIALTY AND NICHE PROVIDERS 87 (2005) (The specialty hospital "approach allows [physicians] to create "focused factories" which have been demonstrated to improve quality and efficiency, thereby benefiting consumers."); Ericksen, *supra* note 40, at 455.

evidence indicates that such specialization helps reduce medical error and improves the efficiency of care.[58]

According to niche providers, physician investment will lead to a higher quality of care because physicians who are financially tied to the specialty hospital will have a greater interest in providing quality services.[59] The growth of "Best Doctors"[60] and "Best Hospitals" ratings services make accountability a key to profit in a competitive marketplace.[61] According to Wales, banning physician investment eliminates the most knowledgeable category of investors in health care facilities, and depletes the supply of capital available to these facilities.[62]

Increased volume and access can provide a direct benefit to patients when physicians are able to hone their skills in a particular area and develop more proficiency in that specialty than they would be able to in other settings.[63] Specialty hospitals' profits can also be invested in new technology. Such resources can enable physicians to better treat patients, and specialized nursing staff may be better trained and equipped to work with the technology available than nonspecialist staff in general hospitals.[64] Some advocates of consumer-directed health care argue that the concentration of doctors and procedures at specialty hospitals help eliminate waste that occurs when care is fragmented, as it often is in general hospitals.[65] Specialty hospitals can negotiate volume discounts from suppliers and dedicate operating rooms to an orderly set of surgeries each day.

---

58. *See generally* Jon Chilingerian, Clinical Focus in Health Care: Some International Lessons, 5–12, *available at* http://council.brandeis.edu/pubs/Specialty%20Hospitals/Chilingerian%20Paper.pdf

59. *See* Physician-owned specialty hospitals: Hearing Before S. Subcomm. on Fed. Fin. Mgmt., Gov't Info., and Int'l Sec. Comm. on Homeland Sec. and Governmental Affairs, 109th Cong. 9 (2005) (statement of Mark E. Miller, Executive Dir., Medicare Payment Advisory Commission), *available at* http://hsgac.senate.gov/public/index.cfm?FuseAction=-Files.View&FileStore_id=d9332a3f-3aec-4834-9b43-5657912358b2 (describing financial incentives for physicians to provide more efficient and better quality care).

60. *America's Top Doctors, available at* http://www.castleconnolly.com/doctors/index.cfm.

61. *See* Avery Comarow, *Birth of A New Methodology, U.S.N.W.R,* Aug 26, 2007 *available at* http://health.usnews.com/usnews/health/articles/070826/3meth.htm (new rules that require reporting of mortality rates, preventable deaths, errors).

62. Steven D. Wales, *The Stark Law: Boon or Boondoggle? An Analysis of the Prohibition on Physician Self-Referrals,* 27 L. & PSYCH. REV. 1, 15, 28 (2003).

63. Materials collected in Jennifer Bartels, *The Application Of Antitrust And Fraud-And-Abuse Law To Specialty Hospitals,* 2006 COLUM. BUS. L. REV. 215 (2006).

64. Cheryl Jackson, *A Hospital of Their Own; Specialists Say Physician-owned Hospitals can Offer Focused Care at Lower Costs. Full-service Hospitals, and the Doctors who Depend on Them, are Leery,* AM. MED. NEWS, OCT. 16. 2000, at 17–18.

65. Jody Hoffner Gitell, *Achieving Focus in Hospital Care: The Role of Relational Coordination, in* CONSUMER-DRIVEN HEALTH CARE: IMPLICATIONS FOR PROVIDERS, PAYERS, AND POLICYMAKERS, 683, 689–90 (Regina Herzlinger ed., 2004). As this language shows, different types of fragmentation rankle different people. When I started this project, I saw

Consumer demand for niche providers appears to vindicate the quality claims of their owners. Doctors at niche providers also appear to be more satisfied with their work environment than peers elsewhere. When physicians own a share of a specialty hospital in which they works, they can make policy and purchasing decisions with more leverage over hospital administrators.[66] When physicians have greater control over their schedules and are able to make decisions regarding hiring and staffing levels, this increases their satisfaction with their work environment and allows for better patient interaction."[67] Additionally, specialty hospitals can develop physician expertise due to the high volume of similar procedures performed. This expertise can lead to innovation, which may reduce costs and increase quality.[68]

Opponents of specialty hospitals dispute these claims about quality. Specifically, they argue that specialty hospitals introduce additional risks to their patients.[69] The CMS has found that patients at cardiac specialty hospitals were significantly more likely to be admitted shortly after discharge because of a complication or ineffective treatment when compared to those at community hospitals.[70] This discrepancy may be explained by the fact that niche providers often lack the capacity to deal with complications that can occur during procedures. The GAO has reported that, only half of all physician-owned hospitals have

---

specialty hospitals and ASCs as centripetal forces in an already fragmented health delivery system. However, CDHC advocates see the concentration of resources on particular problems at these niche providers as a virtue.

66. Cheryl Jackson, *A Hospital of Their Own; Specialists Say Physician-owned Hospitals can Offer Focused Care at Lower Costs. Full-service Hospitals, and the Doctors who Depend on Them, are Leery*, AM. MED. NEWS, Oct. 16. 2000, at 17–18; Julie Piotrowski, *Niche Facilities Hit; Moratorium Raises New Self-Referral Issues for Docs*, MOD. HEALTHCARE, Dec. 22, 2003, at 28 *available at* http://www.modernhealthcare.com/article/20031222/PREMIUM/312220337 (Dennis Kelly, spokesman for MedCath Corp., which operates primarily heart hospitals, says he believes that care is better in specialty facilities precisely because physicians are effectively managing all aspects of care.).

67. Ericksen, *supra* note 40, at 29. Darr argues that "when a physician gains more control over the work environment, she can have more input in the medical device and drug selection. Ultimately, physicians feel that more control over the delivery of services allows them to provide better care to their patients." Kurt Darr, *Physician Entrepreneurship and Hospitals–Part 2*, Hospital Topics, Sept. 22, 2005, at 29.

68. Kelly Devers *et al.*, *Specialty Hospitals: Focused Factories or Cream Skimmers?*, at 2–3 (HSC, Issue Brief No. 62, 2003), *available at* http://www.hschange.org/CONTENT/552/ (last visited April 7, 2008).

69. David N. Heard, Student Comment, *The Specialty Hospital Debate: The Difficulty of Promoting Fair Competition Without Stifling Efficiency*, 6 Hous. J. HEALTH L. & POL'Y 215, 220–21 (2005) (noting that many types of for-profit hospitals don't provide this type of care).

70. Centers for Medicare & Medicaid Services, *Study of Niche providers Required in Section 507(c)(2) of the Medicare Prescription Drug Improvement & Modernization Act of 2003*, (May 2005).

emergency departments, and of those that do have emergency departments, fifty-eight have only one bed.[71]

The Office of Inspector General (OIG) at the Department of Health and Human Services has been especially critical of the inability of specialty hospitals to deal with complications. It has concluded that seventy seven percent of all physician-owned hospitals have insufficient emergency care capacity.[72] Deaths due to complications in specialty hospitals have been documented. On multiple occasions specialty hospitals lacked personnel with the emergency training necessary to provide assistance. In these situations the specialty hospital were forced to dial 911 in order to obtain the requisite emergency assistance.[73] In fact, two thirds of all physician-owned hospitals rely on 911 in case of emergencies that arise during surgeries.[74]

The lack of emergency services in speciality hospitals is not the only indicator that quality may be lacking. Other empirical research commissioned by the U.S. government is equivocal on the quality question. According to a CMS Report, the cardiac hospitals surveyed delivered a level of care that was as good or better than that of their competitors. However, a small sample size deterred CMS from extrapolating these findings to specialty hospitals in general.[75] CMS found that overall patient satisfaction with specialty facilities was as good as or higher than the level of satisfaction with competing community hospitals.[76] Critics might find the CMS findings suspect because a key aspect of the competitive strategy

---

71. Office of Inspector General, *Niche Providers' Ability to Manage Medical Emergencies*, (2008).

72. *Id.*

73. *Id.*

74. *Id.*

75. *Id.* at 112 ("there are several limitations to our findings. First, we could only visit a limited number of specialty hospital markets (given the time and resources available). While we believe the markets and hospitals we chose represent a reasonable cross-section of the specialty hospitals currently operating, our findings cannot be generalized to all markets. Second, again because of resource constraints, our site visits clearly focused on specialty hospitals rather than community hospitals. While we did visit the community hospitals in each of the six markets, *we spent much less time speaking with the community hospitals and therefore do not seek to fully describe their specific operations.* Rather, our focus was on describing specialty hospitals in detail, paying particular attention to policy issues identified in the MMA legislation. Finally, in site visits, we relied on self-reported information."); MedPAC Report, *infra* note 98, at 13 ("The data available to make this comparison are limited. Data are available for only a small number of specialty hospitals, and those hospitals have not been operating for long. Over time, as the hospitals establish themselves and expand their market share, their relative costs could change.").

76. *CMS Report*, at iii.

of specialty hospitals is to treat healthier patients. However, CMS methodology did adjust for "patient mix."[77]

3. The Mechanisms by Which Specialty Hospitals Affect Access to Care Regardless of the ultimate resolution of the cost and quality debates, many community hospitals accuse specialty hospitals of diverting revenues that would have gone toward their public service obligations into the pockets of physician-investors.[78] The community hospital rests on a delicate financial ecosystem of cross-subsidization;[79] specialty hospitals are accused of diverting more and more lucrative cases away from them via patient selection.[80] To the extent that large community hospitals serve as "providers of last resort," specialty hospitals pose an extraordinary financial threat. Cardiac services are the most lucrative for community hospitals; they account for up to forty percent of such hospitals' revenue.[81] Orthopedics often is the highest grossing department in community hospitals that do not have cardiac centers.[82] Specialty hospitals' cardiac and orthopedic patients tend to have better insurance, and to require less recovery time, than community hospitals' patients.[83] Niche providers also target higher income patients that have the clear ability to pay for elective procedures; studies show that thirty percent of niche providers are located in areas that serve residents of higher socioeconomic status (SES) zip codes.[84]

---

77. *CMS Report*, at 38. ("To adjust for patient severity, we used the severity score generated by the APR-DRG risk adjustment grouper, a methodology developed by 3M Corporation. The severity score classified each Medicare claim into one of four subclasses of mortality risk: 1) Minor, 2) Moderate, 3) Major, and 4) Extreme. For each analysis, we stratified results by severity score, examining outcomes of admissions with moderate severity (i.e., those with an APR-DRG severity category of Minor or Moderate) and severe (i.e., those with an APR-DRG severity category of Major or Extreme). We calculated the following measures of quality of care: mortality during hospitalization and within 30 days of discharge from the hospital; complications during hospitalization; readmission within 30 days of discharge; and discharge disposition.")

78. David Armstrong, *A Surgeon Earns Riches, Enmity By Plucking Profitable Patients*, WALL ST. J., Aug. 2, 2005, *available at* http://online.wsj.com/article/SB112294877775102271.html?mod=health_home_inside_today_left_column.

79. Peter Hammer, *Code Blue or Blue Light Special: Where is the Market for Indigent Care?* (2007).

80. Rebecca Bethard, Note: *Physician Self-Referral: Beyond Stark II*, 43 BRANDEIS L.J. 465, 478–79 (2005).

81. Lawrence Casalino, *et al.*, *Focused Factories? Physician-Owned Specialty Facilities*, 22(6) HEALTH AFF. 56, 61 (2003).

82. *Id.*

83. *Id.*

84. *See* American Hospital Association *supra* note 3 at 9 (*citing* Cram P. et al. *Hospital Characteristics and Patient Populations Served By Physician Owned and Non Physician Orthopedic Specialty Hospitals.* BMC Health Services Research, 7(155)).

Physician-owners have several strategies at their disposal in order to draw the most lucrative cases away from community hospitals.[85] First and foremost, specialization itself in certain "diagnosis related groups" can be more lucrative than performing a broad range of services.[86] For example, the range of services associated with cardiac surgery affords a higher "margin" than most routine care. A recent report by the CMS suggests that physician-owners at specialty hospitals can achieve windfalls because of faulty DRG methodology; there are wide discrepancies between the profitability of various fields.

Having "cherry picked" given DRGs, physicians at specialty hospitals are accused of "cream-skimming" even further by focusing admissions on the healthiest and wealthiest patients. According to Maureen Kwiecinski, physicians at specialty hospitals have better access to patients' medical and financial records, and thus are able to engage in "patient credentialing:" referring the lucrative cases to the physician-owned specialty hospital while diverting the less profitable cases to the community hospital.[87] The physician-owners of specialty hospitals are reacting rationally to incentives created by prospective payment reimbursement schemes, which "provide[] a strong financial incentive to decrease the cost of patient care" and encourages physician owners to "select patients who are less medically complicated."[88]

Thus it should be no surprise that some commentators conclude that "[t]he growth of these facilities threatens the viability of the business model underlying the traditional community hospital."[89] If they truly divert resources from general hospitals and further worsen the margins of "hospitals of last resort," the growth of specialty hospitals represents further stratification in health care delivery between payor classes.[90] Competition from specialty hospitals for the dollars of the insured tends to make general hospitals even less capable of treating the uninsured.[91]

---

85. Suzanne Strothkamp, Note and Comment, *Understanding the Physician-Owned Specialty Hospital Phenomenon: The Confluence of DRG Payment Methodology and Physician Self-Referral Laws*, 38 J. HEALTH L. 673, 693 (2005).

86. The "Diagnosis Related Group" (DRG) categorizations are part of the Medicare Prospective Payment System. Under the DRG system, "all human diseases were to be classified into homogeneous categories called diagnosis related groups, or DRGs, with Medicare paying a predetermined amount for each DRG," Strothkamp, 38 J. HEALTH L. at 675.

87. Maureen Kwiecinski, *Limiting Conflicts of Interest Arising from Physician Investment in Specialty Hospitals*, 88 MARQ. L. REV. 413, 423 (2004).

88. *Id.* at 422.

89. Peter J. Hammer, *Medical Code Blue Or Blue Light Special: Where Is the Market for Indigent Care?*, 6 J. L. & SOC. 82, 92 (2005).

90. *Id.*

91. *Id.*

Regardless of the broader goals of the proponents of specialty hospitals and their plans for a broader consumer-directed health care movement,[92] their "cherry picking" and "cream-skimming" raises significant diversionary concerns. According to a Government Accountability Office study, "on average, specialty hospitals treat a lower percentage of severely ill patients than . . . general community hospitals.[93] There is also concern that specialists' own case for SSHs indicates their capacity to undermine the surge capacity necessary for emergencies; SSH physician-owners have repeatedly said that they prefer to work in their own hospital because their schedules are less likely to be disrupted by emergencies. A physician allocating his or her time to an SSH may increase the convenience of patients with non-urgent matters, but also risks denying the general hospital the staff it needs for sudden surges of demand for specialists. This would only intensify an ongoing trend of under-resourced emergency services—an unintended consequence of the Emergency Medical Treatment and Active Labor Act (EMTALA) and the greater comparable profitability of non-emergency services.

Severely ill patients are less profitable to treat under the current DRG reimbursement system, because hospitals are reimbursed on a "per-case" rather than "per-procedure" basis.[94] The Medicare Payment Advisory Commission confirmed that "specialty hospitals treat a mix of patients that, on average, should

---

92. For a full description of CDHC, *see* Timothy Jost, Health Care at Risk: A Critique of the Consumer Driven Movement 17–27 (2007) (summarizing characteristics of CDHC). *See also* Regina T. Jefferson, *Medical Savings Accounts: Windfalls for the Healthy, Wealthy & Wise, available at* SSRN http//ssrn.com/abstract=171973; M. Greg Bloche, *Consumer Direct Health Care and the Disadvantaged*, Health Aff., 26, 5, 1315 (2007) *available at http://content.healthaffairs.org/cgi/content/abstract/26/5/1315?maxtosho w=&HITS=10&hits=10&RESULTFORMAT=&author1=Bloche&andorexactfulltext=and& searchid=1&FIRSTINDEX=0&resourcetype=HWCIT.*

93. U.S. Gen. Acct. Off., GAO-03-683R, Specialty Hospitals: Information on National Market Share, Physician Ownership, and Patients Served 1, 12–13 (2003), *available at* http://www.gao.gov/new.items/d03683r.pdf (last visited June 12, 2007) ("17% of patients at specialty hospitals [were] classified as severely ill by DRG system compared with 26% at general community hospitals"). The report breaks this down further by type of specialty hospital. "The median orthopedic hospital, in terms of patient illness severity, had 5 percent of patients in its most common diagnosis group classified as severely ill. The median general hospital in the urban areas with orthopedic hospitals had 8 percent of patients in the same diagnosis groups classified as severely ill." For cardiac treatment: 17 percent of patients in the most common DRG at Cardiac specialty hospitals were classified as severely ill, whereas 22 percent of cardiac patients in the same DRG at general hospitals classified as severely ill.

94. Betty B. Bibbins, *Medicare Severity Diagnosis Related Groups (MS-DRGS) Set The Stage For Documentation And Coding Paradigm Shifts*, 9 No. 6 J. Health Care Compliance 11 (2007).

result in higher-than-average relative profitability."[95] The constant emphasis of the specialty hospital is to treat low-severity patients who may not need the types of additional services that the very sick would demand.[96]

CMS provided even more empirical data to demonstrate that specialty hospitals treat healthier patients on average. As the MedPAC report summarized, "DRGs that were common in specialty heart hospitals—primarily surgical DRGs—were relatively more profitable than the national average DRG."[97] Moreover, even within DRGs, "the least severely ill Medicare patients generally were relatively more profitable than the average Medicare patient," and specialty hospitals focus on these patients' elective procedures.[98] The MedPAC therefore concluded that "specialty hospitals are benefiting from selection opportunities among and within DRGs that are rewarded by the current [Inpatient Prospective Payment System] IPPS." Given the already difficult circumstances now faced by many general hospitals with disproportionately large numbers of un- and under-insured patients,[99] the siphoning away of the most profitable categories of business raises serious challenges to the cross-subsidization that has kept their public service mission afloat.

III. LEGAL AND POLITICAL BATTLES OVER THE SSH BUSINESS MODEL

General hospitals have engaged in a sustained lobbying campaign to prevent specialty hospitals from undermining their business model and attendant public service obligations.[100] They have partially succeeded by exploiting a labyrinth of

95. MEDICARE PAYMENT ADVISORY COMM'N, REPORT TO THE CONGRESS: PHYSICIAN-OWNED SPECIALTY HOSPITALS (hereinafter MedPAC Report), 32 (2005). Strategies for diversion differ at different hospitals. "Heart hospitals benefit financially from both the mix of DRGs and the severity of patients within them. In contrast, orthopedic and especially surgical hospitals benefit from treating less sick patients and not from the mix of DRGs." *Id.*

96. *Id.* at 33–4. ("Heart specialty hospitals treat patients in financially favorable DRGs and, within those, patients who are less sick (and less costly, on average) . . . by treating a high proportion of low-severity patients within their mix of DRGs, specialty orthopedic hospitals show an overall favorable selection." "Like orthopedic hospitals, surgical specialty hospitals and their peers do not appear to have a favorable mix of DRGs, but show a favorable selection of patients overall (1.15) because they treat relatively low-severity patients within the DRGs."

97. MedPAC Report, 25.

98. *Id.*

99. List of empirical studies confirming their difficulties; *see, e.g.,* Richard S. Saver, *Squandering the Gain: Gainsharing and the Continuing Dilemma of Physician Financial Incentives,* 98 Nw. U.L. REV. 145 (2003); *See* Eyman, *supra* note 22.

100. Sujit Choudhry, Niteesh Choudhry, and Troyen A. Brennan, *Specialty Versus Community Hospitals: What Role for the Law?,* http://content.healthaffairs.org/cgi/

federal and state regulation rife with traps for the unwary. Physician-investors in specialty hospitals have fought back with ferocious lobbying campaigns of their own.[101] As various political battles royal are waged, decisive action will probably only emerge administratively.[102] This part examines extant regulatory responses to these niche providers and their likely future directions.

Though the constantly shifting legal battlefield described below may be daunting to comprehend as a whole, it demonstrates one key point: specialty hospitals are a creature of law, not simply an organic development in the evolution of medical delivery systems. The vast majority of specialty hospitals exist in states without Certificate-of-Need laws, and the current driving force behind specialty hospitals is bias in third-party payment guidelines, which tend to overpay for less intense cases. Both sides in the debate are now beginning to agree that payment guidelines need to be adjusted to better reflect the actual cost of care.

A. Economic Credentialing

General hospitals have implemented specific business strategies to respond to physicians on staff who start SSHs. Most drastically, general hospitals will simply deny or revoke admitting privileges to members of their medical staff who start rival specialty facilities.[103] This is known as a form of "economic credentialing:" granting admitting privileges not on the basis of medical skill or other clinical objectives, but rather because of the economic impact of the physician's presence at the hospital.[104] This aspect of determining staff appointments can prevent

---

content/abstract/hlthaff.w5.361vi. ("The AHA [American Hospital Association] argues that specialty hospitals erode cross-subsidization by 'cherry-picking' relatively well-insured and healthy patients (where profit margins are higher) and by limiting or denying care outright to underinsured, indigent, and less healthy patients.").

101. *See* AAASC.org website; report on *The Attack on Niche and Specialty Providers,* available at: http://www.foundationsurgery.com/voice/Chapter_4/ AAASCAttacksonNicheProviders.pdf.

102. About the only development that appears universally unobjectionable is the disclosure of physician investment. Virtually everyone agrees that physician owners should disclose their stake in the specialty hospital when they refer patients to the facility. Kimbol, at 670.

103. In order to admit and treat patients in a hospital, a physician must apply for "privileges" by submitting comprehensive background about education, residency training, board certification, experience, malpractice insurance coverage, and references. Several general hospitals keep track of the number of patients admitted by a physician and include that among the criteria used in determining whether to render medical staff privileges. Without said "privileges," many physicians would be unacceptable to patients and would not be included in payers' provider networks. Francis Serbaroli, *Hospitals, Physicians, and Economic Credentialing,* N.Y. L. J., May 26, 2004, *available at* http://www.cadwalader.com/assets/article/Serbaroli_052604.pdf.

104. The American Medical Association ("AMA") defines economic credentialing as "the use of economic criteria unrelated to quality of care or professional competence in

physicians from selectively sending the most remunerative cases to their own facilities outside of the general hospital, while reserving low-to-negative margin cases for the general hospital.[105]

Physicians have bitterly opposed economic credentialing, and have developed a number of legal and political responses to the practice. Antitrust law prohibits certain "combinations in restraint of trade," and physicians have alleged that economic credentialing violates both state and federal competition laws. Courts have not been very sympathetic to this argument in the context of specialty hospitals. For example, in *Mahan et al. v. Avera St. Lukes*, orthopedic surgeons who owned a specialized facility charged that a general hospital violated antitrust laws by denying them admitting privileges.[106] The court rejected that argument, noting that the competing physician-owned orthopedic facility quickly captured a large amount of surgical volume and threatened the profitable neurosurgical services that cross-subsidized other unprofitable services for the general hospital.[107] In general, courts have not been receptive to antitrust challenges to

---

determining a physician's qualifications for initial or continuing hospital medical staff membership or privileges." See http://www.ama-assn.org/ama/pub/category/10919. html.

105. David A. Argue, *An Economic Model of Competition Between General Hospitals and Physician-Owned Specialty Facilities*, 20(2) ANTITRUST HEALTH CARE CHRONICLE 1 (July, 2006). ("The complementarity of hospital and physician services results in a mutual dependence between hospitals and physicians. Physicians desire hospital privileges because that allows them to treat patients who need hospital facility services. Without privileges, many physicians likely would be unacceptable to patients and not included in payers' networks. Physicians capture the benefits of their acceptability to patients and payers regardless of the extent to which they actually practice at the general hospital. Hospitals, for their part, depend on patient referrals through the physicians on their staffs. Hospitals capture the benefits of extending physician privileges when the physicians' patients are admitted and consume hospital services. What is unusual about this relationship from an economic perspective is that neither the hospital nor the physician pays the other for the benefits received. In other words, both hospitals and physicians generate positive "externalities" for which they receive no direct compensation. Physicians are not paid by the hospital for referring patients, and hospitals are not paid by physicians for granting admitting privileges (though privileged physicians typically are required to serve on hospital administrative committees and provide call coverage.)"). Specialty physicians' efforts to route profitable cases to their own facilities, and away from the general hospital, may be thought of as a form of "free-riding" from this perspective.

106. 621 N.W.2d. 150 (S.D. 2000).

107. *Id.; see also* Gordon v. Lewistown Hospital, 272 F.Supp.2d 393 (M.D.Pa.2003) (Dr. Gordon, who owned a successful ophthalmic surgery center near Lewistown Hospital in Pa., lost his hospital privileges at the defendant hospital in what he argued was an act of economic credentialing. The court ruled in the defendant's favor.); *but see* Heartland Surgical Specialty Hospital v. HCA Midwest, No. 05-2164-MLB (D. Kan., Oct. 1, 2007) (antitrust claim survived summary judgment). Monica Beck Glover, *A Recent Anti-trust*

economic credentialing, despite criticism of the practice from both the Department of Justice and the Federal Trade Commission.

Apart from antitrust laws, other state policies on economic credentialing also have an impact on the development of niche providers.[108] States are free to outlaw economic credentialing altogether.[109] States that explicitly restrict economic credentialing are more receptive to specialty hospitals than those which permit it. For example, Louisiana and Texas prohibit the economic credentialing that many general hospitals have used to "fight back" against doctors who form specialty hospitals.[110] Georgia allows economic credentialing, but its statute does not allow hospital boards to make the financial associations of a physician the sole basis of a decision on medical privileges.[111] Illinois permits economic credentialing, but requires it to be disclosed—generating evidence for potential antitrust suits.[112]

B. Questioning the Whole-Hospital Exception to Self-Referral Laws

Niche providers emerged because of exceptions in some notoriously complicated statutes. The 1972 federal anti-kickback statute and the Ethics in Patient Referral Act of 1989 (Stark I) and its amendments in 1993 (Stark II) all deter physicians from profiting from the medical services they recommend to patients.

As MedPAC summarizes, the "[1972] anti- kickback law is a criminal statute that broadly prohibits the purposeful offer, payment, or receipt of anything of value to induce the referral of patients for services reimbursable by a federal

---

Lawsuit Brings New Hope to Physician Owners' Battle with Community Hospitals, available at http://www.law.uh.edu/healthlaw/perspectives/2008/(MG)%20anti%20trust.pdf (discussing Heartland case).

108. See CCH.com News & Information, *Physicians obtain relief from hospital economic credentialing policy*, July 20, 2009, http://health.cch.com/news/medicare/072009a.asp (describing a recent Arkansas case where the court ruled that niche providers were entitled to declaratory judgment because the hospital's economic credentialing policy violated state public policy).

109. Michael A. Cassidy, *Legal Issues Involving Economic Credentialing*, HEALTH CARE LAW MONTHLY 20, 208 (July 2002). (listing states that had enacted statutes restricting economic credentialing.)

110. *See* Texas code §241.1015; § Louisiana code §1301.

111. *See* O.C.G.A. § 31-7-7.

112. *See* Illinois statute 210 ILCS 85/2 stating that ". . . it is in the interest of the people of the State of Illinois to establish safeguards that (i) require hospitals and hospital based providers to explain to individual providers the reasons, including economic factors, for credentialing decisions, (ii) allow an opportunity for a fair hearing, and (iii) report economic credentialing to the Hospital Licensing Board for further study. As used in this Section and defined by the American Medical Association, "economic credentialing" means the use of economic criteria unrelated to quality of care or professional competency in determining an individual's qualifications for initial or continuing medical staff membership or privileges."

health care program."[113] However, the 1972 law was difficult to enforce because prosecutors had to "prove beyond a reasonable doubt that the parties involved intended to violate it." This "resulted in few cases being successfully litigated and little discouragement of physician ownership of health care ancillary facilities [such as clinical laboratories and imaging centers]."[114] As physician investment in ancillary facilities grew, both physician-oriented publications (like the NEJM) and the American College of Physicians began to question the ethical propriety of certain ownership arrangements.[115] After the Institute of Medicine proposed new legislation restricting physician self-referral in 1986, Congress addressed the issue.[116]

In 1989, "Stark I" was enacted, and "prohibit[ed] physicians from referring Medicare or Medicaid patients for clinical laboratory services to labs with which they have a financial relationship (either ownership or compensation) unless the relationship fits within a specified exception."[117] Eventually "Stark II" (which took effect in 1995) applied these prohibitions to more health services.[118] However, it did not apply to "ASCs for surgical services only" and to whole hospitals, "as long as the physician's investment interest is in the whole hospital and not a subdivision or part of the hospital, and the physician is authorized to perform services at the hospital."[119] MedPAC claims that "the whole-hospital exception was originally intended to apply to full-service hospitals, [but] many physician-owned single-specialty hospitals now take advantage of it."[120] Yet laws regulating economic relationships between providers may also work against general hospitals: doctors have lobbied the OIG to enforce the Anti-Kickback

---

113. MedPAC Report, p. 62.

114. *Id.*

115. *Id.*

116. *Id.*

117. *Id.*

118. The "designated health services" covered by Stark II included "clinical laboratory, physical and occupational therapy, radiology, radiation, home health care, hospital, outpatient prescription drugs, and many types of equipment and supplies." MedPAC notes that "The law applies to durable medical equipment and supplies; parenteral and enteral nutrients, equipment, and supplies; and prosthetic and orthotic devices and supplies." MedPAC Report, 67.

119. The OIG later clarified the exact bounds of the ASC exception. *Federal Register* 64, no. 223 (November 19): 63517–63557.

120. MedPAC Report, 63. U.S. Rep. Fortney "Pete" Stark, the sponsor of Stark I and II, believes even if physician ownership of specialty hospitals complies with the letter of the law, such arrangements violate the spirit of the law. Stark has stated, "My suspicion is that this is a watered-down lawyer's way to pay doctors kickbacks for the patients they refer." Stark has also articulated concerns about physician-owned services and has said, "I don't think the physicians ought to be investing in the hospitals . . . It troubles me as a patient, as an individual. I would like for my physician to have no incentive one way or the other to send me to the hospital or choose which hospital I go to."

Statute[121] against general hospitals engaged in economic credentialing, on the theory that such general hospitals are essentially using staff privileges as a form of remuneration granted to induce referrals to the general hospital.[122]

Worried by the unintended consequences of this complex legal landscape, Congress passed, as part of the Medicare Modernization and Prescription Drug Act of 2003, an eighteen-month moratorium on referral by physicians of Medicare or Medicaid patients to specialty hospitals.[123] This initial moratorium expired in 2005, leading Congress to temporarily extend it until the Medicare Payment Advisory Commission could recommend action.[124] In 2006, CMS Director McClellan claimed that "CMS does not have the authority to extend the current moratorium," and it expired on Jan. 1, 2007.[125] Physicians may be deterred from further investment given a history of hostility toward specialty hospitals among key Democrats on Capitol Hill. In the meantime, some states have also been able to impose their own moratoria on specialty hospitals.[126] States are also free to develop self-referral laws more strict than their federal counterparts.[127]

Despite this complexity, several commentators have proposed national adoption of some states' strict limits on physician self-referrals.[128] National adoption would expand restrictions on self-referral in states that have relatively loose restrictions to date. These are the states in which the bulk of specialty facilities are located.[129] Bethard has even proposed a total ban on self-referral at the state level,[130] but concedes that self-referral laws are often best left to the federal government because of a potential "race to the bottom:" when one state bans self-referrals and another state permits them, physicians may desert the state with stricter regulations.[131] Kwiecinski has also argued that federal restrictions are the

---

121. 42 USC s. 1320a-7b.

122. 67 Fed. Reg. 72,894–5 (Dec. 9, 2002).

123. As a practical matter, given the dominant role of the U.S. government in financing health care, this moratorium on Medicare/Medicaid support effectively stopped the specialty hospital "movement" at the time.

124. Celestina Owusu-Sanders, *Health Lawyer*, October, 2005.

125. American Political Network, American Health Line Vol. 10 No. 9. May 19, 2006.

126. *See, e.g.,* MONT. CODE ANN. § 50-5-101.

127. For example, Illinois has a complete bar on physician self-referral, with one exemption based on community need. 225 ILCS 47/20 (2001). The exemption allows physicians to make referrals to health services and facilities that the physician administers himself or to facilities that are the only one of their type available. *Id.* Other states base self-referral statutes on federal regulations. For example Nebraska has a federally-modeled self-referral statute, but with separate punishment of reimbursement of all payments received through the illicit referral. Neb.Rev.St. § 68-107 (2007).

128. Kwiecinski, supra note 90, at 437.

129. *Id.* at 438.

130. Bethard, *supra* note 1, at 474.

131. *Id.* at 478.

most effective avenue of enforcement because of the Medicare program's purchasing power.[132]

C. Cooperative Strategies: Ending Physician-Entrepreneurs' Exodus from the General Hospital

The complex legal battles surrounding specialty hospitals have led some commentators to focus on more cooperative strategies. As they did with ASCs, some general hospitals may choose to invest in "joint ventures" with SSHs. General hospitals may also be inclined to give entrepreneurial physicians a share of the financial gains they make via the specialization and efficiencies often claimed by specialty facilities. However, regulations now deter hospitals from sharing profits achieved due to expert or efficient care. Such profit sharing, also known as gainsharing, has been suspect because federal officials have worried that it creates undue incentives for skimping on patient care.

Although anti-gainsharing rules may have been intended to protect patients' interests, the rules also hurt general hospitals' chances of retaining entrepreneurial specialists, especially in the cardiac and orthopedic areas. In a notable article on the OIG's discouragement of gainsharing, Richard Saver notes that "[p]hysician financial incentives, if well-designed and appropriately implemented, provide a necessary, critical step in the process of reform[ing]" a health care system that can unduly discourage competition.[133]

Saver's work suggests that, at its root, the debate over niche providers stems from rival views of the place of profit in medicine.[134] His work suggests that OIG rules against physicians' initiatives to economize *within* hospitals may unduly pressure those services to migrate *outside* of hospitals.[135] Saver believes that repeal

---

132. Kwiecinski, *supra* note 90, at 435. She has also called for the elimination of grandfather clauses governing investment dates and "date of hospital development." Currently, new physician-investors may enter existing physician-owned facilities and are covered by older physicians' 'grandfather' exceptions. *Id.*

133. Richard S. Saver, *Squandering the Gain: Gainsharing and the Continuing Dilemma of Physician Financial Incentives*, 98 Nw. U. L. Rev. 145, 151 (2003) (arguing for an increase in gainsharing arrangements at traditional hospitals).

134. "While there is no fixed definition of a 'gainsharing' arrangement, the term typically refers to an arrangement in which a hospital gives physicians a percentage share of any reduction in the hospital's costs for patient care attributable in part to the physicians' efforts." *Gainsharing Arrangements and CMPs for Hospital Payments to Physicians to Reduce or Limit Services to Beneficiaries*, OFFICE OF INSPECTOR GENERAL SPECIAL ADVISORY BULLETIN (July 1999) (*available at* http://oig.hhs.gov/fraud/docs/alertsandbulletins/gainsh.htm). *See also* David A. Hyman & Charles Silver, *Contingent Fee Contracts and In Vitro Fertilization*, 26 J. LAW MED. & ETHICS 79 (1998).

135. Richard S. Saver, *Squandering the Gain: Gainsharing and the Continuing Dilemma of Physician Financial Incentives*, 98 Nw. U. L. Rev. 145, 225 ("Even if lowered expectations about hospital gainsharing are appropriate, a new overall legal approach is needed, one that encourages gainsharing in its more optimal forms.")

of these rules, and resulting financial arrangements for mutual gain between physicians and hospitals would reduce the financial pressures on physicians to leave community hospitals and invest in specialty centers.

Saver's solution is elegant, and gainsharing has gained support in policy circles.[136] However, it remains to be seen whether gainsharing will get traction at the federal level. The Deficit Reduction Act of 2005 established demonstration projects to assess the impact of gainsharing pilot programs.[137] Even if the demonstration projects succeed, many questions will remain about the appropriate degree of transparency of gainsharing arrangements and their ultimate acceptability among hospitals and patients.[138]

D. Making the Specialty Hospital More Like A "Whole Hospital"

Several initiatives have been proposed to narrow the gap between specialty hospitals and general hospitals. Recent incidents have raised serious concerns about the development of hospitals without full ER capabilities.[139] The Director of the Survey and Certification Group for the Centers for Medicare & Medicaid Services broached a requirement that specialty facilities maintain emergency facilities or provide emergency treatment in a 2007 memo to State Survey Agency Directors.[140] Commentator Anne Kimbol had earlier suggested that specialty hospitals be

---

136. MedPAC Report, vii ("We also recommend an approach to aligning physician and hospital incentives through gainsharing, which allows physicians and hospitals to share savings from more efficient practices and might serve as an alternative to direct physician ownership."). Check: proposed rulemakings or legislation on gainsharing presently?

137. Gail Willensky, Nicholas Wolter, and Michelle M. Fischer, *Gain Sharing: A Good Concept Getting a Bad Name?*, HEALTH AFF. WEB EXCLUSIVE, Dec. 5, 2006, w65 (*available at http://content.healthaffairs.org/cgi/content/abstract/26/1/w58* (DRA of 2005 permits these hospitals to "pay physicians up to 25 percent of the documented cost savings generated from quality improvements").

138. See Health Financial Management Association, *Gainsharing in Health Care— Meeting the Quality-of-Care Challenge*, at 6, *available at* http://www.hfma.org/NR/rdonlyres/B2C351F7-64D9-4327-8118-933CBDFD581D/0/GainsharinginHealthcare.pdf (noting that legislative risks, contractual issues, administrative issues and quality control concerns surround the implementation of gainsharing).

139. Reed Abelson, *Some Hospitals Call 911 to Save Their Patients*, N.Y. TIMES, April 2, 2007, ("As the number of doctor-owned surgical hospitals grows, federal and state officials now acknowledge that the government rules may be too vague about the emergency abilities a hospital must have in place. Regulators are particularly concerned about the very small hospitals that focus on only a few kinds of surgery but perform operations that frequently require an overnight stay. While Medicare's rules currently say a hospital must "meet the emergency needs of patients in accordance with acceptable standards of practice," the details are left largely to the hospital's discretion. Federal and state officials say they are now reviewing the guidelines to toughen the rules and make them more specific.").

140. Memorandum from Thomas E. Hamilton, Dir., Survey and Certification Group, Ctrs. for Medicare & Medicaid Servs. to State Survey Agency Dirs., 1 (Apr. 26, 2007).

required to maintain emergency departments if there are no other emergency care centers within fifteen miles of the specialty center.[141]

By 2007, EMTALA regulations were changed to reflect some of these recommendations.[142] They require every participating hospital[143] to provide some forms of emergency treatment regardless of whether it has an emergency facility.[144] Calling 911 generally will not satisfy a hospital's emergency care obligations.[145] Nevertheless, there are still many details to be worked out as the rule develops, and many possibilities for such "command and control" regulation to end up either over or under-inclusive.

E. Targeted Adjustments of Payment Systems and Tax Obligations

Regulatory complexity has led policymakers to turn to a revenue-focused response to the rise of niche providers. Even staunch defenders of specialty hospitals concede that certain discrepancies in Medicare's administered pricing (based on DRGs) have fueled their growth. The DRG payment system tends to under-pay for complex cases and to overpay for less serious ones. Some DRGs related to cardiac and orthopedic surgery are more profitable generally than most others. Policymakers did not worry about the divergences in profitability when they could assume that gains in one field might be used to subsidize low-margin community service. The rise of SSH's permitted their physician-owners to "cream-skim" and claim the overpayment as profit.

Given these changed conditions, the Medicare Payment Advisory Commission has recommended "improving Medicare's inpatient prospective payment system for acute care hospitals" in order to reduce "financial incentives for patient selection."[146] CMS has very recently revised ASC payments in many ways to better reflect the "true cost" of providing services.[147] The Medicare Payment Advisory Commission identified the "patient selection" of specialty hospitals as part of a much larger problem with the DRGs:

> the evidence suggests that current payment policies create differences in relative profitability both across and within DRGs. Surgical DRGs are generally

---

141. Anne S. Kimbol, *The Debate Over Specialty Hospitals: How Physician-Hospital Relationships Have Reached a New Fault Line Over These "Focused Factories,"* 38 J. HEALTH L. 633, 669 (2005).

142. 42 C.F.R. § 482.

143. A "participating hospital" is one which accepts Medicare or Medicaid funding from the government.

144. 42 C.F.R. § 482.

145. 42 C.F.R. § 482.

146. *See* http://www.kaisernetwork.org/daily_reports/rep_index.cfm?DR_ID=35745; MedPAC report is *available at* http://www.medpac.gov/documents/Mar05_SpecHospitals.pdf.

147. MedPAC Report, *supra* note 99, at 39–40.

relatively more profitable while medical DRGs tend to be relatively less profitable than the overall average. Within DRGs, patients in low severity groups tend to be relatively more profitable. Conversely, those in high severity groups tend to be relatively less profitable. Consequently, hospitals appear to have financial incentives to specialize and to treat low severity rather than high severity patients.[148]

MedPAC urged Congress to give the Secretary of Health and Human Services the authority to adjust DRG weights.[149] Here MedPAC followed the reasoning of many commentators who have urged HHS to update DRG payment methodology to reduce specialty hospitals' ability to "skim" the more profitable DRGs (and the more profitable patients within DRGs).[150] Study of such adjustments has been ongoing.[151]

Recent changes in the payment rates for smaller niche providers—ASCs— provide one model for reform here. The GAO pointed out in 2006 that old rates were out-of-date; at that point "payments [had] not been revised using ASC cost data since 1990."[152] Compared to hospital out-patient departments, ASCs had very few category codes, leaving the ASC billing system comparatively more vulnerable to gaming. Though the CMS did not explicitly address diversionary concerns in its rationale for these changes, it offered the following justification:

> The Government Accountability Office (GAO) studied ASC costs and found that the relativity of costs among ASC procedures was comparable to their relativity of costs in hospital outpatient departments. According to the GAO report, released in November 2006, ASCs experience greater efficiencies in furnishing surgical services than hospital outpatient departments, resulting in surgical procedures being less costly when performed in that setting of care. In the CY 2008 OPPS/ASC final rule, CMS estimates that ASCs should

---

148. *Id.; see also* Stuart Guterman in HEALTH AFF. (are specialty hospitals a problem or a symptom?).

149. *Id.* at 40. ("MedPAC recommended that Congress provide the Secretary with the authority to adjust DRG relative weights so that he may account for differences in high-cost outlier cases. Affecting specialty hospitals and general acute care hospitals, this recommendation would be implemented over a transitional period so that hospitals can adjust to the refined payment system." (*available at* http://physiciansnews.com/law/405miller.html).

150. Strothkamp, *supra* note 7 at 689–90. She notes one striking example from MedPAC report: "for DRG 107-bypass with cardiac catheterization, the cost per discharge can vary from 70% of the average to 170% of the average."

151. 42 C.F.R. § 411 *et seq.*

152. GAO, *Payment for Ambulatory Surgical Centers Should Be Based on the Hospital Outpatient Payment System* (Nov. 2006), *available at* http://www.gao.gov/new.items/d0786.pdf, at 11.

be paid about 65 percent of the OPPS payment rates for the same surgical procedures.[153]

This explanation of the reimbursement change raises difficult questions about the nature of the "efficiencies" found. If the ASCs have found a way to deliver the same services for less cost, it would seem perverse to cut their reimbursement rate as a result. However, the DRG system has long been designed to "ratchet down" payments by turning last year's "profitable cost-cutting" into this year's baseline for payments. It might seem wise for CMS to steer more procedures toward ASCs if they are more efficient. But some of these "efficiencies" may be attributable to patient selection, or to a business model that fails to cross-subsidize services with positive externalities.

Though there is a strong expert consensus on adjusting the DRG system in order to leave less "cream" for the "skimming" by specialty hospitals, those on all sides of the specialty hospital debate may end up considering this a dangerous solution.[154] The process of adjusting DRGs could lead to losses for all hospitals.[155] Cross-subsidization is not a universally approved policy goal.[156] Rather than diverting funds once (over)paid for cardiac procedures to other hospital spending, coverage for the uninsured, or public health measures, it is possible that their downward adjustment would fund other priorities. Given the perilous fiscal situation of most hospitals that serve substantial populations of un- and

---

153. Calendar Year (CY) 2008 Revised Ambulatory Surgical Center (ASC) Payment System Questions and Answers, *available at* http://www.cms.hhs.gov/ASCPayment/downloads/ASC_QAs_03072008.pdf (referring to GAO report, which is available at http://www.gao.gov/new.items/d0786.pdf)

154. Note the AHA's critique, *available at* http://www.cms.hhs.gov/PhysicianSelfReferral/Downloads/Comments_from_American_Hospital_Association.pdf ("While these changes may appear to be a viable option for addressing some of the incentives driving the growth of limited-service hospitals, payment changes alone are not enough. CMS needs to address the growing problem of self-referral. The revision of Medicare inpatient payments would do nothing to address incentives for physician-owners of limited service hospitals to increase use of inpatient and outpatient ancillary services (e.g., lab and imaging services) for which self-referral under the whole hospital exception loophole is currently permitted. And changing Medicare inpatient payments does nothing to change physician-owners' incentives to steer patients to owned facilities, select the most well-insured patients, and avoid Medicaid and uninsured patients.

155. John V. Jacobi, *Dangerous Times for Medicaid*, (2005), 33 J.L. MED. & ETHICS 834.

156. *Id.* (regarding budget cuts); regarding conservative skepticism about cross-subsidization, see *FTC and DOJ Issue Report on Competition and Health Care*, (July 23, 2004), available at http://www.ftc.gov/opa/2004/07/healthcarerpt.htm. ("Competition cannot provide resources to those who lack them, and it does not work well when providers are expected to use higher profits in certain areas to cross-subsidize uncompensated care. In general, it is more efficient to provide subsidies directly to those who should receive them to ensure transparency.").

under-insured patients, downward adjustments to "too-profitable" DRGs could be a more immediate threat than specialty hospital competition.

Targeted state taxation programs offer a more measured approach to redistributing health care spending. For example, some states have taxed niche providers—either to diminish what lawmakers perceive as an unfair competitive advantage, or to directly subsidize indigent care or Medicare and Medicaid patients.[157] New Jersey has taxed ambulatory surgical centers that are not owned by hospitals, imposing a 3.5 percent tax on the first $200,000 of gross revenues of Ambulatory Surgical Centers.[158] New Jersey also adopted a "vanity tax" in 2004, levied on "any medical procedure performed on [an] individual which is directed at improving [his/her] appearance and which does not meaningfully promote the proper function of the body or prevent or treat illness or disease."[159] The tax is 6 percent of gross revenues of cosmetic surgery practices,[160] and carefully draws a distinction between reconstructive and cosmetic procedures.[161]

Ideally, a tax on specialty services would be directly allocated toward funding the community service threatened by SSH's business model. However, just such a tax, imposed by Oklahoma, was deemed violative of state constitutional provisions. However, this tax was deemed unconstitutional in part because it set up an arbitrary distinction between facilities built before and after July 1, 1999.[162] A tax that more rationally spread the burden of uncompensated challenge may well avoid being deemed an unconstitutional "special law" by Oklahoma courts. A Florida court has upheld a Florida statute that taxes niche providers and uses the proceeds to benefit community hospitals with a Public Medical Assistance Trust Fund.[163]

Other forms of taxing a top "tier" of medical services have been attracting support across the political spectrum. For example, in his State of the Union Address in January, 2007, George W. Bush proposed taxing "gold-plated" health

---

157. These programs pay less than the average private insurer, so subsidies might be needed in order to discourage providers from discriminating against Medicare and Medicaid patients.

158. N.J. Stat. Ann. 26: 2H-18.57.

159. N.J. STAT. ANN. § 54:32E-1 (West 2006).

160. Id.

161. Id. Cosmetic surgeons have denounced the tax, but many states are now considering similar measures. Michael D. Ruel, Student Comment, How New Jersey Has Opened Pandora's Box by Elevating Its Moral Judgment about Cosmetic Surgery without Consideration of Fair Health Care Policy, 28 J. LEGAL MED, 119 (2007). State Senator Karen Keiser has upped the redistributive ante in Washington state, with a plan to earmark vanity tax revenue for health insurance for poor children. Such a plan was also proposed in Illinois, with proceeds to benefit both medical research and access to basic medical care. Id.

162. Id.

163. Agency for Health Care Administration v Hameroff, 816 So.2d 1115 (Fla. App. 1 Dist., 2002).

care plans that cost more than $7,500 annually (for individuals) or $15,000 annually (for families).[164] Revenues from the tax were designated to pay for a "deduction of $7,500 for individuals and $15,000 for families who purchase health insurance on their own."[165] One iteration of Senate Finance Committee Chairman Max Baucus's proposed health reform bill of 2009 incorporated similar ideas, with revenues from the tax were designated subsidize access to existing insurance plans for those who could not afford them. Bush's FTC and DOJ provided theoretical support for direct subsidies instead of the cross-subsidization that redistributive regulation encourages. According to the FTC and DOJ report *A Dose of Competition*,

> Competition cannot provide resources to those who lack them, and it does not work well when providers are expected to use higher profits in certain areas to cross-subsidize uncompensated care. In general, it is more efficient to provide subsidies directly to those who should receive them to ensure transparency. [166]

If this policy idea gains traction, we can expect more states to forsake redistributive regulation for a more direct approach. Taxation like that used in New Jersey and Florida would permit some niche providers to flourish, but would require these "high-end" options to allocate some of their revenues to support traditional providers of care for the indigent.

The most attractive aspect of the tiering of taxation is that it can be carefully adjusted to take into account the social usefulness of an activity—or even

---

164. *See* Kaisernetwork.org, *Coverage & Access, President Bush in State of the Union Address To Propose Health Insurance Tax Deduction for Non-Group Coverage and Cap on Tax Preference for Employer Coverage*, Jan. 22, 2007, http://www.kaisernetwork.org/Daily_ reports/rep_index.cfm?DR_ID=42387. The amount of the allowable deduction would increase in future years based on some measure of overall inflation but would not necessarily be indexed with changes in medical or health care costs. Sheryl Gay Stolberg & Robert Pear, *Bush to Urge New Tax Plan for Health Care Coverage*, N.Y. TIMES, Jan. 22, 2007. *available at* http://www.nytimes.com/2007/01/21/washington/21health.html?_ r=2&oref=slogin&oref=slogin.

165. U.S. President George W. Bush, State of the Union Address (Jan. 23, 2007) ("And so, tonight, I propose two new initiatives to help more Americans afford their own insurance. First, I propose a standard tax deduction for health insurance that will be like the standard tax deduction for dependents. Families with health insurance will pay no income on payroll taxes—or payroll taxes—on $15,000 of their income. Single Americans with health insurance will pay no income or payroll taxes on $7,500 of their income. With this reform, more than 100 million men, women, and children who are now covered by employer-provided insurance will benefit from lower tax bills.") *available at* http://www. washingtonpost.com/wp-dyn/content/article/2007/01/23/AR2007012301075_pf.html.

166. *See* FTC and DOJ, *Dose of Competition; but see* Jost Review of *Dose of Competition, and* TIMOTHY STOLTZFUS JOST, HEALTH CARE AT RISK: A CRITIQUE OF THE CONSUMER-DRIVEN MOVEMENT (2007).

micro-targeted to take into account the relative value of different *aspects* of an activity. For example, in an article on the tiering of primary care via retainer medicine, I advocated the taxation of queue-jumping and amenity-bundling, but not preventive care, because such care is not adequately provided in the United States today.[167] Similarly, the ordinary run of ASC procedures merit less taxation than cosmetic ones: the former focus on meeting basic health needs, whereas the latter overwhelmingly amount to a diversion of medical personnel to non-medical ends.

There are many critics who question the wisdom of using revenues from one part of the health care system to subsidize other parts.[168] Perhaps in an ideal world a basic level of health care would be provided by the state for all, and such care would not be a "drag" on higher-end services. In our world, suspicion of general tax increases, even on the wealthiest, has become pervasive.[169] As one tax policy analyst claims, "user-based, selective tax proposals are more palatable than broader ones."[170] Niche providers are in part responsible for the paucity of care options available to the disadvantaged, since competition from specialty hospitals for the dollars of the insured tends to make general hospitals even less

---

167. Pasquale, *The Three Faces of Retainer Care*, 7 YALE J. HEALTH POL'Y, L., & ETHICS 39 (2007).

168. Responding to Bush's proposal, Neil Trautwein, a vice president of the National Retail Federation, said, "This is a classic case of robbing Peter to help Paul pay for coverage. I do not think the president will find many backers in the employer community for this proposal." He added that "we should not start by endangering coverage for people who already have it." Sheryl Gay Stolberg & Robert Pear, *Bush to Urge New Tax Plan for Health Care Coverage*, N.Y. TIMES, Jan. 22, 2007. *available at* http://www.nytimes.com/2007/01/21/washington/21health.html?_r=2&oref=slogin&oref=slogin. There has been a similar reaction to a Schwarzenegger initiative in California. "In California, a key component of Gov. Arnold Schwarzenegger's universal coverage proposal call[ed] for a controversial 2% to 4% surcharge on doctors' and hospitals' revenues. The money would be used to pay for higher Medicaid fees so that doctors will take in more enrollees." *See* Vanessa Fuhrman, *Note to Medicare Patients: The Doctor Won't See you*, WALL ST. J., July 19, 2007, *available at* http://online.wsj.com/article/SB11848016564877o935.html.

169. The difficulties of redistribution founded upon a broad-based tax are explored more generally in Chris William Sanchirico, *Taxes versus Legal Rules as Instruments for Equity: A More Equitable View*, 29 J. LEGAL STUD. 797 (2000); *see also* Frank Pasquale, *Copyright's Distributive Impact*, Posting to Madisonian.net, *available at* http://madisonian.net/2006/09/29/copyrights-distributive-impact/("When claim[ing] that redistributive taxation will address egalitarian concerns voiced by a proponent of regulation, [a proponent of substituting taxation for regulation should] a) identify which tax . . . will [be] raise[d] in order to redistribute income to the intended beneficiaries of the proposed regulation and b) give . . . some sense of the likelihood of that tax and transfer occurring.").

170. Karen Wakefield, *Putting the 'Vanity' in Vanity Tax*, ASSOCIATED PRESS, Jan. 28, 2005 (*available at* http://www.cbsnews.com/stories/2005/01/28/national/main670058.shtml).

capable of treating the uninsured.[171] Taxation helps compensate for this negative externality of tiering in the health care system.

Defenders of specialty hospitals claim that they provide as many or more community benefits than nonprofit general hospitals, since specialty hospitals pay sales tax, personal property tax, and real estate/real property taxes.[172] In addition, owners of specialty hospitals pay state and federal income tax on their share of the income. These taxes are paid at the owner's individual or corporate rate.[173] Some sources view this situation as an unfair competitive advantage of nonprofit general hospitals over already taxed niche providers.[174] In addition, nonprofit hospitals often issue tax-exempt bonds and receive tax-free donations from the public—what some commentators call an ample recompense for public service obligations that are not often met.[175]

Yet after reviewing the array of regulatory options for addressing niche providers, commentator David N. Heard endorsed a tax as the best way of addressing their diversionary effects. He believes that the main benefit of a tax is increasing a state's "eligibility to draw down matching federal funds through the state's Medicaid program," and using this additional revenue to offset revenue losses at general hospitals.[176] Heard also posits that a tax could impose a penalty on facilities that do not provide community benefits such as emergency services, treating Medicaid patients, or similar criteria: "The amount of the tax could be applied on a staged basis depending on the degree of community benefit or desirable service that is performed."[177] This reasonable proposal should complement (and be designed in light of) federal proposals to change Medicare reimbursement rates.

171. *Id.*

172. As of 2006, only about 18 percent of community general hospitals are for-profit; 59 percent are nonprofit, and 23 percent are government owned. AHA, HOSPITAL STATISTICS (2008 edition).

173. Study of Physician-owned Specialty Hospitals Required in Section 507(c)(2) of the Medicare Prescription Drug, Improvement, and Modernization Act of 2003, Centers for Medicare & Medicaid Services paper, *available at* https://www.cms.hhs.gov/ MLNProducts/Downloads/RTC-StudyofPhysOwnedSpecHosp.pdf (2005).

174. Ericksen, *supra* note 39, at 449 (2006).

175. One study concluded that "the total proportion of net revenue that specialty hospitals devoted to uncompensated care and taxes combined exceeded the proportion of net revenues that community hospitals devoted to uncompensated care." Study of Physician-owned Specialty Hospitals Required in Section 507(c)(2) of the Medicare Prescription Drug, Improvement, and Modernization Act of 2003, Centers for Medicare & Medicaid Services paper, *available at* https://www.cms.hhs.gov/ MLNProducts/Downloads/RTC-StudyofPhysOwnedSpecHosp.pdf (2005), at iv.

176. David N. Heard, Jr., *The Specialty Hospital Debate: The Difficulty of Promoting Fair Competition Without Stifling Efficiency*, 6 HOUS. J. HEALTH L. & POL'Y 215 (2005).

177. *See* Heard, *supra* note 9, at 240.

IV. PREREQUISITE FOR PROGRESS: MORE INFORMATION ON GENERAL HOSPITALS' RECORDS OF COMMUNITY SERVICE

Revenue and taxation adjustments address many of the problems raised by specialty hospitals. Unfortunately, it is hard to determine exactly what their fair contribution to community service should be. There is also variation among specialty hospitals in terms of the percentage of severely ill patients they take in; cardiac hospitals are more likely to take on these cases than their peers. Given that SSH's pay taxes which most general hospitals (as nonprofits) do not have to pay, some commentators have argued that specialty hospitals already contribute more to the community than nonprofit general hospital peers. Yet for health policymakers the relevant concern here is health-oriented community service, and the percentage of specialty hospital taxes going to subsidize health care is not clear. It varies state by state, and to some extent all such calculations are called into question by the fungibility of tax revenue.

More troublingly, general hospitals vary greatly in the extent to which they provide care for the indigent, support medical education, and provide other community services. Clearly academic health centers and safety net hospitals have service-oriented missions. On the other end of the spectrum, a for-profit general hospital in an affluent suburban area may avoid the vast majority of non-paying patients whom its inner-city or rural counterpart regularly treats.

These disparities have attracted the attention of tax policymakers as officials at the local, state, and federal levels question whether to continue offering tax exemptions to nonprofit hospitals.[178] As Gregg Bloche notes, "the exemption's cost to federal, state, and local taxpayers almost certainly exceeds the cost of the care that nonprofit hospitals now provide for free to the poor."[179] Nonprofits claim that they provide a more generalized "community benefit," but there is controversy over the precise nature and extent of such positive externalities. Although John Colombo has written a series of articles attacking such claims, Jill Horwitz has conducted empirical research demonstrating a greater role for service at nonprofit hospitals.

Although such scholarly debates are ongoing, some steps taken by federal and state tax authorities may help provide data at a level of granularity necessary to understand the true contribution of nonprofit general hospitals. After several Congressional hearings investigating the level of community benefit provided by nonprofits, the Internal Revenue Service began aggressively investigating many

---

178. Nancy M. Kane, *Tax-Exempt Hospitals: What is Their Charitable Responsibility and How Should It be Defined and Reported?*, 51 St. Louis U. L.J. 459 (2007).

179. M. Gregg Bloche, *Tax Preferences for Nonprofits: From Per Se Exemption to Pay-for-Performance*, Health Aff., June 20, 2006, citing N. Kane and W. Wubbenhorst, *Alternative Funding Policies for the Uninsured: Exploring the Value of Hospital Tax Exemption*, Milbank Quarterly 78, no. 2 (2000): 185–212.

hospitals' nonprofit status.[180] Several states have also begun investigating the degree to which nonprofits "earn" their tax- exempt status.[181] News stories alleging excessive pricing power and excessive personal gain at nonprofit hospitals have provoked many policymakers to demand "demonstrable value" for the tax exemptions they enjoy.

The specialty hospital "wars" thus boil down to competing claims of unearned privilege. General hospitals (which are largely nonprofit) claim that specialty hospitals' owners do not deserve to take advantage of the "whole hospital" exemption from federal laws deterring self-referrals. Specialty hospitals in turn charge that their nonprofit rivals are enjoying tax exemptions they have not earned. Though many studies have assessed specialty hospitals' record in terms of quality of care and accessibility, few promise to break the stalemate apparent in these conflicting distributional claims. More specific information is needed in order to fully assess the impact of specialty hospital entry in any given location.

In several other areas of law, "information-forcing" rules have aided regulators facing extraordinary complexity and a shortage of relevant details about particular externality-generating activities. For example, in environmental regulation, it is often hard to gauge the exact scope of the negative externalities generated by a polluter without gaining access to information that only the polluter is able to provide.[182] A law like California's Proposition 65 requires polluters to bear

---

180. Robert Pear, *I.R.S. Checking Compliance by Tax-Exempt Hospitals: Inquiry May Bring Changes in Standards*, N.Y. Times, June 19, 2006, at A15.

181. Kane, *supra* n. 190, 51 St. Louis U. L.J. at 461 ("In New Hampshire, the legislature set up a committee to study hospital property tax exemptions . . . . In Ohio, the Ohio Tax Commissioner denied a local tax exemption for Cleveland Clinic's newly acquired clinic in a wealthy suburb because it provided minimal charity care. In Illinois, the state passed legislation requiring community benefit reporting in 2003; in 2006, the state Attorney General proposed legislation (H.B. 5000) requiring minimum charity expenditures by nonprofit hospitals. In North Carolina, a bill was proposed that would limit the types of property that can be exempt and would require provision of a minimum level of charity care expenditure. In Kansas, the Attorney General opened an investigation of hospital billing and collection practices. In Utah, Intermountain Health agreed to less aggressive debt collection practices under pressure from the legislature. In Minnesota, the Attorney General investigated aggressive debt collection and inadequate provision of charity care, forcing four hospital systems to agree to discount charges to the uninsured by 40 to 60%.").

182. Bradley C. Karkkainen, *Information-Forcing Environmental Regulation*, 33 Fla. St. U. L. Rev. 861, 862 (2006) ("[V]aried reform initiatives proceed from the common assumption that regulatory agencies have a limited capacity to gather and process relevant information, constraining their ability to specify environmentally effective and economically efficient rules."); see also Baker et al., *The Rat Race as Information-Forcing Device*, 81 Ind. L. J. 53 (2006) (giving qualified endorsement of "revelation tournaments"); Benjamin Duke, *Regulating The Internal Labor Market: An Information- Forcing Approach To Decision Bargaining Over Partial Relocations*, 93 Colum. L. Rev. 932 (1993).

arduous costs unless and until they either give "'clear and reasonable warning' to anyone they expose to listed carcinogens and reproductive toxins" or "'show that the exposure poses no significant risk.'"[183] This shifts the burden of demonstrating safety from the overburdened state enforcement office to corporations that may ordinarily block public access to such information via trade secrets.

In the health sphere, we are primarily concerned with positive externalities—benefits the larger community receives but does not pay for, such as uncompensated care.[184] Given the degree of public criticism they've encountered over the past several years, it might seem odd for nonprofit general hospitals to fail to make transparent exactly how much uncompensated care they are providing. However, there are several operative barriers to transparency. First, hospital pricing itself can be proprietary—either due to the competitive strategies of the hospital itself, or due to efforts of private insurers it contracts with. Second, there is conflict among general hospitals about what should actually count as uncompensated care.[185] The larger category of "community benefit" is even harder to define, though Jill Horwitz has helped clarify the idea in a few recent research projects.

Despite these ambiguities, health law has a few notable "information-forcing" mechanisms for assessing quality and accessibility of care, including licensure requirements and "certificate of need" (CON) laws. CON laws were a response to a perceived surplus of physician and health service supply during the 1960's.[186] In 1974, Congress passed the National Health Planning and Resources Development Act. The Act required new health care facilities, and additions to existing facilities, to obtain a Certificate of Need (CON) from the appropriate state agency as a prerequisite to receiving federal funds via the Medicare and Medicaid programs. This requirement was aimed at controlling health care costs. Policymakers worried that health care costs were rising due to "induced

---

183. *Id.*, at 871–2, quoting Cal. Code Regs. tit. 22, § 12703(b) (2006).

184. In 1997, US hospitals provided about $18.5 billion in uncompensated care. G. Melnick, J. Mann, and A. Bamezai, *Preliminary Findings: Hospital Uncompensated Care Not Keeping Pace with Per Capita Spending*, HCFO NEWS AND PROGRESS (March 2000).

185. One of the most controversial issues here is the degree to which "bad debt" should count as uncompensated care. T. Rundall, S. Sofaer, and W. Lambert, *Uncompensated Hospital Care in California: Private and Public Hospital Responses to Competitive Market Forces*, ADVANCES IN HEALTH ECONOMICS AND HEALTH SERVICES RESEARCH 9 (1988): 113–133. To give a flavor of this dispute: Catholic health care systems generally oppose characterizing bad debt that is written off as "charitable care," while other hospital trade associations disagree and would count it. If the bad debt is reported to credit reporting agencies, the debtors may be "paying" for the care with a declining credit store. New "medical credit reporting agencies" are also emerging, and some hope to give hospitals information about which indigent patients they should consider denying admittance due to inability to pay.

186. 4 DEPAUL J. HEALTH CARE L. 261 (describing history).

demand:" the more doctors and hospitals there were, the more these actors would try to counteract the normal price-depressing effect of increased supply by finding more wrong with patients, thus "inducing" demand for their services.[187] Although such a strategy could rarely work in a normal market, health care is a credence service—it is very hard for the average consumer to "second guess" his or her provider about the amount or nature of care needed. As a result of these laws, those opening new health care entities needed to demonstrate to state commissions that their services are actually needed by the community.

Over time, state boards have started addressing concerns beyond "induced demand" to larger goals of equity and fair distribution of health resources. CON proceedings can also attempt to detect whether a given specialty entity will lead to a dangerous monopolization of services within a specialty. For example, in Seattle "access to orthopedic surgeons is virtually nonexistent for uninsured people and Medicaid enrollees, because a single group of orthopedic surgeons has a virtual monopoly in the community and does not accept Medicaid or uninsured patients."[188] Though Washington's own CON process did not stop that particular outcome, CON certifications might have impeded the development if it had been threatened by the proposed opening of an orthopedic specialty hospital.

Unfortunately, CON laws probably cannot provide an adequate response to specialty hospital entry because virtually all specialty hospitals are located in states without such certification requirements.[189] Lack of CON procedures makes specialty hospital entry much easier.[190] Some public health researchers have expressed support for states to "tighten up" CON processes in order to deter unnecessary specialty hospitals.[191] As a result, some have proposed the reinstatement of federal CON restrictions generally,[192] including a requirement for

---

187. "The premise that unchecked supply creates unwarranted demand" from Wolfson, cited in 4 DePaul J. Health Care L. 261, 264. Network effects can also result in unpredictable changes in demand for professionals' services.

188. Peter J. Cunningham, Gloria J. Bazzoli, and Aaron Katz, *Caught In The Competitive Crossfire: Safety-Net Providers Balance Margin And Mission In A Profit-Driven Health Care Market*, Health Affairs 27, no. 5 (2008): w374–w382 (published online 12 August 2008; 10.1377/hlthaff.27.5.w374.

189. See Appendix A, citing Glenn M. Hackbarth, *Physician-owned specialty hospitals*, report to Subcommittee on Health Committee on Energy and Commerce, U.S. House of Representatives, *available at* http://www.medpac.gov/publications/congressional_testimony/20050512_TestimonySpecHospEC.pdf (2005).

190. David N Heard, *The Specialty Hospital Debate: the Difficulty of Promoting Fair Competition without Stifling Efficiency*, 6 Hous. J. Health L & Pol'y 215, 232 (2005); Stuart Guterman, *Specialty Hospitals: A Problem or a Symptom?*, 24 Health Aff. 95, 99–101, 104 (2006).

191. Choudry, Choudry, & Brennen, Health Aff. (Aug. 9, 2005).

192. David N. Heard, Comment, *The Specialty Hospital Debate: The Difficulty of Promoting Fair Competition Without Stifling Efficiency*, 6 Hous. J. Health L. & Pol'y 215, 235 (2005).

emergency facilities at specialty hospitals whose patients require overnight stays.[193]

Policymakers may want to be cautious about re-instating CON programs nation-wide. Both the Federal Trade Commission and the Department of Justice have seriously questioned the efficacy and efficiency of CON laws, and they have been in decline for some time.[194] In 1987, Congress ended the federal subsidies that flowed to states that implemented CON Programs under the National Health Planning and Resources Development Act. Since that time, at least fifteen states have abandoned their CON programs.[195] Any revitalization of the CON process should be premised on its ability to prioritize the positive types of cross-subsidization discussed in Part II above. CON laws may reduce competition.[196] However, given the nature of the "competition" that many specialty hospitals engage in, it is not always clear that the anti-competitive effects of CON laws are counterproductive here.

A more promising approach might involve state authorities imposing taxes on any facility that fails to treat a certain reference level of charity, Medicaid, and Medicare cases—and to allocate those taxes toward care for the uninsured.[197] As Gregg Bloche has suggested, tax exemptions should be geared toward the perfor-mance of institutions—and not simply a matter of permanent legal status.[198] Medicare also has significant leverage here—virtually no specialty hospitals were completed during the Medicare moratorium. Overly profitable DRGs, this policy could realign incentives for all hospitals to provide for a more optimal mix of patients.

Yet even these types of adjustments may need to be targeted more tightly than either the federal or state governments can manage presently. Blunter instru-

---

193. *Id.* at 239 (citing Tex. Health & Safety Code Ann. § 241.026(f) (Vernon 2004)). Note that the HHS has done a rulemaking very recently on ER issue.

194. One advocacy group claims that "CON does not improve the quality of healthcare or reduce costs." See their report at http://aaasc.org/pub/AHSRHP_Presentation.pdf American Association of Ambulatory Surgical Centers.

195. Many states have abandoned CON licensing. *Mississippi Hospital Association: MHA's Monday Executive Briefing,* (Dec 13, 2004), *available at* http://www.mhanet.org/i4a/pages/index.cfm?pageid=624. ("In the past two decades, 20 states have repealed their acute-care CON programs, while the majority of states that kept regulations saw legisla-tive attempts to either modify or abolish them.").

196. Dr. Roy Cordato, *Certificate-of-Need Laws: It's Time for Repeal,* at 9 (The Macon Series, 2005), *available at* http://www.johnlocke.org/acrobat/policyReports/con_laws-macon_no.1.pdf) ("This is not a healthy economic contest among suppliers of a service attempting to better serve health care customers, but rather a battle to win the favor of a government bureaucracy in an attempt to gain or keep a monopolistic cartel").

197. The "payment to cost" ratio of private payers is, on average, about 125 percent; Medicare's is closer to 92 percent and Medicaid's is closer to 87 percent. AHA, AHA Hospital Statistics (2008) xiii, Chart 8. In other words, private cases tend to cross-subsidize Medicare and Medicaid cases.

198. Bloche, *supra* note 191.

ments may be necessary until relevant data emerge—and nonprofit hospitals are in no hurry to provide it. To create incentives for them to do so, Medicare and state health officials might consider establishing a given threshold of community service at a general hospital a "trigger" permitting it to petition for a share of the revenue of a rival specialty hospital—or for that specialty hospital to be taxed at a rate that will help support the types of community service offered by community hospitals. A safety net hospital could easily satisfy such criteria.

Such distributed enforcement of community service standards might encourage cooperation, instead of endless legal battles, between specialty hospitals and their general hospital rivals. Two schematic narratives help illuminate the dynamics here.

First, consider a wealthy suburb where two nonprofits with a relatively low level of community service obligations are operating. There, the entry of a specialty hospital may bring needed competition. Economic credentialing by the incumbents may simply delay the entry of a competitor institution which promises to bring lower costs and higher quality to patients. One or both incumbents might worry that an exodus of most or all their cardiac or orthopedic surgeons could leave them dangerously ill-equipped to deal with emergencies. If they could make that case compellingly—i.e., if they could force state or federal reconsideration of the revenue profile or tax burden of the specialty institution—they would be in a stronger position to demand that the SSH either open its own emergency room, or agree to help in case of unusual emergencies. Further government intervention would only be necessary if such cooperative arrangements could not be brokered.

Second, consider an urban area where one safety net hospital accepts most of the region's indigent, uninsured, and government-insured patients, and a for-profit general hospital manages to attract most of the more-profitable cases. If an SSH enters this market, it will have a more negative impact on the for-profit general than the safety net institution—though the latter is likely to be more vulnerable to even slight diversions of its paying clientele. To the extent the classic legal maneuvers mentioned in Part II above were the prime avenues for challenge of the SSH, the for-profit general hospital would have every incentive to engage in them in order to delay, deter, or stop the entry of this competitor. If revenue-focused challenges were limited to institutions with a certain reference level of community care, the safety net hospital would have leverage to improve the behavior of both the SSH and the for-profit general hospital. The SSH might offer to take on more indigent care in order to avoid lengthy legal inquiries into its own business model; the for-profit general hospital might do the same in order to encourage the safety net provider to instigate such a challenge. Economic theory predicts that the "least-cost provider" of community services would strike a deal first.

Both of these scenarios show how pilot programs of revenue-focused challenges could encourage community-minded bargaining by hospitals responding to the particular needs of given health care markets. Given the opacity of health care pricing, these parties have more information about their relative ability to care for the underserved than regulators.

Presently, the financially strongest health care institutions are the ones best able to challenge specialty hospitals' entry. Yet from a policy perspective, we are far less concerned with threats to their profitability than we are with the effects of specialty hospital entry on providers of charitable care and other community services. A community service trigger for revenue and tax-based challenges puts the focus back where it should be in the specialty hospital debate—on the struggling safety net hospitals and academic health centers whose operation is vital to the health care of the more than forty-five million uninsured individuals in the United States. Pilot programs by both state and federal authorities would catalyze a frank discussion of the real contributions of health care providers. Though the exact details of such a pilot program would prove complex, HHS is presently administering gainsharing pilot programs. The agency has experience in managing a diverse and variegated regulatory landscape.

Of course, universal health insurance coverage might appear to be a far more direct solution to problems like those posed by specialty hospitals.[199] Yet even if it is achieved, public policy will need to address the payor mix of providers in order to assure that the public program does not become a dumping ground for those least able to pay.[200] Both the Canadian and British health care systems have addressed the difficult balance between provider autonomy and access to care within parallel public and private health care systems. The United States will also need to address this issue, regardless of the extent of health reform. Pilot programs can help start this process by establishing a baseline of obligation to care for the un-, under-, or publicly insured for even the best (and best-paid) physicians and institutions.

Although the fragmentation of U.S. health care policy might frustrate some policymakers, the divergent impacts of specialty hospitals show the constructive role it can play. If all the cardiac surgeons in a given market affiliate into a specialty hospital, state and local officials should worry—who will care for Medicaid patients or the uninsured? The extraordinarily disruptive potential of

---

199. See, e.g., Uwe E. Reinhardt, Letter to the Editor, BMJ 2007;335:1020 (17 November), doi:10.1136/bmj.39398.601655.59 ("Absolutely without intending to do so, the efforts of US healthcare providers to cater to uninsured people have aided and abetted great irresponsibility among the nation's political leaders, thereby perpetuating the plight of the uninsured. This is so because the benevolence of health professionals has provided political leaders with moral coverage for resisting any and all efforts to move the nation at long last to fully universal health insurance.").

200. Medicaid is in danger of becoming such a program; see Frank Pasquale, The Public/Private Balance in Health, Post to Concurring Opinions, at http://www.concurringopinions.com/archives/2008/02/badly_socialize.html. Public subsidies for physician education may provide both a legal and moral foundation for payor-mix mandates.

such moves mean that state bans should be an option for a state where cross-subsidization is under siege.

VI. CONCLUDING REFLECTIONS

Legal battles over specialty hospitals highlight the fiercest ideological conflicts about in health policy. Over the last few decades, entrepreneurial doctors have tried to strip out the most profitable business from general hospitals. Ambulatory surgical centers were the pioneers here; they did not worry general hospitals terribly much at first because patients could not spend over twenty-three hours in such facilities, and the most lucrative procedures took longer than a day to recover from. But then other niche providers started providing services at the core of the general hospital's business model, including cardiac and orthopedic surgery. For various reasons, these are some of the highest margin procedures under the Medicare system, and some general hospitals have long used the margin from these departments to cross-subsidize a mission of care for the uninsured (as well as other community benefits).

When cardiac or orthopedics departments migrate away from the general hospital, it is not easy to find alternative funding for vital public services. Specialty hospitals often do not provide the type of emergency rooms, unsponsored care, or other public health initiatives offered by competing general hospitals. Most specialty hospitals can more easily avoid serving Medicaid patients, costly Medicare patients, and the uninsured than general community hospitals can.

This "cream-skimming" recalls the classic debate about whether insurers should be allowed to "cherry pick" the healthiest consumers as a business model. Just as a growing consensus among health policymakers is rejecting that business practice in insurance, providers should also be required to take on some fair share of cases from the least to most lucrative payor classes. Advocates of consumer-directed health care may claim that specialty hospitals are one more "dose of competition" that will improve the health care system. But real health insurance options for every American need to be available before untrammeled entry by specialty hospitals undermines extant patterns of cross-subsidization that now provide some backstop of access to care.

Defenders of cross-subsidization have used many tactics to stem the flow of dollars and entrepreneurial doctors to niche providers. After convincing Congress to put a temporary moratorium on specialty hospital participation in the Medicare program, general hospitals focused on lobbying the executive branch (and state governments) to stymie their spread. They also used Certificate of Need (CON) laws and other state level regulations to deter entry of niche competitors—and to this day, virtually all specialty hospitals are in states without CON laws.

Though they may protect access to care for the nonwealthy, these tactics have a cost. An on-again, off-again moratorium on specialty hospitals has generated legal uncertainty about their viability. In response to these perceived shortcomings of regulation, a coalescing consensus of scholars and policymakers has begun supporting alterations in tax law or payment levels to supplant these complex regulatory responses to niche providers. If specialty hospitals are "cherrypicking" the healthiest Medicare patients and most lucrative DRGs, then reimbursements should be altered to better reflect the true cost of care. If they are eroding an infrastructure of emergent or indigent care, state authorities can tax them in order to directly subsidize these services (or can decide to directly support the uninsured). Such payment system changes appear to many commentators to be more efficient than direct regulation.

Though such proposals are theoretically attractive, their successful implementation will depend on the development of data we presently lack. Pilot programs permitting re-evaluation of specialty hospitals' reimbursement rates from public insurers and taxation rates on the basis of challenges from providers that engage in a reference level of community service could help develop this data. Taxation (and reduction of payments to) niche providers should be based on their real effects in particular markets, not generalized assumptions.

12. FRAGMENTATION IN MENTAL HEALTH BENEFITS AND SERVICES
A Preliminary Examination into Consumption and Outcomes

BARAK RICHMAN, DANIEL GROSSMAN, AND
FRANK SLOAN

The delivery of mental health services might offer the most paradigmatic window into the fragmentation of health services in the United States. Not only is delivery fragmented across outpatient clinicians, inpatient services, prescription drugs, and other behavioral interventions, but the rise of mental health carve-outs has meant that insurance benefits have been fragmented across mental and physical health services as well. If the financing of health care helps direct outcomes,[1] then carved-out mental health benefits might contribute to the many harms of fragmentation, including poorly coordinated care, overprovision and duplication of certain services, and ineffective restraints on cost.[2]

In this chapter, we examine consumption patterns and health outcomes within a health insurance system in which mental health benefits are administered under a carved-out insurance plan. Using a comprehensive dataset of health claims, including insurance claims for both mental and physical health services, we examine both heterogeneity of consumption and variation in outcomes. Consumption variation addresses the regularly overlooked question of how equal insurance and access does not translate into equitable consumption. Outcomes variation yields insights into the potential harms of disparate consumption and of uncoordinated care. We find that even when insurance and access are held constant, consumption of mental health services varies dramatically across race and class. We are unable, however, to find any evidence that higher levels of consumption correspond with improved health when health status is controlled. We also find some evidence of the costs of fragmentation, such as uncoordinated care, low adherence rates, and variation in sources of care.

---

1. David Hyman, *Health Care Fragmentation: We Get What We Pay For*, in OUR FRAGMENTED HEALTH CARE SYSTEM: CAUSES AND SOLUTIONS _PG?_ (Einer Elhauge, ed. 2010).

2. Alain Enthoven, *Curing Fragmentation With Integrated Delivery Systems: What They Do, What Has Blocked Them, Why We Need Them, and How to Get There from Here*, in OUR FRAGMENTED HEALTH CARE SYSTEM: CAUSES AND SOLUTIONS __PG? (Einer Elhauge, ed. 2010).

These findings have important implications for both the delivery of health services and the administration of health insurance benefits.

FRAGMENTATION IN MENTAL HEALTH INSURANCE

In recent years, insurance for mental health services has been organized by "carve-outs," insurance benefits that are separated from insurance covering physical health services and managed under different contracts.[3] Carve-outs permit administrators of mental health benefits to establish specialty provider networks, negotiate competitive service fees, institute treatment protocols, and monitor consumption of mental health services. Use of carve-outs grew rapidly in the 1990s, increasing coverage from 70 million people in 1993 to 164 million in 2002.[4]

Although there is some debate over how the provision of mental health benefits affects overall insurance expenditures,[5] cost containment has been the primary motivation behind the rise of carve-outs. Separate administration of mental health benefits has been shown to reduce the costs of mental health care,[6] in large part by reducing mental health inpatient days and the cost of hospitalizations.[7] Although some of these costs appear to be pushed onto other insurance coverage, there is evidence that carve-outs reduce overall health care costs. For example, although carve-outs have been shown to increase psychotropic drug use,[8] such increases have been shown to decrease overall health care costs by reducing psychotherapy treatments in favor of drug use.[9]

One reason carve-outs might reduce overall health care costs is because mental health benefits have been associated with wasted dollars. In a study of the

---

3. Kyle L. Grazier & Laura L. Eselius, *Mental Health Carve-outs: Effects and Implications*, 56 MED. CARE RES. & REV., 37 (1999).

4. *Id.;* Colleen L. Barry, Richard G. Frank, & Thomas G. McGuire. *The Costs of Mental Health Parity: Still an Impediment?*, 25 HEALTH AFFS. 623 (2006).

5. Julie M. Donohue & Richard G. Frank, *Medicaid Behavioral Health Carve-outs: A New Generation of Privatization Decisions*, 8 HARVARD REV. OF PSYCHIATRY 231 (2000).

6. Richard G. Frank & Rachel L. Garfield, *Managed Behavioral Health Care Carve-outs: Past Performance and Future Prospects.* 28 ANN. REV. OF PUB. HEALTH 303 (2007); Barry, Frank & McGuire, *supra* note 4.

7. *Id.;* Donahue & Frank, *supra* note 5.

8. Susan H. Busch, *Specialty Health Care, Treatment Patterns, and Quality: The Impact of a Mental Health Carve-out on Care for Depression.* 37 HEALTH SERVICES RES. 1583 (2002); Alisa B. Busch et al, *The Impact of Parity on Major Depression Treatment Quality in the Federal Employees' Health Benefits Program After Parity Implementation*, 44 MEDICAL CARE 506 (2006).

9. Ernst R. Berndt, *Changes in the Costs of Treating Mental Health Disorders—An Overview of Recent Research Findings*, 22 PHARMACOECONOMICS 37 (2004).

value of mental health treatment, Richard Frank and colleagues report findings from a panel of psychiatrists, psychologists, and primary care physicians that examined the records of mental health patients.[10] The panel concluded that nearly 25% of the mental health services provided were unsupported by clinical evidence and were clinically equivalent to no treatment at all for treating depression.[11] To the degree that carve-outs permit better monitoring of the consumption of mental health services, they might reduce health care costs without compromising health outcomes.[12] However, because carve-outs have made mental health benefits more affordable, they also have fueled the expansion of mental health insurance coverage, including many efforts by legislatures to require "parity" between insurance coverage for mental health and physical health services.[13] One recent manifestation of legislative efforts to mandate mental health benefits is the Mental Health Parity Act of 2007, which purports to expand mental health benefits to 118 million workers. The 2007 Act extends the Mental Health Parity Act of 1996, and most states have instituted their own mental health parity mandates.

Carve-outs therefore appear to have had a dual effect on health care costs. While they might be responsible for eliminating some unnecessary and costly care, they also have helped fuel the expansion of mental health insurance. It remains to be seen whether parity under carve-outs leads to improved quality of care or simply better financing of care.[14] Susan Busch and colleagues, for example, found that although there were modest increases in quality of care and the timeliness of administering follow-up care following the implementation of parity legislation, quality of care still fell well short of adequate quality standards as defined by the American Psychiatric Association and the Agency for Healthcare Research and Quality.

However, unconsidered in debates over expansions in mental health insurance benefits, and debates over parity in particular, are the distributional consequences of expanded mental health benefits on individual workers. If increases in insurance coverage are fully shifted to employees as equal reductions in take-home pay, akin to a head tax,[15] and thus workers of all wages contribute equally

10. Richard G. Frank et al, *The Value of Mental Health Care at the System Level: the Case of Treating Depression*, 18 HEALTH AFFS. 71 (1999).

11. *See id.;* Berndt, *supra* note 9.

12. Richard G. Frank & Thomas G. McGuire, *Savings from a Medicaid Carve-Out for Mental Health and Substance Abuse Services in Massachusetts*, 48 PSYCHIATRIC SERVICES 1147 (1997); Kyle L. Grazier et al., *Effects of a Mental Health—Carve-out on Use, Costs, and Payers: A Four-Year Study*, 26 J. OF BEHAV. HEALTH SERVICES & RES. 381 (1999); Frank et al., *supra* note 10.

13. Grazier & Eselius, *supra* note 3; Frank & McGuire, *supra* note 10.

14. Busch et al., *supra* note 8.

15. Jonathan Gruber, *Health Insurance and the Labor Market.* (Nat'l Bureau of Econ. Research, Working Paper No. 6762, 1998); Jonathan Gruber, *Statement Before the Senate*

to receive mental health insurance benefits, then equity and fairness compel us to investigate whether these insurance expansions distribute benefits equally as well. As the combination of carve-outs and parity create an increasingly common profile of mental health insurance coverage, it becomes important to consider the distribution and effectiveness of those benefits.

DESCRIPTION OF THE DATA

We explore these questions through the lens of a valuable database of health care claims from a heterogeneous population with identical health insurance, including a mental health carve-out, and ready access to physical and mental health care services. The data provides a rare opportunity to investigate differences in health care consumption when the unfortunately common inequalities in access to care are not present. It also offers a valuable opportunity to examine how a carve-out mental health insurance scheme affects a heterogeneous population, and it provides a window into understanding more generally how vulnerable populations—who frequently are the intended beneficiaries of insurance mandates—actually fare when coverage is uniform across a heterogeneous population.

Duke University and Duke University Health System (Duke) provide health insurance to more than twenty thousand employees in over six counties in central North Carolina.[16] Duke's Human Resources provided limited access to deidentified records of each employee's health claims from 2001 through 2004, yielding almost 92,000 person-year observations. Each health claim includes information on the services provided, the associated diagnosis, and the amounts paid by both the insurer and patient. The data also reveal each individual's race, job category (from which education and income are derived[17]), and insurance benefits.

Finance Committee, July 31, 2008; Clark C. Havighurst & Barak D. Richman. *Distributive Injustice(s) in American Health Care.* 69 LAW & CONTEMP. PROBS. 7 (2006).

16. Duke has employees living in 97 of North Carolina's 100 counties, but 95% live in the six counties surrounding the Raleigh-Durham area. The region is home to many urban, suburban, and rural residential areas.

17. To protect employees' privacy, and to ensure that the data remained deidentified, individual salaries were not released. However, Duke HR categorizes each position by job code, each with a fairly precise salary range and required levels of education, which permitted imputing education and annual income for each individual. Income was determined by the mid-point of the income range for each job code, coded in units of $10,000 in 2004 dollars. For job codes for which wages are hourly, the hourly rate was multiplied by the individual's full-time equivalent. Job code salary ranges were not available for 2001, so 2001 incomes were imputed for each job code from the salary ranges in 2002-04. Finally, faculty member salaries and the salaries of certain administrators are not determined by job code, thus individuals with these positions are not included in the sample.

The demographic profile of the population remains stable for the period under study. Approximately sixty eight percent of the sample is White and twenty four percent is African-American, the median annual earnings of the sample member rises gradually from about $36,000 to $40,500 over the four years, and the seventy fifth and twenty fifth percentile incomes range from approximately $47,800 to $51,000 and $28,600 to $30,500, respectively. These figures are roughly reflective of the demographic profile of both Durham County (in which Duke University is located) and North Carolina.[18]

Duke offers its employees a menu of insurance coverage options for different employee-paid premiums, including an HMO (selected by over seventy percent of employees), a more expensive PPO with a wider network of participating providers (selected by about fifteen percent of employees), and other managed care options, some of which were terminated and replaced during the period of study. The different plans offer slightly varying copayments, deductibles, and rates of coinsurance for most medical services, and they also present different copayments for going to out-of-network providers. However, most of these insurance plans offer the same carve-out package of mental health benefits, including identical copayments, network, and coverage of services, so there is far less variation across plans for these benefits. In 2004, for example, three of the four insurance plans, subscribed collectively by eighty seven percent of the employees, offered a common carve-out for mental health and substance abuse benefits, with the remaining thirteen percent with a BCBS plan enjoying almost identical financial coverage but for a wider network.[19]

The dataset offers an unusual opportunity to examine health care consumption in a racially and economically diverse population that enjoys equal access and insurance coverage. Most data sources on health care consumption, such as the Medical Expenditure Panel Survey (MEPS), rely on self-reported surveys of populations in which individuals have different insurance benefits and confront

---

Anecdotal evidence suggests that results would be even stronger if these high-income individuals remained in the data. Also omitted from the analyses were individuals with missing race data (N=784).

18. The dataset is skewed by gender since women are heavily represented in health care occupations. Approximately 65% of the individuals in the dataset are female. Female median income in the sample is nearly identical to median income for males, which is just above the median for males in Durham County.

19. The BCBS plan imposes $35 copayments for unlimited outpatient office visits, whereas the other three plans impose $35 copayments for up to twenty in-network visits and a $100 deductible plus 50% coinsurance for all out-of-network visits. The non-BCBS plans also impose some precertification requirements and laboratory and outpatient charges. However important or unimportant these cost-sharing differences are, we control in each analysis for insurance plan, including controlling separately for the three plans, enjoyed by 87% of the population, that offer identical coverage.

assorted barriers to care.[20] In contrast, all of the individuals in the Duke dataset have comprehensive health insurance with nearly uniform mental health coverage. Moreover, the Raleigh-Durham metropolitan area is home to many providers (including two academic medical centers), so individuals in the data live near a hospital and a physician practice, and since the data includes Duke University Health System employees, a great number of individuals work at or right next to health care institutions. Thus, the Duke population faces very few logistical and institutional barriers to care, and observed consumption disparities can be primarily attributed to other factors.[21]

CHARTING REGRESSIVE REDISTRIBUTIONS THROUGH MENTAL HEALTH BENEFITS

In "Insurance Expansions: Do They Hurt Those They Are Designed to Help?" ("*Insurance Expansions*"), one of us examined the Duke data to investigate the basic—but, from the perspective of economic policy, crucial—question of whether mental health insurance redistributes wealth in desirable directions.[22] Since all insureds are paying equal amounts (or, more precisely, are receiving equal reductions in their take-home pay) in exchange for employer-sponsored insurance, determining which employees are receiving more, and which are receiving fewer, insurance dollars in the form of mental health services reveals whom the benefits package favors.

Insurance Expansions focused on how mental health benefits redistribute wealth across race and class, in large part because mental health parity legislation—like most legislative efforts to expand health insurance—is often characterized as an effort to benefit low-income and traditionally vulnerable populations. Accordingly, the empirical tests examined whether low-income and non-White individuals use fewer mental health benefits than Whites and high-income individuals.[23] Measuring utilization benefits requires two distinct

---

20. For a description of the Medical Expenditure Panel Survey, *see* http://www.meps.ahrq.gov/mepsweb/

21. It should be noted that the benefits offices of most large employers should have access to similarly useful data, but very few share their data with researchers. Benefits data of this kind is a valuable resource both to understand health care consumption and to explore important health policy questions. We are deeply grateful to Duke Human Resources for its cooperation in exploring research questions of both local and national importance. Medicare claims data exhibits some of these advantages, since it follows heterogeneous individuals with known insurance benefits, but it does not cover the working population.

22. Barak D. Richman, *Insurance Expansions: Do They Hurt Those They Are Designed to Help?*, 26 HEALTH AFFS. 1346 (2007).

23. *Id.*

but related calculations: (1) the probability an individual filed a claim in a given year, and (2) given the probability of filing a claim, an individual's estimated annual health expenditures. Since the relevant policy question asks who extracts benefits from insurance coverage, the empirical study focuses on the insurer's expenditures on behalf of individuals, rather than the individual's out-of-pocket expenses.

The four years of data were aggregated into 92,000 person-year observations, with all dollar amounts converted into 2004 dollars. Ordinary least-squares estimated the probabilities that individuals would receive an insurance benefit within a given year.[24] Then a two-stage smearing technique estimated annual individual expenditures. The two-stage technique first calculates a transformed estimation of annual expenditures only for those individuals who exhibited positive expenditures, and then the mean of these smearing estimates are multiplied by the fraction of individuals that have positive expenditures.[25] This two-part approach—rather than a one-step estimation of consumption—is appropriate when a substantial portion of the population has zero consumption since a one-step estimation would then generate biased results. Control variables presumed to correlate with health care consumption were age, gender, years of education, and years of work experience. A dummy variable (Exemption Status) indicated whether the employee was an hourly or salaried worker, and individual dummy controls were also added for each of the available health insurance plans. Huber-White standard errors were generated to determine the statistical significance of the parameter estimates.

The regressions measured the effects of two distinct variables (race and income) on the consumption of two separate insurance benefits (mental health and pharmaceuticals). Separate regressions were run on the consumption data for each benefit. Regressions first examined the effect of race variables alone, then income alone, then both together (to determine whether the separate effects are independent), and then gradually additional control variables were added for a robustness check.

The regression results illustrate that non-Whites and low-income individuals receive significantly fewer benefits from the mental health insurance coverage made available to them. Exhibit 1 reveals that both race and income independently

---

24. Logit estimations were also used to estimate the probabilities of consumption, and the same variables were found to be statistically significant. OLS is employed instead because of the ease of interpreting OLS coefficients.

25. The smearing estimate is $[\exp(X_o\beta) \times n^{-1}\Sigma[\exp(e_i)]]$ where $X_o\beta$ is the predicted values from an OLS regression of log dollars consumed and e_i, is the residuals from that regression. This is the same 2-stage smearing estimation method used previously in William G. Manning et al, *Health Insurance and the Demand for Medical Care: Evidence from a Randomized Experiment*, 77 AMER. ECON. REV. 251 (1987).

EXHIBIT 1: DEPENDENT VARIABLE: PROBABILITY OF AT LEAST ONE MENTAL HEALTH CLAIM[26] IN A YEAR

Model	Race Only	Income Only	Race AND Income	Race, Income & Education	All Variables[27]
Intercept	0.077***	0.028***	0.071***	−0.011	0.0188
Sex[28]	−0.022***	−0.016***	−0.015***	−0.014**	−0.016***
Age	0.0005***	0.0002^	0.0003*	0.0003^	0.0002
African-American	−0.064***		−0.060***	−0.055***	−0.056***
Asian	−0.059***		−0.058***	−0.072***	−0.069***
Annual Income[29]		0.0087***	0.0026**	−0.0043*	−0.0073***
Education				0.0077***	0.0062***
Exemption Status[30]					0.024***

Source: Duke Human Resources

*** p<.001
** p<.01
* p<.05
^ p<.10

contribute to an individual's likelihood of consuming mental health care. The "Race Only" model indicates that Whites are significantly more likely to file a claim for mental health benefits than African-Americans and Asians.[31] When controlling for age and sex, the race variables are highly significant and—in relation to the intercept—of very large magnitude. For example, a 40-year-old White male has an estimated probability of 7.5% of receiving mental health

---

26. Some of the claims in the data were for zero dollars. Probability estimations were made both for claims greater than $0 and for claims of any amount, including $0. Results were consistent and robust. Estimates shown here are for claims of any amount.

27. The "All Variables" model includes, but does not show, dummy controls for the available insurance plans and years of work experience, and each model includes the race category of "Latino" and "Other," but these results also are not shown. See FN6 for an explanation why Latinos are removed from the sample.

28. Male = 1, Female = 0.

29. Annual income, in units of $10,000.

30. Salaried Worker = 1, Hourly worker = 0.

31. The Latinos in the dataset appear to be misrepresentative of other Latinos in Durham and North Carolina. Median incomes for Latinos in the sample hold steadily at approximately $34,000 throughout the sample, just slightly below the overall median, and Latino's median education is at least one year higher than the sample's overall median. Many Latino low-wage earners working at Duke are employees of subcontractors and are not Duke employees, which might explain this skewed sample. Since few generalizable conclusions can be drawn from studying the Latinos in the sample, results for that group are omitted.

services within a year while a forty-year-old African-American male has an estimated probability of 1.1% and a forty-year-old Asian male has an estimated probability of 1.6%. These results remain extremely robust even as income, education, exemption status, and dummies for the insurance plans are added to the model. Exhibit 1 also reveals that income has a significant and independent effect on seeking mental health care, as an additional $10,000 in annual income increased the likelihood an individual receives mental health care by nearly 0.9%. The income variable also remains robust as other control variables are added. The results suggest that race and income have independent and very significant effects on consumption. The race variables remain significant even after controlling for income and education, and income remains significant even after controlling for race.

Of perhaps greater interest is how these differences in the propensity to seek care translate into disparities in receiving dollar benefits from the insurer. Exhibit 2, showing the estimates from the two-stage smearing techniques,[32] indicates that Whites can expect to receive nearly four times the annual insurance dollars from mental health benefits that African-Americans expect to receive and more than three times the dollars that Asians expect to receive. Similarly, individuals with the seventy fifth percentile income receive about two-thirds more than individuals at the twenty fifth percentile. Like the results in Exhibit 1, both the race and income variables remain independently robust in the smearing estimates.[33]

Insurance Expansions puts a dollar figure on what most observers surely suspected: that Whites and high-income individuals take greater advantage of, and thus extract more financial gain from, a given menu of insurance benefits. Prior research confirms that high-income insured parties are less deterred by copayments and other cost-sharing burdens than lower-income individuals with the same insurance benefits.[34] Affluent individuals also are better at navigating through medical bureaucracies to obtain desired providers, high-quality

---

32. *See* Manning et al., *supra* note 25, for a description of the two-stage smearing techniques.

33. Duke also provides employees short-term counseling, or "Personal Assistance Services" (PAS), free of charge. Utilization of PAS is not captured in the claims data, but since they constitute another form of employer-provided mental health care, a complete understanding of employee mental health care utilization requires taking PAS into account. Data on PAS consumption are not at a level of detail that would allow a replication of the analyses executed on the claims data. Overview statistics of PAS consumption are available, and they suggest that the findings on race and income would not measurably change if PAS consumption were included in the larger sample. For example, PAS data reveal that White employees visit PAS in greater proportions than African-American or Asian employees (no income data is available for PAS clients).

34. Emmet B. Keeler et al. *The Demand For Episodes of Medical Treatment in the Health Insurance Experiment*, 7 J. OF HEALTH ECON 337 (1988); JOSEPH P. NEWHOUSE, THE

EXHIBIT 2: ESTIMATED ANNUAL INSURANCE EXPENDITURES FOR MENTAL HEALTH CLAIMS, USING TWO-STAGE SMEARING

Control Variables	White	African-American	Asian
Age, Sex, Race	$62.97	$17.68	$20.60
Age, Sex, Race, Income	61.20	16.26	20.66
Age, Sex, Race, Income, Education	66.07	16.34	13.27
All controls	66.17	16.71	13.27

Control Variables	25th Percentile Income	75th Percentile Income
Age, Sex, Income	$33.30	$55.77
Age, Sex, Income, Race	33.87	55.83
Age, Sex, Income, Race, Plans	33.74	56.48
All controls (including education & exemption)	42.82	50.07

Source: Duke Human Resources

treatment, and medical advocacy,[35] and there remains significant evidence that African-Americans receive inferior care and attention in the U.S. health system.[36] Moreover, consumption disparities in mental health services are further explained by different attitudes towards mental health care. Non-Whites have been shown to attribute a larger stigma to mental illnesses and seeking mental health care than Whites,[37] and there is evidence that non-Whites are more likely than Whites to use social support systems and religious participation as alternatives to seeking care from mental health care providers.[38]

Nonetheless, despite the consequent wealth transfer, mandating coverage for mental health care might still be a desirable policy. If it is determined that receiving outpatient mental health care prevents costly mental health hospitalizations, or if receiving services from an outpatient mental health provider is shown to have greater benefits (at lower costs) than receiving services from alternative

INSURANCE EXPERIMENT GROUP. FREE FOR ALL? LESSONS FROM THE RAND HEALTH INSURANCE EXPERIMENT (1993)

35. M. Gregg Bloche. *Race and Discretion in American Medicine*. 1 YALE J. HEALTH POL'Y L & ETHICS 95 (2001).

36. INSTITUTE OF MEDICINE. UNEQUAL TREATMENT: CONFRONTING RACIAL AND ETHNIC DISPARITIES IN HEALTHCARE (2003).

37. UNITED STATES SURGEON GENERAL, MENTAL HEALTH: CULTURE, RACE, AND ETHNICITY (1999), *available at* http://www.surgeongeneral.gov/library/mentalhealth/cre/

38. David R. Williams & Harold W. Neighbors, *Social Perspectives on Mood Disorders. in* TEXTBOOK OF MOOD DISORDERS 145 (Dan J. Stein et al., eds., 2006).

sources, then perhaps coverage is desirable and low-users of mental health care should be encouraged to consume more. We report our analysis of these questions on efficacy in the following section.

EVALUATING EFFICACY: HOSPITALIZATIONS, REHOSPITALIZATIONS, AND FOLLOW-UP CARE

To examine both the effect and efficacy of insurance coverage for outpatient mental health services, we investigate whether low-income and non-White individuals seek substitutes to mental health services. We then discuss whether those substitutes, or forgoing mental health care altogether, lead to adverse health outcomes. We also report results from testing, more generally, whether disparate consumption of outpatient mental health services leads to disparate mental health outcomes.

Consumption Patterns

In "Mental Health Care Consumption and Outcomes: Considering Preventative Strategies Across Race and Class" (*"Consumption and Outcomes"*), we sought to determine whether race or income is systematically associated with variation in mental health care seeking behavior.[39] Our claims data reveal at least three ways that insureds can use insurance benefits to obtain outpatient mental health care: receiving care from a mental health care professional, filling prescriptions for psychotropic pharmaceuticals, or visiting a general practitioner. The claims data determined whether an insured sought care from a mental health provider or a general practitioner. We separated pharmaceutical claims for psychotropics from other prescriptions based on their NDC codes, and we used International Classification of Diseases ninth edition (ICD-9) diagnoses codes—relying only on the primary codes—to determine whether an insured's visit to a general practitioner included treatment for a mental illnesses.

Insureds were separated into four mutually exclusive categories: (1) individuals who sought care from an outpatient mental health care provider (including those who also obtained psychotropic pharmaceuticals and/or sought care from a general practitioner and received a mental illnesses diagnosis), (2) individuals who filled a prescription for psychotropics (including those who sought care from a general practitioner and received a mental illnesses diagnosis) but did not obtain care from an outpatient mental health care provider, (3) individuals who sought care from a general practitioner and received a mental illnesses diagnosis but neither obtained care from a mental health care provider nor filled a

---

39. Barak D. Richman et al, *Mental Health Care Consumption and Outcomes: Considering Preventative Strategies Across Race and Class* (Duke University Law School Working Paper, 2008).

prescription for psychotropics, and (4) individuals who received no form of mental health care. We labeled these categories Outpatient Mental Health (OMH), Psychotropics/No-OMH, GP-Only, and No Care.

We employed a multinomial logit test to compare how race and income affected an individual's probability of being in one of the three consumption categories. Exhibit 3 shows the relative risk ratios (RRRs) that capture the comparative probabilities. The 0.29 RRR for African-Americans in the OMH category is the probability an African-American will consume outpatient mental health care divided by the probability he/she will not consume any care. Since Whites are the reference group, it means African-Americans are only twenty nine percent (p < 0.001) as likely as Whites to be in the OMH group compared to the No Care group. Asians are even less likely than Whites to be in the OMH group compared to the No care group, and income is found to increase the relative probability of consuming mental health care. These findings, with their significant magnitudes, corroborate those in *Insurance Expansions*.

One question raised in *Insurance Expansions* is whether non-Whites and low-income workers obtained mental health care through alternative sources. Exhibit 3 indicates that African-Americans and Asians are also much less likely to obtain mental health care from mental health providers and through psychotropic prescriptions than Whites, but are more likely to see a general practitioner for a mental health problem (RRR: 1.24; p<0.001) than not seek treatment at all, compared to Whites. Income, however, appears to have an opposite effect on these alternative sources, and lower incomes are associated with greater likelihoods of receiving care from general practitioners and psychotropic

EXHIBIT 3: MULTINOMIAL LOGIT: RELATIVE RISK RATIOS (RRR) OF RECEIVING MENTAL HEALTH CARE FROM VARIOUS SOURCES OF CARE COMPARED TO RECEIVING NO MENTAL HEALTH CARE

	Outpatient Mental Health (OMH)		Psychotropics/ No OMH		General Practitioner Only	
	RRR	P value	RRR	P value	RRR	P value
Male	0.56	0.000	0.46	0.000	1.05	0.328
Age	1.02	0.000	1.05	0.000	1.03	0.000
African-American	0.29	0.000	0.43	0.000	1.24	0.000
Asian	0.24	0.000	0.23	0.000	0.65	0.001
Income	1.03	0.002	0.94	0.000	0.91	0.000

Source: Duke Human Resources
N = 31640
Omitted reference group is "No Care"
RRR—Relative risk ratio
Covariates not shown include type of insurance, income missing, year of service
* p<0.05, ** p<0.01, *** p<0.001

prescriptions compared to not seeking help, while higher incomes are associated with greater likelihoods of receiving care from mental health professionals compared to not seeking help. So, while non-Whites are less likely than Whites to consume mental health care from mental health providers or through prescription medicines, low-income individuals appear to substitute GPs and prescriptions for mental health providers.

Exhibit 4 further explores different consumption patterns by executing a multinomial logit only for those who seek some kind of care for a mental illness and excludes the No Care group. These findings confirm that rising incomes are associated with declining use of general practitioners for mental health care and increasing use of mental health care providers. Also, both Asians (RRR: 2.84; p<0.001) and African-Americans (RRR: 2.91; p<0.001) are nearly three times as likely to seek care for mental illnesses from GPs than through psychotropic prescriptions compared to Whites, while African-Americans are just two-thirds as likely (RRR: 0.65; p<0.001) to seek care from mental health providers than through psychotropic prescriptions compared to Whites.

These results illustrate that both the race and income variables independently (i.e., when each one is controlled for the other) are associated with different patterns of health care consumption. As a general matter, we see major differences in how individuals of different races and with different incomes seek health care for mental illnesses, as low-income and non-White individuals are more inclined compared to Whites to obtain care from GPs than mental health professionals. We also observe that non-Whites are less likely than Whites to seek outpatient mental health care or prescription medications, whereas low-income individuals, compared to their more affluent coworkers, appear to

EXHIBIT 4: MULTINOMIAL LOGIT: RELATIVE RISK RATIOS (RRR) OF RECEIVING ALTERNATIVE FORMS OF MENTAL HEALTH CARE FROM VARIOUS SOURCES FOR THOSE WHO OBTAIN SOME FORM OF MENTAL HEALTH CARE

	Outpatient Mental Health (OMH)		General Practitioner only	
	RRR	P value	RRR	P value
Male	1.26	0.000	2.31	0.000
Age	0.97	0.000	0.98	0.000
African-American	0.65	0.000	2.91	0.000
Asian	0.99	0.936	2.84	0.000
Income	1.10	0.000	0.96	0.065

Source: Duke Human Resources
N = 11129
Omitted reference group is "Psychotropics/no MH"
Covariates not shown include type of insurance, income missing, year of service
*p<0.05, **p<0.01, ***p<0.001

substitute care from GPs and prescriptions for psychotropics for outpatient mental health care.

Incidence of Mental Illness and Effectiveness of Mental Health Care

Differences in consumption patterns are difficult to interpret meaningfully without evaluating the effectiveness of the alternative forms of care. In *Consumption and Outcomes*, we investigated the effectiveness of various mental health services by examining whether outpatient mental health care, compared to GP visits and psychotropics (which are covered in standard care, not by a mental health care benefit) reduce the likelihood of an adverse outcome. We used hospitalizations associated with mental illnesses as an indicator of an adverse outcome, which we gathered from three sources. We identified any individual hospitalized with a primary diagnosis of mental disorder (ICD-9 codes 290-319), any insured who sought treatment at an emergency room and received a primary diagnosis of mental disorder, and any patient who received mental health care with a service code that denoted inpatient treatment (which largely included hospital patients who had an inpatient mental health consult). With these three sources, we identified 297 individuals who were hospitalized at least once.

Since mental illnesses prevent many individuals from maintaining their employment, we employed a competing risk model to compare the probability of hospitalization with the likelihoods that individuals will leave our sample, which occurs when an employee leaves the Duke workplace. The competing risk model permits a comparison of two alternative risks for identical groups while controlling for differences in the sizes of the groups of interest. The results in Exhibit 5 reveal that the probabilities of African-Americans, Asians, and Whites being hospitalized for a mental illness are statistically indistinguishable, while low-income employees are more likely to be hospitalized than their higher-income co-workers

EXHIBIT 5: COMPETING RISK BETWEEN THE LIKELIHOOD OF HOSPITALIZATION VERSUS EXITING THE SAMPLE

	Hospitalization		Exiting Sample	
	HR	P value	HR	P value
African-American	0.80	0.148	1.12	0.477
Asian	0.71	0.286	1.63	0.137
Income	0.82	0.001	1.10	0.096

Source: Duke Human Resources
N= 31640
Notes: HR—Hazard ratio
Covariates not shown include gender, type of insurance, income missing, age, year of service
* p<0.05, ** p<0.01, *** p<0.001

(Hazard ratio (HR): 0.82; p=0.001) (high-income employees are also more likely to leave the employment sample, probably because of better outside labor market opportunities).

Exhibit 5 therefore dispels, in part, one potential explanation for the results in Exhibits 3 and 4, that differences in consumption across race reflect differences in need. Exhibit 5 instead suggests that non-Whites are about as likely to require hospitalization as Whites, and thus their lower levels of consumption cannot be solely attributed to differences in the incidence of mental illness. The combined results in Exhibits 3–5 also conform to research relying on survey data revealing that ethnic and racial minorities experience lower prevalence rates of acute mental illnesses than Whites but are equally likely (and often more likely) to present severe major disorders and debilitating mental illnesses.[40]

The bigger question by Exhibit 5 is whether interventions by medical professionals can reduce the probability of a hospitalization associated with a mental illness and whether some interventions are more effective than others (Exhibits 3–5 also suggest that low-income individuals are more likely to be hospitalized yet are less likely to seek outpatient mental health care, which additionally invites further testing of the efficacy of interventions). Exhibit 6 introduces interventions into the competing risk model and examines how out-patient interventions are associated with hospitalizations. It indicates that individuals who consume outpatient mental health care are more than nine times

EXHIBIT 6: COMPETING RISK BETWEEN THE LIKELIHOOD OF HOSPITALIZATION VERSUS EXITING THE SAMPLE: EFFECT OF MENTAL HEALTH CONSUMPTION

	Hospitalization		Exiting Sample	
	HR	P value	HR	P value
African-American	1.22	0.190	0.70	0.017
Asian	1.20	0.572	0.89	0.728
Income	0.80	0.000	1.12	0.071
Outpatient mental health (OMH)	9.01	0.000	0.08	0.000
Psychotropics/No OMH	3.23	0.000	0.22	0.000
General practitioner only	1.60	0.101	0.43	0.003

Source: Duke Human Resources
N= 31640
Notes: HR—Hazard ratio
Covariates not shown include gender, type of insurance, income missing, age, year of service
* p<0.05, ** p<0.01, *** p<0.001

40. David R. Williams et al, *Prevalence and Distribution of Major Depressive Disorder in African Americans, Caribbean Blacks, and Non-Hispanic Whites—Results form the National Survey of American Life*, 64 ARCHIVES OF GEN. PSYCHIATRY 305 (2007).

as likely to be hospitalized as individuals who receive no care, and individuals who fill prescriptions for psychotropics are more than three times as likely to do so.

Of course, Exhibit 6's results are readily explained by the endogeneity of the consumption patterns, since individuals who seek mental health care of any sort are revealing some mental illness, and individuals with some form of illness are more likely to be hospitalized. Moreover, some individuals might receive inpatient care following a referral or admission by the provider from which they receive outpatient care, so receiving outpatient care might also facilitate inpatient care. It is very difficult to control for underlying conditions if the only data available are insurance claims, and given the unobservable heterogeneity of underlying health status, it is empirically challenging to determine how outpatient services might impart benefits to subscribers.

We begin controlling for health status by constructing our own "severity index," in which a psychiatrist assigned a 1–10 value for each mental illness-related ICD9 diagnosis, with 10 being the most severe (for a discussion of the severity index, see *Consumption and Outcomes*). In Exhibit 7, we add this severity value to the competing risk model. Each individual who received a diagnosis from either a general practitioner or an outpatient mental health care provider thus received a severity score, and in order to allow the severity index to predict hospitalizations, we based the severity score on the diagnosis individuals received before they were hospitalized (if they were hospitalized at all). The problem with employing this metric, aside from its reliance on approximations, is that it assigns a zero to all individuals who do not receive any diagnosis. Thus, since more than one-quarter of those hospitalized did not visit a GP or mental health provider before being hospitalized, and consequently did not receive a diagnosis, the metric is necessarily biased downward. Nonetheless, in Exhibit 7 the severity index is positively associated with the likelihood of hospitalization, and including it in the model makes the medical interventions less positively associated with hospitalizations. This suggests that the severity measure does help solve some of the endogeneity problem. When controlling with the severity index, the results suggest that only one of the three outpatient interventions reduce the likelihood of hospitalizations. Receiving care from a general practitioner—a service covered by standard insurance benefits, not by mental health benefits— does appear to reduce the probability of hospitalization. The results do not, however, indicate that receiving care from outpatient mental health providers reduces the likelihood of hospitalization.

For a robustness check, and to pursue another path to control for the severity of the underlying medical condition, we examined only the 297 individuals who were hospitalized for a mental illness. Even though these individuals were hospitalized under different conditions and for different illnesses, their severity is much more homogeneous than that of the whole sample. Moreover, each hospitalized individual is, at time of discharge, given an appointment to see an outpatient mental

EXHIBIT 7: COMPETING RISK BETWEEN THE LIKELIHOOD OF HOSPITALIZATION VERSUS EXITING THE SAMPLE: EFFECT OF MENTAL HEALTH CONSUMPTION AND SEVERITY INDEX

	Hospitalization		Exiting sample	
	HR	P value	HR	P value
African-American	1.24	0.152	0.68	0.012
Asian	1.24	0.513	0.86	0.661
Income	0.82	0.001	1.09	0.144
Outpatient mental health (OMH)	0.77	0.429	0.93	0.828
Psychotropics/No OMH	0.58	0.073	1.24	0.490
General practitioner only	0.20	0.000	3.58	0.001
Severity	1.48	0.000	0.67	0.000

Source: Duke Human Resources
N= 31640
Notes: HR—Hazard ratio
Covariates not shown include gender, type of insurance, income missing, age, year of service.
* $p < 0.05$, ** $p < 0.01$, *** $p < 0.001$

health care provider within the first few weeks of discharge, with regular visits scheduled thereafter. We therefore can test to see if these post-hospitalization instructions are followed, and we can test to see if race or income affects the probability an individual will miss, or refuse to attend, those follow-up appointments.

To test for "failure" to attend post-hospitalization outpatient appointments, we determined whether within the first four months of discharge there is a ninety-day period in which a formerly hospitalized patient did not visit an outpatient mental health provider. We employed a competing risk model that compares the probability of an adherence failure across race and income, with results shown in Exhibit 8. Here again, African-Americans and Asians, controlling for income, exhibit a lower propensity to visit outpatient mental health care providers, even shortly after being discharged for a hospitalization (though the small sample size keeps the Asian coefficient from being statistically significant, with a p-value of 0.23). Income does not affect follow-up behavior, suggesting that the refusals of non-Whites might be a function of cultural preferences rather than financial means.

In Exhibit 9, we tested whether the failure to follow post-discharge instructions has adverse consequences. We used rehospitalization as an adverse outcome, and we determined whether discharged individuals are hospitalized after fourteen days (to ensure that the second admission reflects a second event, rather than a recurrence) but within one year of the date of initial discharge. We then employed a competing risk model to calculate whether the likelihood of rehospitalization is affected by race, income, or failure to pursue post-discharge outpatient mental health care. Exhibit 9 reveals that there is little evidence that

EXHIBIT 8: COMPETING RISK: HAZARD RATIOS (HR) OF FAILURE TO ADHERE TO POST-HOSPITALIZATION FOLLOW-UP TREATMENT VERSUS EXITING THE SAMPLE

| | Treatment Failure | | Exiting Sample | |
	HR	P value	HR	P value
Male	1.21	0.265	1.23	0.653
Age	0.99	0.326	0.97	0.073
African-American	1.92	0.000	0.52	0.201
Asian	1.64	0.231	2.75	0.287
Income	0.92	0.191	0.66	0.059
Severity	0.83	0.000	1.41	0.012

Source: Duke Human Resources
N=297
Notes: Treatment failure is not seeking mental health outpatient care for a period of longer than 90 days
Included covariates were year of service, type of insurance, and income missing. None were significant.
* p<0.05, ** p<0.01, *** p<0.001

EXHIBIT 9: COMPETING RISK: HAZARD RATIOS (HR) OF REHOSPITALIZATION WITHIN 1 YEAR FOLLOWING INITIAL HOSPITALIZATION VERSUS EXITING THE SAMPLE: EFFECT OF TREATMENT FAILURE

| | Rehospitalization | | Exiting Sample | |
	HR	P value	HR	P value
Male	1.52	0.186	1.20	0.660
Age	1.02	0.186	0.96	0.036
African-American	1.05	0.908	1.68	0.357
Asian	1.00	0.997	3.80	0.234
Income	0.92	0.480	1.00	0.982
Severity	1.12	0.277	0.97	0.809
Treatment failure	0.65	0.263	0.36	0.070

Source: Duke Human Resources
N=293
Treatment failure is failure to see mental health provider for a period of 90 days within in the first four months following initial hospitalization.
Included covariates were year of service, type of insurance, and income missing. None were significant.
* p<0.05, ** p<0.01, *** p<0.001

failure to follow up increases the probability of a rehospitalization. In fact, a "failure" to follow up with an outpatient mental health provider is closer to decreasing, rather than increasing, the likelihood of a rehospitalization (p-value is 0.26), although this also might be a problem of unobserved severity—individuals who fail to follow-up might have less severe illnesses. These analyses that focus on hospitalized insureds, however, have a much smaller sample size, and thus are less likely to produce significant results.

Exhibit 10 reveals where discharged patients sought care, including those who fail to follow up with mental health care providers. Here again, like the results in Exhibits 3 and 4, African-Americans appear to prefer seeking care from general practitioners (or forgo care altogether) than from mental health care providers. These results are even more striking than Exhibits 3 and 4 since they follow a severe event that was accompanied by instructions to see a mental health care provider. Exhibit 11 offers similar results for the six months prior to an initial hospitalization. Of individuals who are hospitalized for mental illnesses, African-Americans were far less likely to seek care from mental health providers and receive psychotropics.

EXHIBIT 10: MULTINOMIAL LOGIT: RELATIVE RISK RATIO (RRR) OF RECEIVING MENTAL HEALTH CARE FROM VARIOUS SOURCES IN THE FOUR MONTHS AFTER INITIAL HOSPITALIZATION VERSUS EXITING THE SAMPLE

	Outpatient Mental Health		Psychotropics or General Practitioner (No OMH)		Exit Sample	
	RRR	P value	RRR	P value	RRR	P value
Male	0.57	0.187	0.74	0.514	1.06	0.903
Age	1.02	0.318	1.01	0.518	1.00	0.953
African-American	0.27	0.004	0.57	0.249	0.24	0.008
Asian	0.21	0.177	0.44	0.470	0.66	0.694
Income	1.14	0.346	1.09	0.603	0.97	0.862
Severity	1.38	0.013	1.14	0.366	1.25	0.129

Source: Duke Human Resources
N=297
Notes: Omitted reference group is "No Care"
*p<0.05, **p<0.01, ***p<0.001

EXHIBIT 11: MULTINOMIAL LOGIT: RELATIVE RISK RATIOS (RRR) OF RECEIVING MENTAL HEALTH CARE FROM ALTERNATIVE PROVIDERS IN THE 6 MONTHS PRIOR TO INITIAL HOSPITALIZATION

	Outpatient Mental Health		Psychotropics/No OMH		General Practitioner Only	
	RRR	P value	RRR	P value	RRR	P value
Male	0.50	0.117	0.38	0.035	1.64	0.505
Age	1.04	0.087	1.04	0.087	1.03	0.439
African-American	0.08	0.000	0.19	0.000	4.07	0.162
Asian	0.87	0.323	0.94	0.651	0.61	0.179
Income	1.09	0.553	0.96	0.748	0.82	0.512
Severity	0.50	0.117	0.38	0.035	1.64	0.505

Source: Duke Human Resources
N=220
Notes: Omitted reference group is "No Care"
Asians were excluded from this analysis due to insufficient sample size
*p<0.05, **p<0.01, ***p<0.001

DISCUSSION & CONCLUSION

Although the rise of mental health carve-outs might deserve credit for reducing the costs of providing mental health care, including reducing wasteful treatment and substituting costly care with less expensive alternatives, there has been little investigation into how carve-outs might contribute to the shortcomings of fragmented care. Moreover, if carve-outs have facilitated the spread of mental health insurance benefits, the efficacy and distributive consequences of such insurance also deserve greater scrutiny. Our investigations into consumption patterns and health outcomes under carved-out mental health insurance suggest that mental health carve-outs are associated with many of the costs of fragmentation.

We first find that insureds vary widely in how they receive mental health care. Care is received from GPs, hospitals, and mental health outpatient providers, and the consumption rates of each of these services vary widely across race and class, with non-Whites and low-income workers less likely to receive specialized care. We also find low and varied adherence rates following hospitalization, with non-White and low-income workers exhibiting a lower likelihood of receiving outpatient care following a hospitalization for a mental health diagnosis. The post-hospitalization findings are striking because upon discharge, every patient is instructed to seek outpatient mental health care.

Moreover, if mental health carve-outs, in addition to fragmenting the delivery of care, are also responsible for the expansion of mental health insurance, we observe that those benefits channel more benefits to White and high-income individuals than their non-White and low-income coworkers. Non-Whites and low-income individuals do not take advantage of their mental health benefits at the same rates as their White and more affluent coworkers, and to the degree that they seek care for mental illnesses, they are more likely to seek care from general practitioners, whose services are generally covered by standard insurance benefits. Differences in consumption patterns across race are also evident among those who are hospitalized, both before and after hospitalization. These findings sound a sharp warning to those who advocate mental health parity legislation or other mandates of mental health insurance—especially those who do so claiming that mandates equalize health benefits across race and class—since these results suggest that expanding mental health benefits increases regressive and undesired wealth transfers.

Perhaps most intriguing are our findings concerning how consumption disparities translate into health outcomes. Despite significant differences in consumption patterns, especially between African-Americans and Whites but also between Asians and Whites and across income, we find no evidence that these differences affect the probability of hospitalizations for mental illnesses. Specifically, receiving care from a mental health provider does not reduce the probability of hospitalization, and following a hospitalization, receiving outpatient care from a mental health provider does not reduce the probability of rehospitalization. In sum, we find that White and affluent workers take greater advantage of the mental health insurance benefit than their non-White and lower-income co-workers, that non-Whites, especially African-Americans, are significantly more likely to seek care from general practitioners than from mental health care providers, and that there is no statistically significant evidence that receiving outpatient care from a mental health care provider reduces the likelihood of adverse mental health. In short, we find nothing to temper the provisional conclusions in *Insurance Expansions*.

The limitations of these results should be recognized. The studied population works in a university setting, and it is unclear how generalizable the findings are. Moreover, relying on hospitalizations as a measure for adverse mental illnesses is fairly coarse, and more sensitive measurements—such as lost workdays or surveyed responses—would improve our ability to measure effectiveness. More important, it is not clear what drives these results. The potential causes for the consumption disparities range from different attitudes towards necessary care, enmeshed in ethnic histories with health care providers or cultural attitudes towards mental illnesses, to different preferences and needs for care, to discriminatory referral practices and the effectiveness of care. Much more needs to be known about how individuals engage with their insurance benefits and health care providers and whether those benefits and providers meet the needs of the insureds. Many of these questions can be further explored with employer claims data, and we also hope to supplement these econometric investigations with surveys and focus groups that inquire into attitudes and practices that shape health care-seeking behavior. Given the complexity of the behavior we studied, employing multiple methodologies and several data sources might be necessary before arriving at meaningful conclusions about mental health interventions and benefits policies.

Nonetheless, these studies yield findings that raise serious questions about the provision of mental health insurance. Carve-outs appear to facilitate some of the downsides of fragmentation, and mandating mental health benefits, as Congress (like many state legislatures) has done again, amounts to transfer payments from non-Whites to Whites and from low-income to higher-income workers. Before insurance expansions spread further, in part fueled by carve-outs, serious attention should be given to studying how insurance benefits and our fragmented health care system can improve mental health outcomes without charging vulnerable populations for services they do not want or need.

13. FROM VISIBLE HARM TO RELATIVE RISK
Centralization and Fragmentation of Pharmacovigilance

ARTHUR DAEMMRICH AND JEREMY GREENE

INTRODUCTION: EFFECTS OF ADVERSE REACTIONS

At the age of three when my mother began to sew small coats and ponchos for me and my arms pretty much didn't even stick out, people would stop in front of my stroller, stare, and say, "Oh, my God!" I mean, at that point you figure out pretty quickly that something isn't right![1]
– Carina Hedtke, radio interview, June 2007

My Doc took me off Avandia. I was only taking 2.5mg daily. After about 10 days my fasting BG is up about 15 points and after meal readings seem higher than before. Wish for some solid info on this drug, but probably will have to wait a couple of years.[2]
– "RB" posting to alt.support.diabetes, July 2007

Adverse drug reactions pose distinct but potentially catastrophic risks to patients, physicians, pharmaceutical firms, and regulators. Between the early 1960s and the present, national systems were built to collect, standardize, and respond to individual reports of side effects, with the Food and Drug Administration (FDA) playing the central role in the United States. In recent years, however, this centralized approach to the collection and analysis of adverse events through doctor-initiated case reports has been superseded by innovative, though episodic pharmacoepidemiological studies of large databases that identify the probability of side effects in a population. This chapter advances a historical comparison of these two methods—individual case reports and population-based studies—and draws attention to the fragmentation of the institutional basis for

The authors gratefully acknowledge helpful comments from Einer Elhauge, Jerry Avorn, Daniel Carpenter, Harry M. Marks, Charles Rosenberg, and participants of the conference "Our Fragmented Healthcare System" at Harvard Law School's Petrie-Flom Center in the preparation of this chapter

1. Oli's Abendshow, Internet radio interview of 20 June 2007, *available at* http://www.yourjournal.de/artikel/95-50-jarhre-contergan.html(last visited May 2008).

2. RB posting to Google Group, 1 July 2007 http://groups.google.com/group/alt.support.diabetes (last visited May 2008).

assessing pharmaceutical risk. Our analysis of the evolution of techniques for identifying and responding to adverse drug reactions suggests the need for greater regulatory state involvement in the integration of case report and statistical analysis. Despite the appeal of fragmented post-market drug safety studies, centralization may be necessary to achieve faster and better integrated pharmacovigilance in the present era of large-scale pharmaceutical use for chronic conditions.

Over fifty years ago, in fall 1957, the small pharmaceutical manufacturer Chemie Grünenthal introduced Contergan (thalidomide) to the German market. Initially marketed as a sedative and sold over-the-counter until 1959, once pregnant women began to use it to mitigate morning sickness it caused arguably the twentieth century's worst drug disaster. Ms. Hedtke, quoted above, is one of approximately ten thousand children born with thalidomide-induced deformities in the early 1960s. Even though cases were concentrated in northern Europe, especially Germany, thalidomide children visibly demonstrated a failure of medical and government authorities worldwide to protect a vulnerable population from drug side effects. In the aftermath of the drug's withdrawal, many countries tightened standards for pre-market clinical testing, established formal approval procedures for new drugs conditional on proof of safety and efficacy, and designed systems to collect reports of adverse reactions and warn physicians of high-risk drugs.

"RB," also quoted above, is a diabetic whose physician changed his/her medication in the wake of reports warning of increased cardiovascular risks from Avandia (rosiglitazone). First marketed in the United States in 1999, by 2007 some sixty million prescriptions had been written for this oral glycemic control agent. Several studies in 2006 and early 2007—the findings of which were disputed by the manufacturer, GlaxoSmithKline—suggested that the drug was associated with an increased risk of myocardial infarction. Concern with Avandia's safety grew to the point that when Henry Waxman (D-California) held a Congressional hearing in May of 2007, he began by suggesting "millions of diabetics who have taken Avandia have not been well served by our regulatory system."[3] An FDA advisory committee convened to address the issue of rosiglitazone's safety voted twenty to three that it increased cardiac ischemic risk, but then recommended in a twenty-two to one vote that the drug remain on the market.[4]

What unites these two cases is the tremendous power that prescription drugs have to help or harm the bodies of their consumers. What differentiates them

---

3. H. A. Waxman, Hearing on FDA's Role in Evaluation of Avandia's Safety, 110th Congress, House of Representatives Committee on Oversight and Government Reform (6 June 2007): 3.

4. C. J. Rosen, *The Rosiglitazone Story—Lessons from an FDA Advisory Committee Meeting,* 357(9) NEW ENG. J. MED. 844–846(2007).

are fifty years of changes in pharmaceutical research, regulation, marketing, and approaches to post-market risk identification. In the thalidomide case, proof of the drug's embryopathy was established through the compilation of thousands of individual case reports and documentation of a correlation between sales and rates of birth defects. The ascribed link between heart attacks and rosiglitazone, in contrast, was uncovered primarily through statistical analyses that differentiate drug-caused events from ones that occur for other reasons in a high-risk patient population. Contrasts between these approaches are deeply intertwined with changes in the institutional structure of regulating post-market risk. A critical challenge for pharmaceutical regulation in coming years, especially in light of the emerging "sentinel initiative" at the FDA, will be to integrate these two methods and overcome fragmented approaches to post-market data capture and analysis.[5]

CONTEXTUALIZING RISK AND REGULATION

Side effects from prescription drugs confound public expectations for safety in today's era of advanced technological medicine. In light of the media attention given to Vioxx, Avandia, and other recent cases, many consumers feel that adverse drug reactions are occurring at an increasing rate of frequency.[6] In fact, voluntary and mandated market withdrawals comprised just 3.2 percent of approved drugs in the decade between 1980 and 1990, and 3.5 percent between 1990 and 2000. This figure has not changed significantly since 2000. Although drug withdrawals are not rising by statistically significant measures, seven blockbuster drugs with annual sales of $1 billion or greater were pulled from the market due to adverse reactions since 2001.[7] The occurrence of unexpected side effects on such a large scale, which even extensive pre-market testing was unable to prevent, has implications for nearly every component of the health care system. In the United States, adverse drug reactions are estimated to cost $10 billion annually in additional health care costs, and international studies have indicated they generate 6.5 percent of new hospital admissions.[8]

---

5. Food and Drug Administration, "The Sentinel Initiative: National Strategy for Monitoring Medical Product Safety," (Washington, D.C.: FDA, 2008).

6. S. Frantz, "Pharma's Year of Trouble and Strife," *Nature Reviews Drug Discovery* 5 (January 2006): 7–9; S. Wang, "Drug Safety Data: Too Much Information?" *The Wall Street Journal* (9 December 2008).

7. G. Steven Burrill, "Biotech 2006 Life Sciences: A Changing Prescription," presented at BIO 2006; *see also*: G. Steven Burrill, *Biotech 2006—Life Sciences: A Changing Prescription* (San Francisco: S. Burrill & Co., 2006): 260–315.

8. L. Kohn, J. Corrigan and M. Donaldson (eds.), *To Err is Human: Building a Safer Health System* (Washington, D.C.: Institute of Medicine, 1999): 26–48; M. Pirmohamed, et al.,

Adverse reactions concern patients, regulators, physicians, and the industry for other reasons as well, ranging from the worry that patients will discontinue pharmaceuticals and turn to less rigorously studied treatments to the disquieting notion that over a half-century of risk mitigation efforts have not produced accurate early warning signals of adverse reactions to approved pharmaceuticals. Despite extensive pre-market testing of new pharmaceuticals, side effects continue to pose a health risk for individuals, a financial risk to drug companies, a visible challenge to physicians' mandate to "do no harm" and a political risk to the FDA.[9] These are different kinds of risk and are part of what makes the post-market arena so difficult to monitor and regulate. This chapter explores efforts at capturing risk signals and reducing adverse drug reactions for drugs on the market in the United States since the thalidomide tragedy of the early 1960s. Specifically, it draws a longitudinal contrast between monitoring pharmaceuticals by collecting individual case reports and new approaches to pharmacoepidemiology, including meta-analysis.

Pharmacovigilance has drawn significant scholarly and policy attention in recent years ranging from studies of the costs of side effects to proposals for new or reformed government regulation of the post-market.[10] Yet little scholarly attention has contextualized recent events or analyzed post-market risks in light of institutional trajectories. This chapter thus contributes to the emerging work on adverse reaction monitoring systems through a historical-institutional analysis. Our goal is to suggest how physicians, industry, and regulators can assess risks and respond effectively, especially in light of the fragmented institutional structure of the U.S. healthcare system.

A central question to post-market regulation concerns the evidentiary threshold for withdrawing a drug from the market, either voluntarily by the company or under FDA mandate. Market withdrawals are significant interventions that pose financial and reputational challenges to manufacturers. The history of pharmaceutical regulation suggests they are infrequent and not undertaken lightly. Likewise, identifying drugs as risky, especially when harm is visible only at the level of the population, poses a dilemma for medical practice. Physicians are trained from early on to reason by analogy; a drug that works in a patient with a

---

"Adverse Drug Reactions as cause of Admission to Hospital: Prospective Analysis of 18,820 Patients" *British Medical Journal* 329 (3 July 2004): 15–19.

9. A. Daemmrich, *Pharmacopolitics: Drug Regulation in the United States and Germany* (Chapel Hill: University of North Carolina Press, 2004): 116–150.

10. C. L. Bennett, et al., "Evaluation of Serious Adverse Drug Reactions," *Archives of Internal Medicine* 167 (2007): 1041–1049; Institute of Medicine, *Adverse Drug Event Reporting* (Washington, D.C.: National Academies Press, 2007); Institute of Medicine, *The Future of Drug Safety* (Washington, D.C.: National Academies Press, 2007); Institute of Medicine, *To Err is Human: Building a Safer Health System* (Washington, D.C.: National Academies Press, 2000).

particular profile will work in another with the same disease and similar characteristics.[11] But translating data from populations to patients has long posed a challenge to physicians in practice, and many clinicians are uncertain about how to incorporate findings from pharmacoepidemiology into their prescribing decisions for individual patients.[12]

A useful analogue to the present situation is found in the scholarly literature on environmental risk, which examines how to regulate in light of probabilistic rather than directly observed risks. Numerous studies have explored miscalculation by the lay public and even by experts of which activities or technological systems pose greater risks and under what circumstances they may fail.[13] Research in the field of science and technology studies has extended this work with findings that the lay public identifies risk both related to individual decision choices and to more holistic views of human interactions with hybrid social and technical systems.[14] Using statistical probabilities to guide human choices or behaviors often requires counter-intuitive thinking, and case narratives frequently dominate policy discussions. Adverse drug reactions as identified through new methods of pharmacovigilance illustrate a similar disconnect between general probabilistic risk and specific individual decisions. Furthermore, the epistemological transformation of pharmacovigilance currently underway will have follow-on impacts in other domains of risk management within the fragmented U.S. healthcare system.

CONTROLLING VISIBLE HARM

Although largely unregulated by governments in the nineteenth and early twentieth centuries, pharmaceutical firms have long operated under controls instituted by professional bodies, including national formularies that set manufacturing standards and occasionally exposed fallacious claims made concerning

---

11. C. Rosenberg, "The Tyranny of Diagnosis: Specific Entities and Individual Experience," *The Milbank Quarterly* 80 (2002): 237–260.

12. J. Greene, *Prescribing by Numbers: Drugs and the Definition of Disease* (Baltimore: Johns Hopkins University Press, 2007).

13. P. Slovic, B. Fischhoff, and S. Lichtenstein, "Rating the Risks," *Environment* 2 (1979): 14–39; C. Perrow, *Normal Accidents: Living With High-Risk Technologies* (New York: Basic Books, 1984); A. Wildavsky, *Searching for Safety* (New Brunswick: Transaction Books, 1988).

14. U. Beck, *Risk Society: Towards a New Modernity* (London: Sage Publications, 1992); B. Wynne and A. Irwin *Misunderstanding Science? The Public Reconstruction of Science and Technology* (Cambridge: Cambridge University Press, 1996); S. Jasanoff, *Designs on Nature: Science and Democracy in Europe and the United States* (Princeton: Princeton University Press, 2005).

medical ingredients. The development of diphtheria antitoxin in the 1890s and subsequent cases of inactive or contaminated doses led Health Ministries in Germany and France to test and oversee biologicals; likewise, the U.S. Hygienic Laboratory was authorized to license manufacturers under the 1902 Biologics Control Act.[15] Government authority to remove medicines from the market or constrain advertising claims, however, was limited because legislatures at the time were eager to foster national industrial champions in the face of international competition.[16]

The American Medical Association (AMA), by contrast, took steps to monitor the array of new pharmaceuticals coming on the market and to intervene in cases of significant side effects by forming the Council on Pharmacy and Chemistry in 1905.Council members, who included pharmacologists, chemists, and physicians, published standards for drug quality and created a voluntary "Seal of Acceptance" program in 1930 to evaluate drug safety and efficacy.[17]

In 1938, in the wake of the much-publicized Elixir of Sulfanilamide disaster—in which over one hundred people died from a liquid form of an antibiotic sulfa drug that had been prepared using ethylene glycol as a solvent—the U.S. Congress passed the Federal Food, Drug, and Cosmetic Act.[18] The Act expanded the FDA's earlier 1906 mandate to prevent misbranding and check products for adulteration. Manufacturers now had to carry out tests before marketing new pharmaceuticals and the FDA had sixty days to review applications, file objections, and request additional information. The post-market arena also began to take shape as the FDA established a boundary between testing and market. Nevertheless, the FDA had little authority and no resources to collect and act on reports of side effects or mandate withdrawals.

---

15. C. Gradmann, *Redemption, Danger, and Risk: The History of Anti-Bacterial Chemotherapy and the Transformation of Tuberculin, in* THE RISKS OF MEDICAL INNOVATION: RISK PERCEPTION AND ASSESSMENT IN HISTORICAL CONTEXT, 53–70 (Ulrich Tröhler & Thomas Schlich eds., 2006); Ramunas A. Kondratas, *Biologics Control Act of 1902, in* THE EARLY YEARS OF FEDERAL FOOD AND DRUG CONTROL, 8–27 (James Harvey Young ed., 1982).

16. BIG BUSINESS AND THE WEALTH OF NATIONS (Alfred D. Chandler, Jr., eds., 1997); ULRIKE BAUMHEIER, STAAT UND PHARMAINDUSTRIE: SICHERHEITSKONTROLLE, PREISREGULIERUNG, UND INDUSTRIEFÖRDERUNG IM INTERNATIONALEN VERGLEICH (1994); JOHN J. BEER, EMERGENCE OF THE GERMAN DYE INDUSTRY (1959).

17. For more on the Council's history, see HARRY M. MARKS, THE PROGRESS OF EXPERIMENT: SCIENCE AND THERAPEUTIC REFORM IN THE UNITED STATES, 1900–1990 at 32–41 (1997); HARRY F. DOWLING, MEDICINES FOR MAN: THE DEVELOPMENT, REGULATION, AND USE OF PRESCRIPTION DRUGS 154–185 (1970).

18. CHARLES O. JACKSON, FOOD AND DRUG LEGISLATION IN THE NEW DEAL (1970); Marks, *supra note* 17.

By the mid-1950s, the AMA increasingly found itself caught between acting as a non-governmental regulator and serving as a formal voice of the profession. In 1955, the Council dropped its Seal of Acceptance Program and started to compile a registry of adverse reactions. In place of evaluating new drugs as they came on the market, the renamed Council on Drugs sought to position itself as a national monitor of patients' experiences with pharmaceuticals. Severe side effects associated with the antibiotic chloramphenicol provided additional justification for this organizational change.[19] The Council collected reports and developed an AMA policy that recommended restricted use of the drug.

The Committee's name was changed in 1960 to the Committee on Adverse Reactions and its mandate was broadened to include the compilation and review of all side effects from marketed drugs. Committee members worked with the AMA to develop an official registry of side effects and expected physicians in private practice to report to the centralized site. In Germany and other European countries, national medical associations established similar registries in the 1940s and 1950s. As events associated with the Thalidomide tragedy would reveal in 1961, however, these registries were incomplete. Even when they could identify a risk, the associations could only influence physician prescriptions; they lacked any authority to force manufacturers to withdraw products.

Two methodological issues plagued side effects registries maintained by medical associations and would carry over to challenge efforts at the FDA and other national regulators monitoring approved drugs. First, they relied on physicians to volunteer information. Studies carried out in the mid-1960s, however, revealed that the AMA registry had received case reports from only 2 percent of American physicians.[20] As a professional association, the AMA had no mechanism to enforce data collection.

Second, the dilemma of a missing denominator undermined efforts to turn registries operated by medical associations into a tool for influencing physicians' prescriptions. AMA committees could not determine how many patients had taken a questionable drug. Efforts to calculate risk profiles were hampered because reports of side effects did not reveal the incidence or frequency of adverse reactions. Although the Council on Drugs assembled a cadre of physicians with practical experience and broad medical expertise, it lacked the organizational structure, financial support, and regulatory authority necessary to operate a successful warning system about drugs on the market.

---

19. THOMAS MAEDER, ADVERSE REACTIONS (1994); Cases were tabulated some years later: *Blood Dyscrasias Associated with Chloramphenicol (Chloromycetin) Therapy* 172 JAMA 2044–45 (30 April 1960); C.M. Huguley, et al., *Drug-related Blood Dyscrasias* 177 JAMA 23–26 (8 July 1961).

20. *The Suspect and the Innocent*, 196 JAMA 160 (2 May 1966).

A VISIBLE TRAGEDY: THALIDOMIDE

Thalidomide was first synthesized in Germany in 1953, underwent laboratory, pharmacological, and clinical testing, and then was marketed by Chemie Grünenthal as an anti-anxiety treatment and sedative starting in fall 1957. Reports in medical and scientific journals prior to its marketing emphasized its safety. Scientists at the firm were unable to determine a lethal dose (LD_{50}) for half of the test animals, and tests in mice, rats, guinea pigs, and rabbits over thirty days revealed no visible changes to white or red blood cells.[21] Clinical studies suggested that it produced a "natural" sleep with no grogginess or other "after-effects."[22] Arriving in the midst of West Germany's post-war economic boom, the sedative seemingly offered an escape from the stresses of modern life. Grünenthal picked up on this notion and advertising for the drug in medical journals shifted gradually from lists of conditions against a simple background to depictions of bucolic nature scenes.

By 1960 the combination of increasingly sophisticated advertising and widely disseminated reports of low toxicity made thalidomide the top-selling sedative in Germany. Its sales of DM 12.4 million were five times those of the leading competitor.[23] According to one estimate, 700,000 Germans took it on a regular basis. Some parents even gave the drug to their children, earning it the nickname "West Germany's baby-sitter."[24] Adverse reactions were rare, though a few patients complained of persistent tingling in their extremities and the feeling that their arms and legs had gone to sleep. Nerve specialists Ralph Voss and Horst Frenkel reported those cases of "peripheral neuritis" cases to the company and to the German Medical Association in 1959, after which thalidomide was shifted to prescription-only status.[25]

In 1959 and 1960, a wave of children were born with abnormalities that included stunted arms and legs, misshapen hands and feet, and damaged internal organs. Because of diminutive long bones between the shoulder and hand or hip and foot, victims' extremities appeared to connect directly to their torsos.

---

21. W. Kunz et al., *N-Phthalyl-glutaminsäure-imid: Experimentelle Untersuchungen an einem neuen synthetischen Produkt mit sedativem Eigenschaften*, 6 ARZNEIMITTELFORSCHUNG 426–430 (1956).

22. H. Jung, Klinische Erfahrungen mit einem neuen Sedativum, 6 ARZNEIMITTELFORSCHUNG 430–434 (1956).

23. T. STEPHENS AND R. BRYNNER, DARK REMEDY: THE IMPACT OF THALIDOMIDE AND ITS REVIVAL AS A VITAL MEDICINE (2001).

24. D. WENZEL & K. WENZEL, DER CONTERGAN-PROZEβ (I): VERURSACHTE THALIDOMID NERVENSCHÄDEN UND MIβBILDUNGEN? (1968); H. Taussig, *A Study of the German Outbreak of Phocomelia*, 180 JAMA 1106–1114 (30 June 1962).

25. H. SJÖSTRÖM AND R. NILSSON, THALIDOMIDE AND THE POWER OF THE DRUG COMPANIES 71–110 (1972); H. Frenkel, *Contergan-Nebenwirkungen*, 86 Deutsche Medizinische Wochenschrift 970–975 (6 May 1961).

German physicians confronted with these children discussed cases at professional meetings; however no obvious causal agent was identified in the initial reports.[26] The pediatrician and chair for Human Genetics at the University of Hamburg, Widukind Lenz, gradually emerged as a pivotal figure as he began compiling detailed index cases from his own patients as well as from other clinics in the area.

Among other queries, Lenz began specifically asking mothers if they had taken the popular new drug Contergan during the autumn of 1961. As the number of cases increased, his suspicions coalesced around a pharmaceutical rather than environmental cause. Based on the case reports, he focused on drug use during the second month of pregnancy, when the limbs are formed.[27] He also contacted fellow doctors and directors of medical institutes around Hamburg and Kiel to ask if they had seen similar cases. Within a short time, Lenz had collected reports of thirty-nine deformities linked to thalidomide use and then reported his findings in a conference talk at the 1961 meeting of the Society for Pediatric Medicine. The following week, officials from the Federal Health Office brought Lenz together with Grünenthal representatives for a six-hour meeting concerning thalidomide's market status. Company officials disputed Lenz's data and even succeeded in having him removed from the room for part of the meeting. Nevertheless, the company withdrew thalidomide from the German market on 26 November 1961.[28]

During the next several years, Lenz and other physicians accumulated and analyzed further evidence linking thalidomide to birth defects. Their initial publications relied on individual case studies and noted the association with thalidomide as tenuous. For example, in a January 1962 *Lancet* article, Lenz claimed that he had observed over fifty cases. In addition, he invoked a network of contacts in Germany, Belgium, England, and Sweden that compiled 115 cases in which thalidomide was thought to be the causal agent.[29] By the mid-1960s, he had compiled information on several thousand cases. In a criminal case that German federal prosecutors brought against company scientists and executives starting in 1967, Lenz testified that he knew of 1,963 cases from West Germany alone, and had additional records of cases in England, Japan, Sweden, and the Netherlands.[30] Findings published in 1970 included graphs correlating striking

---

26. W. Kosenow and R. Pfeiffer, "Micromelia, Haemangioma and Duodenal Stenosis Exhibit," *Monatsschrift für Kinderheilkunde* 109 (1961): 227.

27. Strafkammer des Landgerichts Aachen, *Contergan-Prozeß*, Testimony by Widukind Lenz (12 August 1968): 32.

28. G. Gemballa, *Der dreifache Skandal: 30 Jahre nach Contergan, eine Dokumentation.* (Hamburg: Luchterhand Verlag, 1993).

29. W. Lenz, "Thalidomide and Congenital Abnormalities," *Lancet* (6 January 1962): 45.

30. Strafkammer des Landgerichts Aachen, *Contergan-Prozeß*, Testimony by Widukind Lenz (12 August 1968): 32–40.

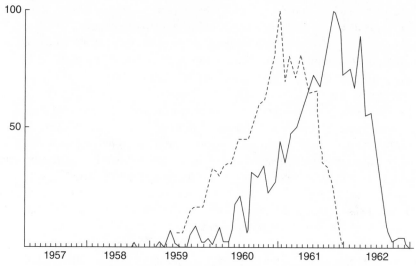

Graph showing the relation between the malformations of the thalidomide type and the sales of the thalidomide (figures for Germany excluding Hamburg)

- - - - - Thalidomide sales (January 1961 = 100)
———— 845 abnormalities of the thalidomide type (October 1961 = 100)

peaks and equally stark declines in the numbers of phocomelia cases and amount of thalidomide sold between the late 1950s and mid-1960s.[31] While Lenz's data was widely accepted in the medical community, and the biologically causal link between thalidomide and birth defects was later demonstrated in laboratory studies, some critics argued that case evidence could only show correlation, not causation. Yet this methodological dispute between case reports and proof of causation was overwhelmed by the visible appearance of birth defects and their sharp decline once thalidomide was withdrawn.[32]

The wave of birth defects that resulted from pregnant women taking thalidomide forced physicians and regulators to confront the risks that accompany therapeutic advances. The failure of governments to protect a vulnerable segment of their population—mothers and infants—led many countries to strengthen regulatory controls over drug testing and marketing. In the United States, the drug had been delayed from broad marketing by a vigilant FDA official.[33] Though prevented from wide marketing, the U.S. licensee had sent

---

31. W. Lenz, "Übersetzungsfehler, falsche Zitate und Widersprüche," *Deutsches Ärzteblatt* (12 September 1970).

32. A. Daemmrich, "A Tale of Two Experts: Thalidomide and Political Engagement in the United States and West Germany," *Social History of Medicine* 15 (2002): 137–158.

33. P. J. Hilts, Protecting America's Health: The FDA, Business, and One Hundred Years of Regulation (2004).

samples to 1,200 doctors with the recommendation that they give it to any patient complaining of stress or having trouble sleeping. According to government tabulations made in August 1962, nearly 16,000 patients, 624 of whom were pregnant, took thalidomide tablets; through good fortune only 12 children were born with phocomelia.[34] The resulting scandal precipitated the 1962 Kefauver Harris Act, which strengthened the FDA's role as gatekeeper and guarantor of efficacy and safety of pharmaceutical products. When implementing the Act, the FDA focused its regulatory authority primarily on structuring pre-market testing into phases I, II, and III, and setting procedures for reviewing new drug applications. The post-market arena, by contrast, was largely left to opportunistic case reporting.

STANDARDIZING THE CASE REPORT

The 1962 Kefauver-Harris Amendments to the Food and Drug Act marked a significant turning point in pharmaceutical regulation with the FDA gaining responsibility also for ensuring safety and efficacy after approval of a new drug application. In fact, the notion of "post-market monitoring" hinges on a formal approval, which largely dates to the 1962 Act. The FDA could prevent or delay marketing before 1962, but as long as test results had been sent to the agency for a 60-day review period, companies did not need a formal statement of approval in order to begin marketing. Among other provisions, the 1962 Act included a new subsection stating that for approved drugs, the manufacturer must establish records and make reports to FDA of "data relating to clinical experience and other data or information, received or otherwise obtained."[35]

The agency previously had begun to monitor drugs on the market through a pilot program with five hospitals launched in the mid-1950s. Unlike the AMA's effort to convince doctors in private practices to submit reports, the FDA initiated its adverse reaction program by collecting data from government-affiliated hospitals. Within a few years, the network expanded to include university clinics and large private hospitals. Thin national coverage was provided through the participation of six hundred hospitals by 1964, though fewer than one hundred were under formal contract by the end of the decade.[36] Also, unlike the AMA, the

---

34. U.S. Department of Health, Education, and Welfare, Food and Drug Administration, For Immediate Release 4 (1962), FDA Files AF 1-542, Accession #72A 2957, v. 10–14.

35. Kefauver-Harris Amendments to the Food and Drug Act, Pub. L. No. 87-781, 76 Stat. 783 (1962).

36. George Saiger, The Food and Drug Administration Information Center on Adverse Reactions and Hazards, presented at Drug Information Services Conference, Lexington, Kentucky, (24 February 1964); Albert Esch, *Food and Drug Administration Drug Experience*

FDA did not rely on volunteers from the medical profession; instead the agency had the resources to hire full-time staff. Yet, officials nevertheless found it a challenge to establish consistency across reports and to convince physicians and hospital administrators to send reports to Washington.

Along with criteria for clinical testing and other regulations under the 1962 Act, the agency published detailed definitions and interpretations for post-market monitoring in June 1967.[37] Manufacturers were responsible for maintaining unpublished case reports of side effects along with published reports from the medical literature. Firms also were told to keep files on the quantity of a drug in distribution. Experienced by this point with challenges to data analysis, FDA officials requested that reports be transmitted "in a manner and form that facilitates estimates of the incidence of any adverse effects reported to be associated with the use of the drug."[38] The agency also distinguished among degrees of severity of adverse reactions, and the speed with which companies were required to report to the government. Cases in which a drug caused an "unexpected" side effect, injury, toxicity, sensitivity, or in which the expected pharmacological activity did not occur were to be reported within fifteen days. Other kinds of information "pertinent to the safety or effectiveness of the drug" were to be reported quarterly for the first year after approval, twice in the second year, and annually thereafter.[39]

In order to evaluate and draw conclusions from the mass of resulting data, the agency developed a standardized medical terminology to codify reports. The FDA grouped adverse reactions into one of sixteen primary categories, based on individual organs or biological systems. Medical officers also could select among twenty-two secondary categories to describe impacts on patients, such as addiction or withdrawal symptoms. This process of translation and data conversion produced numerical data about the severity of any given reaction. Over the course of the next several decades, FDA officials expanded the terminology associated with adverse reactions into a complex "dictionary" that could handle wide variability in drug names and different methods for data entry that persisted despite attempts to create bureaucratic uniformity.[40]

Starting in the late 1980s, FDA's activities in the post-market area came under greater scrutiny associated with efforts to speed AIDS and cancer therapies to market. As certain pre-market testing requirements were loosened under the

Reporting System, JOURNAL OF CHEMICAL DOCUMENTATION 9 (1969): 66–70; Irvin Kerlan, *Adverse Drug Reaction Reporting: Approach to Better Patient Care,* 34 JOURNAL OF THE AMERICAN HOSPITAL ASSOCIATION 65 (1960).

37. 32 FEDERAL REGISTER 8080–89 (1967).

38. *Id.* at 8086.

39. *Id.* at 8086–7.

40. Mary B. Forbes et al., *FDA's Adverse Drug Reaction Drug Dictionary and its Role in Post-Marketing Surveillance,* 20 DRUG INFORMATION JOURNAL (1986): 135–145.

"fast-track" and "parallel-track" review systems, the agency made commitments to re-invigorate post-market monitoring.[41] Seeking to increase physicians' awareness of side effects and to recruit broader participation in voluntary reporting, FDA launched MEDWatch in 1993. The MEDWatch program was designed to simplify reporting and enroll more physicians and other health professionals in the process of gathering data on adverse reactions. According to then FDA Commissioner David Kessler, "it is not in the culture of U.S. medicine to notify the FDA about adverse events or product problems."[42] However, since the agency had no authority to regulate physician behavior, it had few options to change the culture of non-reporting other than an information campaign.

Recent changes to the doctor-patient relationship and American healthcare have compounded the agency's historical difficulties with reports about side effects. The culture of American individualism and diversity of medical information and misinformation available on the internet support patients who seek out their own treatment. According to a recent poll, eighty percent of American internet users, comprising over one-third of the total population, have searched for medical information on-line, and eight million American adults research health information on the Internet daily. Three-quarters of them do not check the date or source of health information they find online.[43]

By the 1990s, the FDA was changing its definition of patients from passive recipients of prescriptions into active consumers who required information in order to make rational choices. MEDWatch today combines data collection with information and warnings about drugs on the market. Furthermore, it is not targeted exclusively to physicians. Instead, the FDA now accepts reports directly from patients and provides public access to aggregate data on side effects. The agency recommends that patients with serious drug reactions should take the MEDWatch form to their doctor. Since "not all patients feel comfortable discussing side effects with their physicians, or have easy access to doctors," the agency devised a web-based form that the lay public can submit directly.[44] To avoid direct competition with physicians, the agency does not suggest alternative treatments or recommend palliative measures for patients' complaints. Nevertheless, in an era when patients rarely establish long-term relationships with physicians, the FDA offers itself as a trustworthy confidant for intimate medical details. At the same time, it now accepts patients as reliable and trustworthy sources of information about the effects of drugs on their bodies.

41. D. Kessler and K. Feiden, "Faster Evaluation of Vital Drugs," *Scientific American* (March 1995): 48–54.

42. D. Kessler, "Introducing MEDWatch," *JAMA* 269 (1993): 2765–2768.

43. S. Fox, *Pew Internet and American Life Project: Online Health Search 2006* (Philadelphia: Pew Charitable Trusts, 2006).

44. www.fda.gov/medwatch/report/consumer/consumer (accessed August 2009).

Operating largely in parallel to the MEDWatch program, the FDA also came to rely on post-market clinical trials sponsored by pharmaceutical companies as a means to identify adverse reactions. Widely perceived as an integral component of changes in approval procedures designed to speed drugs to market, the agency significantly increased "phase-IV" study agreements with industry during the 1980s.[45] These post-approval tests were intended to identify drug interactions and resolve questions that arose during advisory committee meetings that FDA officials found significant, but not of sufficient concern to delay an approval by requiring additional pre-market tests.

In a 1986 NEW ENGLAND JOURNAL OF MEDICINE article, an FDA official explained, "FDA monitoring of adverse reactions is primarily based on 'spontaneous' reports from practicing physicians—i.e., reports that originate from observations made in the usual practice of medicine (not derived from a formal study)".[46] Within a short time, however, FDA was requesting that sponsor firms carry out structured post-approval studies on some 45 percent of new drugs.[47] Two decades later, the voluntary nature of these studies came to the fore and both FDA and the industry came under fire. Of 1,231 post-market studies that FDA believed pharmaceutical firms had agreed to carry out, 65 percent had not even begun as of September 2006.[48] By late 2009, publicity of this fact had spurred the industry to action though over 50 percent of post-approval study commitment were either pending or delayed.[49]

Thus, in the nearly five decades since thalidomide's adverse impacts were identified, the FDA has continued to rely on spontaneous reporting of adverse events by manufacturers and physicians and a limited number of industry-funded post-marketing clinical trials to determine the risks of approved drugs.[50]

---

45. B. Richard, A. Melville, and L. Lasagna, "Postapproval Research as a Condition of Approval: An Update, 1985-1986," *Journal of Clinical Research and Drug Development* 3 (1989): 247–257.

46. Gerald Faich, *Adverse Drug Reaction Monitoring*, 314 NEW ENG. J. MED. 1589–92, quote at 1589–90 (12 June 1986).

47. OFFICE OF TECHNOLOGY ASSESSMENT, PHARMACEUTICAL R&D: COSTS, RISKS, AND REWARDS 150–51 (1993).

48. 71 FEDERAL REGISTER 10978–79 (2006); *See also*: U.S. GOVERNMENT ACCOUNTABILITY OFFICE, DRUG SAFETY: IMPROVEMENT NEEDED IN FDA'S POSTMARKET DECISION-MAKING AND OVERSIGHT PROCESS 28 (2006); THE FUTURE OF DRUG SAFETY: PROMOTING AND PROTECTING THE HEALTH OF THE PUBLIC 55 (Alina Baciu et al. eds., 2006).

49. Author's search of FDA database, "Postmarket Requirements and Commitments for Human Drugs," http://www.accessdata.fda.gov/scripts/cder/pmc/index.cfm (last visited September 2009).

50. M. COHEN, MEDICATION ERRORS 2nd edition (2007); A. Daemmrich, *Pharmacovigilance and the Missing Denominator: The Changing Context of Pharmaceutical Risk Mitigation*, 49 PHARMACY IN HISTORY 61–75 (2007).

This method, suited perhaps for detecting another thalidomide, has proven insufficient in our current era of extensive use of prescription drugs for chronic disorders.

IDENTIFYING RELATIVE RISKS

Since the early 1990s, pharmacoepidemiology has developed techniques for carrying out therapeutic assessments falling between single case reports and structured clinical trials.[51] Although its origin as a field dates to observational studies carried out in the 1960s and 1970s, it has more recently taken center stage in post-market surveillance through new methods for studying large human populations.[52] Seeking to solve the longstanding dilemmas of the missing denominators from case reports and the wide variety of potential confounders in observational studies, pharmacoepidemiologists have developed sophisticated techniques for calculating the rate at which side effects occur in populations that take a particular drug. FDA generally has welcomed this approach. A 2005 guidance document thus detailed what the agency considers appropriate methods for estimating the number of patients and time of exposure to a drug. It also suggested ways of avoiding "confounding by indication," provided a general protocol for pharmacoepidemiologic studies, and suggested that practitioners carry out more than one study to ensure robust results.[53] By more accurately calculating populations that have actually taken a drug and the frequency of specific adverse reactions, pharmacoepidemiology has made important contributions to drug safety. Yet the use of findings from the field of pharmacoepidemiology by practicing physicians is often complicated by the distance between the tangible individual patient and the abstraction of population-based results.

Controversy concerning the GlaxoSmithKline drug Avandia illustrates some of the tensions arising from our current era's simultaneous attention to consumers as individual patients and as data points in probabilistic risk assessments. Avandia belongs to the thiazolidinediones, a relatively new group of antidiabetic drugs believed to act by increasing cellular receptivity to insulin. The first thiazolidinedione, Pfizer's Rezulin, was released with much fanfare in 1997 and was one of the first new drugs launched after FDA loosened restrictions on broadcast

---

51. B. L. Strom, *Pharmacoepidemiology*, 2nd edition (Chichester: John Wiley and Sons, 1995): 3-13; see also, J. Avorn, *Powerful Medicines: The Benefits, Risks, and Costs of Prescription Drugs* (New York: Alfred A. Knopf, 2004), 102–125.

52. A. Hartzema, "The Beginnings of Pharmacoepidemiology in The Annals," *The Annals of Pharmacotherapy* 40 (2006): 1647–8.

53. FDA, "Guidance for Industry: Good Pharmacovigilance Practices and Pharmacoepidemiologic Assessment" (March 2005).

advertising for pharmaceuticals.[54] Despite reports of drug-associated fulminant liver toxicity that began to accumulate the same year it was launched, Rezulin was heavily promoted through direct-to-consumer (DTC) advertisements along with traditional physician-specific marketing. Two years after its launch, Rezulin had become one of the ten most commonly mentioned drugs in physician office visits.[55] At the time of its withdrawal from the market in 2000 at the request of the FDA, Rezulin had captured nearly one of every three prescriptions for oral antidiabetic medications.

Although Avandia was launched as a second-entry into the thiazolidinedione market in 1999, it developed a large market after Rezulin's withdrawal. Like Rezulin, it was promoted in print and on television, including a well-known series of advertisements featuring the actress Jane Seymour and singer Della Reese. Although some deaths from liver disease were noted in patients once the drug was approved, a follow-up FDA review did not find sufficient evidence for a class warning.[56] Correspondingly, the manufacturer sought to reassure consumers of its safety: "There's a safer way to help treat your type-2 diabetes," a full page ad in the Wall Street Journal announced, claiming Avandia was "a much safer alternative to Rezulin."[57] Although its safety profile would be somewhat marred by associated weight gain and the risk of exacerbating congestive heart failure, Avandia quickly rose to the top of GlaxoSmithKline's portfolio. By 2002, Avandia was the fourth most-advertised pharmaceutical in the U.S. market and by 2006 sales had risen to $3.4 billion, putting it second only to Advair for GlaxoSmithKline sales and into the therapeutic regimen of millions of diabetes patients worldwide.

In June 2007, Steven Nissen and Karen Wolski of the Cleveland Clinic published an influential meta-analysis in the *New England Journal of Medicine* suggesting that Avandia use was associated with a 43 percent increase in risk of heart attack or associated cardiovascular events.[58] A prior meta-analysis of eighteen clinical trials by the Cochrane Collaboration had raised similar concerns of increased cardiovascular risk in 2006, and the Nissen analysis had access to

---

54. *Federal Register*, 62, no. 155 (August 12, 1997): 43171.

55. J. Dickinson, "DTC Boosts Prescribing of New Drugs," *Medical Marketing and Media* 36, no. 10 (October 2001): 36–38.

56. "Avandia Liver Reports won't Affect Labeling," *Medical Marketing and Media* 35, no. 3 (March 2000): 32.

57. "Firms Quick to Promote Alternatives to Rezulin," *Medical Marketing and Media* 35 no. 5 (May 2000): 18–20.

58. S. E. Nissen and K.Wolski, "Effect of Rosiglitazone on the Risk of Myocardial Infarction and Death from Cardiovascular Causes," *New England Journal of Medicine* 356 (14 June 2007): 2457–2471; A. Von Eschenbach, "Avandia," 110th Congress, House of Representatives Committee on Oversight and Government Reform (6 June 2007) http://www.fda.gov/ola/2007/Avandia060607.html (accessed 30 October 2007).

additional unpublished trials made public in the wake of a lawsuit against GSK.[59] Though not publicly known at the time, GSK had already performed patient-level analyses of their clinical trials in 2005 and 2006 which suggested an increase in ischemic events. Nevertheless, GlaxoSmithKline publicly disputed the Nissen findings by citing results from three prospective multi-center randomized controlled trials, ADOPT, DREAM, and RECORD and by suggesting that meta-analysis lacked suffieicnt rigor to reach conclusions about adverse events.[60] As of fall 2007, the RECORD trial's independent Safety Monitoring Board had not found cases of safety risk among the trial population.[61] But as Nissen and others countered, analysis of data GSK previously supplied to the FDA suggested a 30 percent increase in the risk of heart attack associated with Avandia.

Practically overnight, newspapers and popular magazines projected estimates of how many preventable cardiovascular events had conceivably occurred as a result of the drug's consumption, and enterprising tort lawyers sought to recruit Avandia consumers who had suffered heart attacks while on the drug. At the same time, critics of the Nissen meta-analysis suggested that the relative risk increase of 43 percent was a misleading statistic and the situation should instead be understood in terms of the much smaller-appearing 0.1 percent increase in absolute risk.[62] Others argued that meta-analysis had no place in the assessment of a drug's safety profile. In contrast to the monstrous imagery of deformed babies associated with thalidomide, these contested numerical markers of risk required intellectual work and contextualization on the part of physicians and patients before they could be transported from a level of population risk into pragmatic decisions about whether or not to continue a particular therapeutic regimen in an individual patient. Nonetheless, many physicians proceeded with caution and in the financial quarter following the Nissen article and the special meeting of the FDA advisory committee, Avandia's sales fell by 31 percent, leaving it with 7.4 percent of total retail prescriptions in the oral antidiabetic market, down from 11.7 percent at its peak in May 2007.[63] Sales dropped by an additional 29 percent in 2008.[64]

---

59. B. Richter et al., "Rosiglitazone for type 2 diabetes mellitus," *Cochrane Database of Systematic Reviews* 2 (2006).

60. GlaxoSmithKline, "GlaxoSmithKline Responds to NEJM Article on Avandia," 21 May 2007, www.gsk.com/media/avandia-in-the-news.htm (accessed October 2007).

61. P. D. Home et al., "Rosiglitazone Evaluated for Cardiovascular Outcomes—An Interim Analysis," *New England Journal of Medicine* 357 (2007): 28–38.

62. C. Arnst, "The High Cost of the Diabetes Controversy," *Business Week* online edition (1 June 2007).

63. GlaxoSmithKline, "Results Announcement for the Second Quarter 2007," 25 July 2007, www.gsk.com/investors/quarterly_results.htm (accessed October 2007).

64. GlaxoSmithKline, *Annual Report 2008*, available on-line at http://www.gsk.com/investors/annual-reports.htm (accessed August 2009).

A technical discussion regarding appropriate methods for carrying out meta-analysis, especially the weighting of different studies, proved central to discussions about Avandia at the FDA and in physicians' offices around the country. For example, questions were raised about lumping patients with very low risks for cardiovascular events with those of higher risk. On the one hand, this method could overstate risks to some patients by linking them to the overall average. On the other hand, if those same patients tended to benefit less from the therapy, they could be taking on unnecessary risk.[65] A related dispute emerged regarding the exclusion of studies with zero events in the treatment and control groups from the meta-analysis; as some critics noted, the absence of safety events was itself useful data.[66] Correlating between second-order analysis of clinical trials or pharmacoepidemiological analyses of health databases and individual patients was a stretch for most physicians.

For regulators, the situation was no less perilous. The FDA had only recently sought to gain access to health databases amenable to meta-analysis and to evaluate drugs based on electronic data tracking prescription use, medical utilization, and complications among specific populations. As a result, medical reviewers within FDA were divided on how to respond to Avandia's putative risks. Additional data had come into the agency regarding Avandia's cardiovascular risks as a result of phase-IV studies, but with few adverse event case reports, there was no clear consensus on label warnings or restricting the approved indication. This sequence featured prominently in Henry Waxman's congressional hearings into the FDA's handling of Avandia, and ultimately contributed to passage of an FDA reform act in September 2007.[67] FDA's response has been to raise the bar for approval; a February 2008 guidance document for diabetes drugs recommends that manufacturers increase the minimum number of patients exposed to a drug pre-market from 1,500 to 2,500 and extend controlled trials by 6–12 months.[68]

---

65. R. I. Misbin, "Lessons From the Avandia Controversy," *Diabetes Care* 30 (2007): 3141–3144; K. M. Kent and R. A. Hayward, "Limitations of Applying Summary Results of Clinical Trials to Individual Patients," *Journal of the American Medical Association* 298 (12 September 2007): 1209–1212.

66. G. A. Diamond, et al., "Uncertain Effects of Rosiglitazone on the Risk for Myocardial Infarction and Cardiovascular Death," *Annals of Internal Medicine* 147 (2007): 578–582; D. Jones, "Of Medicine and Meta-analysis," Nature Reviews Drug Discovery 7 (May 2008): 376–377.

67. H. A. Waxman, "Hearing on FDA's Role in Evaluation of Avandia's Safety," 110th Congress, House of Representatives Committee on Oversight and Government Reform (6 June 2007): 3; H.R. 3580, 110th Congress, 1st Session, "Food and Drug Administration Amendments Act of 2007," (19 September 2007).

68. Food and Drug Administration, *Guidance for Industry: Diabetes Mellitus: Developing Drugs and Therapeutic Biologics for Treatment and Prevention* (Washington, D.C.: FDA, 2008) www.fda.gov/cder/guidance/7630dft.htm (accessed May 2008).

The 2007 FDA Revitalization Act will further advance broad surveys and quantitative analysis over case reports. Created under the Act, the new Reagan-Udall Foundation for the Food and Drug Administration has a mandate to fund large-scale statistical pharmacovigilance studies and establish a new post-market surveillance system. Illustrative of the tense political atmosphere relating to drug safety, its funding was blocked for 2008 due to concerns about transparency and industry influence over decision-making.[69] In addition, the FDA is required under the act to establish a "validated and integrated post-market risk identification and analysis system" that includes twenty-five million patients by 2010 and one hundred million by 2012.[70]

In May 2008, the FDA announced a "sentinel initiative" to enable analysis of electronic medical records from federal payors with claims data (including the Veteran's Administration and the Centers for Medicare and Medicaid Services), along with plans to include records from private electronic health records once issues of access and privacy were resolved.[71] Under scenarios advanced by the FDA, queries or even automated analysis of data in the public and private systems will detect higher-than-expected rates of side effects or confirm signals from other sources. Yet the reliance on datasets created for other purposes, such as reimbursement or admission to a hospital, and the wide variation found in use of drugs and outcomes could generate spurious safety signals or mask real harms.[72] The new data on relative risks generated by the sentinel initiative—and questions concerning what to report to physicians and the public—are central elements in the transformation of pharmacovigilance currently underway.

The Avandia case and its aftermath thus raise substantive issues for the contemporary management of post-market pharmaceutical risk. First, when drugs are approved on the basis of biomarkers such as the ability to lower blood sugar and glycosylated hemoglobin, the FDA must ensure that these promising indicators are followed with actual clinical outcomes. Second, if current standards of proof favor randomized prospective clinical trials as the most desirable means for settling questions of long-term risk, then FDA, the medical profession, and the public are dependent on the timely conduct of post-market studies. Such studies require vast numbers of patient-years (and significant funding) in order to be sufficiently powerful to render risks visible. Observational studies and meta-analyses, offer more immediate and cost-efficient approaches to adverse

---

69. BNet.com, "Controversy, Distrust Surround Reagan-Udall Foundation" (15 January 2008).

70. 110th Congress, First Session, "Food and Drug Administration Amendments Act of 2007" H.R. 3580, 19 September 2007, 183–207.

71. Food and Drug Administration, "The Sentinel Initiative," www.fda.gov/downloads/Safety/FDAsSentinelInitiative (accessed August 2009).

72. J. Avorn and S. Schneeweiss, "Managing Drug-Risk Information: What to do with All Those New Numbers," *New England Journal of Medicine* 361 (2009): 647–649.

event identification than multi-year randomized controlled trials (RCTs). However, with Medicare data based on billing codes and representing an older and less healthy population, pharmacoepidemiologists must remain vigilant that their work not drive potentially useful drugs off the market. This risk is partly offset by the increasing use of private health insurer data which tend to over-represent younger and healthier populations. Third, the Avandia case suggests that to help restore public trust in the FDA's ability to effectively render risks visible, the agency and industry need to agree upon earlier use of black-box warnings, improved compliance with recommended post-marketing risk surveillance studies, and tighter standards for the use of outcomes data in place of biomarkers.[73]

CONCLUSION: COMPARING VISIBLE AND PROBABILISTIC RISKS

A methodological fragmentation of post-market monitoring is currently occurring on two levels. The first schism lies between physician or patient-initiated reports of visible side effects (adverse event reporting) and proactive surveillance studies of risk in populations (pharmacovigilance). The second split lies between proponents of targeted, phase-IV clinical trials and advocates of observational studies and meta-analyses. Structured RCTs can be lengthy and costly to carry out; they typically rely on industry funding and can require up to three years or more between trial initiation and the publication of findings. Observational trials and meta-analyses are more immediately feasible but are nonetheless faced with problems of confounding. Their methodologies are more frequently contested and produce moments of highly-publicized regulatory difficulty for the FDA. Clearly both techniques are vital to a sound pharmacovigilance policy, but at present there is no consensus on the relative apportionment of resources between the two approaches.

Post-market monitoring is fragmenting compared to the centralized processes FDA put in place from the 1960s through the 1980s. The realization that adverse effects are in some ways an inevitable byproduct of the expanded pharmacotherapy of chronic disease has led to a shift in policy away from risk *prevention* strategies and towards risk *evaluation and mitigation* strategies, or REMS.[74] Recent initiatives at the agency also include the proposal of a new Drug Safety Board, a renewed effort to publish drug safety information on the internet, a plan to assess

---

73. D. H. Solomon and W. C. Winkelmayer, "Cardiovascular Risk and the Thiazolidinediones: Déjà Vu All Over Again," *Journal of the American Medical Association* 298, no. 10 (2007): 1216–1218.

74. Department of Health and Human Services. 2008. " Identification of Drug and Biological Products Deemed to have Risk Evaluation and Mitigation Strategies." *Federal Register* 73 (2008): 16313–16314.

the safety of all new drugs eighteen months after approval, and the sentinel initiative to generate signals of adverse events from diverse electronic medical health records.[75] At the same time, greater access to data from clinical trials and in public and private electronic patient records is enabling and even encouraging analysis by physicians, biostatisticians, and others. With little uniformity in analytical methods, the fragmentation of post-market monitoring is resulting in a wide diversity of findings, in turn leading to confusion among physicians and patients.

Regardless of whether data is gathered through post-market clinical trials, meta-analyses of prior trials, or observational studies using available claims data, risk categories are changing. As opposed to the visible emergence of a birth defect or the symptomatic appearance of fulminant liver failure, the emerging era of relative risk of drugs taken daily for chronic disease and risk factor prevention relies primarily on the statistical analysis of data sets. Identified through the analysis of large populations, these risks are only visible to statisticians and epidemiologists. Even when such risks are well-documented, they lead to cognitive dissonances between patient and practitioner-based measures of health such as symptom relief or immediate control of diabetic blood sugar levels, and more abstract measures such as population rates of cardiovascular mortality.

Comparing the epidemiological work of Lenz and Nissen offers insight on the evolution of epidemiology and pharmacovigilance over the past half-century. Lenz's case-oriented methodology reflects the classic tools of infectious disease epidemiology, which originates with an outbreak of unusual events and works outwards to find root causes. Nissen's work, by contrast, is characteristic of the contemporary population-based study of chronic disease mortality. Heart attacks, though abnormal in the life of an individual, are found in a relatively normal distribution within a population (and are especially prevalent among populations with diabetes). The study of causative factors for heart attacks therefore requires vast numbers of patients over several years before putative risks of potential agents can be ruled in or out. Data does not flow in from the clinic; rather, the investigator must actively reach out to produce this data through RCTs, case-control or cohort analyses, or meta-analyses of the above.

This is particularly significant today because of the sheer volume of pharmaceuticals that are consumed for indefinite periods after an approval based on a few years' testing. All of the top 10 selling pharmaceuticals in 2008 were for chronic conditions.[76] The analytical power of the large "n" used to identify risks

---

75. Food and Drug Administration, "FDA Drug Safety Initiative Fact Sheet," www.fda. gov/oc/factsheets/initiative.html (accessed August 2007); FDA Center for Drug Evaluation and Research, "Drug Safety Oversight Board Manual of Policies and Procedures" (2 March 2007); Food and Drug Administration, *Guidance: Drug Safety Information—FDA's Communication to the Public*. (Washington, D.C.: FDA, 2007).

76. IMS Health, "2008 Top-Line Industry Data: Top 10 Products by U.S. Sales," www. imshealth.com (accessed August 2009).

in therapeutics for chronic disease lies in a complex jump from the individual patient to the level of the population. However, this same detachment often proves a liability when translating the results of such studies into terms that can be incorporated into practice by doctors and patients and into regulatory decisions by government officials.

Thalidomide is remembered worldwide as a basis for mandating pre-market safety testing. However, in the fifty years that separate thalidomide from rosiglitazone, little systematic effort was invested in monitoring drugs post-market. As our pharmaceutical economy has overwhelmingly shifted from drugs for acute disease to drugs for chronic disease, the need for new techniques to render risks visible has become increasingly important. Yet even as the shift from clinical observation of individuals to statistical analysis of populations will increase the disciplinary reach of pharmacoepidemiology, it also will require rigorous specification of subgroup risks and communication to patients and physicians responsible for translating statistical probabilities into individual treatment decisions. Differences between Contergan and Avandia highlight the progress that has been made in a half century of pharmacovigilance. Nevertheless, in our current era of consumer access to information and patients' more active role in the disease process, additional steps are needed to effectively monitor and intervene in the post-market arena. A challenge remains to make individual case reports more useful alongside the current enthusiasm for building databases and carrying out meta-analyses.

Finally, the fundamental source of information about adverse reactions is the patient who takes medicines. Properly informed and enrolled as participants, prescription drug users could help to generate both individual case reports and the large datasets that would provide comprehensive information to FDA and its advisory groups. Patients have forged communities defined by disease, in some cases with deep databases on experiences with treatments.[77] This trend could be fostered in a more formal way by providing password-controlled access to dedicated websites for every pharmaceutical. Patients who have been prescribed the drug could then log on and in a matter of minutes provide both quantitative (check boxes for a variety of reactions and ratings of severity on an appropriate scale) and qualitative experiential information about their experience with the drug. At quite modest cost, this would generate extensive information and provide critical risk information that may be missed using current approaches. Such a system could also benefit manufacturers and patients as it validates (or inexpensively disproves) expanded indications for medicines currently only approved for narrow uses.

---

77. T. Goetz, "Practicing Patients," *New York Times* (23 March 2008); see also www.patientslikeme.com (accessed May 2009).

14. THE U.S. HEALTH CARE SYSTEM
A Product of American History and Values

DAVID W. JOHNSON AND NANCY M. KANE

INTRODUCTION

If change is to be for the better, it should be based on an understanding of why things are the way they are.[1]

The U.S. health care system stands apart from those of other industrialized nations. It costs more, employs more technology, generates remarkable medical innovation, emphasizes specialty care, underserves over twenty percent of its people, and avoids standardization. Hundreds of thousands come each year to receive advanced care not available in their home countries. Yet we suffer disconnections across the continuum of care; disparities in care across population subgroups; lack of information or care integration even within legally structured "systems" of care; disparities in insurance coverage and benefit structures; excess availability of some services and scarcity of others in communities throughout the United States.

How can we explain American tolerance for these contradictory outcomes? And why is the American model for health care delivery so different from other developed nations? American exceptionalism has been a part of our national character from the country's origin. It was on his way to America in 1630 that the Puritan John Winthrop gave his famous sermon outlining his vision for the Massachusetts Bay Colony in which he said, "For we must consider that we shall be as a city upon a hill. The eyes of all people are upon us." American ideology is unique in its reverence for the individual, its suspicion of authority, its broad optimism, and its belief in national destiny. Although these American virtues give us our unique history and accomplishments, they also bring with them ironies:

Irony consists of apparently fortuitous incongruities in life which are discovered, upon closer examination, to be not merely fortuitous. . . . If virtue becomes vice through some hidden defect in the virtue, if strength becomes weakness because of the vanity to which strength may prompt the mighty man or nation, in all such cases the situation is ironic.[2]

---

1. V.R. FUCHS, WHO SHALL LIVE? 7 (2002).

2. R. NIEBUHR, THE IRONY OF AMERICAN HISTORY xxiv (University of Chicago Press 2008) (1952).

Our authors' contention is that fragmentation is an ironic by-product of our virtues. Although other forces (advocacy groups, political parties) affect the design of the U.S. health care system, core American values shape the health care policy debate and influence its outcome. Failure to understand these values and their impact will compromise the ability of reformers to address the system's shortcomings.

At one level, our contention is a truism. Health care consumes 15% of national GDP, employs millions, touches all citizens and communities. How could health care not reflect our national beliefs, attitudes and experience? At the same time, the system's size and complexity combined with its structural anomalies (the independence of physicians, the predominance of nonprofit hospitals, the third-party payment system, governmental regulations, the powerful academic influence, rising consumerism) make it difficult to discern the importance of values and history. The following chart arrays quintessential American values on a national map and distills the results that derive from them.

These value relationships are complex, interrelated and deeply held. They shape our national character, identity, and approach to policy development. Unfortunately our national values frequently work in opposition to policy initiatives designed to integrate our health care financing and delivery systems. Exploring their history will illuminate the contours of the policy debate shaping health care reform and will identify sources of fragmentation. Specifically, we

American Healthcare is a Product of Our History, Values and Experience.

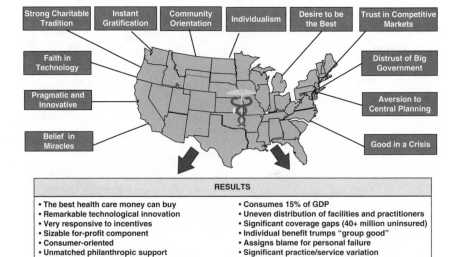

RESULTS	
• The best health care money can buy	• Consumes 15% of GDP
• Remarkable technological innovation	• Uneven distribution of facilities and practitioners
• Very responsive to incentives	• Significant coverage gaps (40+ million uninsured)
• Sizable for-profit component	• Individual benefit trumps "group good"
• Consumer-oriented	• Assigns blame for personal failure
• Unmatched philanthropic support	• Significant practice/service variation
• Strong volunteer support	• Over/Under treatment patterns

FIGURE 1 AMERICAN HEALTHCARE, HISTORY, VALUES AND EXPERIENCE

will investigate the following six areas where American values contribute to the uniquely fragmented nature of the U.S. health care system:

- Individual versus Collective Responsibility for Health
- Health Crisis Management versus Managing Health
- Faith in Markets versus Distrust of Government
- Being the Best versus Collaboration
- Philanthropy for Buildings not People
- Community Orientation versus Lack of Accountability

INDIVIDUAL VERSUS COLLECTIVE RESPONSIBILITY FOR HEALTH

Thomas Jefferson envisioned America as a nation of agrarians who, due to an open frontier with unlimited opportunity, would never be subject to the over-crowded conditions of Europe. European governments had to impose greater restrictions on "men steeped in vices which the situation generates," or, more specifically, when class rebellion erupted over the distribution of scarce resources. According to Jefferson,

> Here, every man may have land to labor for himself, or preferring the exercise of any other industry, may exact for it such compensation as not only to afford a comfortable subsistence but wherewith to provide a cessation from labor in old age.[3]

The economic opportunity to support oneself in a land of plenty was glorified into a personal virtue by writers such as Ralph Waldo Emerson, whose 1841 essay, "Self-Reliance," proclaimed,

> Discontent is the want of self-reliance: it is infirmity of will. Nothing can bring you peace but yourself.[4]

Emerson's version of self-reliance included a healthy dose of anti-collective invective, such as,

> Society everywhere is in conspiracy against the manhood of every one of its members. Society is a joint-stock company in which the members agree, for the better of securing of his bread to each shareholder, to surrender the liberty and culture of the eater.[5]

---

3. *Id.* at 27–28.
4. R.E. EMERSON, *Essay II: Self Reliance,* from ESSAYS: FIRST SERIES (1841), *available at* http://www.emersoncentral.com/selfreliance.htm.
5. *Id.*

This American virtue of self-reliance has generated great wealth and opportunity over the last two hundred years and created "individualistic" cultural icons from Horatio Alger to Wyatt Earp to Charles Bronson's vigilante hero in "Death Wish." However, in recent decades, it has also produced disparities in income and health that approach those of a third-world country. A recent study indicates that life expectancy is decreasing for low income and less educated Americans.[6] This pattern of decline is not seen in most other industrialized countries. The study concluded that "because policies aimed at reducing fundamental socioeconomic inequalities are currently practically absent in the U.S.,"[7] remedies would lie primarily with the public health community, and focus on managing risk factors causing chronic disease.

In the United States, the predominant political view is that health is an individual rather than a collective responsibility. We view the obese individual as a product of over-eating and under-exercising. Ubiquitous marketing by the diet industry encourages the overweight to "invest" (and they spend billions) in diets and exercise programs. Meanwhile our laws and social norms allow the food industry to inundate Saturday morning children's television shows with 40,000 ads each year for sugary cereals, soft drinks, and candy. These ads target children at ages too young to know the difference between advertising and education.[8] Opponents of public health laws that would curtail such advertising object to "paternalistic interventions into lifestyle choices," which "enfeeble the notion of personal responsibility" and constrain our constitutional right of free speech.[9] Instead, they urge public health policymakers to exercise their right of free speech by giving consumers the information they need, through counter-advertising and food labeling, to make better food purchasing decisions. As one observer concludes, "the law is slow to realize that choices in the market may not be totally free."[10] Meanwhile, other countries have statutory guidelines on advertising to children; one recent article found that 63% of 73 countries reviewed had such guidelines.[11] The United States has only self-regulatory guidelines on advertising to children.

The undertone of individual responsibility colors today's political debate over universal health insurance. Health insurance is a "voluntary" benefit for most Americans, and close to fifty million people "choose" not to purchase it. Conservative policymakers advocate using economic incentives, such as tax

---

6. K. Sack, *The Short End of the Longer Life*, N.Y. TIMES, April 27, 2008, at 4.

7. *Id.*

8. M.M. Mello et al., *Obesity—The New Frontier of Public Health Law*, 354 NEW ENGLAND JOURNAL OF MEDICINE, 2601–10 (2006).

9. *Id.* at 2610.

10. *Id.* at 2602.

11. C. HAWKES, MARKETING FOOD TO CHILDREN: THE GLOBAL REGULATORY ENVIRONMENT, WORLD HEALTH ORGANIZATION (2004), http://libdoc.who.int/publications/2004/9241591579.pdf.

credits and high-deductible health plans funded by tax-favored savings accounts, to convince individuals to buy health insurance. In reality, it is difficult to convince young, healthy, but low-earning people to spend money that they don't have on something that they feel they don't need. On the other end of the spectrum, no politician to date has recommended tax credits sufficient to pay for health insurance premiums and out-of-pocket costs for higher risk people (e.g., those over age 45, of child-bearing age, or with pre-existing conditions). Insurance works effectively when the healthy pay for the sick, not when individuals establish medical savings accounts tailored to their unique personal needs. It works best as a mandated, collective good, something the advanced industrialized nations of the world concluded decades, and in some places, centuries ago.

In 1881, Otto von Bismarck had just finished a decades-long battle to unify Germany. Social unrest generated by rapid migration to cities posed a significant threat to the new German empire. Bismarck pacified that social unrest by enacting a series of government-sponsored social benefits:

> Whoever has a pension for his old age is far more content and far easier to handle than one who has no such prospect.[12]

In 1883, Germany passed the first compulsory health insurance program, which has grown to insure all but the country's *wealthiest* 10%. They can choose to opt out of the system.

Let's hope it doesn't require open class warfare in America before we see the wisdom of providing health insurance to all our citizens.

HEALTH CRISIS MANAGEMENT VERSUS MANAGING HEALTH

We respond generously in a crisis, but become miserly when paying for routine care or chronic disease management: We fly conjoined twins from Bangladesh to the United States for advanced separation surgery, but underfund basic prenatal care. Elderly citizens living with several chronic conditions see multiple specialists, none of whom talk to one another. This requires the patient to integrate his or her care and sort through the conflicting advice, including prescriptions for drugs that shouldn't be taken together. We frequently ignore the wishes of dying patients regarding their end-of-life treatment. Too many elderly die in a hospital ICU surrounded by high-technology equipment rather than comfortably at home surrounded by family.

To better understand why we favor the acute, dramatic, and highly technical care over preventive, primary, chronic, and even palliative care, it is instructive to review the origins of the Blue Cross and Blue Shield plans, which played a

---

12. A.J.P. TAYLOR, BISMARCK, THE MAN AND STATESMAN 158 (1985).

dominant role in the structure and design of today's health care financing system. As Sylvia Law pointed out in her 1974 book, *Blue Cross—What Went Wrong*, "Blue Cross is most accurately characterized today as the financing arm of American hospitals."[13] As the "child of the Depression and the American Hospital Association"[14], Blues plans were born of hospitals' need to achieve financial stability as the Depression reduced both patients' out-of-pocket payments and philanthropic contributions from benefactors. At the same time, hospitals were rapidly moving from almshouses caring for the poor to modern, high-technology hospitals curing diseases afflicting everyone, and were in need of substantial new capital investment. During the 1930s, twenty-seven of the thirty-nine new Blues plans received all or part of their initial financing from hospitals. For decades, hospital representatives dominated Blues boards; by 1970, forty-two percent of the members of local plan boards were hospital representatives and 14% were doctors. Given this governance structure it's not surprising that Blue Cross plans guaranteed payment to hospitals for the full cost of services provided to subscribers. Full cost reimbursement from insured patients enabled hospitals to grow and adopt new technologies at explosive rates. These spending habits continue today despite shifts to a more independent Blues plans and more restrictive prospective payment systems.

From its inception through the 1970s, Blue Cross's responsibility to offer subscribers affordable health care benefits were subservient to, and at times undermined by, their determination to keep American hospitals financially healthy and technologically advanced. Not atypical was the frustration expressed by a New York court in 1964 to a 33% rate hike by Blue Cross of New York. The judge criticized the superintendent of insurance for failing to exercise adequate control over rate increase requests, commenting:

> Both Blue Cross and the Superintendent seem intent on adopting the notion that no matter how costly operations become, for whatever reasons, eventually and inevitably, Blue Cross subscribers will shoulder the load. Small wonder that subscriber rates have increased 124% in the past five years.[15]

During the debate to establish Medicare in the early 1960's, the AHA dropped its early opposition to a federal program of hospital insurance on the condition that only a Blue Cross plan could administer it. At the same time, Blue Cross and the AHA became the technical experts in designing the Medicare payment system, particularly the payment to hospitals for their reasonable costs, ensuring rapid technology-driven hospital expansion for decades. Also not surprising given the AHA/Blue Cross influence, the compulsory part of Medicare, Part A, covered only acute inpatient care.

---

13. SA. LAW, BLUE CROSS: WHAT WENT WRONG? 2 (1974).
14. *Id.* at 6.
15. *Id.* at 15.

Concentration of the power of resource allocation in the hands of the providers and their captive insurers naturally resulted in a hospital-dominated system that is more responsive to its own needs than the needs of their communities. As Victor Fuchs pointed out,

> The desire . . . of the physician to practice in the best-equipped hospital is understandable. But to the extent that the [physician] fails to recognize the claims of competing wants or the divergence of his priorities from those of other people, his advice is likely to be a poor guide to social policy.[16]

Physicians took much longer than hospitals to accept health insurance coverage for their services, seeing in it such "evil practices" as "solicitation of patients, destructive competition among professional groups, inferior medical service, loss of personal relationship of patient and physician, and demoralization of the professions,"[17] as the editor of the Journal of the American Medical Association (JAMA) wrote in 1933. However, patient demand for physician services rose as the Depression continued to erode income and more physician work required a hospital setting, in which patients were covered under Blue Cross plans for hospital but not for physician services. The greatest motivator for coverage for physician services was the horrible specter (to conservative medical practitioners) of compulsory, state-sponsored medical insurance. Repeated state and federal proposals for compulsory health insurance in the 1930s finally led the American Medical Association (AMA) to encourage state medical societies to sponsor medical plans, particularly for payment of professional bills incurred during a prolonged or emergency illness. Thus, in 1939, the first medical service prepayment plan, the California Physician's Service (now Blue Shield of California), was born. Its primary purpose was to stave off compulsory public insurance, rather than to enhance the health of populations served. Primary and preventive care was not a focus of the early plans; the concept of preventive care did not take root in American health insurance coverage until the spread of health *maintenance* organizations in the 1980s.

In contrast to the acute care, provider-dominated financing systems of the United States, the British financing and delivery system established in 1948 maintained public control over health care benefits and payments. General practitioners in Great Britain were also suspicious of government control, but their solution was to maintain private practice while accepting capitated payments for National Health Service (NHS) patients. The NHS's payment design created incentives for general practitioners to manage the *health* of their patient populations. Later reforms (in the 1990s) enhanced the power of the

---

16. FUCHS, *supra* note 1, at 5.

17. R. CUNNINGHAM & R.M. CUNNINGHAM, THE BLUES: A HISTORY OF THE BLUE CROSS AND BLUE SHIELD SYSTEM 38 (1997).

general practitioner. A core principle of the NHS, stated in 2000, was that it will help keep people healthy and work to reduce health inequalities.

In the German system, the federal government designed a generous benefit package payment levels for health care benefits results from negotiations among powerful coalitions representing the doctors, hospitals, and pharmaceutical companies on the provider side, employers and unions (through the sickness funds) on the financing side, with government playing the role of rule maker and protector of citizens' interests. This balancing of conflicting interests favors patients and population health more than in the United States. For instance, the German government recently passed legislation requiring sickness funds to implement primary care-based chronic disease management for diabetes and other chronic conditions.

The United States relies on the private market to develop innovative ways to provide primary care and disease management. In our **"highly fragmented"** system, dominated by specialists, this has proven to be a difficult task. The effort in the early 1990s to allocate a higher proportion of physician spending into primary care/evaluation and management (E&M) services under the Medicare-sponsored Resource-Based Relative Value System (RBRVS) has failed to achieve its goals, as the share of Medicare payments going to primary/E&M services today is the same as it was before Medicare implemented the RBRVS. A recent Medicare demonstration in which specialized disease management companies worked directly with patients to manage their care, without involving their doctors, may be cancelled due to the lack of compelling results. Meanwhile, the supply of primary care physicians continues to dwindle despite a growing need as the baby boom population ages. A popular market-based response is for primary care doctors to ration their services on an economic basis by forming "concierge practices" that require patients to pay thousands of dollars up-front (not covered by insurance) to guarantee access to their doctors. Others will manage their care using Web MD. Inadequate routine care will result in more "crisis care" where people become seriously ill, go to the emergency room and "fortunately" have insurance cover the cost of their subsequent care.

FAITH IN MARKETS VERSUS DISTRUST OF GOVERNMENT

America has had a tortured relationship with government since the country's origin. Thomas Paine, the author of the influential 1776 pamphlet "Common Sense," which spurred a generation of American patriots, captures this ambivalence in the following two quotations:

> "Government even in its best state is but a necessary evil; in its worst state, an intolerable one,"; and "The government is best which governs least."

The colonists' struggle to overthrow British rule bred a natural distrust of authority that found sustenance in a vast land populated by rugged individualists.

Our citizens have never easily accepted the benefits of centralization. Jefferson dismantled the national army and navy. Jackson dismantled the national bank. The South seceded in the belief that states' rights reigned supreme. The existence of term limits and recall petitions reveal that distrust of government continues unabated. Echoes of this sentiment carried into President Bill Clinton's 1996 State of the Union Address when he declared the end of the era of big government.

The same cannot be said of markets and business. Though unusually taciturn for a politician, President Calvin Coolidge made himself clear on the importance of business in 1925 when he proclaimed "the chief business of the American people is business." And why not? Markets have proven effective at allocating resources, generating wealth, funding innovation, improving life quality and separating winners from losers. Markets seem robust while government appears ineffective. Business leaders seem decisive while government leaders appear out-of-touch, incompetent or corrupt. The country hailed the arrival of Ford CEO Robert McNamara and his whiz kids in 1961 when they brought professional management science to the Department of Defense. In 1982 President Reagan created the private sector Grace Commission to eliminate waste in the Federal Government. He instructed them to:

"Be bold. We want your team to work like tireless bloodhounds. Don't leave any stone unturned in your search to root out inefficiency."[18]

Leave it to mudraking journalist H.L. Mencken to describe the relationship between business and government in words with which most Americans would agree,

Capitalism undoubtedly has certain boils and blotches upon it, but has it as many as government? Has it as many as religion? Has it as many as marriage? I doubt it. It is the only basic institution of modern man that shows any genuine health and vigor.[19]

This business-government dynamic also leads American policymakers to incorporate and protect a role for the private sector in government financed health care services. Medicare and Medicaid proposals in the early 1960s appeared defeated until House Ways and Means Chair Wilbur Mills embedded Blue Cross's "cost plus" reimbursement into the hospital payment formula and awarded the adminstrative contract to Blues plans; also written into the legislation was a promise that Medicare would never interfere with the private practice of medicine (Patashnik and Zelizer, 2001).[20] Medicare's preferential payment

---

18. Remarks at a White House luncheon on March 10, 1982, with Chairman and Executive Committee of the Private Sector Survey on Cost Control *available at* http://en.wikipedia.org/wiki/The_Grace_Commission#References (last visited May 23, 2008).

19. H.L. Mencken, from *The Library*, THE AMERICAN MERCURY, September 28, 1924.

20. E. Patashnik & J. Zelizer, *Paying for Medicare: Benefits, Budgets, and Wilbur Mill's Policy Legacy*, 26 (1) JOURNAL OF HEALTH POLITICS, POLICY AND LAW 7–36 (2001).

structure for entrants in privately run, managed care plans and its requirement that Part D beneficiaries purchase their drugs through private insurance plans are recent examples. For Medicare Advantage Plans, this provision of public benefit through private channels has led to higher costs without the anticipated improvement in efficiency. Consistent with this outcome, Part D provides a new benefit to seniors, but the law's prohibition against governmental pricing negotiation with drug providers increases the program's cost.

American's reverence for private markets has had a defining role in shaping our complicated and fragmented model for providing health care services. The predominant belief is that market-based strategies are best equipped to deliver value; however, health care economics defy conventional economic wisdom. In other industries, companies invest in technology to increase efficiency and reduce cost. Investment in medical technology increases cost. In other markets, demand for products and services drives supply. In health care, the demand for health care services is a function of the supply of facilities and practitioners. More cardiac catheterization labs and more cardiac surgeons generate more cardiac catheterization procedures irrespective of patient need. This latter phenomenon is termed "Roemer's Law" in reference to the work of Milton Roemer, a former professor at the UCLA School of Public Health. He concluded in the early 1960s that "supply may induce its own demand in the presence of third-party payment."[21] The undermining of effective market functions by third-party payment for services operates throughout American health care. It causes fragmentation in several ways:

1. It compensates "reimbursable care" whether or not is appropriate;
2. It discourages "appropriate care" when it is unreimbursable;
3. It complicates the determination of what constitutes proper care, which in turn increases administrative costs;
4. It separates the recipient of health care services from their payment.

This blending of public and private activity without the normal clarity provided by efficient markets has led to a high cost system with significant coverage gaps. Hospitals and payors engage in a zero-sum game to maximize revenue within a closed payment system. Each sector is consolidating to improve its negotiating leverage. The result is that higher payments go to hospitals with the most negotiating leverage, not those that deliver the highest health care "value." Payors use their leverage and enrollment systems to maximize revenue and minimize payment for care services (the "medical loss" ratio). This pattern of payment and service provision generates confusion and uncertainty for patients within the system. The lack of pricing transparency and the limited availability

---

21. M.I. Roemer, Bed Supply and Hospital Utilization: A Natural Experiment, HOSPITALS, November 1, 1961, 36–42.

of outcomes data frustrate the ability of consumers to make informed decisions regarding health care purchases.

Americans believe in markets and their ability to operate within them to purchase goods and services at fair prices; however, with few exceptions, Americans cannot make market-based decisions regarding health care services. Reform without private sector involvement will be difficult for Americans to accept given their historic distrust of government. Reform that relies on private sector involvement without transparency regarding pricing and outcomes will continue a legacy of high-cost services that don't deliver value to patients.

BEING THE BEST VERSUS COLLABORATING

America's obsession with winning is legendary. Vince Lombardi, the iconic Green Bay Packers football coach from the 1960s, famously observed "Winning isn't everything; it's the only thing." He also said "Show me a good loser and I'll show you a loser."[22] America is the only nation whose professional teams declare themselves world champions despite never competing against teams from other countries. Being "the best" or being "number one" is a constant theme across industry, entertainment, education, and health care. Americans rank everything from schools to restaurants to doctors to employers. This focus on winning feeds a national identity that has emerged from centuries of history where American virtue has triumphed against lesser adversaries: from independence (beat the British) through development (manifest destiny) through war (from Indians to Iraqis) into space (beat the Soviets to the moon) and to the current day ("winning the war on terror"). Under pressure, Americans rely on this shared history of victory and its supporting philosophies ("when the going gets tough . . .") to marshal the energy and will to compete. It motivates our corporations, fuels our drive for growth, and sustains our national belief that competitive markets are the best method for allocating resources.

This faith in competition works. Americans have created an economic model that has generated unprecedented productivity, innovation and wealth. This American model has transformed health care delivery. Americans have pioneered most of the breakthrough science that has revolutionized diagnostics, cured disease, and improved life quality. Our absolute and per-capita investment in health care facilities, research, and treatment dwarfs that of all other nations. Yet our fragmented approach to health care doesn't deliver benefits commensurate with this level of national investment. Unlike other industries, competition in health care delivery doesn't always create value through more efficient resource allocation. Instead our competitive system creates fragmentation that affects

---

22. D. Maraniss, When Pride Still Mattered: A Life Of Vince Lombardi (2000).

patient care throughout the care continuum: with uneven care access; with over- and under-treatment; without adequate coordination; with uneven information flow; and without systematic chronic care management.

Ironically, organizations that emphasize collaboration have better outcomes and more efficient care. These include the Veterans Administration; integrated systems; and medical foundations, such as the Mayo Clinic that employ physicians, share information, and follow protocols. These organizations also are more likely to practice "logical care" (e.g., preventive care, promotive care, and disease management).

Christus Health has a Futures Task Force that is exploring social and economic trends to assist in shaping the organization's strategic direction. After a recent study mission to Toronto, the Committee concluded that Canadian society is less competitive and its people believe there is "enough health care to go around." Canadians have a high level of trust in their health care system and tolerate some rationing and treatment delay. Unlike Canadians, Americans want their treatment without delay and they want to receive it from the best institutions. Hospitals go to enormous effort to differentiate their services through advertising and by competing for recognition awards. Pass by any hospital and you're likely to see a banner highlighting its recognition as a superior care provider by a respected independent organization. Here's a partial list of organizations that recognize/rank hospital care:

- U.S. News and World Report rankings of the best U.S. hospitals by specialty
- Health Grades
- Health Leaders
- Solucient Top 100 hospitals
- Thompson Top 100 hospitals
- J.D. Power and Associates
- Magnet Designation for Nursing Excellence
- Cleverly and Associates "CVI Five-Star Hospitals"
- Leap Frog
- Baldrige Award

Americans want "the best" health care for their families and they rely upon well-developed consumer instincts to evaluate care alternatives. Hospitals employ sophisticated marketing strategies to attract patients. The trouble is that there is too much extraneous information, too many awards, and limited reliable data. True measures related to cost and outcomes are difficult to find and interpret. Consequently, consumers cannot make value judgments for health care services like they can in all other areas of their economic lives. Instead consumers rely upon anecdotal information including awards, advertisements, and personal referrals to make health care decisions.

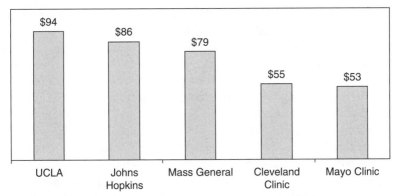

FIGURE 2 CHRONIC CARE COST LAST TWO YEARS OF LIFE (000'S)

A recent study contained in the 2008 Dartmouth Atlas of Health Care examined spending by Medicare for chronic illnesses in the last two years of life.[23] Over one third of Americans have chronic illnesses and approximately 70% die from them. Most Medicare spending relating to chronic illness in the last two years of life occurs in hospitals. In an interesting research twist, the report focused on the five academic medical centers ranked highest (the "winners") by the U.S. News and World Report survey. The results presented in Figure 2 from the 2008 Dartmouth Atlas are striking:

Of the five, UCLA had the highest cost at $93,842 per patient and Mayo Clinic had the lowest at $53,432 per patient. Other academic centers, including NYU and Cedars-Sinai, had costs exceeding $105,000 per patient. The cost differential resulted from higher-cost institutions performing more tests and procedures. Defenders of these organizations highlight their aggressiveness in "going the extra mile" for patients and/or maintain their patients are sicker. More likely, the higher costs result from uncoordinated care and a system that rewards activity over outcomes. Two quotations from a New York Times article describing the study are illuminating. The first comes from Dr. Denis A Cortese, the president of the Mayo Clinic, explaining their less aggressive approach to medical care management, "Our physicians are salaried. They have no financial incentive to do more than is necessary for the patient. In each case, multiple doctors and nurses make decisions collaboratively with the patient and family members. We really try to understand the patient's wishes for end-of-life care." At the other end of the cost spectrum, the Chief Medical Officer for NYU, Dr. Robert A. Press, acknowledged the findings but noted, "It's not an easy fix. We are dealing with a

---

23. Dartmouth Atlas of Health Care, Tracking the Care of Patients with Severe Chronic Illness (2008), http://www.dartmouthatlas.org/atlases/2008_Chronic_Care_Atlas.pdf.

culture of physicians who have been very aggressive in their care and a patient population that has desired this type of care."[24]

To a remarkable extent, a typical patient's values (wanting the best and wanting it now) coalesce with the values of prestigious delivery centers (wanting to "win" by doing whatever it takes for their patients). Unfortunately, this "values alignment" leads to high-cost, inefficient care absent a strong organizational culture that enforces care coordination based on shared information. Since we won't change our national fixation on winning, we need to redefine winning to mean care that produces the best outcomes consistent with patient wishes in the most efficient manner. This will require greater emphasis on care coordination through collaboration and meaningful data sharing. There can still be (and should be) competition, but it must center on delivering true cost and outcome value to patients.

PHILANTHROPY FOR BUILDINGS NOT PEOPLE

Americans give and give generously. U.S. charitable giving approached $300 billion in 2006 and represented over 2 % of gross domestic product. Americans give their time. 55 % of Americans volunteer and over 90 % believe it is important to promote volunteerism. American giving is widespread. 89 % of U.S. households donate with an average contribution exceeding $1600. Americans give as individuals. Including bequests, 83 % of philanthropic contributions in 2006 came from individuals.[25] Recipients include over 1 million U.S.-based charitable organizations that employ over ten million people (7 % of the American workforce). This pattern in philanthropy is unique among industrialized nations and another example of American exceptionalism. In other developed countries, governments, corporations, and private foundations are the primary funding sources for charitable activity. Japanese corporations, for example, fund over 75 % of Japan's charitable contributions.[26] American philanthropy reflects a national value system that reveres the individual, distrusts big government, and believes in free markets. Individuals direct their philanthropy to organizations of their choosing. Organizations solicit donations using sophisticated marketing strategies that include direct mailing, sponsorships, personalized appeals, and telethons. Philanthropy has become "big business," in which charitable organizations compete for contributions in a freewheeling

---

24. R. Pear, *Researchers Find Huge Variation in End-of-Life Treatment*, N.Y. TIMES, April 7, 2008, at A17.

25. National Philanthropic Trust, http://www.nptrust.org/philanthropy/philanthropy_stats.asp.

26. New AFP-Funded Research Compares U.S., Japanese Fundraising, http://www.afpnet.org/ka/print_content.cfm?folder_id=2326&content_item_id=24350.

marketplace and then distribute their largess in accordance with organizational priorities.

This American form of philanthropy has its origins in American history, in which diverse immigrant groups came together to build a new nation on a vast, undeveloped land. America's innate optimism, frontier spirit, comfort with mobility, innovative character, penchant for pragmatic solutions, and belief in individual virtue evolved as the country spread westward and overcame a remarkable array of challenges. Results rather than heredity became the true measure of an individual's community standing. In 1835 Alexis de Tocqueville published *Democracy in America*, his insightful essay on the character of civic life in America. The following passage from the National Philanthropic Trust's website summarizes de Tocqueville's thoughts on voluntary associations in America.

> Among his most important observations was the American disposition to organize and join voluntary associations which helped to provide charitable relief to those in need, and to discuss and offer solutions to societal problems. De Tocqueville noted that early America had no distinct class of wealth that could be turned to in times of need to relieve suffering. Associations necessarily formed to create the means to deal with problems and reflected a compassion for all those in trouble.[27]

American "solutions" for philanthropy were as new and innovative as those that transformed American industry. America's most famous industrialist and self-made man, Andrew Carnegie, wrote the "Gospel of Wealth" in 1889, in which he advocated distributing personal wealth to fund benevolent causes. In 1913, Carnegie donated $125 million to create the Carnegie Corporation of New York, one of the nation's first grant-making organizations. Many followed including foundations endowed by the Rockefeller and Ford families. The first community foundation originated in Cleveland in 1914. Over six hundred such foundations exist today. Contributions to charitable organizations became tax deductible in 1917, providing another stimulant for American giving. Today nonprofit organizations are among America's most dynamic and innovative organizations. The Lance Armstrong Foundation began in 2004 and already has over fifty-five million people wearing yellow LIVESTRONG wristbands to support cancer research.[28] With assets now exceeding $37 billion, the Bill and Melinda Gates Foundation is designing innovative approaches to eradicating disease, protecting the environment, improving education and increasing agricultural production.[29] The Gates Foundation is the largest of a vanguard of new

---

27. History of Philanthropy, 1800-1899, http://www.nptrust.org/philanthropy/ history_philanthropy_1800s.asp.

28. History of Philanthropy, 2000-present, http://www.nptrust.org/philanthropy/ history_philanthropy_2000s.asp.

29. http://www.gatesfoundation.org/MediaCenter/FactSheet/default.htm

philanthropic organizations that increasingly exercise leadership in areas where governmental initiatives are lacking or inadequate.

Hospitals are among the largest not-for-profit organizations and recipients of charitable contributions. Hospitals employ sophisticated market research and personalized appeals to design and execute fundraising campaigns. Many of these campaigns center on raising philanthropy for new health care facilities and strategically employ naming rights. The University of Colorado Hospital renamed its new campus the "Anschutz Medical Campus" in recognition of contributions exceeding $50 million by the Philip Anschutz Foundation.[30] This was the largest philanthropic gift to a charitable organization in Colorado history. Ann Lurie has donated $100 million to Children's Memorial Hospital in Chicago. In recognition for her gift, Children's will name its new 288-bed hospital the "Ann and Robert Lurie Children's Hospital of Chicago."[31] Philanthropy will pay for roughly half of the hospital's $850 million construction cost. At almost $3 million per bed, this will be among the most expensive hospitals ever constructed.

There is no equivalent philanthropic support for funding health care services for indigent patient populations. Most safety net hospitals rely upon local and Federal government funding to cover the capital and operating costs of providing care to medically indigent patients.

At the margins, providing unreimbursed care strains a hospital's financial profile and restricts capital access. Not surprisingly, hospitals over-invest in areas and services that promise a positive financial return and under-invest in areas and services that do not. Thus metropolitan Chicago is projected to spend in excess of $6 billion to build new/replacement hospitals at academic medical centers and in affluent areas while making minimal new facility investment in the region's most medically underserved areas. Illinois just approved a sixth heart transplant program even though no Illinois program completes more than twenty-five heart transplants annually, well below national averages.[32] This market "logic" is a principal factor in the uneven distribution of health care facilities and practitioners. As hospitals both shape and respond to the wishes of major donors, the gap between needed and provided health care services widens.

It is an anomaly of history that U.S. health care relies so heavily on individual charity to finance its delivery system. Many not-for-profit systems trace their origins to civic-minded founders who established philanthropically supported care centers where none previously existed. However, in the mid-1960s, medicine

---

30. The Anschutz Medical Campus, http://www.uch.edu/about/anschutz-medical-campus.aspx.

31. Ann Lurie's Transformational Gift, http://www.childrensmemorial.org/newsroom/new_hospital_donation.aspx.

32. J. Graham, *Too Many Heart Centers, Not Enough Heart Transplants*, CHI. TRIB., April 13, 2008.

shifted from being supported by philanthropy and patient self-payments to selling services to large third-party payors. Philanthropy has remained an important source of hospital capital for buildings, but is unevenly distributed and subject to the proclivities of donors. Large tax deductions support such giving, while removing from tax revenues funds that might otherwise be used to provide capital to safety net hospitals or provide subsidies to low-income people for purchasing health insurance.

STRONG COMMUNITY ORIENTATION BUT LACK OF ACCOUNTABILITY TO THE COMMUNITY

Pennsylvania Hospital, the oldest hospital in the U.S., was among Benjamin Franklin's many legacies. He raised money to found the hospital in 1751 and served on its first Board of Managers. A hospital to treat the sick and poor was one of many community activities promoted through Franklin's Junto, a Friday evening discussion club devoted to self-improvement through enlightened group discussion. One of the standing questions used to guide the discussions of the group was: "Do you think of any thing at present, in which the Junto may be serviceable to mankind? To their country, to their friends, or to themselves?" Thus was born the idea of a community hospital for purposes of housing and treating the "distempered poor" who came to the city to seek medical advice but had difficulty finding lodging, as well as for the local poor residents, who were "badly accommodated in sickness, and could not be so well and so easily taken care of in their separate habitations as they might be in one convenient house, under one inspection and in the hands of skilful practitioners. . . ."[33]

Besides helping to keep the lunatics off the street, where they terrorized the neighbors, the hospital provided wealthy Christian citizens with the "greater opportunity of exercising towards each other that virtue, which most of all recommends us to the Deity, I mean charity."[34] In the founders' accounts of the Pennsylvania Hospital's beginnings were repeated stories illustrating the Christian virtue of helping the sick as the way to be admitted to the "happiness of heaven." For those with means, not helping the sick would be a sure way to **not** get into heaven:

> I was sick and ye visited me, is one of the terms of admission into bliss, and the contrary, a cause of exclusion.[35]

---

33. B. Franklin, *Some Account of the Pennsylvania Hospital; from its First Rise to the Beginning of the Fifth Month, Called May, 1754*, U.S. GAZETTE, 1817, 3–4.

34. *Id.* at 31.

35. *Id.* at 32.

Private donations to the proposed Pennsylvania Hospital quickly matched the public donation approved by the Pennsylvania Assembly, and a Board of Managers was elected annually from among those who had donated at least ten pounds to the hospital. Thus began the American philanthropic tradition of donor-dominated boards which govern local community hospitals. One task of the Board of Managers was to determine who was worthy of admittance as a patient; prospective patients were asked to obtain letters of reference from the "overseers" of the poor in their local township, who would verify their residency, indigency and worthiness, and describe their symptoms.

Since 1751, and primarily since World War II, thousands of cities and towns across the United States have founded local tax-exempt, nonprofit hospitals. These hospitals are often the "crown jewel" of local civic life. Service on hospital boards is still generally reserved for members of high social, religious, and/or professional standing in the community, and board members are generally benefactors. Although boards no longer decide who is "worthy" to be a patient, they play a significant role in determining what services and markets their hospital will serve—in other words, which community "needs" are deserving. Thus unlike the British NHS, which requires that its delivery system be centrally planned by government and remain, "through the body politic"[36], accountable to the population it serves, American hospitals serve whomever their private boards decide to serve in a market-based environment. As described earlier, particularly when there are significant philanthropic dollars available, many community hospitals end up with a set of services that are quite inconsistent with any objective determination of "community need." For example, a small one hundred-bed nonprofit hospital in a remote resort community with over three thousand uninsured citizens raised gifts from wealthy board members to build a cardiac catheterization lab, even though the hospital had no full-time cardiologists available to staff it, while many of the local community's health care needs were ignored.

Local civic pride and the pursuit of personal salvation through charity are commendable virtues; however, these "virtues" in American not-for profit hospitals often convert into a stubborn self-righteousness that resists public accountability. Modern hospital boards, their management teams, and their political lobbyists have a history of stonewalling government and local community efforts to make their use of charitable resources transparent to the public. They also have a reputation for failing to engage in meaningful dialog regarding service provision and community benefit.

Given the historic mission of tax-exempt hospitals and the multi-billion dollar value of hospital tax-exemptions, it is remarkable that there is no place on the

---

36. D.A. MATCHA, HEALTH CARE SYSTEMS OF THE DEVELOPED WORLD—HOW THE UNITED STATES SYSTEM REMAINS AN OUTLIER 75 (2003).

two major federal filings by tax-exempt hospitals (the Medicare Cost Report and the IRS Form 990) for the reporting of charity care provided by our nation's tax-exempt hospitals. Only recently, in 2007, did the IRS revise the IRS Form 990 to require hospitals to report standardized charity care and other community benefit information (starting in 2009). At the same time, detailed financial reporting is not universally available to the public. For many years, nonprofit hospitals viewed their audited financial statements as "private" and therefore not accessible to the public. Some states prohibited individual citizens from accessing hospital audited financial statements. As a hospital chief financial officer once said to one of the authors, "why would you want to make our financial data public?" Following the refusal of the Cleveland Clinic Foundation in the mid-1990s to provide timely financial statement updates to bondholders, the Securities and Exchange Commission (SEC) required nonprofit hospitals to file annual statements publicly once they have issued tax-exempt debt. Filings still are not timely in many cases, and many are not freely available without paying a fee for downloading statements. Nor are financial statements as timely, transparent, and comparable as creditors would like. This lack of transparency may explain why nonprofit hospitals pay higher risk and tax-adjusted interest rates than for-profit hospitals—creditors find the nonprofit statements less rigorously presented and more difficult to interpret.

In the 1990s several states began requiring hospitals to file "community benefit" reports for public viewing; but many of those filings lacked a common definition of community benefit. Efforts to define community benefit by state and local governments often deteriorated, after intensive lobbying by local hospitals and their associations, into meaningless categories of "benefit" that even for-profit, tax-paying hospitals provided, such as paying employee salaries, giving to the United Way, or landscaping improvements to the hospital grounds.[37] The AHA is still battling the IRS over whether or not Medicare "shortfalls" (payments below hospital costs) should be reported as a "community benefit," even though such shortfalls befall tax-paying and tax-exempt hospitals alike, may represent inefficiency rather than underpayment, and can hardly be said to be freely or charitably given.

Thus our country is served by over three thousand nonprofit hospitals that view themselves as *private* enterprises, whose philanthropic boards are free to determine who in their community to serve with minimal accountability to the broader body politic. Not surprisingly, the result is enormous variability in the availability of services and facilities and in the willingness of our hospitals to truly address community needs.

---

37. A. Noble et al., *Charitable Hospital Accountability: A Review and Analysis of Legal and Policy Initiatives,* 26 JOURNAL OF LAW, MEDICINE, AND ETHICS, 116–137 (1998).

CONCLUSION

We have met the enemy and he is us[38]

It is easier to blame some evil "other guy" (bad government, greedy insurers, arrogant administrators, rich doctors, inept boards) than recognize that our fragmented health care system is a by-product of our strongly ingrained American belief system. Reformers ignore these beliefs at their peril. At a minimum, policies directed at integrating the broken connections of our health system must accommodate this value system, not confront it head-on.

Globalization creates an opportunity for policymakers to encourage a slow cultural shift toward different values. This does not mean a rejection of the value and importance of competitive markets or respect for individual rights, but a deeper appreciation, born of a more mature nation, of the need for collaboration, collective action, accountability, building trust in needed government programs and permitting effective regulatory power to bring about a more integrated, affordable health care financing and delivery system. The recent collapse of global financial markets may create a window of opportunity for a fundamental reassessment of the values underlying American exceptionalism. In essence, Americans must redefine winning to compete effectively in a more complex game.

Redefining core values can help solve some of America's most vexing social problems. While we can't reform the health care system any faster than our social DNA allows, recognizing that we must change is a critical first step. Solutions will still have to be pragmatic, more bottom-up (communities and states have been the locus of most reform activity to date) than top-down. We will still have a uniquely American health care system, but one that acknowledges there are real limits to what we can do and how fast we can do it. With more maturity and honesty will come the admission that our system is broken, too expensive, leaves too many citizens unprotected, unduly rewards vested interests and causes too much physical, emotional, and financial harm to patients. Throughout its history, Americans have responded to crisis with a sense of purpose, creativity and bold action. Failure to address the underlying values of the U.S. health care system will contribute to a decline in America's global competitiveness and a reduction in our national standard of living. That unfortunate result would represent an "ironic" manifestation of American exceptionalism.

---

38. We Have Met the Enemy, http://en.wikipedia.org/wiki/Pogo_(comics)—.22We_have_met_the_enemy. . . . 22.

15. AMERICAN HEALTH CARE POLICY AND POLITICS
Is Fragmentation a Helpful Category for Understanding Health Reform Experience and Prospects?

THEODORE R. MARMOR

INTRODUCTION

The continuities of American medical politics, despite the surges of reform enthusiasm, are impressive. As the presidential election of 2008 drew closer, all the candidates felt compelled to offer plans for universal health insurance. That had also been true in the buildup to the presidential election of 1992, and what had followed was the birth and death of the Clinton reform plan. Now, as then, huge majorities of Americans claim they want reform—universal insurance coverage—and disagree about what that would be. Then, as now, interest groups mobilize for battle, trading sound bites and horror stories attacking and defending particular reforms. At the same time, the more quiet politics in health care continue to unfold off the front page and the evening television news: the moral disputes over abortion, euthanasia, and stem-cell research, the distributive, intense local politics of hospital closures and clinic openings, the Washington and state capital fights in hearing rooms over the rules governing the practices of nurses, chiropractors, and physicians, let alone the armies of lobbyists struggling to start or stop health insurance reforms in the states. The cost of health insurance—public and private—dominates the surface of discussion, but the distributive realities of who bears those costs (and should) continue to agitate or bewilder many commentators. To make sense of these diverse topics on the American medical political agenda, it is essential to use categories that separate the fundamental from the incidental. One option is to employ the ordinary categories of policy and political conflict, which will be my approach. But, throughout, I will ask whether and how the notion of fragmentation—the focus of this book—helps or hinders. In short, what follows is a running commentary on American health care politics over the past four decades interpreted with and without the focus on fragmentation.

The essay proceeds in parts. The first reviews—in broad brush—the highlights of health policy disputes, changes and continuity from the 1970s to the present. The second elaborates on the contemporary scene, placing the United States in some comparative perspective. Part III discusses the regulation versus competition debate that has been so much a part of the American medical care dialogue since the 1970s. Part IV uses the issues surrounding the reform of Medicare—its affordability, its fairness, and the claimed need for modernization—as an illustration of an important policy dispute that the conception of fragmentation, if useful, should illuminate. Part V returns to the theme of contemporary health reform with my conclusions.

I. LOOKING BACK, LOOKING NOW: 1970–2007

The broad history of American medical care from the 1970s to the first decade of the twentieth century is one of diverse conflicts, turbulent change, and a persistent sense that the vast health expenditures of these decades failed to provide good value for money.[1] Senator Edward Kennedy's 1972 book, *In Critical Condition: The Crisis in America's Health Care*,[2] reflected in its title the atmosphere of urgency at the time. Indeed, this sense of trouble—of seemingly continuous inflation, a complex and *fragmented* organization of care, and both under-insurance and lack of coverage for many millions—was so widespread that Republicans and Democrats, liberals and conservatives, competed over which form of national health insurance to offer in response. The regulations that emerged, however, were *dispersed* bureaucratically, disconnected from the major public programs financing care and celebrated with visions of eventual success that no reasonable analyst should have accepted. Professional Standards Review Organizations (PSROS), for instance—established by the federal government to monitor quality of care—were relegated in 1972 to a different set of agencies, dominated by physicians and *disconnected* in practice from the payment systems of Medicare, Medicaid, or private health insurance plans. Medicare and Medicaid, once separate organizationally, were *technically joined* in an agency known as the Health Care Financing Administration (HCFA). But this new organization (now the Center for Medical Services) failed to *unify* Medicare and Medicaid administrations, much less have an impact on health planning. In all these cases, the political struggles were intense, dominated by groups with financial and professional interests in the policies and reported in the trade press and

---

1. The sketch of American medical politics and policy is drawn from my previous work: *Commentary*, on Kenneth R. Wing, *American Health Policy in the 1980s*, CASE WESTERN RESERVE LAW REVIEW 36, 4 (1985–86): 608–85, at 686–92, and a review of ROBERT G. EVANS, STRAINED MERCY: THE ECONOMICS OF CANADIAN HEALTH CARE (1984), in JOURNAL OF HEALTH POLITICS, POLICY, AND LAW 11, 1 (1986): 163–66 (for an expanded version, *see* PERSPECTIVES IN BIOLOGY AND MEDICINE 30, 4 (1987): 590–96).

2. EDWARD M. KENNEDY, IN CRITICAL CONDITION: THE CRISIS IN AMERICA'S HEALTH CARE (1972).

professional medical journals. But they all fell short of the national attention that debates over universal health insurance always prompt.[3]

All through the 1970s, commentators complained about the uneven distribution of care and the high rates of inflation in medicine, but few fundamental changes were made. The Nixon administration tried wage and price controls, but gave up on them. The Carter administration supported legislation to contain hospital costs, but was defeated by opposition from hospitals and general skepticism that the federal government could accomplish what it promised. Inflation continued unabated amid naïve rhetoric about a "voluntary effort" to control costs by the health industry. It all seems very long ago, looking back from the perspective of 2008 to this earlier flurry of proposals and stalemate over universal, government-financed health insurance. From the standpoint of fragmentation, however, there was a fundamental development. The celebration of health maintenance organizations (HMOs) as a model emphasized the unification of medical care financing and delivery in the same legal organization. This was but a rhetorical renaming of the conceptual fundamentals associated with the previous generations' pre-paid group practices whether called Kaiser-Permanente, Group Practice of Puget Sound, or HIP in New York. Here at least was one institutionally clear instance of a unified as opposed to a dispersed model of delivering and financing care.[4]

---

3. The italicized terms in this paragraph all touch on two ordinary meanings of fragmentation: namely, broken into parts as opposed to kept whole, and dispersed as opposed to unified. So, the formal unification of Medicare and Medicaid in HFCA during the 1970s did not in practice work as a unified administration of a program with common rules. This is quite independent of whether it should or should not have been unified in practice; the reality was and is that the programs are quite separately administered for perfectly understandable statutory reasons. These understandings are not quite parallel with, for example, the idea of fragmentation in health care markets discussed by Greaney, where fragmentation is supposed to act, "at times, at cross purposes with competition policy." Fragmentation at the level of the American "healthcare system" is the topic throughout, but, as I will try to illustrate, it plays very different roles in the various papers and falls short of a consistent meaning throughout. So, for instance, a paper entitled "The Role of the Payment System in Causing Fragmentation" raises the obvious question: fragmentation of what exactly? The fragmentation of the "delivery of health services," we are told, is "likely driven by a variety of factors," . . . but the author concentrates on those "caused or exacerbated by the law." The desired alternative is "quality-and efficiency-enhancing *integration*," which is the favored antonym of fragmentation in this paper. Given these differences, I will proceed with my own exploration of where and when it seems useful to treat fragmentation—in one or more of its meanings—as central.

4. In 1974, for instance, the now forgotten Kennedy-Mills proposal received extended consideration in the finance committees of the Congress, as did the Nixon CHIP plan and the catastrophic health insurance bill of Senators Long and Ribicoff. The politics of this period are reviewed in Lawrence D. Brown, POLITICS AND HEALTH CARE

In the 1980s the picture was different, politically, economically, and intellectually. Few prominent figures promoted government-financed universal health insurance, either for the nation or for a particular state. Following the 1980s, the deficits of the Reagan and Bush years continued to dominate political discourse, and reformers turned first to bureaucratic realignments as a means to rationalize medical care provision and then to financing through such policies as diagnostic-related group payments to hospitals (DRGs). When those strategies failed, many reformers looked to competition and privatization as their panacea, appealing both to the ideology of market competition and to the grief caused by the persistent relative inflation in the costs of health care. Here, an immediate conceptual issue arises. The notion of competition in American medical care has at least three distinct expressions. One is returning the purchase of most medical care to consumer decisions, with substantial deductibles (and possibly co-insurance), so as to have suppliers compete for the custom of patients as if, for most dealings, in an ordinary consumer market. Major risk insurance has been the favored policy reform of that perspective. A second perspective, strongly associated with the work of Clark Havighurst, emphasizes anti-trust enforcement to make the supplier side of the market more competitive. Finally, there is the very different level of competition associated with "integrated delivery systems" competing for customers—whether at the level of the insurance firm, the employer, or the individual. There the emphasis is on bringing together—as opposed to dispersing—the range of delivery, financing, and day-to-day regulation of medical care. It is the more recent expression of the ideas emphasized in the HMO movement of the 1970s.[5]

The earlier attention to national health insurance gave way to a wide variety of other initiatives. At the state level, there were earnest but unsuccessful efforts to expand insurance coverage. At the business level, there were noteworthy attempts to broaden the benefits in employment-related health insurance. And there were innovative experiments in financing second opinions, wellness programs, prepaid group practice plans, and exercise facilities at the workplace. Medicare and Medicaid tried a variety of payment reforms, including the diagnosis-related group method of paying hospitals and complex formulas to adjust physician fees to standards of relative value.

But the fundamental reform of the rules of the American medical game was off the political agenda, and the major changes that were attempted were basically private initiatives. Attracted by the gold mine of funds flowing through a system of retrospective, cost-based reimbursement, the captains of American capitalism came to see opportunity where the politicians had found causes for complaint.

ORGANIZATIONS: HMOs AS FEDERAL POLICY (1984); and T.R. MARMOR, POLITICAL ANALYSIS AND AMERICAN MEDICAL CARE (1983).

5. *See*, for instance, HENRY J. AARON AND WILLIAM B. SCHWARTZ, THE PAINFUL PRESCRIPTION: RATIONING HEALTH CARE (1983).

In the hospital world, small chains of for-profit hospitals—the Humanas and Hospital Corporations of America, to name but one—grew into large companies. HMOs—the Republican-backed variant of the pre-paid group practice model of American liberals noted earlier—had important consequences. On the one hand its language of integration increasingly dominated the discussion of the delivery and financing of care for Americans. On the other hand, its earlier nonprofit status gave way over time to profit firms and the organizational label expanded rapidly. The reality, however, is that most of the organizations calling themselves HMOs or "integrated delivery systems" were no such thing.[6] Industrial giants like Baxter-Travenol and American Hospital Supply took their conventional dreams of competitive growth and extended them to vertical and horizontal integration.[7]

All of these changes in the structure of American medicine took place within the context of increasingly anti-regulatory and anti-Washington rhetoric. Democrats and Republicans alike had been influenced by a generation of academic policy analysts—mostly economists—who ridiculed the costliness and captured quality of the decisions taken by supposedly independent regulatory agencies in Washington. The Civil Aeronautics Board and the airlines industry came to represent the distortions likely when government regulates industry and, with time, the convention of describing any set of related activities with economic significance as an "industry" demythologized medicine as well. So, even before the Reagan administration came into office, the time was ripe for celebrating "competition" in medicine, getting government off the industry's back, and letting the fresh air of deregulation solve the problems of access, cost, quality, fragmentation, and the sheer complexity of health care. The irony is that the most consequential health initiative of the 1980s—Medicare's prospective payment system by diagnosis-related groups—was an exceedingly sophisticated, highly regulatory form of administered prices. Although this irony strikes me as worth emphasizing, it is obvious that the deregulation movement had huge effects on the understanding of medical care among selected groups of scholars, commentators and reformers. (For example, in the McCain proposals for health insurance reform in 2008, the competition themes return to the 1970s and 80s, but not to the ideas of 'integration' of delivery and finance.)

---

6. *See* for an extended discussion of this development, T.R. Marmor & Hacker, Michigan Law Reform article, in T.R. Marmor, FADS, FALLACIES, AND FOOLISHNESS IN MEDICAL CARE MANAGEMENT AND POLICY (2007).

7. For a varied discussion of these new elements in American medicine, *see* Jeffrey Goldsmith, *Death of a Paradigm: The Challenge of Competition*, 3 HEALTH AFF. 7–19 (1984); PAUL STARR, THE SOCIAL TRANSFORMATION OF AMERICAN MEDICINE (1984); and T.R. Marmor et al., A NEW LOOK AT NONPROFITS: HEALTH CARE POLICY IN A COMPETITIVE AGE, 3 YALE JOURNAL OF REGULATION 313–49 (1986).

II. THE CONTEMPORARY SCENE: PLACING THE UNITED STATES
COMPARATIVELY

After more than thirty years of talk about an American medical world in critical condition, little progress has been made in arriving at consensus about a major policy change. The United States is, of course, now the only major industrial nation without universal or near-universal health care program. Rather, Americans get their health insurance from a mix of private and public sources— employers (60%), private individual plans (9%), and various governmental financing programs (27%). Medicare insures more than 40 million elderly and disabled Americans and Medicaid provides financing for some 38 million low-income Americans. The public share of financing constitutes more than half of the 2.1 trillion dollars spent on healthcare in 2006. The public share is not only for the major programs noted above, but the Veterans Administration network of hospitals and clinics, special programs for Native Americans and the Armed Services, and the tax expenditures that help to finance the employment based coverage for most working Americans.

At any one time, some 46 million Americans are without health insurance, though emergency care at hospitals is legally available to all, whether they can pay or not. Still, medical bills remain the second major cause of personal bankruptcy. The problems of access have worsened, and the list of the uninsured and the under-insured has grown. (The number of those who are uninsured within a two-year period, it is estimated, is nearly twice the 46 million noted above.) The relative rate of medical inflation has continued, and its relentless rise shows no signs of slowing, despite the extraordinary changes that have been made in the rules of the professional medical game: America spent about 7 percent of its national income, or GNP, on health in 1970, over 9 percent by 1980, more than 11 percent by 1990, and something close to 16 percent in 2008. With the highest health cost per capita of any country in the world, the United States was ranked 37th in overall performance by the World Health Organization (WHO). (The WHO did evaluate American health care first in the world in level of responsiveness and 72nd in general health.) Since Canada was 33rd in overall performance, and Oman was 8th, one should use these figures with caution. It is simpler to say that Americans spend the most and feel among the worst about their value for money.

Before elaborating on this contemporary portrait of American medical care and its politics, there are some analytical preliminaries to address. First, there is no such thing as a common politics of American medicine. One can rightly emphasize the politics *in* the nation's medical care, but not a politics *of* American medical care. In practice, that requires distinguishing among the most prominent varieties of political dispute and resolution. This analytic breakdown—rather than the causes, consequences, and reform of a fragmentary medical care system—proceeds from a political scientist's approach to policy analysis:

- System reform: ideologically controversial disputes about whether and how to change the major features of a medical care system—whether financing, quality, costs, or delivery. The struggles over state insurance reform in Massachusetts and California in 2007–2008 exemplify these politics.
- Rationing: disputes about the extent to which and the explicitness with which medical care is apportioned at any one time—a topic of differential intensity across national borders and within them. These struggles are usually dominated by professional medical care groups but find expression in the mass media, as with the denial of access to organ transplantation.
- Prevention: disputes about the effectiveness and cost implications of efforts to prevent illness, disease, and injury, as well as conflicts over the benefits and costs of so-called healthy public policies. There is great variability over time and space in the salience of these disputes, with current attention in the United States focused on wasteful treatment as compared to possible improvements in preventive care.
- Professional accountability, autonomy, and power: the extent to which the medical profession is being subjected to external scrutiny and losing control over its own activities. These issues are obviously of greatest interest to the affected professional parties.
- Panics: issues where public anxiety and governmental action are generated by unexpected or unpredicted epidemics or health crises (e.g., AIDS, BSE, contaminated blood, SARS). These episodes result initially in a period of strict order, followed by intense politics, and struggles that dominate the mass media for a time before they disappear.
- Consumer empowerment: disputes over efforts to increase the role of ordinary citizens, whether patients, taxpayers, or caregivers, in the making or implementation of policies in health care. While highly variable in salience over time and space, this topic emerged in the Bush administration under the rubric of "consumer-directed healthcare." In practice, that euphemistic phrase refers to high-deductible health insurance plans with or without the tax incentives represented by medical savings accounts (MSAs).
- Moral crusades: disputes about abortion, stem-cell research, euthanasia, smoking bans, alcohol control, and other contentious issues of individual versus social choice.

These categories should help us to explore the distinctive configurations of interests, institutions, and processes shaping current debates about specific health care issues.

III. COMPETITION VERSUS REGULATION IN THE PRESENT REFORM DEBATE

Is the idea of complete government control over and administration of medical care financing the answer to the continuing debate over containing health care expenditures? Some Americans—policy-makers and medical care professionals as well as ordinary citizens—think that the only way to get the problems of America's health care system under control is to follow the model of the British National Health Service.[8] That model, however, invokes the unhappy image of severe rationing of care and long waits for all but the most pressing medical problems. It also conjures up images of "socialized" medicine, with all the loss of individual control and freedom of choice for both practitioner and patient that the slogan implies. The widely acknowledged seriousness of American medicine's present problems has not produced clear public support for the British policy. By contrast, considerable support has been expressed at various times for versions of national health insurance modeled on Medicare, the Canadian national health insurance program. Interestingly, that was less so in 2007–2008 than in either the early 1970s or the period leading up to the Clinton reform struggle of 1991–1994. The absence of substantial support for the NHS model of financing and delivering medical care is worth noting in connection with the theme of fragmentation. All complex, national systems of medical care raise problems of interpretation. Figuring out whether what is claimed is actually so regarding other national arrangements regularly produces caricatures, not characterizations. But the NHS is one organization—huge as it is—and is held accountable for the performance of the decentralized delivery arrangements for fifty million plus citizens. In that sense it is the model of unification as opposed to political fragmentation.

At the other ideological extreme in American health policy is a different model. By that I mean the set of ideas often described as the "competitive health strategy."[9] Though their arguments vary, advocates of competition believe that restructuring the financial incentives of patients is crucial to restraining medical inflation and controlling both public and private health expenditures. Their central policy prescription is the introduction of greater price competition in medical care. In the presence of widespread health insurance, these advocates argue, there is scope for price competition in premiums. They also argue that substantially increased cost-sharing by patients is helpful on the demand side of the market. This version of a competitive strategy is, as noted, but one, and is very different from what has already been identified as an integration and competition variant.

---

8. *Supra* note 5.

9. *See* ALAN C. ENTHOVEN, HEALTH PLAN: THE ONLY PRACTICAL SOLUTION TO SOARING HEALTH CARE COSTS (1980); Clark C. Havighurst, *Competition in Health Services: Overview, Issues, and Answers,* 34 VANDERBILT LAW REVIEW 1115–78 (1981); and T.R. Marmor et al., *Medical Care and Procompetitive Reform,* 34 VANDERBILT LAW REVIEW 1003–28 (1981).

The eventual outcome of any thoroughgoing competitive health care strategy has been and remains uncertain. The strategy has not been implemented on a wide scale anywhere in the postwar period. For all these reasons, the reality of health politics from the 1980s on has been comprised of incremental steps of both a regulatory and a competitive variety—what we might call "agitated incrementalism."[10] There has been and continues to be little coherent public concern about the rising costs of health care in the United States, though polls revealed continuing public anxiety. The concerns that mattered were the costs of care to individuals (in premiums or cost sharing when ill), to firms (in increased expenditures for employee health insurance), and to governments (in rising outlays for particular programs—Medicare for federal officials; Medicaid for state and federal officials). Concern about relative inflation in medical care— the concern that the society is spending more for care in the aggregate than its citizens receive in benefits—is an academic's problem. America may well be, as Brian Abel-Smith wrote some years ago, a country where we receive insufficient "value for money."[11] But, where medical care is concerned, the public worries more about access, financial protection, and quality than about value for money. And that is why, at this point, the concern about the dismantling of employer-related health insurance has prompted so much national attention. (Dismantling—or fraying—might, for some, be synonyms for fragmenting. If so, one could say that employment-related health insurance has become more fragmented. But, that interpretation does not seem central to this book. The changes in employment coverage of health insurance were, however, central to the health reform debates of 2007-9). Cost containment, when seriously attempted, arises from actions to control the rising burden of medical care to particular payers, most prominently the federal government and hardly less so to particular states and corporations.[12] The problems with that approach are all related to the obvious fact that actions that save federal (or state or corporate) dollars do not necessarily constitute anti-inflationary successes. Indeed, actions that have substantially shifted costs among payers have had little or no effect on total health care expenditures. Viewed through this lens, the absence in the United States of a unified payer—a monopsonist on the model of a Canadian province—is consequential, a topic to be discussed momentarily.

Turning now to delivery, the dispensing of American medical care "can be simultaneously described as a system on the brink of crisis and as a strong and growing industry, with seemingly equal accuracy."[13] In attempting to explain this situation, we need first to emphasize the enormous influence of providers in the

10. These ideas are drawn from T.R. Marmor and Jon B. Christianson, HEALTH CARE POLICY: A POLITICAL ECONOMY APPROACH (1982).

11. Brian Abel-Smith, VALUE FOR MONEY IN HEALTH SERVICES (1976).

12. For an extended presentation of the politics of medical inflation, see Wing, *American Health Policy in the 1980s*.

13. *Id.* at 612.

imbalanced political marketplace of many of the health policy struggles. And worsening that imbalance is the lack of sustained public opinion marshaled around any one of the various formulations of the problems of cost, access, and quality of American medicine. A large part of the explanation for the United State's current health situation is the pluralism of American politics and the parallel dispersion of countervailing power in both the political and the economic marketplaces. Our federalism has spread the authority for regulating medical care between the national government and the many states. Our financing splits private and public payers, with considerable discrepancies among them in each sector. Here is the language of federalism and dispersal, language that could quite easily be converted into fragmentation as opposed to a unified political structure.

Two explanatory factors for the cost pressures in American medicine become central. Medical care is widely regarded as a merit good, still widely insured through work, and a part of the American private and public welfare state. The *fragmentation* of finance has meant that, once payers are aroused, the problem they separately address is that of their own costs, not of American medicine. Pluralistic finance, combined with extensive third-party coverage, is a predictable recipe for inflation. Only those regimes that have concentrated the stakes of medical payers—Great Britain, Canada, Germany, for instance—have been better able to restrain the forces of medical inflation. And such countervailing power is but the necessary condition for restraint. Political will is also essential. In some instances, as in Sweden, the governments with concentrated authority have chosen to spend more on medical care—as government has, too, in recent years, in Canada. Those countries made these choices through balancing the gains and losses of increasing expenditures. In the United States, in contrast, we have discovered our inflated health outlays, not chosen them. Financial fragmentation as understood here is indeed of crucial policy importance.

Rapidly increasing medical care costs are not only a central problem that reformers must address but also a major barrier to sensible reform debate in the United States. The controversies over the Medicare program in the period after the Clinton reform failure (1995 to the present) illustrate clearly this feature of contemporary health politics. Budget politics provided the setting, but the themes were much broader. They help us to understand the context of the U.S. presidential battles of 2008.

IV. MEDICARE: AFFORDABILITY, FAIRNESS, AND MODERNIZATION

Medicare, largely ignored in the battle over health care reform in the early 1990s, returned to center stage following the Republican congressional victories of 1994. Given bipartisan calls for reductions in the nation's budget deficits and hostility among some Republicans to Medicare's social insurance roots, it was almost certain that this program would again generate intense and very public debate and conflict. Moreover, like Social Security pensions, long-term projections of Medicare spending prompted worries about unsustainable budget outlays—especially in light of the aging population and the hugely expensive medical technologies and prescription drugs increasingly becoming available.[14] The public commentary about Medicare in the 1990s incorporated arguments that were to reappear in vivid language over the next decade and more. Unaffordability, unfairness, and somewhat masked ideological objections—operating under the banner of "modernization"—all these terms were applied to social insurance itself and, by extension, to "government medicine."[15]

Affordability

The truth is that fearful projections of Medicare's fiscal future reflect a problem of U.S. medicine, not a crisis caused by Medicare's structure. In fact, for most of Medicare's history, program spending grew about as rapidly as outlays in the private medical economy. Figure 1 shows a number of temporal shifts, which helps explain particular episodes of fearfulness. From the early 1990s, per capita medical costs grew much faster than per capita gross domestic product (GDP) in both the private sector and Medicare. But from about 1993 through 1997, private health outlays grew far less rapidly than Medicare outlays. This discrepancy itself

EXHIBIT 3
Trends In Health Care Costs Per Capita, United States, 1991–2003

	Percent change by spending category			
	GDP per capita	Non-Medicare health services	Large employer premiums	Medicare per enrollee
1991–1993	3.3	6.2	10.1	–[a]
1994–1997	4.4	2.4	2.4	–[a]
1998–2000	4.6	6.7	5.0	0.3
2001–2003	2.8	9.0	13.3	7.2
1990–1995	3.7	(4.5)	(7.4)	(8.7)
1995–1997	4.8	(2.6)	(1.3)	(6.5)

SOURCE: J. White, "Transformations of the American Health Care System: Risks for Americans and Lessons from Abroad" (Unpublished manuscript, 2006).
NOTE: GDP is gross domestic product.
[a] Not available.

FIGURE 1 TRENDS IN HEALTH CARE, 1991–2003

14. Boards of Trustees of the Federal Hospital Insurance and Federal Supplemental Health Insurance Trust Funds, *2005 Annual Report*, March 23, 2005, http://new.cms.hhs.gov/ReportsTrustFunds/downloads/tr2005.pdf (accessed February 27, 2006).

15. J. Oberlander, The Political Life of Medicare (Chicago: University of Chicago Press, 2003); and T.R. Marmor, The Politics of Medicare. (New Jersey: Tranaction Books, 2000, 2nd edition).

prompted many cries of alarm. Since then, however, the relationship has shifted back and forth. The important reality in the period after 1997 is rapid inflation in U.S. medical care generally, not just, or even particularly, in Medicare.

Over the long run—from 1970 to 2001, for instance—Medicare spending per enrollee grew less rapidly (9.6 percent per year) than spending for the privately insured (eleven percent). Over the period 1990–2003, spending rose at similar rates for both Medicare and private insurance.[16] These data give no reason to be complacent about the costs of U.S. medical care. But nor do they support the claim of Medicare's incapacity to control medical inflation.

Yet, whenever there has been a more rapid rate of increase in Medicare spending in combination with projected deficits in the Medicare Part A Trust Fund, critics use projections of Medicare's future outlays to suggest that the program must be fundamentally reformed now. Suggestions for reform are often fabulously complex, but they tend to have these common features: the explicit or implicit claims that the "common pool," or social insurance features, of Medicare are the cost-control culprit; and the idea that adding choice, competition, and individual responsibility ("consumer-driven health care" now) will solve the problem.

The common pool feature of Medicare cannot plausibly be a cause for fiscal concern. In other developed countries, experience has repeatedly demonstrated the superior capacity of more universal social insurance programs to restrain growth in overall medical spending. As noted earlier, any comparison of growth in health spending of the United States and social-insurance nations like Germany, the Netherlands, and France would show American spending growing more rapidly in recent decades. And these other countries have older populations and more widespread use of health care than is the case in the United States.[17]

One might argue more plausibly that fiscal restraint is difficult because Medicare does not cover everyone. Medicare has indeed few instruments to control capital spending. But its powerful constraints on payments to hospitals and doctors spill over onto pressures on private payers. The latter fight back by adapting some of Medicare's techniques, which then increases political pressures from providers to ease up on cost control. The experience of the past thirty or more years demonstrates that fragmented U.S. arrangements for financing medical care are comparatively weak instruments for controlling spending growth. That does not indict Medicare, but it does highlight a serious problem that Medicare (and the rest of the medical economy) will have to confront.

---

16. C. Boccuti and M. Moon, *Comparing Medicare and Private Insurers: Growth Rates in Spending over Three Decades*, 22 HEALTH AFF. 235 (2003).

17. T.R. Marmor, *From the United States, in* DUTCH WELFARE REFORM IN AN EXPANDING EUROPE: THE NEIGHBOURS' VIEW 111–34 (E. de Gier et al., eds., 2004).

Critics—especially those concentrated in the pro-market wing of the Republican Party—have increasingly appealed to individual responsibility, choice, and competition as the "solution" to the problems of both U.S. medicine generally and Medicare's fiscal problems in particular.[18] One response is the broad proposal for health savings accounts (HSAs). Instead of participating in group insurance at the place of employment or paying the health insurance portion of *Federal Insurance Contributions Act* taxes, Americans are urged to contribute, tax free, to health savings accounts to cover their medical care needs. A version of such accounts was included in the 2003 *Medicare Prescription Drug, Improvement, and Modernization Act (MMA)*. The buildup in these accounts, along with an inexpensive "high-deductible" or "catastrophic" insurance policy, would, it is claimed, provide sufficient reserves for medical care both while employed and during old age.

There are major transitional problems with this scheme, but those need not distract from the main line of argument. For the young, the healthy, and the affluent, a health savings account approach is a great deal, particularly so if, as is virtually certain, these tax-free savings could be tapped for other purposes once a sufficient cushion was achieved. What happens to the rest of the population is only slightly less clear but broadly predictable. With "good risks" now not in the insurance pool, bad risks must be "insured" by general taxation. In short, instead of medical care as a part of a national pool of social insurance financing (or its Canadian equivalent), the system would move rapidly toward segmentation: private insurance for the young, healthy, and relatively well-off; welfare medicine for everyone else. Here is the sharp contrast between broader insurance "pools" contrasted with the individualization of risk-bearing. Looked at through a fragmentation lens, HSAs would qualify as the opposite of a policy of holding together.

An alternative "privatization" approach retains Medicare's social insurance coverage for the elderly but attempts to save public funds by having privately managed care plans compete for Medicare patients. This alternative poses no direct threat to social insurance. Rather, the worrisome issue is whether managed care can both save money and deliver decent medical care at the same time to the elderly, or to anyone else. These are crucial questions for the whole of U.S. medicine, not just Medicare.

Fairness
A more fundamental issue than fragmentation is financial fairness in medical care. Should the insurance risks of ill health be dealt with in a universal, contributory, or tax-financed "public insurance" program or left to a patchwork system of private

---

18. For some illustrations, *see* S. Butler and D.B. Kendall, *Expanding Access and Choice for Health Care Consumers through Tax Reform*, 18 HEALTH AFF. 45–57 (1999); and H.J. Aaron & R.D. Reischauer, *The Medicare Reform Debate: What Is the Next Step?* 14 HEALTH AFF. 8–30 (1995).

payment, private insurance, and diverse public subsidies for veterans, the aged, the poor, participants in employment-based health insurance, and so on?

The place of Medicare in this more fundamental discussion was, in 2008, odd. From the standpoint of universal protection, Medicare remains conceptually divided. It separates retired workers from those still on the job, thus breaching one version of social solidarity and giving rise to concerns about unfair special treatment for one segment of society. And because Medicare covers only three groups of the population—those "retired" because of age, disability, or renal failure—it can all too easily take on the coloration of interest-group politics. These politics are not the vitriolic struggles of us versus them welfare policy. But it is quite easy to claim as "unfair" the relatively generous treatment of Medicare beneficiaries compared with the circumstances of ordinary American families flailing in the sea of either uncertain insurance coverage or added constraints on their choices within insurance coverage. The question is whether the rest of the population shares this vision of unfairness, as opposed to wanting Medicare's security and choices in their own coverage. Little of this debate connects to the fragmentation theme.

Developments during the past two decades have undermined a common experience of health insurance coverage. Traditional private, non-profit Blue Cross, Blue Shield plans have largely disappeared. Where they exist, they mostly use commercial health insurance practices.

There is no evidence that any substantial number of Americans accepts "unfairness" claims or favors moves to align Medicare's coverage with what has emerged in the private market. Nor, as the discussion of affordability reveals, is there any reason to believe that competition yields cost savings that will permit a "fairer" distribution of coverage. Indeed, the only "modernization" movement that has gained traction was the complaint about Medicare's failure to respond to changes in the nature of medical care, not changes in insurance plans. There the critics had obvious grounds for their charge. In 1965, drugs used outside the hospital were a modest part of the medical budget, and, in any case, Medicare reformers assumed that there would be persistent expansions of populations and services covered. Neither development took place according to plan. As pharmaceuticals came to play a larger role in medical care and as the world of private American health insurance diverged from the older Blue Cross, Blue Shield model, Medicare became an outlier in form and, in substance, fell short of the breadth of services covered by many private plans. Medicare beneficiaries were not getting the drug coverage that had become standard for other insured Americans.

Modernization
As of 2003, Medicare could be perceived as unfair in two ways: Medicare beneficiaries had more comprehensive coverage and choice of providers than many insured non-retired people had, but less coverage of increasingly important and expensive prescription drugs. Enter the *Medicare Prescription Drug, Improvement,*

and Modernization Act of 2003, a fantastically complex piece of legislation designed to combat both "unfairnesses" by rolling them into a common call for "modernization." Medicare beneficiaries would obtain drug coverage, but in a "choice of plans" form that relied on private insurance provision, competition, and consumer choice. Moreover, the statute went beyond drug coverage to pursue the "modernization" of other health insurance areas. These included a complex set of incentives and financing arrangements intended to promote movement out of traditional Medicare into private plans more like those available to most other insured Americans. "Modernization" in this form implicitly promised cost containment through competition. Indeed, the statute went so far as to prohibit the one proven cost-constraint mechanism in Medicare's arsenal: use of its market power to bargain down prices, a technique too close to government price setting to satisfy the Bush administration and its allies in the 2003 Congress.

This Act was, in many respects, legislation by stealth. Here, and elsewhere, "modernization" has become a code word that masks ideological hostility to the public social insurance structure with which Social Security and Medicare began. It holds out the hope that truly modern systems of social provision will be both more affordable and fairer than "relics" of our New Deal and Great Society past that have outlived their usefulness. And in the current U.S. political context, to be modern means to hold a distinctive ideological position—at least to every one of the Republicans who sought their party's nomination in 2007–2008. It is the power of individual choice, market competition, and personal responsibility to remake social policy to fit the demands of the twenty-first century.

I believe these "hopes" to be profoundly misguided. *Fragmenting risk pools* will not increase the fairness of American medical care.[19] And choice and competition have no proven record of cost control in medical care either in the United States or elsewhere. Modernization in this guise is a Trojan horse. Inside is a complex set of devices that increase individual risk bearing and decrease the economic security traditionally provided by government health insurance in its social insurance or tax-financed form. Nonetheless, the contemporary debate has been profoundly influenced by the struggle over Medicare in the period after the Clinton reform failure. What appears sensible to promote is constrained by the interpretations of affordability, fairness, and modernity just discussed.

V. HEALTH REFORM IN 2007–2009

Americans are not well served by their current medical care arrangements. Compared to our major trading partners and competitors, we are less likely to be

---

19. It should be obvious by now that this is the central meaning of fragmentation that I think bears on the reform debates of the past few years.

insured for the cost of care, and the care that we receive is almost certain to be more costly. Though the leader in expenditures for medical research, American medicine is not the undisputed leader in medical innovation; except in the costliness and ubiquity of high-technology medicine. Most Americans "covered" by some form of health insurance still worry about its continuation when they or a close family member become seriously ill. Some are locked into employment they would gladly leave but for the potential catastrophic loss of existing insurance coverage. Something needs to be done, as the presidential candidates all acknowledge.

One fact remains obvious, however. Americans have long been dissatisfied with the nation's medical arrangements, but our political system has been unable to come up with a solution that satisfies enough of the public to overwhelm the institutional and interest group barriers to reform.[20] There is now once again a remarkable consensus that American medical care, particularly its financing and insurance coverage, needs a major overhaul. The critical unanimity on this point bridges almost all the usual cleavages in American politics: between old and young, Democrats and Republicans, management and labor, the well-paid and the low-paid. The overwhelming majority of Americans (including Fortune 500 executives) told pollsters in 2008 that the medical system requires substantial change. This level of public discontent was good news for medical reformers in 1993, just as it has been again.[21]

The bad news for reformers, then and now, is that, for ideological and institutional reasons, American politics makes it very difficult to coalesce around a solution that reasonably satisfies the requirements for a stable and workable system of financing and delivering modern medical care. Agreement on the seriousness of the nation's medical ills will not necessarily generate the legislative support required for a substantively adequate and administratively workable program. That is as true in 2007–2009 as it was in 1948, 1971, 1993, and 2000.

---

20. While substantial change took place in the United States in the decades from 1980 to 2000, most of it was privately generated. What is called the "managed care" movement altered the way most American physicians practice and get paid, and it had a lot to do with the changing ownership and shape of American hospitals. These changes stand in contrast to the publicly organized reforms in the United Kingdom (internal markets in the 1990s) or Canada (national health insurance in the period 1957–71). For more on health reforms, especially "nonpublic change," see CAROLYN H. TUOHY, ACCIDENTAL LOGICS: THE DYNAMICS OF CHANGE IN THE HEALTH CARE ARENA IN THE UNITED STATES, BRITAIN, AND CANADA (1999).

21. For more on the public desire for substantial change in health care, see Robert J. Blendon & John M. Benson, American's Views on Health Policy: A Fifty-Year Historical Perspective, 20 HEALTH AFF. 33–46 (2001). A New York Times/CBS news survey in February 2007 confirmed this historical pattern, with "an overwhelming majority" saying that "the healthcare system needs fundamental change or total reorganization." Robin Toner, U.S. Guarantee of Care for All, Poll Finds, NEW YORK TIMES, March 2, 2007.

The most obvious point is that the presidential competition for 2007–2008 recapitulated the run-up to its parallels in earlier struggles. Contenders—particularly among the Democratic hopefuls—felt compelled to propose detailed plans or are put on the defensive for not doing so. The result had been depressingly familiar in a number of ways. Not one candidate had stated straightforwardly the core values health reform should express. Rather, the enumeration of complaints had dominated. The result was a pattern of problem identification and gestures toward complicated steps to broader health insurance coverage. The differences in values between a plan presented by Governor Schwarzenegger and any of the Democratic contenders are not easy to identify. None of the plans discussed—whether the expansions of child health insurance mentioned by Senator Clinton, the appeal to mandated coverage by Clinton and John Edwards (and incorporated in the California and Massachusetts plans), the Obama proposal of incentives for health insurance expansion, or the Bush administration's embrace of medical savings accounts and changes in the tax code's treatment of employer-arranged health insurance celebrated by Republican policy experts—seriously addressed persistent medical inflation. Yet it is the contemporary costs (16 percent of national income) and the rate of increase (1.5 to 2 times the growth of American incomes) that is at the core of the coverage problems the United States still face.

The gap between diagnosis and remedy was not an oversight, however. Candidates understandably were wary of announcing who the losers would be if their favored approach were actually to become a program fact. After all, if our medical arrangements are to become more affordable, some of those whose incomes constitute health expenditures must get less in the future than they might like. The presidential campaign of 2007–2008 showed no sign of improvement over the Clinton period and had less clarity, about values or program structure, than the campaign of the early 1970s. That is not a healthy sign, but it is a good reason to reconsider the serious values debate: over values at stake, international experience, and a sober review of the United States' own history with public and private financing of medical care. In that review, fragmentation should have, I believe, a modest, but not insignificant place. But, to play that role, the very notion requires stipulation of meaning and context. Without that context, fragmentation too easily turns into a buzzword. Sadly, the health reform debates of 2009 generated confusion more than clarity, leaving the American public largely bewildered by the clash of buzzwords and outright misrepresentation.

INDEX